ENCYCLOPEDIA OF MANAGEMENT DEVELOPMENT METHODS

To
Janet, Sophie and Gregory

Encyclopedia of Management Development Methods

Andrzej Huczynski

Gower

Reprinted 1984, 1986

Published by
Gower Publishing Company Limited
Aldershot, Hants, England

Huczynski, Andrzej
    Encyclopedia of Management Development Methods
    1. Executives — Training — Dictionaries
    I. Title
    658.4'0431   HF5549.5.T7

    ISBN 0-566-02334-2

Typeset by Activity
Salisbury, Wilts
Printed in Great Britain by
Redwood Burn Limited, Trowbridge, Wiltshire

CONTENTS

There are no bad methods of instruction. The use to which each is put largely determines its effectiveness. Selecting the proper method and preparing for its use are paramount in successful instruction.

J. H. Proctor and W. M. Thornton (1960), *Training: A Handbook for Line Managers*, New York: American Management Association

We would be in a fine fix if the surgeon only performed those operations he is 'comfortable with', or if the carpenter refused to use any tool but the hammer because he likes the 'feel' of it. Since it is true that the teacher is unlikely to work effectively unless he does feel comfortable with a method, he should, as a professional, be constantly at pains to extend his repertoire, and should learn to like the feel of an ever widening range of media and techniques.

R. F. Mager and K. M. Beach (1967), *Developing Vocational Instruction*, Palo Alto, California: Fearon Publishers

Teaching methods do not seem to make much difference, or to phrase it more appropriately, there is hardly any direct evidence to favour one method over another.

N. E. Wallen and R. M. W. Travers (1963), 'Analysis and Investigation of Teaching Method' in N. L. Gage (ed.) *Handbook of Research on Teaching*, Chicago: Rand McNally.

FOREWORD

by Cary L. Cooper
Professor of Organisational Psychology
University of Manchester, Institute of Science and Technology

There are many managers who feel that 'behavioural scientists are incapable of telling us anything we don't already know' and that 'the bag of tricks (or management learning methods) used by management training specialists is as effective as a magician's wand'. This was amply illustrated in *The Financial Times* some years ago:

> Good evening, gentlemen, welcome to the X management education establishment. You will have noted, perhaps with relief, the absence of faculty or curriculum. This is a regular feature of this programme and a closely guarded secret of its alumni, present and past. If you should require any inducement to keep this secret, you may be influenced by the £500 in crisp ten-pound notes which are to be found in a brown envelope in your bedroom. This represents half the fee paid by your employers and approximated expenditure that would otherwise have been incurred with respect to teaching staff salaries and related costs. In the meantime, meals and other services will be provided and the bar will remain open at normal opening times. You will have discovered that your colleagues are drawn from similar organizations to your own and contain amongst them a wealth of practical experience in all manner of managerial roles. There is also a first rate library at your disposal. How you decide to pass these six weeks is your own managerial decision; we trust you will enjoy it and find it beneficial. Thank you.

On the other hand, there are those who feel that 'the last quarter century has seen the emergence of "the manager" as a recognised occupational role in society' (C. Handy, *Understanding Organizations*, 1976). Handy goes on to suggest that managers seem to be increasingly playing two primary sets of roles: the manager as a person and the manager as a GP. In the former, more and more skills are required to deal with people at work, while in the latter he/she is the 'first recipient of problems' which demand solutions and decisions. This GP role is composed of four basic activities of work: (*a*) symptom identification, (*b*) diagnosis of the cause of the trouble, (*c*) decision making about how to deal with it and (*d*) creating action plans or treatment.

The variety of skills necessary to perform all of these functions requires creative and innovative training approaches. Management trainers and educationalists must now possess an armoury of techniques and methods to meet the needs of the contemporary manager. This book is designed to help the training specialist by providing a comprehensive compendium of management learning methods between the covers of one book. Not only does it summarise the essence of a variety of different techniques and methods, but it also makes available further detailed readings in the area. This encyclopedia will be an essential part of the library of any management training specialist and management educationalist of the future.

PREFACE

Soap and education are not as sudden as a massacre,
but they are more deadly in the long run.

Mark Twain

In this book I have tried to describe briefly some of the methods that can be used by teachers and trainers in their work with managers and management students. I have found it difficult to draw any precise boundaries between the three spheres of management education: training and development; organisational development; and psychotherapy. However, an attempt is made to specify the subject field dealt with.

My aim has been to provide a source of information and ideas for the educational decision maker. This term encompasses students, course designers, tutors, teachers, training personnel in companies, consultants and indeed anybody who has to make a decision about any learning event or system which they are about to embark on or to design. It is perhaps easiest to talk about the company trainer to illustrate the types of decisions he has to make. Whether meeting individuals' training needs or solving a specific organisational problem, the trainer has the choice of doing the training himself by designing his own course and teaching it, or he can send the manager concerned on an externally run course. He can buy a training package together with a consultant to run it on an in-company basis, or buy a package which he then runs himself. If he believes that an off-the-shelf training package may be the answer then this encyclopedia describes some of the most popular ones, together with supplementary reading which can help him to make his final choice. If on the other hand he decides to run the course himself, then he has to make a choice between a bewildering variety of methods. The book suggests some of the criteria that need to be considered when making such a choice.

While I believe that the field of management development is an innovative one in its adoption of new techniques, developments have taken place in other areas. For this reason the encyclopedia includes descriptions of teaching and learning methods taken not only from management education but also from other areas such as medicine, biology, geology, languages and physics. These approaches are selected in the belief that they have a potential application to the work of management trainers.

In the encyclopedia readers will find entries at five levels of application:

1 Those methods which can be applied by the trainer following a reading of the description with no further preparation.

2 Those methods which, although directly applicable, nevertheless require the trainer to do some reading of the recommended literature in order to gain greater familiarity with the objectives and the steps involved.

3 Those methods which, if they were to be applied by the trainer himself, would require him to have gained first-hand experience of them in a learner role. Alternatively, they should be used by the trainer under the guidance of someone skilled in their use.

4 Those methods which require the engagement of an experienced professional, because the trainer himself lacks the necessary skills and knowledge or does not wish to develop such expertise.

5 Those packaged or copyrighted training programmes which are run by an outside consultant who may do the training on an in-company basis or else to whom individual managers or a group of managers might be sent.

As a general rule, where the training methods focus on affective issues, i.e. those concerned with people's feelings, values and emotions, the trainer will need to have developed the relevant skills to lead such a learning activity successfully.

The following brief description of the content of each of the encyclopedia's sections may help readers to select the ones which are of most immediate relevance to them.

Definition of the field
The subject is defined and distinguished from the related fields of organisational development and psychotherapy. This section concludes with a discussion of the way in which the concept of method has been used in the literature on management development and examines why the classification of different teaching and learning methods presents so many difficulties.

Criteria for method selection
While there is no simple and automatic procedure for the selection of

appropriate methods, it is nevertheless important for the tutor to think systematically about which methods to use. A number of key variables which influence method choice are presented here and the major ones are discussed in depth.

Directory of methods

A brief description of each method is provided together with some of the alternative names by which it is also known. References are given both to related methods and to relevant reading.

Resources for teaching and learning

Included in this section is an annotated bibliography of management teaching. This is followed by the names and addresses of organisations whose work and publications are a source of useful ideas for the management teacher. Finally, a number of journals are listed which regularly carry articles on teaching and learning methods, course design and programme evaluation.

Analytical framework for method assessment

The final section offers an analytical framework which the trainer can use to consider his philosophy of learning which is reflected both in his course design and in his choice of methods.

Note to readers

The purpose of this book is to produce a comprehensive source of references on teaching and learning methods for my colleagues in the management development field. Despite careful research, it is inevitable that I will have missed some. In addition, new approaches are constantly being developed.

In order to keep the encyclopedia as comprehensive as possible, I should like to hear from readers who use (or have had used on them) any methods in their work which significantly differ from any described in this book. Method descriptions can be sent to me at the publisher's address and, where appropriate, should include references to published descriptions of their uses. I shall undertake to collate and edit these contributions which will be included in any future editions of the encyclopedia.

A. A. Huczynski

ACKNOWLEDGEMENTS

Many people have contributed, both directly and indirectly, to this book. Space prevents me from formally acknowledging the contributions of them all. However, I should like to express the debt that I owe to the individuals who developed and described the teaching and learning methods that are contained in this book. In summarising their ideas in order to make them more widely available, I hope that I have not distorted them in the process.

The original idea for this book came from a meeting of management teachers who were discussing available teaching methods. I should like to thank David Antoine, Jenny Budden, Ann Caro, Edward Mallett and Sheila Evers for putting the idea of a book into my mind and for contributing some ideas as to what might go into it.

Throughout the writing of the book I have received suggestions and advice from many people and I should like to express my debt of gratitude to Dave Boud (University of New South Wales), Brigitte Berendt (Free University of Berlin), Dietrich Brandt (Hochschuldidaktisches Zentrum, Aachen), Gaye Manwaring (Dundee College of Education) and Chris de Winter Hebron (Newcastle-upon-Tyne Polytechnic). The most difficult part of the whole book was the production of a methods classification system. The original categories and their definitions were suggested by Rolf Schulmeister (University of Hamburg), a complementary listing was supplied by John Burgoyne (University of Lancaster) and these two listings were synthesised and developed further by Alex Main (University of Strathclyde) who produced the framework for the analysis of methods.

The original draft of the manuscript was entered on to the word processor by Maureen Christie, and David Buchanan spent many hours patiently explaining what I was doing wrong as I tried to edit the text. My editors at Gower Publishing Company were Malcolm Stern and Ellen Keeling who supplied both advice and encouragement.

Throughout this book, masculine pronouns have been used for succinctness and are intended to refer to both females and males.

The following publishers were kind enough to give their permission for me to reproduce material:

Blandford Press for Figure 3.1, Algorithmic approach to sales training, from Jinks, M., *Training*, Blandford Management Series, 1979.

Kogan Page Ltd for Figure 2.7, Cornwall's steps in student autonomy, from Cornwall, M., 'Independent Learning in a Traditional Institution', in Boud, D. J. (ed.) *Developing Autonomy in Student Learning*, 1981, p. 191.

Dr. K. Macharzina for Figure 1.2, Branching hierarchy of management education decisions, from Burgoyne, J. G. and Cooper, C. L., 'Research and Teaching Methods in Management Education: Bibliographical Examination of the State of the Art', *Management Education Review*, 1976, vol. 4, no. 1, pp. 95–192.

MCB Publications Ltd for Figures 2.1, Domains or areas of learning behaviour, and 2.2, Analysis of negotiating behaviour by learning domains, from Pedler, M., 'Negotiating Skills Training. Part 4: Learning to Negotiate', *Journal of European Industrial Training*, 1978, vol. 2, no. 1, pp. 20–25; and for Figure 2.5, Learning Methods by Level of Learning, from Pedler, M., 'Learning in Management Education', *Journal of European Training*, 1974, vol. 3, no. 3, pp. 182–94.

McGraw-Hill Book Company (UK) Ltd for Figure 32, Example of a Decision Table, from Davis, I. K., *The Management of Learning*, 1981, p. 143; and for fifteen lines (quoted on page 39) beginning 'They draw out the' and ending'... for their people.' from Mumford, A., *Making Experience Pay*, 1980.

Society for Research into Higher Education for twenty-four lines (quoted on page 15) beginning 'A possible conceptualization ...' and ending '... pace and choice' from Percy, K. and Ramsden, P., *Independent Study: Two examples from English Higher Education*, 1980, p. 6.

AAH

INDEX OF METHODS

1
DEFINITION OF THE FIELD

The delineation of boundaries between management development, management education, management training and organisational development has in the past been an area of not very fruitful debate. Nevertheless, since this encyclopedia will avoid dealing with what have been labelled organisational development methods or OD intervention techniques, it is necessary to specify the subject area which will be addressed. The focus will be on the teaching and learning methods which have a potential application in the field of management development. The term management development has itself been defined in a number of ways. Morris (1971), for example, saw it as 'the systematic improvement of managerial effectiveness within the organization assessed by its contribution to organizational effectiveness'. Ashton and Easterby-Smith (1979) identified a number of perspectives included within management development which they viewed as an organisational function within which '... activities such as training, coaching, career planning, appraisal, job rotation might all have some part to play'. These writers saw management development as involving the continuing education of the individual manager at all stages of his career. Thus management development was considered as not only being concerned with education and training, but also '... with a broader concept of development which implies improvement'. The breadth of this definition allows one to use it to refer to a wide range of different activities. It can be used to apply to both in-company and extra-company development programmmes, to short as well as to long courses, to periods of training and education, to those which lead to formal qualifications as well as those which do not. It is an all-embracing concept of management development which is being used in this book. A more detailed examination follows of what is included under the label of management development.

Burgoyne and Cooper (1976) conducted a study on the research that had been done on management teaching methods and identified journal references concerned with teaching methods. In doing this they produced a hierarchy of decisions concerning management education which was used by them as a basis for classifying the research studies they found. Their five-level hierarchy is summarised in Figure 1.1. While the authors did not explicitly define the term teaching method which they used, they did nevertheless present a useful framework with

1

1 Policy – decisions on issues concerning national approaches to education.

2 Strategy – decisions on issues concerned with management education at the institutional or departmental level.

3 Programme design – choices of approaches relevant to learning objectives and to how people learn.

4 Choice of methods – within-programme choices between different teaching/learning methods.

5 Intra-method decisions – 'here-and-now' choices made by tutors during the teaching session itself.

Figure 1.1 Hierarchy of management decision making

which to begin to sort out some of the confusion which surrounds the use of terms such as management development, education and organisational development. They achieved this by raising the terms management education and development to an abstract level and in their place referred to different types of programme designs. Their description of a branching hierarchy of decisions is shown in Figure 1.2.

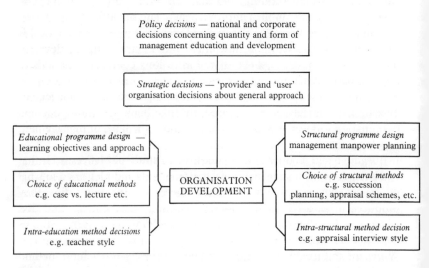

Figure 1.2 Branching hierarchy of management education decisions

The attractiveness of the Burgoyne-Cooper hierarchy is that at a stroke it sidesteps the arid debate over nomenclature referred to earlier. It is based on decisions to be taken by different people at different levels. In terms of methods or 'what people actually do' there is likely to be a high degree of overlap between what happens in educational programmes and in structural programmes. This encyclopedia focuses on the two aforementioned educational and structural programme designs on levels 3, 4 and 5. Burgoyne and Cooper see organisational development activities as deriving from both these strategies. However, the encyclopedia does not attempt to deal explicitly with organisational development methods although some of these OD techniques are included if they are capable of being extracted and used outside of their usual OD context. Similarly, psychotherapies are excluded, other than those which have already established themselves in management development (e.g. Transactional Analysis). Such therapies have been dealt with in great detail in other books (Herick, 1980; Winn, 1980; Clare and Thompson, 1981).

What exactly does the term 'method' refer to in the context of teaching and learning? Wesley and Wronski (1965) commented on the lack of specificity in the use of the word. They quoted a study in which students were asked to list the methods they knew. In addition to listing traditional, well-known ones such as the lecture and seminar, other methods listed included curricular materials, organisation schemes, activities and devices. All these were equated with the term method. A brief survey of the literature on teaching and learning methods in management development can show whether the connotations of the word method are equally broad in this field. In the Burgoyne and Cooper (1976) article mentioned earlier, the authors produced a 'list of teaching methods' which consisted of the following: lecture, texts, programmed instruction, role playing, case studies, games and simulations, projects, packages, T-group/social skills training and 'specials'. In a second paper on teaching and learning methods in management development, Burgoyne and Stuart (1978) discussed the lecture, seminar, business game, encounter group, T-group, joint development activities, action learning, autonomy lab, learning community, guided reading and programmed instruction. The final example is taken from some work by Pedler (1978) on negotiating which will be referred to in greater detail later. In discussing the teaching of information or situational knowledge he argued that 'the more traditional methods of teaching or training would seem to apply best'. He went on to list these as being lectures, talks, seminars, films, books, handouts and discussions. From these few examples it is clear that the term method is used in the same broad way in management development as elsewhere.

Being such a difficult concept to pin down, it is not surprising that there has been little success in producing a meaningful method classification system. According to Wesley and Wronski (1965) such a classification task is impossible:

> the complex and inclusive nature of method defies epigrammatic condensation. It is composed of diverse elements and is scarcely susceptible to logical analysis.

Nevertheless, the attempt at classifying or grouping different methods in some way is useful in that, as these same authors state:

> it clearly demonstrates the futility of devoting oneself wholly to one method. It appears desirable not only to use different methods, but to take care that those grounded in different bases are employed. And the analysis also furnishes an inclusive viewpoint that will prevent one from assigning undue merit or inclusive qualities to any one method.

There is yet to be produced an adequate procedure whereby one can automatically select an approprite method to fulfil a particular training need. It is also very unlikely that any such satisfactory procedure will ever be developed. Why should this be? Knowing what exactly is meant by the term group discussion or lecture well enough to be able to classify it is rare. On its own the label says nothing about the nature of the interactions between the persons involved. Two group discussions or two lectures may be conducted in two such radically different ways that it would be wrong to refer to these two activities using the same label. Binsted, Stuart and Long (1980) reported that management teachers tended to perceive the same teaching method label in different ways. They concluded that, 'This diversity strongly suggests that the label we give to a management teaching method, be it the lecture or action learning, is insufficient to convey the detail or the spirit of the event, and that this spirit is itself a function of the particular teacher and his audience'. While this criticism is generally valid, it is nevertheless also true that confronted with the term lecture or group discussion, most teachers recognise both the denotation of the word or phrase and some of its connotations. Each term does conjure up in their minds a picture of specific activities and behaviours which are guided by certain communication sequences and interaction rules. However, beyond this very general level there is unlikely to be sufficient agreement between different people to produce a useful classifications of methods.

Some writers see method as referring to a series of teacher-directed activities that result in learning. Since method is a process, it consists of several steps. Many of the elements or steps used in a particular method may also be used in other methods. Hence the overlap between educational programme designs, structured programme designs and organisational development activities. Educational psychologists have also argued that methods are tutor-initiated, are based on an educational philosophy which states the values to be achieved and on a theory of how people learn. They are said to list a set of learning principles which have relevant applications in the classroom and indicate the behaviour that the teacher should maintain in order to make effective use of these principles. While a method consists of several steps or elements, it is the tutor who combines or synthesises the elements into an effective process. Wallen and Travers (1963) have written that research on teaching methods is the study of the consistencies in the behaviour of teachers and the effect of these consistencies on the learning process. Teacher behaviour which might be considered could include the amount of information provided by a teacher, the emphasis he places on assessment and so on. These writers use the terms 'teaching method' and 'pattern of teacher behaviour' interchangeably. Burgoyne and Stuart (1978), who investigated the relationship of learning theories to teaching methods, reported that:

> the idea that one teaching method always embodied the same learning theory was wrong. We found, rather, that different learning theories illuminated different aspects of the same teaching methods, and that different applications of teaching methods 'implemented' assumptions from different learning theories, depending on the manner or style of application of the method by the person applying it.

To date the attempts to classify different teaching and learning methods have met with little success. Those offered by Wesley and Wronski (1965) and Joyce and Weil (1980) either tend to omit many of the entries described in this encyclopedia altogether or else place them into categories where experience and common sense suggest that they do not belong. Simplistic categorisation systems are likely to fail for at least two reasons. First, a method label carries no agreed indication of the interactions it is likely to describe and second, in order to produce any classification system one needs criteria with which to establish the categories. Numerous such criteria are possible. But after one's interest is stated, it is then impossible to apply a single-criteria classification system universally. Given these difficulties, one needs to ask what is the purpose of classifying these methods in the first place? At one level, the answer may be to indicate to the reader which methods are operationally similar to each other so that he can choose between several which are likely to achieve similar objectives, or else those which are similar in their mechanics but which can be used to achieve a variety of objectives. At another level the purpose may be to indicate that the entries in the encyclopedia differ qualitatively from each other. Some are learning principles, while others might be described as recipes, interaction rules, feedback systems and so on. This would allow the tutor to reflect on the suitability of any particular method in relation to the objectives and participants being worked with. For this reason, an analytical framework is offered in preference to a classification system and is described in Chapter 5.

2
CRITERIA FOR METHOD SELECTION

There are numerous criteria which one can use in order to choose between different teaching and learning methods. This chapter outlines three important bases for such a choice. These are objectives of the learning, the size of group and the level of student autonomy. It will be argued that there is no single, simple criterion which one can use to select a method, but that it is nevertheless important to evaluate and use different methods rather than be wedded to a single one.

LEARNING OBJECTIVES AS A BASIS FOR CHOICE
There has been a belief in management training circles, that if one specified the learning objectives to be achieved, this would somehow lead one magically to the selection of the appropriate method. This is rather too simplistic an approach. Nevertheless, a consideration of objectives remains an important criterion, along with others, on which a choice between teaching methods can be made. The aim, goal, purpose or objective of any learning situation, whether defined by the tutor, the students or both, constitutes one of the guiding considerations. While the stating of the objectives of learning is universally considered a good thing, there has been less agreement on the classification system to be used or on the degree of specificity which is relevant and appropriate. The attempt to produce a comprehensive list of educational objectives has a long tradition in educational psychology. The taxonomy developed by Bloom and his collaborators (Bloom *et al.* 1956; Krathwohl *et al.* 1964) is perhaps the best known. Bloom's taxonomy identified three areas or domains of learning. These were the cognitive (concerned with knowledge, facts and their manipulation), the affective (dealing with feelings, emotions and values) and the psychomotor (concerned with movement). For anyone involved in education and training, the discipline of stating one's objectives is of tremendous value. Too often a single learning event or an entire course attempts to achieve incompatible objectives. A study of Bloom's taxonomy, or the less elaborate one developed by Gronlund (1971) well repays the time and effort spent.

In discussing objectives in management educational training, the author has found Pedler's classification (1978) particularly useful. In this section, it is proposed to use Pedler's scheme as a basis for thinking about objectives in management development. In addition to Bloom's original classification of three domains or areas of learning, Pedler added two more. The full list is reproduced in Figure 2.1.

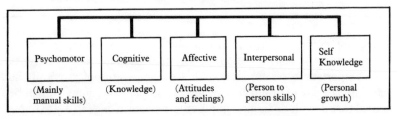

Figure 2.1 Domains or areas of learning behaviour

'Interpersonal' refers to skills associated with face to face interactions. It is a blend of specific cognitive, affective and even psychomotor skills. 'Self Knowledge' focuses on objectives concerned with a better understanding of oneself, in particular regarding personal knowledge of one's own strengths and weaknesses. Despite some overlap in the domains, this framework is perhaps particularly useful in areas of management training and development. The classification scheme helps one to think about different objectives and it is clear that when one considers a typical managerial behaviour, a number of these separate learning areas come together. Gage and Berliner (1979) made this point when they wrote:

> None of these kinds of behaviour is isolated from the others. While we are thinking, engaged in intellectual activity, we also experience emotions and display certain movements. When we are lost in feeling, swept away by a symphony or a poem, we are nonetheless thinking and posturing, i.e. engaged simultaneously in certain cognitive and psychomotor behaviours. And whenever we perform certain bodily movements – such as high diving or piano playing – we also think about how we move and have feelings about our performance.

Pedler (1978) provided an example of how a complex managerial behaviour such as negotiating spanned a number of areas of learning behaviour (see Figure 2.2).

In the preceding paragraphs a horizontal division of learning objectives was described. In order to make the discussion of educational objectives even more specific, Bloom and others further developed the domains by specifying objectives within them into

Knowledge of procedures, rules and regulations at various levels; issues at stake etc.	Cognitive Area
Feelings and beliefs about the issues; your case, other side's case; fairness, justice etc.	Affective Area
Ability to express self clearly; respond appropriately to other side; develop trust and understanding with own team and other team.	Interpersonal Area
Knowledge of own behaviour under different conditions; strengths and weaknesses; likes and dislikes etc.	Self Knowledge Area

Figure 2.2   Analysis of negotiating behaviour by learning domains

sequences or hierarchies. For example, within the cognitive domain, objectives were divided into knowledge, comprehension, application, analysis, synthesis and evaluation. For day to day design purposes, the writer has found Pedler's 'levels of learning division' sufficiently detailed when dealing with the cognitive aspects of learning. It is a vertical division which is similar to one developed by Fyfe and Richardson (1974) (see Figure 2.3).

4   Transfer, Value and Self Expression
3   Application
2   Understanding
1   Memory

In discussing this hierarchical system, Pedler made several comments about the differences betwen the levels in terms of the implications of the differences for the choice of teaching methods. At all levels below the fourth, certain 'right answers' existed which could be taught. Beyond these there were no content free right answers. As one moved upwards, the methods used tended to become less structured and feedback to learners increased. Moving up through the levels, the outcomes became more difficult to specify or even to recognise. It was therefore more

9

Level 1: Memory

The Memory level, or what others have called the Knowledge level concerns the ability to recall knowledge, recognise basic facts, procedures, principles and methods. It is the first and most basic level. Here the manager may need to recognise the names of major motivation theorists or of some statistical techniques used in business. Memory level objectives frequently need to be achieved before the student can progress to higher levels of learning.

Level 2: Understanding

Understanding involves integrating or relating bits of knowledge. Thus the student may be asked to explain the Expectancy Theory of Motivation or justify the use of a particular statistical test on some data. Attainment of objectives at this level depends on the achievement of the corresponding objectives at the Memory Level.

Level 3: Application

Application can be thought of as 'doing with understanding'. For this reason it has also been termed the Skills level. In our example, the manager may be required to apply the motivation theory or use the chosen statistical techniques to complete a task that is set for him.

Level 4: Transfer

Pedler defined this level as one at which the learner was able to select and use the appropriate skills and knowledge in a range of new and different situations. To this idea, I would wish to add the notion of the learner accepting what he has learned, valuing it and showing some preference for it. For example, having learned about some statistical technique such as correlation, the learner will try it out at work and will apply it in circumstances which appear to require it in order to solve problems. This fourth level might be relabelled as Transfer, Value and Self Expression.

Figure 2.3 Hierarchy of cognitive learning objectives

difficult to select the 'appropriate' methods. As the tutor's uncertainty regarding content increased, so he relinquished his expert role and

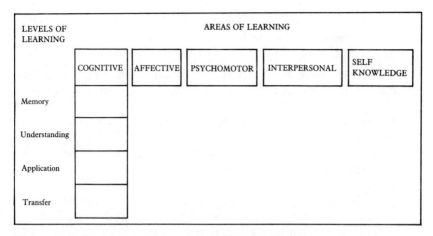

Figure 2.4   Domains and levels of cognitive learning

learning increasingly became a cooperative venture between the learner and the teacher. In the first three levels, traditional learning sequences appeared to work as one moved from the rules of the theory to practice; from the learning of parts to an understanding of the whole; from simple to complex learning. At these levels one could distill the theory from the experiences of practice. It was the fourth level which was significantly different. Whereas at the first three levels the learning methods dictated the nature of the learning, at the fourth, it was the nature of the learning which dictated the method. Figure 2.4 summarises the five domains of learning referred to earlier, as well as the four hierarchical levels relevant to the Cognitive domain.

It would be pleasant to suggest at this point that once objectives had been specified, either horizontally or vertically, or both, then all one had to do was to look up a chart in order to select the appropriate teaching method. Unfortunately, it is not that simple for at least two reasons. Firstly, the selection of a method is based on the personal philosophy of the teacher. Burgoyne and Stuart (1978) noted that the

> design of management development programmes is usually seen by practitioners in the field as a matter of choosing the methods appropriate to the content of what they want to teach or the learning they hope to bring about.

There is a widespread belief that the methods used by a tutor reflect his assumptions about how people learn. These writers added:

> Methods can be seen as ready-made assumptions about learning

11

processes ... the assumptions can be varied by the manner in which the methods are applied.

Thus for the teacher, the methods may not be 'out there' to be chosen but are instead inside of him. A second reason why a simple objectives-method link does not exist is related to the nature of learning in general and to the many faceted tasks of management in particular. The behaviours required of a successful manager are so complex that they span the different learning domains and the different levels. It is therefore not possible to select a single appropriate method on the basis of objectives alone. It is important to add that consideration of objectives should not blind one from considering other important dimensions. For example, the learner's learning style, the resources available for teaching and learning, and the location in which the learning takes place.

While it may not be possible to state which method is 'best' rough guidelines can be provided. Thus objectives are often one of several dimensions that the tutor can consider in selecting between different methods. Since the label of a method, for example, the lecture, says nothing about the way it is used, any classification of methods by objectives must employ some stereotype of the method referred to (e.g. lectures allow no student involvement, while discussions allow student expression of views). Pedler (1974) has offered a classification which related objectives to method (see Figure 2.5). He offered it with the proviso that it should not be taken too literally.

GROUP SIZE AS A BASIS FOR CHOICE

Since the number of students or trainees to be catered for can impose severe limitations on the methods which can be used, or indeed on the objectives that can realistically be achieved, the size of group is a second and equally important dimension against which a choice of methods is to be made. Gage and Berliner (1979) refer to the 'quantitative and powerful determiner or at least correlate of teaching methods, namely, group size'. The focus of the work of these authors is on the American secondary school system. In management development, the numbers involved tend to be smaller. For this reason, Gage and Berliner's classification by group size has been somewhat adapted and is summarised in Figure 2.6. The choice of methods based on the size of the group being trained is as realistic as one based on objectives to be achieved.

Number of students	Label
25 +	Aggregate
17–24	Large Group
3–16	Small Group
1–2	Individual/Dyad

Level of learning	Description	Learning methods Off-the-job	On-the-job
1 *Memory*	Learner can recall facts, definitions, procedures, actions, behaviours. He can identify, define and describe.	Lectures Talks Programmed learning	Algorithms Checklists Information maps
2 *Under-standing*	Learner has grasp of concepts, ideas procedures and techniques. He can explain, compare and justify.	Talk Discussion Case study Business games In tray exercises Incident studies Action maze Information maze Group feedback analysis	Assignments Projects
3 *Application*	Learner can use the concepts, ideas, techniques etc. in standard situations. He can use or apply things in the 'correct' prescribed way.	Demonstration and practice Role play Some case studies Simulations In tray exercises Discussion	Demonstration and practice Supervised practice Coaching Assignments Projects Job rotation
4 *Transfer*	From all the concepts, ideas, procedures and techniques ever learned, the learner can select the one most appropriate to a new, non-standard situation. He can modify or create new theories, ideas or tools to cope with unique situations where there are no 'right' answers.	Experimental learning situations Discovery learning Brainstorming Discussion Dialogue Group exercises Sensitivity training Diagnostic instruments and feedback	Counselling Job rotation Assignments Self diagnostic instruments Process consultation Discovery learning

Figure 2.5   Learning Methods by Level of Learning

DEGREE OF STUDENT AUTONOMY AS A BASIS FOR CHOICE

The author's personal choice for a third dimension is that of the degree of student autonomy. Wallen and Travers (1963) have argued that 'probably on no other dimension do teaching methods differ more than on the matter of the exercise of control'. In recent years there has been an increasing interest in management development with 'self-development approaches' (Boydell and Pedler, 1981). Such an interest has been paralleled in other areas of higher and post-experience education with discussions on how to increase autonomous student learning. The emphasis of these movements has been away from teaching towards an increased responsibility on students for their own learning. Boud (1981)

Individual/dyad (1–2 persons)

It may be that it is only one or at most two individuals who have a particular training need. For example, the deputy managing director of a company plant who is being groomed for a more senior job. Because of the low numbers involved, certain methods become feasible.

Typical methods: Development Assignment; Programmed Learning.

Small group (3–16)

The upper figure here is arbitrary. Sixteen is selected because small group work which involves four groups of four reporting back in a plenary session is just possible within a ninety-minute class session. Any more groups reporting back and the other members appear to lose interest.

Typical methods: Discussion method; Role playing, some experiential exercises.

Large group (17–24)

This is the upper limit, not only of group work but also of face-name associations. Unless a group of 24 is met by the tutor on a regular basis, at least once or twice a week, it is difficult for him to remember everyone's name. Twenty-four is also frequently a seating limit. Few college rooms (although more custom-built training centres) can handle this number of people sitting around tables in groups. Problems also arise with teacher-student eye contact.

Typical methods: Case Study; Syndicate method.

Aggregate (25 plus)

Here one comes up against nameless faces and the many lectures where numbers of students and frequently time available as well as room and furniture constrain what can realistically be attempted.

Typical methods: Lecture, Talk, Buzz groups.

Figure 2.6 Learning methods by group size

has written that 'Autonomous learning is not an absolute standard to be met but a goal to be pursued; what is important is the direction – towards student responsibility for learning – not the magnitude of the changes in a given direction'. A framework for considering the degree of autonomy is provided by Percy and Ramsden (1980). It considers the dimensions of freedom of choice available to students when they are confronted with a defined learning situation. The dimensions provide a straightforward way of analysing learning methods to determine the degree of freedom, and thus autonomy which they offer to the learner:

> A possible conceptualization of the relationship between individualized and 'independent' study and of degrees of student independence ... marks out four linked stages of student independence.

1   Pace – Student can work at his own pace and choose the times (and sometimes the places) at which he finds it most appropriate to learn. Examples: Keller Plan courses; parts of many traditionally organized university courses (e.g. essay writing and individual reading) some project and laboratory work.

2   Choice – Student chooses to work or not to work at a course, or at a part of a course. Examples: Keller Plan (to a limited extent): choice between a number of courses offered by a department during an academic year; modular course structures; choice of major and minor options.

3   Method – Student can decide the method of learning he finds most suitable. Examples: independent study programmes; parts of some traditionally organized courses and individualized packages (e.g. choice between video presentations or texts; choice between different textbooks).

4   Content – Student chooses what he wants to learn according to his own goals and interests. This may or may not imply working within established academic disciplines or structures. Examples: some project work, independent study programmes.

The notion of student control over content and method in this scheme necessarily subsumes that of control over pace and choice.

The dimensions mentioned, pace, choice, method and content of study are those which immediately come to mind whenever student autonomy is discussed. There are, however, several others, which have been mentioned by Cornwall (1981) but which were omitted by Percy and Ramsden. Cornwall suggested a hierarchy of independence in learning (see Figure 2.7). He wrote: 'My criterion for the suggested order of the "steps" is the extent to which the provision of choice in each of these aspects of the curriculum is likely to require reorganization of a conventional "teacher prescribed, teacher presented, teacher paced and teacher assessed course".' He was primarily concerned with learning in

Steps to independence in learning?

A hypothetical hierarchy of choice in learning in terms of aspects of the curriculum.

Independence in Learning

Criteria for Success
Assessment Methods
Study Objectives
Mode of Study
Pace of Study
Decision to Enrol

Increasing levels of choice for the learner

Figure 2.7 Cornwall's steps in student autonomy

traditional institutions such as universities, but this hierarchy does offer a set of questions which can assist in the categorisation of student autonomy in general.

The key differences in the Cornwall scheme are at the top and bottom of the hierarchy. At the bottom, managers may have little or no choice in becoming involved in a management development exercise. They may be sent or else pressured to 'volunteer'. At the top of the hierarchy the references are to criteria to be used for assessing success. To what extent are learners involved in setting and agreeing such criteria and in choosing how they wish to be assessed? These crucial elements appear to be missing in the Percy and Ramsdem listing mentioned earlier. Cornwall's levels of autonomy are described in Figure 2.8.

CONCLUSION

It is not being argued that these dimensions are necessarily the main or only criteria which a tutor should use in selecting an appropriate teaching or learning method. Educational contexts differ and it may be that an entirely different set are appropriate elsewhere. The three dimensions

Level 1   Decision to enrol

Shall I join the course? Shall I participate in the activity?'

The most basic level is concerned with choice in participation. In the college or university the question may be whether the course is compulsory or an option which is chosen. In the company the manager may be allowed to volunteer or else be required to participate.

Level 2   Pace of study

'When and how fast will I study?'

Is the training programme of a pre-specified duration, e.g. 3 years, 1 term, 20 meetings? Is there flexibility which would allow the learner to finish earlier or later than the appointed time? To what extent is there the recognition that students learn at different speeds?

Level 3   Mode of study

'In what way will I study?'

Is there a choice of teaching and learning methods? Can the student decide about books and resources to be used?

Level 4   Study objectives

'What specific objectives will I pursue in my study?'

What particular knowledge, skills and attitudes do I wish to acquire or develop? What influence do I have over specifying the objectives?

Level 5   Assessment methods

'How do I wish these objectives to be assessed?'

Is the assessment system for checking on the achievement of objectives open for discussion and negotiation between students and learners, or is it unilaterally imposed by teaching staff?

Level 6   Criteria for success

'What should be the criteria for my success or failure?'

Is the learner involved in the setting of the criteria or does someone else make the judgement whether the person has done well or not?

Figure 2.8   Levels of student autonomy   17

offered here are those which the author has found particularly relevant. The application of such criteria helps to narrow down the choice to manageable proportions. Once this has been done, one may apply a second order sifting system provided by perhaps second order criteria. Binsted, Stuart and Long (1980) for example, presented some criteria for assessing and selecting teaching methods in terms of their ability to deal with problems of translation and transfer of learning into the trainee's work environment. In concluding this section, it may be appropriate to quote Gage and Berliner (1979):

> Not all teaching methods are equally appropriate for helping students to attain all instructional objectives ... The question – what method of teaching is best? – really has no answer unless one

Student Autonomy	
Level	Label
6	Criteria for success
5	Assessment methods
4	Study objectives
3	Mode of study
2	Pace of study
1	Decision to enrol

Objectives		Group Size	
Level	Label	Number	Label
4	Transfer, Value and Self Expression	25+	Aggregate
3	Application	17–24	Large group
2	Understanding	3–16	Small group
1	Memory	1–2	Individual/dyad

Figure 2.9 Summary of key variables in method choice

specifies the characteristics of the students and the objectives of the teaching. The student's age, intelligence, motivational background of previous learning and achievement in the subject matter of the teaching are important factors to consider.

REFERENCES

Ashton, D. and Easterby-Smith, M. (1979) *Management Development in the Organization*, London: Macmillan

Binsted, D., Stuart, R. and Long, G. (1980) 'Promoting Useful Management Learning: Problems of Translation and Transfer' in Beck, J. and Cox, C. (eds) *Advances in Management Education*, Chichester: John Wiley and Sons

Bloom, B. S., Engelhart, M. B., Furst, E. J., Hill, W. H. and Krathwohl, D. R. (1956) *Taxonomy of Educational Objectives. The Classification of Educational Goals Handbook 1: Cognitive Domain*, New York, Longmans Green

Boud, D. J. (ed.) (1981) *Developing Autonomy in Student Learning*, London: Kogan Page Ltd

Boydell, T. and Pedler, M. (eds) (1981) *Management Self-Development: Concepts and Practices*, Aldershot: Gower

Burgoyne, J. G. and Cooper, C. L. (1976) 'Research on Teaching Methods in Management Education: Bibliographical examination of the State of the Art' in *Management Education Review*, vol. 16, no. 4, pp. 95–102

Burgoyne, J. G. and Stuart, R. (1978) 'Teaching and Learning Methods in Management Development' in *Personnel Review*, vol. 7, no. 1, pp. 53–58

Clare, A. W. and Thompson, S. (1981) *Let's Talk About Me*, London: BBC Publications

Cornwall, M. (1981) 'Putting It Into Practice: Promoting Independent Learning in a Traditional Institution' in Boud, D. J. (ed.), op.cit.

Fyfe, T. W. and Richardson, R. (1974) *Educational Technology*, Programmed Text, Dundee College of Education

Gage, N. L. and Berliner, C. (1979) *Educational Psychology*, 2nd edition, Chicago: Rand McNally

Gronlund, N. E. (1971) *Measurement and Evaluation in Teaching*, New York: Macmillan

Herick, R. (1980) *The Psychotherapy Handbook*, New York: Meridian

Joyce, B. and Weil, M. (1980) *Models or Teaching*, 2nd edition, Englewood Cliffs, New Jersey: Prentice Hall

Krathwohl, D. R., Bloom, B. S. and Masia, B. B. (1964) *Taxonomy of Educational Objectives, Handbook 2: Affective Domain*, New York: David McKay Co. Inc.

Morris, J. (1971) 'Management Development and Development Management' in *Personnel Review*, vol. 1, no. 1, pp. 30–43

Pedler, M. (1974) 'Learning in Management Education' in *Journal of European Training*, vol. 3, no. 3, pp. 182–94

Pedler, M. (1978) 'Negotiating Skills Training Part 4: Learning To Negotiate' in *Journal of European Industrial Training* vol. 2, no. 1, pp. 20–25

Percy, K. and Ramsden, P. (1980) *Independent Study: Two Examples from English Higher Education*, Guildford, Surrey: Society for Research into Higher Education

Wallen, N. E. and Travers, R. M. W. (1963) 'Analysis and Investigation of Teaching Methods' in Gage, N. L. (ed.) *Handbook of Research on Teaching*, Chicago: Rand McNally

Wesley, E. B. and Wronski, S. P. (1965) *Teaching Social Sciences in the High Schools*, D. C. Heath and Co.

Winn, D. (1980) *The Whole Mind Book*, Glasgow: Collins/Fontana

3
DIRECTORY OF METHODS

ACCEPTING POSITIONS OF RESPONSIBILITY IN COMMUNITY ORGANISATIONS

A number of companies have encouraged managers to take up positions of responsibility such as chairman, secretary or treasurer in civic, community, church, social and political organisations. Some have given staff time off to attend the meetings of these organisations. The belief is that such involvement can develop a broader view of situations in the manager which will have long term benefits for his job performance. This can become a much more valuable learning experience if the manager is told to look for certain things, keep a log of his experiences, try out different strategies and so on. While the company can express its positive attitude to these types of activity and view them as learning opportunities which can be used by their managers to develop their skills and broaden their outlook, in general, managers tend to view them as a social duty or a social occasion.

See also: Assignment to community organisation; Assignment to customer as representative; Assignment to government body study group; Service in professional organisations; Logging critical incidents

ACTING ASSIGNMENT

In an Acting Assignment the manager is given a role to enact over a fixed time period, usually in connection with a specific problem. Thus a production department manager may be attached to the industrial relations staff during a period when the annual wage negotiations take place. Alternatively, the assignment may be bounded by time limits with the manager waiting to see what problems come up while he is occupying the position.

See also: Research assignment; Sick leave/holiday replacement assignment; Planned delegation; Manager exchange; Manager shadowing; Job swop; Job rotation; Exposure to upper management; Development assignment; Assignment to manager with high development skills

ACTION CENTRED LEADERSHIP

Action Centred Leadership courses were developed by John Adair on the basis of what he calls the 'functional approach' to leadership. His ideas developed out of the deficiencies he saw in the 'qualities approach' to leadership. This held that 'leaders were born'. Adair claims that no common list of personality traits had been revealed by research which could indicate who might be a good leader. Adair also felt that the 'situational approach' which emphasised the importance of the situation in which leadership was carried out, as well as the task being performed, was equally unhelpful. This approach implied a need for a constantly changing leadership to match the constantly changing tasks.

Adair's 'functional approach' is based on the identification of the functions that need to be performed in a team if it is to be successful. He lists three different sets of needs. Firstly, there are the Task Needs. Since a work group comes together to achieve certain objectives, it has a need to move towards the achievement of those objectives. If some measure of success is not achieved, the group may disintegrate. Secondly, there are the Group Needs. The cooperation of team members is necessary if the group's goals are to be achieved. For this reason motivation and group morale need to be maintained. Finally, there are the Individuals Needs. In taking part in groups, individual members seek to fulfil their own needs which are unique to them. Failure to meet these individual needs may lead to the members withdrawing from the team or perhaps leaving the group altogether. Adair views these needs as interdependent and sees the leader's job as being to ensure that all three sets of needs are met. The development of this form of leadership is the objective of Action Centred Leadership courses.

The courses themselves consist of a series of group tasks in which the objectives are specified and feedback on success or failure is clear. Group members take up and relinquish leadership roles as they work at the task depending on their personal characteristics. Debriefing sessions focus on the extent to which individual, group and task needs were met, the degree of task success, problems of communication and the problem solving approaches used.

Smith, E. P. (1975) 'Action Centered Leadership' in Taylor, B. and Lippitt, G. L. (eds) *Management Development and Training Handbook*, London: McGraw-Hill

Adair, J. (1978) *Training for Leadership*, Aldershot: Gower

Adair, J. (1978) *Training for Communication*, Aldershot: Gower

Adair, J. (1978) *Training for Decisions*, Aldershot: Gower

Adair, J. (1979) *Action Centred Leadership*, Aldershot: Gower

Adair, J. (1979) 'Training Leaders' in Babington-Smith, B. and Farrell, B. A. (eds) *Training in Small Groups: A Study of Five Methods*, Oxford, Pergamon Press.

See also: Grid training; 3–D Organisational effectiveness training

ACTION LEARNING

Action Learning as an educational approach is based on the principle of 'learning by doing'. Developed by Reg Revans, the approach in some ways stands in direct contrast to traditional, business-school-based management development programmes for experienced managers. In essence, groups of managers come together periodically to work on real life organisational problems. They form a group which has a 'Set Advisor' available who acts not as a teacher but as a facilitator/resource person.

The following principles apply: those best qualified to solve problems are those who have them; the best opportunities to develop managers occur in their own organisations; the self-help climate of Action Learning groups encourages the solving of problems; Action Learning is action based and not concerned with recommendations for possible future implementation. The aims of Action Learning are to develop managers' skills to pose entirely new questions; to help them recognise their existing experience for future problems; to develop and change organisations by helping managers to see their strengths and weaknesses and creating a momentum to go on dealing with future problems through a continuous process of learning and development.

Different models of Action Learning exist. Generally, a manager or supervisor joins a set of four or five people who are facing broadly similar problems. They may come from the same or different companies or plants. Each group has a professional set advisor who may be an academic, consultant or trainer. His job is to develop the set into a learning group so that the managers learn primarily with and from each other rather than from a professional educator. While originally devised for use with managers, large elements of the Action Learning model are capable of being applied to independent student learning programmes.

Foy, N. (1977) 'Action Learning Comes to Industry' in *Harvard Business Review*, September–October

Elgin, R. (1977) 'Business Schools Come Under Fire from Action Man' in

Industrial Management, May, pp. 25–27

Revans, R. W. (1976) 'Management Education: Time for a Re-think' in *Personnel Management*, vol. 8, no. 7, July, pp. 20–24

Revans, R. W. (1972) 'Action Learning – A Management Development Programme' in *Personnel Review*, vol. 1, no. 4

Boddy, D. (1981) 'Putting Action Learning into Action' in *Journal of European Industrial Training/MCB Monograph*, vol. 5, no. 5

Casey, D. and Pearce, D. (eds) (1978) *More Than Management Development*, Aldershot: Gower

Boddy, D. (1980) 'An Action Learning Programme for Supervisors' in *Journal of European Industrial Training*, vol. 4, no. 3, pp. 10–13

Revans, R. W. (1975) 'Action Learning Projects' in Taylor, B. and Lippitt, G. L. (eds) *Management Development and Training Handbook*, London: McGraw Hill

See also: Project-based management development; Joint development activity; Student-planned learning

ACTION MAZE

An Action Maze is a printed description of an incident for analysis which is followed by a list of alternative actions. Each action choice that is taken by the learner directs him to a new page which gives him the results of his action and presents him with a new set of alternatives from which to choose. The results which the student receives after each step may give him more information as well as providing his reaction to his action choice. It is possible that this set of choices may lead him to a dead end and send him back to make another choice from another set of alternatives.

Action Mazes borrow ideas from programmed learning although they differ significantly from it. In particular the idea of scrambled pages (which are not read consecutively) and that of making a selection of one choice from a number of alternatives (each leading down a different path) are utilised. Programmed learning involves the teaching of a correct response both through reinforcement when the correct response occurs and by re-teaching when an error is made. Although some of the facts of management may be susceptible to that approach, the attitudes and behaviours which compose the major elements in management training and development are not.

While Action Mazes come in book form, the individual pages can be duplicated, placed in pocket files and distributed around the floor of the training room or on tables. Individual trainees work their way through the maze and report their route as well as their exit point (of which there may be several) to the tutor. Groups can be formed consisting of different route takers who then discuss the reasons for their choices. An alternative approach is to put each page on an overhead transparency for group discussion, both at the 'decision-making' and 'de-briefing' stages. Since learners receive immediate feedback on their progress, Action Mazes are frequently found to be interesting to students and tend to provoke intense discussion. Mazes reflect the real life mode of decision making and confirm that we have control only before we take action. Once this has been taken it provokes reaction which in turn creates new situations which need responding to. Mazes exist on topics such as dealing with a regular work absentee and disciplining staff.

Zoll, A. A. (1969) *Dynamic Management Education*, Reading, Mass.: Addison Wesley, chapters 11–12

Elgood, C. (1980) 'The Use of Business Games in Management Training' in *The Training Officer*, vol. 16, no. 12, pp. 332–4

See also: Programmed simulation; Game; Simulation; In-basket exercise

ACTION PROFILING

This approach is based on the idea that every individual may be considered to have three modes of operating which are termed Thinking, Acting and Feeling. We 'energise' ourselves by making things happen. There are different types of effort required. The first type is that of Giving Attention. This may involve answering a query or presenting a problem. Before decisions can be made, attention needs to be given. The second effort is that of Forming an Intention. This is the building of resolve; a basis of purpose and determination on which to proceed. The last stage is the effort of Making a Commitment to pass through a moment of decision to a point of no return. This approach then suggests that each individual has a preference for one or other of these stages and energises himself in that way. Individuals' energy preferences are labelled Action Motivations. The energy preference is held to be a motivating force because of its compelling nature and the satisfaction reported by people as they act in their preferred ways. The Action Profiles of individual managers are assessed and each manager, it is claimed, has his own unique pattern of strengths in action motivation which is called his Action Profile. This Action Profile is diagrammatically described by allocating '100 units of energy' on criteria which are unclear, across the three action stages of Attending, Intending and Committing. The Action Profile is not claimed to measure a manager's performance, but the basic motivating forces within his personality. It has been used as a basis to develop both individual managers, teams and individuals within teams.

Ramsden, P. (1978) 'Top Team Planning and Management Motivation' in *BACIE Journal*, vol. 32, no. 10, November, pp. 173–5

Ramsden, P. (1973) *Top Team Planning – A Study of the Power of Individual Motivation in Management*, London: Associated Business Programmes/Cassell

Rose, C. L. (1978) *Action Profiling – Movement Awareness For Better Management*, London: MacDonald and Evans

ACTION TRAINING
Action Training was originally developed as a means of helping new managers to learn those social skills required for appraising and counselling their subordinates. It evolved from the dissatisfaction with the existing lecture approach (which dealt only with knowledge about appraisal) and role playing (which dealt with skills in an artificial and unreal situation). With Action Training, classroom situations are created in which managers can be themselves and are able to explore and develop the desired social skills. Subsequently, this same approach came to be used in the development of group skills.

Action Training involves the trainee in a group dealing with behaviour by working at a task which is carried out under time pressure and which leads to behaviour such as frustration, curiosity, etc. It utilises a systematic approach which includes a regular review and it encourages participants to learn by experience. An Action Training course usually lasts between two and three days, has between 15 and 18 people participating and is staffed by two tutors.

Drinkwater, A. (1972) 'Group Training and Consulting Approaches in IBM' in Berger, M. L. and Berger, P. J. (eds) *Group Training Techniques*, Aldershot: Gower

Peach, L. (1979) 'Developing High Fliers at IBM' in *Personnel Management*, vol. 11, no. 9, pp. 32–5

See also: Coverdale training

ACTIVE CASE STUDY

Active Case Studies seek to overcome the problem of the time needed for managers to conduct work-related projects on extra-company management development programmes. When project teams have to meet, work pressures and travelling difficulties can all interfere with the successful completion of the task. To overcome this problem, project work conducted by groups of managers is based around a case study which has been researched before the beginning of the management development programme. Project team participants are given access to operating data, have the opportunity to visit the site concerned and view prerecorded interviews with the managers involved. They are required to make a report on their findings and proposals which are based on both inputs received during the course as a whole and on their own detailed group study of a particular problem.

Margerison, V. and New, C. (1980) 'Management Development by Inter-Company Consortium' in *Personnel Management*, vol. 12, no. 11, pp. 42–5

See also: Case study method; Critical incident analysis; Participative case; Personal case study; Incident process method

ADVANCED SEMINAR

The term Advanced Seminar is used here to refer to a particular type of seminar design which was first described by Nisbett. Its distinguishing characteritic is the alternation of a session in which students have a relatively high degree of freedom with one in which there exists a greater degree of discipline. Organisationally the design of the seminar programme proceeds along traditional lines. Topics for study are selected and students in the group are then allocated to a seminar topic. However, one difference is that while each student has a single topic, he is allocated two consecutive seminar sessions, and he is responsible for providing material for them both. Each topic is organised along the following lines. The student begins by deciding on six 'statements worth making' about his subject. Such statements have the following characteristics: (*a*) they are clear, specific and important, (*b*) they are controversial enough to need careful discussion prior to acceptance or rejection by the group, and (*c*) they represent the author's personal belief, based on his study experience and reflection. These statements avoid triviality and vagueness. They are not platitudes. Neither are they mere opinions based on the author's ignorance or the type of assertions with which one is likely to agree without further discussion. Once developed, the student circulates his list of statements to the other seminar participants at least one week before the first of the two meetings. A list of pertinent reading references is also appended with the statements.

During the first meeting, the author of the statements devotes about a quarter of an hour to introducing each in turn, explaining its meaning and justifying his belief that it is 'a statement worth making'. The group discussion which follows is concerned with the clarification of the meaning of the statements and on testing the responses of group members to the list in a generally unstructured and free-wheeling way. The second meeting is more disciplined through being more task-orientated. The job of the group is to arrive at a consensus on the six statements or any modifications of them. Because the original statements were controversial, it is rare for there to be initial agreement on any of them. Individuals in the group become involved in a process of mutual persuasion in which the statements are modified to satisfy objectors while they retain the support of those who originally agreed with them. At the end of this process of negotiation, the ensuing list of statements must continue to conform to the criterion of what constituted a 'statement worth making'.

When group unanimity is impossible, the dissenting minority group produce a reasoned report to the majority statement. At any time during this second seminar, statement supporters have to assess the relative advantage of pursuing their own viewpoints and giving up some of them in order to gain a unanimous agreement on a statement which is close to their own but which may not exactly mirror it. Agreement is reached by disciplined discussion. The tutor's involvement is crucial here. Since consensus depends both on members stating their case and on having their views considered by others, the tutor has to foster a climate in which the receiving and considering of views is accorded equal status with the giving of them.

There are a number of benefits to the students from an Advanced Seminar. The selection of the original six statements is an exercise in individual learning. The student is required to read, think about his reading and exercise his judgement. The two contrasting types of sessions allow the learner to consider the advantages and disadvantages of each. In the first, open discussion, there are similarities to a brainstorming group where new ideas and perspectives are evolved. In the second, there is the need for greater self discipline and group management if the learning task is to be achieved. In addition to developing skills in reasoned argument, it also develops members' group/committee skills as well as influencing skills, especially in negotiating and bargaining situations where the task may be to check tactfully how far apart the positions of the two sides are and to assess the degree to which differences have a substantive, emotional or semantic base.

Nisbett, S. (1965–66) 'A Method for Advanced Seminars' in *Universities Quarterly*, vol. 20, pp. 349–55, June

Nuffield Foundation (1976) *Small Group Teaching*, Selected Papers

See also: Seminar; Group discussion; Small group teaching; Tutorial

AGENDA METHOD

The Agenda Method is one of several autonomous learning approaches available to students. Under this technique, most of the course sessions take place in the tutor's absence. He attends only for the purpose of handing out and defining the task. He returns later to receive reports of the solutions or decisions that have been arrived at and to lead a discussion on them. The Agenda Method gives a lot of autonomy to students, but it has, nevertheless, a firmly directed line of enquiry, content and activity. The tutor's skill is that of defining the task for the group and helping them work through the different stages. The tutor's role is similar to that of the Set Advisor in the Action Learning approach. In using this method, group members obtain the satisfaction of reaching solutions and making decisions without the lecturer's involvement. The greatest difficulty of the approach lies in choosing a suitable task for the group to work on. If the teacher is not to take over the directing role then the task must contain some internal feedback mechanism that gives the students a check on their progress. A task which may be suitable for a group of college students may be that of designing a question paper for their end-of-year examination.

See also: Instrumented team learning; Creative dialogue; Learning cell; Parrainage; Media-activated learning group; Tutorium; Action learning; Examination; Structuring seminars

ALEXANDER TECHNIQUE

The Alexander Technique is a method for correcting destructive habits such as bad posture and bad breathing. Certain body actions, such as tensing the whole arm instead of just the wrist, can become so habitual that they end up as automatic reactions. In consequence we become unaware of them. The Alexander Technique aims to make people conscious of their bad habits, thereby helping to control them. The approach was developed by F. M. Alexander, an Australian actor. While observing himself in the mirror one day he noticed that when he spoke he involuntarily jerked back his head and made a gasping sound through sucking in his breath. By controlling his head movement he found that he could improve his breathing and the functioning of his larynx.

In management training this technique has been applied by Thame. She believes that the biggest obstacle to learning in adults is their habitual patterns of behaviour which prevents them from responding in new ways to new situations and in new ways to familiar situations. The aim of the technique is to help adults to overcome these habitual responses. It is concerned with the development of our ability to gain conscious control over ourselves, by means of the teacher using his hands to communicate directly how this conscious control can be developed through the sensory system. Unlearning precedes new learning. Once a manager learns what habits are hindering his ability to learn something new, he can go on to remove these and thereby become more effective in the future.

Carrington, W. H. M. (1963) 'The F. Matthias Alexander Technique, A Means of Understanding Man' in *Systemics*, vol. 3, December

Maisel, E. (1969) *The Resurrection of the Body: The Writings of F. Matthias Alexander*, University Books

Thame, S. (1978) 'A Means of Understanding Human Learning: The Alexander Technique' in *Management Education and Development*, vol. 9, no. 3, pp. 202–5

Barlow, W. (1981) *The Alexander Principle*, Arrow Books Ltd

See also: Bio-energetics; Re-evaluation counselling

ALGORITHM

Algorithms are communication strategies, other than the spoken word, that the teacher/manager can use either in teaching or in normal company business. Algorithms are a way to help solve complex rules and procedures. They guarantee that a correct solution will be selected provided that the necessary information is accurate. They are recipes or sets of instructions which are usually presented in the form of a family tree. An algorithm is a systematic plan which reduces problem solving to a series of comparatively simple operations and indicates, for a variety of contingencies, the order in which the operations should be carried out. The student need only work through that part of the procedure that is directly relevant to his problem. In this way, the time spent in decision making is systematically reduced and the job thereby simplified. Any set of rules can be represented diagrammatically, though it is best when the number of interaction/outcomes is limited. Although they may become unwieldy if they get very large, algorithms have been found to be useful in dealing with procedures and routines which have to be carried out by organisational personnel. However, one of the dangers of using algorithms for instruction is that the learner can get the right answer without understanding how or why. For this reason they are often called 'anti-teaching devices'. They can be very useful so long as one does not assume that the learner is necessarily doing more than following a simple, usually dichotomous, key.

Keyworth, R. (1977) 'Communicating Complex Information' in *Industrial and Commercial Training*, vol. 9, no. 11, pp. 455–61

Cook, M. H. (1980) 'Algorithmization – A Shortcut to Learning (and to Savings)' in *Training and Development Journal*, Part 1 in vol. 34, no. 4, pp. 4–8; Part 2 in vol. 34, no. 6, pp. 4–7

Landa, L. (1974) *Algorithmization in Learning and Instruction*, Englewood Cliffs, New Jersey: Educational Technology Publications

Landa, L. (1976) *Instructional Regulation and Control; Cybernetics, Algorithmization and Heuristics in Education*, Englewood Cliffs, New Jersey: Educational Technology Publications

Lewis, B. N. and Woolfenden, P. J. (1969) *Algorithms and Logical Trees: A Self Instruction Course*, Cambridge, Algorithm Press

Gane, C. P., Horrabin, I. S. and Lewis, B. N. (1966) 'The Simplification and Avoidance of Instruction' in *Industrial Training International*, July

Unwin, A. (1977) 'Algorithms in Public Service' in *Industrial and Commercial Training*, vol. 9, no. 9, pp. 357–62

Wheatley, D. M. and Unwin, A. W. (1972) *The Algorithm Writer's Guide*, Longman

See also: Decision table; Heuristic; Flowchart

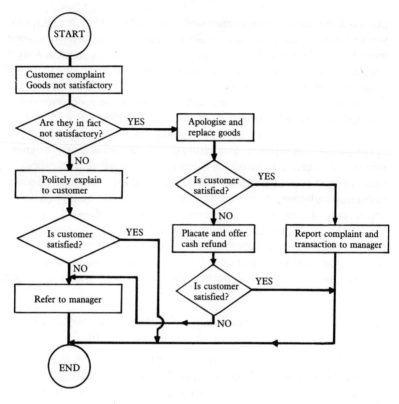

Figure 3.1 Algorithmic approach to sales training

APPERCEPTION–INTERACTION METHOD

This is a projective approach to learning. The tutor begins by identifying problem themes in the daily lives of learners. This may be done through interviews, group discussion or by an analysis of essays completed by students on an appropriate topic. On the basis of these results, a set of learning materials focusing on the themes identified are prepared. These may consist of a provocative picture, an open-ended problem drama or a brief story. Students begin by relating their own feelings and experiences to the photograph or story ('apperception') and then go on to explore a particular problem projected in the narrative through a group discussion ('interaction'). The role of the tutor is that of a discussion leader helping students to explore the options open to the characters in the story or photograph. This approach is a way of assisting students to work in the affective domain of learning (values, feelings, emotions, beliefs) while having a relatively strong cognitive base. It encourages students to think for themselves and to explore creative solutions to problems and issues that are uppermost in their minds. The learning materials contain multiple stimuli in the form of motives, situations and characters and visual material.

For example, an important issue at present is that of women in management. The course designer might interview actual and potential managers of both sexes within a company in order to identify the relevant issues and concerns. Views may be expressed by male managers regarding interaction with a female colleague of equal status, their perception of the role of women in society, their capability with regard to their role etc. Female staff may express their hesitance at applying for managerial and supervisory positions or their anxieties about 'being the only woman there'. The tutor can then write a few brief vignettes describing some of the situations described, obtain photographs of female world leaders, collect relevant feminist literature etc. These can be used with Sociodrama, Role Playing and various Group Discussion methods.

See also: Confluent education; Gestalt techniques; Values clarification; Jurisprudential model; Trigger film

APPLICATION DISCUSSION GROUP (Praxis Group)

An Application Discussion Group is one in which students are encouraged to draw relationships between experiences in the group and similar experiences outside. In 1947, after Kurt Lewin and his colleagues had stumbled across the T-Group method of training, there were established Action Groups (A-Groups) whose aims were to consider this question of application. While these quickly died out in the American model, A-Groups or Application Study Groups continue to be a regular feature of the Tavistock Institute's 'Leicester Conferences'. The term Associative Discussion can more loosely refer to any small group activity which has as its topic the application of learning previously acquired.

See also: Training transfer training; Post-course follow-up; Tavistock conference method

APPRAISAL MODULE

The Appraisal Module is a method useful for structuring group discussion. The task to be performed is the evaluation of something. It may be an object (e.g. microcomputer), an event (e.g. staff appraisal), a statement (e.g. from the Government) or a proposal (e.g. from the Managing Director). There are two elements involved in this activity. The first is the acquisition of a 'warrant'. A warrant is a proposition that serves to support or justify the evaluation of the thing as good or bad, desirable or undesirable, fair or unfair. In some cases the warrant will be the same as the criteria for evaluation. The second element of the model consists of a set of facts that connect the thing being evaluated to the warrant, and thus support the given evaluation of it. How does this process work?

Taking a proposition as the focus of the exercise, the warrant might be, 'Any staff selection technique that predicts high employee performance and success in the job should be used as a basis for recruiting people to the company'. The set of facts would be those which showed the validity of a certain selection technique in predicting employee performance. By applying the warrant and the facts to the question of whether a particular technique should be used or not, serves the purpose of structuring a discussion. Let us consider another application of making an appraisal.

A group of trainees prepares a checklist/appraisal form against which the performance of an individual or a group of individuals can be judged. The students first work individually and then in groups to produce such a checklist. Following this, one member of the trainee group does something which is appraisable, e.g. gives a short talk, interviews a job applicant, gives a stranger directions. The other class members then appraise the volunteer's performance of the set task. Individual assessments can then be compared and discussed. This method can be useful for either highlighting the key success elements in the performance of certain tasks, or can be used to emphasise the subjectivity and consequent variability in the assessment of performance. The exercise can be applied to objectives setting, appraisal for improvement, appraising someone else's performance and so on.

Meux, M. O. (1963) 'The Evaluating Operation in the Classroom' in Bellack, A. A. (ed.) *Theory and Research in Teaching*, New York: Bureau of Publications, Teachers College, Columbia University

Stewart, V. and Stewart, A. (1978) *Practical Performance Appraisal*, Aldershot: Gower

Stewart, V. and Stewart, A. (1978) *Managing The Manager's Growth*, Aldershot: Gower

See also: Performance review; Self appraisal; Management audit; Jurisprudential model

APPRENTICESHIP PROGRAMME

The Apprenticeship Programme is one of the oldest known forms of education. Strictly defined it refers to a contractual relationship between an employer and an employee in which the latter is trained for prescribed work by obtaining personal experience under the supervision of a master craftsman or by formal instruction. In common usage, the term is used to describe any form of on-the-job experience and is sometimes equated with the common form of learning called 'sitting by Nellie'. As a management learning and development approach it can, and has been, used on occasions when an individual takes over the job of another person. Prior to the takeover, the new incumbent works with the expert as an understudy to the person he will succeed. A period of supervised practice can also be provided in cases where the trainee will not succeed the expert. The term Manager Shadowing is sometimes used to refer to a process where the learner works with the manager, following him as he carries out his daily duties to learn about the problems and the tasks and how these should be executed.

Revans, R. W. (1968) 'The Management Apprentice' in *Management International Review*, vol. 8, no. 6, pp. 29–42

Williams, G. (1977) 'Apprenticeship Revisited' in *Journal of Further and Higher Educational*, vol. 1, no. 2, pp. 65–73

See also: Sitting by Nellie; Assignment to manager with high development skills; Manager shadowing; Internship

ASSERTIVENESS TRAINING

Assertiveness Training was developed by Andrew Salter in 1949 and has recently become fashionable in management development and training. The approach aims to help people to avoid embarrassment in communicating their legitimate grievances to others. For example, returning unsatisfactory goods to a shop or complaining to a neighbour about the noise he is making. The purpose is not to make participants aggressive, but more assertive; that is, take account of their own and other people's feelings and in so doing preserve their self-esteem. The training method itself takes people through those situations in which they find it difficult to assert themselves. They role play those situations. The training illustrates how we can allow ourselves to be manipulated into feeling guilty, giving in to unreasonable requests and then harbouring hostilities and resentments. It teaches people to change their expectations and behaviour by encouraging a more assertive approach. Lack of assertiveness can come from not wishing to upset people since it can lead to our not being liked. Management situations such as disciplinary interviews, staff appraisals and interdepartmental communications can provoke the need among some managers for this type of training.

Kelley, C. (1979) *Assertion Training: A Facilitator's Guide*, University Associates of Europe Ltd

Alberti, R. E. (1977) (ed.) *Assertiveness: Innovations, Applications, Issues*, Impact Publishers Inc.

Dawley, H. H. and Wenrich, W. W. (1976) *Achieving Assertive Behavior*, Brooks/Cole Publishing Company

Cotler, S. B. and Guerra, J. J. (1976) *Assertion Training*, Research Press

Paul, N. (1979) 'Assertiveness Without Tears: A Training Programme for Executive Equality' in *Personnel Management*, vol. 11, no. 4, pp. 37–40

See also: Confidence-building training; Motivation training

ASSIGNMENT ATTACHMENT

Assignment Attachment can be seen as a structured way of giving feedback on written assignments to students. The different aspects of the assignments which carry marks or grades are listed so that assignments which are marked by a whole range of people are done so on the basis of an agreed list of specified points. For example, such points may include 'ability to specify the question', 'adequate definition of the key terms' and so on. These criteria for evaluation are communicated to the students beforehand and form the basis of the subsequent written and oral feedback. Thus the tutor makes written comments to the students under each of these headings. However, Assignment Attachments are not merely a way of structuring the feedback that is given to students. Their second and equally important task is to standardise the grade given to an assignment between a range of different staff who are doing the marking. For instance, if a course is team taught and assignments are being given out by different members of the team to different seminar/syndicate groups within the course, then the resulting assignments have to be marked/graded to the same criteria and require feedback about the same criteria because these are the actual learning objectives for the exercise.

To some extent therefore, Assignment Attachments force one into specifying learning objectives.

See also: Essay

ASSIGNMENT TO COMMUNITY ORGANISATION

In this form of development the manager may be seconded to a civic, community, voluntary or social organisation for a continuous period of up to perhaps a year. A major international electronics company has, for example, lent promising managers with development potential to organisations to solve inner-city problems. While no financial return accrues to the organisation lending the manager, the individual concerned does return to his home organisation having learned something and the company has pursued its goal as a good corporate citizen. The problem here is to ensure that the manager involved is clear about his learning goals and does not allow these to be swamped by the demands of the new job and the glamour of being involved in a (necessarily) rare form of staff development.

With this approach, the company needs to ensure that the secondment involved, in addition to perhaps being good public relations, will actually teach the manager something that is relevant to what the company has in mind for him in the future (or what he has in mind for himself in the organisation). For example, there would be little point in a polytechnic seconding one of their teaching staff to the local authority's Social Services Department to learn counselling skills unless the polytechnic were sure that they were going to develop the counselling side of their services to students, and intended making that a bigger part of the lecturer's job description on his return. This is of course different from clarifying the lecturer's own objectives for participating.

See also: Development assignment; Assignment to customer as representative; Assignment to government body study group; Service in professional associations; Accepting positions of responsibility in community organisations

ASSIGNMENT TO CUSTOMER AS REPRESENTATIVE

In this form of development a manager may be assigned to work closely over a period of time with one of the company's major customers. The customer company gains the benefit of having its particular problems examined in depth by a company which supplies some part of its major equipment. The individual manager benefits by being placed in a new and challenging work environment. This approach avoids the difficulty of Assignment to Community Organisation because here one cannot avoid developing oneself in a way which will benefit one's own firm on returning.

See also: Assignment to community organisation; Assignment to government body study group; Development assignment; Service in professional associations; Accepting positions of responsibility in community organisations

ASSIGNMENT TO GOVERNMENT BODY STUDY GROUP

A manager may be requested or invited to participate on some governmental or quasi-governmental committee which is investigating a particular problem or issue. Frequently such bodies may require the type of specialised knowledge that the manager concerned possesses. With this approach, the company involved needs to be clear what the developmental needs of its own staff are. However, when such requests come from the government or its agencies, firms may not be in a position to refuse it for all sorts of political reasons. A recent example in the United Kingdom involved such a study group being formed under the leadership of a Cabinet Minister following a period of rioting in inner-city areas. On this occasion representatives of leading investment institutions were invited to join. Banks, building societies, insurance companies and pension funds sent chief executives, chairmen of boards of trustees and senior property executives. When, as in this case, the issue concerned is politically volatile, both the company and the individual manager involved may express resentment at being included.

See also: Development assignment; Service in professional associations; Accepting positions of responsibility in community organisations

ASSIGNMENT TO MANAGER WITH HIGH DEVELOPMENT SKILLS

Within an organisation a manager may be identified as having the skills, knowledge, ability and temperament to develop his subordinates to a higher degree or at a faster rate than others. Such a person may possibly, although not necessarily, be a 'backbone' manager (to use Alistair Mant's term). This person can become involved in staff development by having staff assigned to work with him for this reason. The manager, if he takes the job on, must be clear about his responsibilities, and may require training and development himself to carry out his new role. The act of developing a junior staff member may itself be considered a developmental activity for the senior manager concerned.

How does one identify an individual with such skills? Mumford (1980) offered a list of the characteristics of managers whom he believed were good, conscious developers of their staff. He argued that such individuals were few and far between, which would make this form of in-company development approach a rare one. According to Mumford, the behaviour characteristics of such managers were as follows:

> They draw out the strengths and weaknesses of their subordinates rather than suppressing them. They reward their people both materially and psychologically for the risks they take in attempting to develop themselves. They positively seek to identify learning opportunities for their subordinates. They give personal time to the development of subordinates – for example, for reviewing and analysing an activity for learning purposes. They involve the subordinates in some of their own important tasks (not just delegate Mickey Mouse tasks). They share some of their problems and anxieties with their subordinates, in the interests of their subordinates' development rather than simply as relief for themselves. They listen rather than talk. They do not say or imply 'be more like me'. They take risks on the desired results of their unit in pursuit of relevant learning opportunities for their people.

If an organisation does contain any managers with the characteristics that Mumford suggests, then they may be the ones to whom junior staff might usefully be assigned.

Mumford, A. (1980) *Making Experience Pay*, London: McGraw-Hill, p. 4

Leigh, D. R. (1966) 'Development or developers — Developing others as a management development method' in *Training and Development Journal*, November, pp. 42-6

See also: Acting assignment; Development assignment; Expanding job assignment; Exposure to upper management; Sick leave/holiday replacement assignment

ASSOCIATIVE DISCUSSION GROUP
Abercrombie defines 'free' or 'associative' discussion groups as ones

which are organised with the purpose of enabling each participant to become aware of the tacit assumptions which are relevant to the topic at hand. Groups of between 6 and 12 students meet for about one and a half hours in a series of eight or more weekly meetings. Members are free to participate as they wish and to follow up their own and others' associations with the topic. Each participant can then see how his past experience and habitual ways of reacting to the content, influences his own process of perception and interpretation of current events. He analyses his own reactions in comparison and contrast to the variety displayed by other members and changes his own if he so chooses.

Abercrombie, M. L. J. and Terry, P. M. (1978) *Talking to Learn: Improving Teaching and Learning in Small Groups*, Guildford, Surrey: Society for Research into Higher Education

Abercrombie, M. L. J. (1960) *The Anatomy of Judgement*, London: Hutchinson; Harmondsworth: Penguin (1969)

Abercrombie, M. L. J. and Terry, P. M. (1971) 'The First Session: an introduction to associative group discussion', Appendix in 2nd edition of Abercrombie, M. L. J. *Aims and Techniques of Group Teaching*, Guildford, Surrey: Society for Research into Higher Education

Abercrombie, M. L. J. (1981) 'Changing Basic Assumptions About Teaching and Learning' in Boud, D. J. (ed.) *Developing Autonomy in Student Learning*, London: Kogan Page Ltd

See also: Leaderless group discussion; Group discussion; Small group teaching; Free discussion method; Creative dialogue

AUDIENCE REACTION/WATCHDOG TEAM (Concept Moderators)

If one is having a large meeting which includes a number of platform speakers and a large audience, the involvement of the latter can be achieved by bringing representatives of the audience on to the platform to serve as a reaction or watchdog team. An Audience Reaction Team is asked simply to listen to the presentation and then to give their reactions, either in a series of statements or through a panel discussion. A Watchdog Team is asked to listen for language or concepts which they think members of the audience might not fully understand and to interrupt the presenter at any time and ask for clarification. If the people selected to serve on the team represent the main characteristics of the audience, the audience will identify psychologically with the interaction on the platform.

An application of this general idea has been developed by de Winter Hebron and is labelled Concept Moderation. If one has a large group such as a total conference membership, which is working in a number of small sub-groups and the organiser suspects that there may be valuable things for a Watchdog Team to look at, then he can assign one participant in each of the sub-groups the additional role of looking out for this point as the group works – for example, how particular labels are being used by group members. In addition, one or more persons are assigned to go round all the groups, visiting their individual meetings. In this way, each group has a Concept Moderator, who knows the whole of the group's work, and also one or more Concept Moderators who know some of the things that have been going on in all the sub-groups. These then meet together and examine which problems run through the whole of the seminar/conference, and which are peculiar to particular groups. This team then reports to all the conference participants in plenary session about halfway through the proceedings, and the report is followed by a discussion. The sub-groups then reform and continue working having clarified and shifted perceptions of what is being said.

See also: Listening team; Interrogation of experts; Reaction panel

AUDIO TAPE

Audio Tapes can be used either as a method of breaking up a period of lecturing or to stimulate and provoke students in a seminar or small group discussion. Tapes are easily homemade, and since the teacher controls the content, they have many potential applications. For example, an item can be taken from a radio current affairs programme such as an interview with a politician or union representative, and then replayed to the lecture class or small group. The item needs to be short enough to have an immediate impact. In a lecture class, the teacher can comment on aspects of the views expressed and then ask for audience reaction through votes of agreement or disagreement. Alternatively, buzz groups can be asked to discuss the views expressed. In small group discussion more in-depth questioning techniques can be used. Many other 'stimuli for discussion' can be put on to a tape such as short dramatic sequences (similar to Trigger Films), a scripted discussion between two people with opposing views on a key issue, analysis of telephone conversations etc.

Rahmlow, H. F. and Langdon, D. G. (1977) 'Ubiquitous Audio' in *Programmed Learning and Educational Technology*, vol. 14, no. 1, pp. 9–12

McDonald, R. and Knights, S. (1979) 'Learning from Tapes: the experience of home based Students', *Programmed Learning and Educational Technology*, vol. 16, no. 1 pp. 46–51

Engel, C. E. (1971) 'Preparation of Audio Tapes for Self Instruction' in *Medical and Biological Illustration*, vol. 21, no. 1, pp. 14–18

See also: Tape-assisted learning programme; Audio tutorial method; Tape stop exercise; Media-activated learning group; Television programme; Trigger film; Buzz group

AUDIO TUTORIAL METHOD

For the individual student, the Audio Tutorial Method will involve individual work in carrels, group working and attending lectures. The key thing is the balance of the different activities that the learner is required to do. The method is used mainly where one cannot make all the resources available at a single time or continuously. It contains administrative techniques and procedures which allow slow and active learners to absorb course material while freeing the rapid learner to proceed as quickly and in as much depth as he requires.

In an ATM programme, a whole group of students moves along through the same set of materials in the same order and at the same rate for the group as a whole. Individual learners spend more or less time, as necessary to complete the work. Basically everyone is expected to finish the same work in a given amount of time equal to a 'grading period'. The grade given is related to the amount of material covered as verified by criterion tests which are often of the multiple choice variety.

Students usually work alone in individual booths, which consist of a chair, table and some shelves housed in a small carrel or cubicle. The booth will contain a tape recorder, some kind of colour slide viewer and other assorted equipment, e.g. maps, books, prepared slides. Courses organised primarily on an ATM model frequently also have large group meetings scheduled so that learners will feel less isolated and can have more contact with the 'voice on the tape'. Discussion groups or quiz sessions may also be scheduled, which can be optional or compulsory.

Although formal lectures are often integrated into the course, these are not mentioned on the tape. The tape tends to be a guide only to what is in the carrel or in the audio tutorial lab. A printed study guide is also very common and contains objectives, questions, spaces for answers, diagrams, etc. The value of this is that the student retains it as a record of the audio-tutorial session.

Postlethwait, S. N., Murray H. and Novak, J. (1972) *The Audio Tutorial System – An Integrated Experience Approach to Learning*, Minneapolis: Burgess

Garland, P. B., Dutton, G. J. and MacQueen, D. (1977) 'Audio Tutorial Aids for Teaching Bio-chemistry' in *Studies in Higher Education*, vol. 2, no. 2, pp. 167–71

Postlethwait, S. N. and Hurst, R. N. (1972) 'The Audio Tutorial System Incorporating Mini-courses and Mastery, in *Educational Technology*, September

Carre, C. G. (1969) 'Audio Tutorials as Adjuncts to Formal Lecturing in Biology Teaching at Tertiary Level' in *Journal of Biological Education*, vol. 3, no. 1, pp. 57–64

Pressey, S. L. (1964) 'Audio-Instruction: perspectives, problems, potentials' in Hilgard, E. R. (ed) *Theories of Learning and Instruction, 63rd Yearbook of the National Society for the Study of Education*, University of Chicago Press.

Meyer, C. R. (1972) 'Audio-tutorials: an overview' in Simpkins, W. S. and Miller, A. H. (eds) *Changing Education, Australian Viewpoints*, Sydney: McGraw Hill

The Audio-Tutorial System, Film Library for Teacher Education, Caxton Place, Gipsy Road, London SE27, Educational Catalogue Number TE 72, Colour, 25 mins.

See also: Autonomous group learning; Personalised system of instruction; Media-activated learning group

AUTONOMOUS GROUP LEARNING

Autonomous Group Learning (AGL) combines programmed instruction and the participative group activity of the case study method. It is used to provide an environment which can motivate effective learning for managers over two days without any formal instruction taking place. It is based on a view which sees instruction as a specific means of controlling and manipulating a sequence of events to produce a change of behaviour through learning. AGL uses simple technology such as books, papers, tapes and 35 mm slides. It emphasises group methods rather than individual instruction because of the motivation to be derived from the variety in the size and composition of different learning groups. By building slack into the learning system, group interaction can make up for instructional design deficiencies. There is no formal group instruction with the AGL method.

The learning is designed in a group environment which does not direct nor teach the learner but which stimulates and reacts to him in conditions of self discovery and mutual help. The learning process is designed to be a cyclical and rhythmic activity of information input and application clearly relevant to the learner's business environment which rewards him by providing continuous group activity and knowledge of results, thereby motivating the learner to continue. Incorporated in the design is the element of surprise with tests and quizzes to challenge the learner and reward him. The learning structure of an AGL has two eight-hour parts each of which contains two learning cycles of approximately four hours each. Thus learners have a sense of achievement and completion every four hours and further when they complete part one before moving on to part two. A typical sequence consists of a personal welcome by the trainer, audio visual presentation indicating objectives and methods, a quiz completed individually, individual work, audio visual lecture and a case study group discussion.

Boland, R. G. A. (1977) 'The Design of the Autonomous Group Learning System' in *Programmed Learning and Educational Technology*, vol. 14, no. 3, pp. 233–9

See also: Audio tutorial method; Personalised system of instruction; Independent learning; Instrumented team learning; Media-activated learning group

AUTONOMY LAB (Creativity Laboratory, Peer Learning Community, Learning Community)

The 'Laboratory in Autonomy, Initiative and Risk Taking' (Autonomy Lab) is an educational event which is used to encourage autonomous learning and which is based on the view that managers are neither born, nor 'made' by others, but in fact create themselves. Throughout the lab, individuals are encouraged to find their own motives, strengths, interests and patterns of development. These decisions help them to choose and learn from the wide variety of materials which characterise the lab. A unique aspect of the programme is the lack of any constraints on the students which tend to be a part of most other teaching-learning situations. Labs are designed on the principle that participants should be in control of their own learning; that the design should allow them to choose activities which they consider appropriate (based on their experience, background, method and speed of learning); designs should meet members' own needs, motives and values. Finally, it is important that there should be an acceptable level of risk taking, and thereby stress, for each learner.

Physically, the Autonomy Lab room(s) is laid out with a wide range of learning resources which may include exercises, books, games, audio-cassettes, case studies, handouts, articles and self-completion question-naires. Each participant is also encouraged to see both himself and other participants and tutors as learning resources. Managerially, the tutor's role is that of guiding members to the resources that are available and giving advice on how they can be used to the greatest effect. The lab may begin with a brief introductory talk and there will be a full group meeting daily in which everybody shares experiences and assesses progress. Labs are usually run on a residential basis and last between 3–7 days. In them, members are encouraged to take risks, set personal goals and generally take initiatives about their own development without depending upon teachers. An additional facet is the encouragement of the ability of 'learning how to learn', i.e. the development of a framework for solving hitherto unmet problems.

Harrison, R. (1973) 'Developing Autonomy, Initiative and Risk Taking Through a Laboratory Design' in *European Training*, vol. 2, pp. 100–17

Megginson, D. F. (1975) 'An Autonomy Lab in Identifying Training Needs' in *Youth in Society*, November/December

See also: Learning community; Learning organisation; Instrumented laboratory; Community of enquiry

BASIC ENCOUNTER (Rogerian Group Method)

Basic Encounter was developed by Carl Rogers and his colleagues in Chicago. Participants usually sit on chairs throughout and there is little or no physical interaction. The leader who is called a 'facilitator' offers no techniques and does not have to adopt any particular role except that of an open participant ready to reveal his feelings and show interest, care and involvement in the talk and actions of group members. He may also share his intuitions or fantasies about other members, not as truths about other people, but as truths about what is going on around him.

Rogers formulated three requirements for the group leader. Firstly, he shows acceptance of other people and the way they are, not judging or evaluating them. Secondly, he cultivates accurate empathy – hopefully being able to sense feelings that are just below the surface. Finally, genuineness, the sense of being aware of what is going on in him and doing justice to it. Rogerian groups tend to be very 'slow' but sure. Whatever happens in them, little or much, is very real. There is no space for phoneyness to creep in. Basic Encounter is a good starting experience for someone who has never been to an encounter group. The participant will not be pushed into extreme experiences before he or she is ready. One can progress at one's own pace.

Rogers, C. (1967) 'The Process of Basic Encounter' in Bugental, J. F. T. (ed.) *Challenges of Humanistic Psychology*, chapter 28, pp. 261–76, New York: McGraw Hill

Rogers, C. (1970) *Encounter Groups*, Harmondsworth: Penguin Books

Rogers, C. (1961) *On Becoming a Person*, Boston, Mass.: Houghton Mifflin

See also: Encounter group; Open encounter

BEHAVIOUR MODELLING

The most elaborate system of thought on imitation, identification and modelling as concepts of teaching has been developed by Albert Bandura at Stanford University. He labels the system Social Learning. In teaching by modelling, the teacher behaves in ways that he wants the learner to imitate. The teacher's basic technique is role modelling. The effects found were *modelling effect* – where the learner acquires new kinds of response patterns, e.g. teachers show learners how to listen empathically by listening empathically themselves; *inhibitory/disinhibitory effect* – where the learner increases/decreases the latency/intensity of previously acquired responses, e.g. the teacher tells learners through modelling that it is/is not approved behaviour to express their feelings openly thus inhibiting or disinhibiting an old response; *eliciting effect* – learner receives from the model a cue for releasing a response that is neither new nor inhibited, e.g. through modelling, the teacher teaches the art of giving and receiving feedback by inviting learners to criticise their own performance helpfully, thus providing a cue eliciting a response that is neither new nor inhibited.

Social Learning has been applied to behaviour modification in therapeutic settings. It is equally applicable to the development of attitudes, beliefs and performance skills. Every teacher employs modelling as one of his techniques, whether consciously or unconsciously. His potency as a model will be influenced by characteristics like his age, sex, socio-economic status, power and intellectual status. In the field of management development, Mumford (1980) has described the way that the boss and colleagues provide role models for the individual to emulate. He explains that they model their behaviour by observing him and working jointly with him. He suggests that such modelling can be either conscious or unconscious, done in the expectation of reward or from fear or punishment and can be both valuable and not valuable. The modelling is based on the boss's actions, i.e. on what he does rather than what he says. Thus for example, the junior may observe that his boss keeps all information to himself and does not share it with others. He then models his behaviour on this observation. Alternatively, he may notice that his boss asks him and his department colleagues for ideas on a problem and in consequence tries to emulate this behaviour. In the same way, peers constitute a further source of role models for the manager. Mumford noticed that individuals can constitute negative models for others as examples of how not to do it. Like the parents of young children, all managers need to be aware of the fact that they are 'teaching' their juniors whether they are aware of it or not.

Bandura, A. (1969) *Principles of Behaviour Modification*, New York: Holt, Rinehart and Winston

Bandura, A. and Walters, R. H. (1963) *Social Learning and Personality Development*, New York: Holt, Rinehart and Winston

Mumford, A. (1980) *Making Experience Pay*, London: McGraw Hill, chapter 8

Johnson, P. D. and Sorcher, M. (1976) 'Behaviour Modelling Training: Why, How and What Results' in *Journal of European Training*, vol. 5, no. 1, pp. 62–70

'Behaviour Modelling: A new approach to supervisory training' in *People and Profits*, 1975, vol. 2, no. 11, pp. 28–31

Smith, P. E. (1976) 'Management Modelling Training to Improve

Morale and Customer Satisfaction' in *Personnel Psychology*, vol. 29, no. 3, pp. 351–9

Moses, J. L. and Ritchie, R. J. (1976) 'Supervisory Relationships Training: A behavioural evaluation of a behaviour modelling programme' in *Personnel Psychology*, vol. 29, no. 3, pp. 337–43

Kraut, A. I. (1976) 'Developing Managerial Skills via Modelling Techniques: Some positive research findings – a symposium' in *Personnel Psychology*, vol. 29, no. 3, pp. 325–8

Tosti, D. T. (1980) 'Behaviour Modelling: A Process' in *Training and Development*, vol. 34, no. 8, pp. 70–74

See also: Behaviour modification; Interaction management

BEHAVIOUR MODIFICATION

Behaviour Modification is based on B. F. Skinner's work and ideas which emphasise that people will be most likely to engage in desired behaviour if they are rewarded for doing so. The rewards are most effective if they follow immediately the desired behaviour response. One aspect of these ideas is reflected in the use of teaching machines and programmed learning which use the same theory. Behaviour which is not rewarded or is punished is less likely to be repeated. Since punishment is known to have many undesirable side effects it is often less efficient than reward in developing the desired behaviour. It is possible either to reward individuals after every time they behave in a desired way or only after some of the responses. Evidence suggests that the latter method produces the more rapid behaviour changes. Behavioural engineering through the use of positive reinforcement has been criticised on ethical grounds in that it manipulates behaviour. Respondents argue that managers attempt to manipulate the behaviour of their employees all the time (in subtle and less subtle ways) otherwise they would go bankrupt.

The purpose of Behaviour Modification is to change the behaviour of a person in a particular direction. Modification is achieved through a process called Behaviour Therapy. Its focus is the changing of actions and responses rather than the location and analysis of the underlying causes of those actions and responses. Thus for example, in dealing with a staff absenteeism problem, the focus is on the reduction of absentee behaviour, rather than on the analysis of the work motivation, personal needs, beliefs etc. about work. The approach is based on learning and its key elements include reinforcement, conditioning and extinction. If a manager solves a worker's problem every time he has one, the worker 'learns' that the best way to get his problems solved is to give them to his boss. By providing solutions the manager reinforces the problem-passing behaviour. By a process of negative reinforcement (telling him to solve his own problems himself) or positive reinforcement (congratulating him when he solves his own problems), the manager produces an extinction in the undesired problem bringing behaviour.

Operant Conditioning is the term given to this and consists of a set process. A piece of behaviour takes place spontaneously in the company by the employee, i.e. the behaviour was not elicited by the presentation of any stimulus. That behaviour is immediately followed by a reward or reinforcing stimulus, with the nature of the reward depending on circumstances. The behaviour which has been rewarded is then more likely to occur again when similar circumstances prevail. By linking rewarded behaviour in this way, a much larger behaviour pattern can be established. The changing of behaviour patterns by Operant Conditioning when applied to human beings is labelled Behaviour Modification. Parents concerned with bringing up their children will be familiar with the preceding description.

Luthans, F. and Kreitner, R. (1975) *Organizational Behaviour Modification*, Glenview, Illinois: Scott, Foresman and Company

Miller, K. L. (1975) *Principles of Everyday Behaviour Analysis*, Monteray: Wadsworth Publishing Company

Connellan, T. K. (1978) *How to Improve Human Performance: Behaviourism in Business and Industry*, Harper and Row

Sherman, A. R. (1973) *Behaviour Modification: Theory and Practice*, Brooks/Cole Publishing Company

Skinner, A. R. (1953) *Science and Human Behaviour*, New York: Macmillan

Goodall, K. (1972) 'Shapers at Work' in *Psychology Today*, vol. 6, November, pp. 53–62 and 132–8

Johnson, P. and Sorcher, M. (1976) 'Behaviour Modelling Training: How, Why and What Results?' in *Journal of European Training*, vol. 5, no. 1, pp. 62–70

Gullett, C. R. and Reisen, R. (1975) 'Behaviour Modification, A Contingency Approach to Employee Performance' in *Personnel Journal*, vol. 54, no. 4, April

See also: Behaviour modelling; Interaction management

BIOENERGETICS

Bioenergetic Analysis is a therapeutic method developed by Alexander Lowen aimed at discharging the tensions and feelings which may be frozen in areas of the body. Using stress postures, breathing, sound and vigorous body movement, this method aims to leave one more open to experience and expression. Bioenergetics is one of the 'growth therapies' that has begun to be used in management training. It is focused on the individual who wishes to change and uses a psycho-physical approach to achieve this. Underpinning the method is the idea that a person's beliefs, attitudes and habits rigidly structure his thoughts, feelings and behaviour. In order to change, an individual must explore himself at a deep level. In this way, the 'unfinished business' from past experiences can be identified and worked on. It is believed that such unfinished business draws what exponents term the 'life energy' from the current tasks the person has to deal with. He wastes a lot of energy holding down the feelings that he has been conditioned not to express. The equal emphasis on the physical dimension arises out of the belief that psychological rigidities of behaviour are reflected in the body. Thus, it is argued, the training must focus on the cognitive as well as the affective dimensions. As with other growth therapies, bioenergetics aims to help the individual to respond to change, become more self-regulating, deal better with feelings and generally to cope better with problems.

Lowen, A. (1976) *Bioenergetics*, Harmondsworth: Penguin Books

Lowen, A. (1971) *The Language of the Body*, New York: Macmillan

Cassius, J. (1980) *Horizons in Bioenergetics*, Promethean

See also: Alexander technique; Re-evaluation counselling

BIOGRAPHY (Autobiography)

The object of biography work is to help people reach a better understanding of and relationship to their personal life patterns, events and circumstances. These are then used as the basis from which to plan the future. This work at the individual level is capable of being integrated with management development. Its primary aim is to develop the participant and is a form of development that a person might use and repeat. Managers may work on the forces of professional formation and deformation, creativity, life patterns and rhythms. In a Biography seminar participants work with other participants to explore their total life field taking into account education, talents, profession, career, organisational culture, personal biography, marriage, family situation and health. Programme approaches include counselling, group discussion, individual reflection on personal questions, exercises and lectures.

Leary, M. (1981) 'Working with Biography' in Boydell, T. and Pedler, M. (eds) *Management Self-Development: Concepts and Practices*, Aldershot: Gower

Abbs, P. (1974–5) 'Autobiography and the Training of Teachers' in *Universities Quarterly*, vol. 29 pp. 104–12

See also: Career life planning; Values clarification

BLOCK METHOD

The central emphasis in the Block Method is upon the differentiated assignment. It is based upon the assumption that students in a single class fall into three or four relatively homogeneous groups with respect to ability. The teacher provides a set of graded assignments and the students are encouraged to select one of the 'blocks' or 'levels' and endeavour to meet its requirements. A student may achieve one level during a certain term or part of a term, and advance or recede to another in the next period.

The determination of what constitutes a block is a difficult process. The teacher usually proceeds on the basis of the minimum of essentials and adds projects and other extra work. There is no principle against which to determine the difficulty of the blocks except by experience, for example:

Block D Test assignment and tests
Block C D plus four oral reports
Block B C plus one written report
Block A B plus one oral book report

The method can have a stimulating effect on students, encouraging those of mediocre ability to endeavour to reach the higher levels. It also provides variety in procedure and in activity. There is no limit on the kinds of blocks utilised.

See also: Worksheet

BOOK REVIEWING

Students are asked to consider the different functions of book reviews which appear in publications such as popular magazines, newspapers, learned journals, hobby and leisure magazines. Their task is to agree a range of criteria against which a review may be judged. They then take a book that is related to the course and, using the criteria previously identified, they write a 'relevant' review of that book. If time and resources permit, the same book title may be reviewed by several students, and the similarities and differences in perceptions and judgements examined. The approach can be used to practise the skills of abstraction and the processing of unpleasant information. Stewart and Stewart (1978) give the example of how books, papers and reports can be given to trainees who have to prepare a précis for a given purpose. For example, an ITB document is studied in order to discover what implications there are in it for the managing director. This is followed by a review and a further practice session. Few adults have any skills in précis, so the review can be vocabulary enhancing, concentrating on methods of skipping, page layout, marking documents etc.

Another aspect highlighted is the review of information one does not like or which is presented in an unpalatable way, while understanding what it says. In management education, the products of Marxist literature are particularly suitable and Stewart and Stewart (1978) recommend a book such as *The Hazards of Work* by P. Kinnersley, Pluto Press, 1973 which is an anti-capitalist guide to safety and health at work. It illustrates how safety regulations are flouted in the interests of convenience. When a text such as this is given to managers to review in writing with a specified word limit, it can distinguish between those who are put off by the politics of the presentation, and those who can nevertheless understand what it is saying. Such an exercise can be followed by a trainer-led discussion on the subject.

Stewart, V. and Stewart, A. (1978) *Managing the Manager's Growth*, Aldershot: Gower

Stewart, A. and Stewart, V. (1976) *Tomorrow's Men Today*, London : Institute of Personnel Management, chapter 5

See also: Re-writing; Reading; Reading parties; Literature search; Guided reading

BRAINS TRUST

Asking the right questions is often as important a part of the learning as getting the right answers. When the subject-matter is non-controversial and does not raise issues that can easily be discussed or when students are unwilling to express their difficulties in class, buzz groups may be instructed to agree a question they wish to ask a lecturer, to write it on a sheet of paper and pass it anonymously to the front. The technique provides the teacher with feedback on his effectiveness and provides clarification of the lecture points. It can also be used when a guest speaker or speakers are invited. Students are requested to research and prepare questions, the answers to which form the basis of the session. Also the Brains Trust can be the first level of audience participation at a large meeting, as in the famous radio programme. Questions are directed from the audience through a chairman or directly, verbally, to panel members.

The approach can be used to provide a background knowledge or a general survey of a subject. It can thus be designed to replace the general standard lecture. Within a company it can be used to give junior staff an insight into the scientific and research aspects of the firm. Persons on the Brains Trust panel must be of high calibre and expert in their subject in order to be capable of standing up to the questioning.

See also: Interrogation of experts; Questioning; Reaction panel; Interview meeting; Buzz group

BRAINSTORMING

Brainstorming is a permissive teaching style based on the assumption that a group of people can produce more ideas than individuals working by themselves. It was first developed by Alex Osborn in 1938. The dictionary defines Brainstorming as the practice of a conference technique by which a group attempts to find a solution for a specific problem by amassing all the ideas spontaneously contributed by its members. The technique, which has been widely used in creativity training, consists in essence of a problem-solving situation in which the participants are given a problem and then asked to bring into the discussion any ideas which come to mind, irrespective of how outrageous or far fetched. At this point no evaluation of ideas takes place. In this way the group encourages rather than discourages strange and unusual suggestions. At a later point, all suggestions are analysed, synthesised and evaluated. A unique and practical solution is then fashioned by the group from what originally may have been a bizarre idea.

Within the teaching situation, Brainstorming can be a useful way to encourage group participation even in a large group situation. Any topic can be introduced with the injunction to the class group of 'What might be the advantages of ...?' or 'What problems might this raise?'. The lecturer can then either ask members to shout out their ideas which are

53

chalked up on the board, or else ask participants to compare answers in small groups. It has been argued that Brainstorming is simply one particular sub-class of the kind of teacher questioning which elicits a whole hidden agenda/response from the student. The Brainstorm Question is thus merely one of several similar questioning strategies.

Andrews, D. J. W. (1980) 'The Verbal Structure of Teacher Questions: Its Impact on Class Discussion' in *Professional and Organizational Development Quarterly*, nos. 2, 3 and 4, Fall/Winter, pp. 129–63

Clark, C. H. (1958) *Brainstorming*, New York: Doubleday and Co. Inc.

Rawlinson, J. G. (1981) *Creative Thinking and Brainstorming*, Aldershot: Gower

Bosticco, M. (1971) *Creative Techniques for Management*, London: Business Books

See also: Questioning; Lateral thinking; Creativity training

BUBERIAN DIALOGUE

Buberian Dialogue is a way of presenting ideas and is named after the philosopher Martin Buber. People with opposing views on a subject are invited to present and discuss their views in front of a group. However, a group rule is that no one is allowed to argue with anyone else on the panel. Discussants may seek clarification of points and identify areas of common agreement, but they must accept any viewpoint presented by another panelist without contradiction or argument. The discussion is then opened to the public with the same ground rules; no arguments only clarification. This dialogue helps people to understand each other's viewpoints. In a Buberian Dialogue everybody wins and the negative competitive aspects of formal debate are minimised.

See also: Debate; Think and listen session; Creative dialogue; Group with ground rules

BUZZ GROUP

A Buzz Group consists of two to six persons who discuss an issue or problem for a short period of time, once or several times, during a lesson or lecture. In a lecture hall, a row of students can be asked to face the row behind or two or three people in the same row can be asked to get together. Groups of three should be used when there are likely to be individual viewpoints to be posed. Buzz Groups tend to be popular with students but they may need to be carefully introduced to learners who are only, or mainly, familiar with didactic methods. They have been used both formally and informally with between 6–200 students. They are flexible and do not require a great deal of preparation. They can be used in an impromptu way for as little as five minutes.

Amongst the aims of the Buzz Group method are the following: (*a*) clarification – lecturer checks that he has got his point over by getting students to work in threes and fours on a problem which requires the use of the knowledge; (*b*) feedback – lecturer checks on students tackling the problem set and receives feedback on the effectiveness of his teaching; (*c*) consolidation of learning and understanding – a task is set which aims to get the students to relate different parts of the lecture together or to their common experiences; (*d*) learning concepts and terminology – an exercise is given to groups in order to check that they have understood the terms taught; (*e*) information application/analytical/evaluative/critical thinking – here Buzz Groups work on questions such as 'What are the advantages of ...?' or 'What is the difference between...?' (*e*) to give the lecturer a breathing space; (*f*) to encourage reticent students to put forward their ideas and views, and (*g*) to foster a cohesive class spirit.

The Buzz Group idea can be developed into a 'Snowball' process. In this variation a question or problem is first discussed by students in pairs, then two fours join up to make a group of eight. A spokesman can be appointed from each group who reports back to the entire large group in a plenary type session.

Improving Teaching in Higher Education, University Teaching Methods Unit, University of London, 1976

Bligh, D. A. (1972) *What's the Use of Lectures?* Harmondsworth: Penguin books

See also: Cross over group; Large groups as small groups; Phillips 66 technique

CAREER LIFE PLANNING

Management career development is a continuous process of change in activities, positions and values. People may feel caught in an 'organisational trap' because their personal goals and sense of meaning may be lost. The career problems of many individuals may be symptoms of larger organisational problems such as a rigid bureaucratic structure. As an individual develops within an organisation, his career path reaches crisis points when he is faced with a choice between jobs or organisations. At this point there is a need for the individual to apply some form of planning in order to determine how best to achieve his career goals. One such method is Career Life Planning. Managers can attend non-company programmes or, if their organisations offer the opportunity, in-company programmes. The purposes of the latter are to develop and promote high potential employees into channels where their abilities will be utilised to the fullest. Extra-company courses focus more on the individual's ability to identify his current life goals and to assess the extent to which his job and his general life style helps him to achieve these. Career Life Planning is one of several forms of career development approaches and involves the application of laboratory learning techniques to career development. All approaches tend to use the idea of individual goal setting, values clarification and achievement motivation as a means of helping the participant to gain greater control of his life.

Hopson, B. (1976) 'Personal Growth and Career Development' in Cooper, C. L. (ed.) (1976) *Developing Social Skills in Managers*, London: Macmillan

Swartz, D. H. (1975) 'Life Goals Planning for Managers' in Taylor, B. and Lippitt, G. L. (eds.) *Management Development and Training Handbook*, London: McGraw Hill

Hopson, B. (1973) 'Career Development in Industry: The Diary of an Experiment' in *British Journal of Guidance Counselling*, vol. 1, no. 1, pp. 51–61

Hopson, B. and Hough, P. (1973) *Exercises in Personal and Career Development*, Cambridge: CRAC/Hobsons Press Ltd

Kirn, A. G. (1974) *Lifework Planning: Workbook and Trainer's Manual*, La Jolla, Calif.: University Associates Inc., 3rd edition

Ford, G. A. and Lippitt, G. L. (1976) *Planning Your Future: A Workbook for Personal Goal Setting*, University Associates of Europe Ltd

See also: Biography; Values clarification

CASE CONFERENCE
Used mainly in fields such as medicine, nursing and social work, the Case Conference involves a meeting of between eight and twelve people.

The primary purpose of any Case Conference is to assist a group of people who all have inputs into the treatment of a particular case (e.g. hospital patient) to reach an accurate and informed decision on what step to take next or an accurate and informed opinion as to the quality of the results achieved in dealing with the case so far. In such meetings participants describe some of their work activities and problems which have caused them difficulties. The others listen and offer advice and suggestions. Each Case Conference involves one or more senior staff or workers who have had extensive experience of the problems being discussed. Such an approach might be used by a group of managers each contributing to the fulfilment of some major export order. While the focus of a Case Conference is on the specific professional/work task involved, it can be directed towards the meeting of individual/group development needs if some form of process review is added to become a regular dimension of each case meeting.

See also: Illuminative incident analysis; Conference method; Group discussion; Problem-centred group; Process analysis

CASE HISTORY

A Case History is a specific and straightforward account of an actual event or situation which is intended to inform the reader or listener of the essentials. The Case History may merely record a series of events or be a distillation of a trainee's experience brought to the group or tutor for discussion. It can be made the subject of study or analysis in any desired way. The Case History approach should not be confused with the Case Study Method which is described below.

Reid, D. D. (1969) 'Case History Methods in Seminar Teaching' in *Innovations and Experiments in University Teaching Methods*, Proceedings of the Third Conference, University Teaching Methods Unit, University of London, April, 1968

See also: Case study method; Critical incident method; Personal case study; Active case study; Incident process method

CASE STUDY METHOD

Developed originally by the Harvard Business School, the Case Study Method is amongst the most used approaches in the teaching of management. A case is a written or filmed description of an actual or imaginary situation which is usually presented in some detail. It may deal with an entire organisational problem or that of a single department. It may consist of a single page or fifty. Cases are written to highlight specific aspects of a situation. The restriction of case information to one aspect is caused partly by the attempt to break up the total situation into manageable or teachable units. A case study approach assumes group discussion and cases tend to be sufficiently involved and detailed so as to produce a wide range of opinions concerning who was to blame, what caused the situation/person to behave in that way and what the best corrective action might be. It is claimed that the case method approach discourages students from making snap judgements about people and situations or in believing in a universal 'right answer'. It shows how the same set of facts can be seen differently and stresses practical thinking. Since they emphasise the importance of facts and their interpretation, case studies are concerned with high level cognitive objectives of analysis, synthesis and particularly evaluation. A case study can promote attitude change provided that it generates the personal involvement of the learner.

The unique characteristic of a 'Harvard case' as opposed to others is that all of them are developed from actual situations. The student is expected to learn through independent thinking how his skills may be used in solving the problem presented. The approach is non-directive with the instructor presenting the case problem to the students, giving them sufficient time for study, and then creating an environment in which group discussion can take place. The instructor's role is to guide the discussion and act as a catalyst in the group. He helps the students to discover for themselves what the answers or solutions may be. He helps the group by skilfully asking questions which aim to draw out, direct or guide them in their thinking. Because of the diversity of approaches possible, the first step in the case discussion may be the presentation of a series of alternative solutions to the same problem.

Other case methods differ in their presentation. In some, a group rather than an individual works on a problem. Cases may be filmed or possibly 'live'. Filmed cases tend to present open-ended problems and they offer considerable detail about real life settings in which emotional relations, as well as facts may also play a part. A 'live' case is one which is a continuing situation. There have been a number of developments and modifications to the original Harvard case method. Nevertheless, the criteria for what constitutes a good case are generally still agreed. It should be based on first hand observation for realism; it presents facts, not opinions disguised as facts; it shows more than it tells; provides organised information; shows both formal and informal relationships where appropriate; describes the key people involved and shows the effects of change indicating that the situation was changing when the observation stopped.

The Case Study as a Training Method: A Select Bibliography, London: Commonwealth Secretariat, 1981

Willings, D. R. (1978) 'How to use the case study method' in *Training for Decision Making*, Business Publications Ltd

Andrews, K. R. (1953) (ed.) *The Case Method of Teaching Human Relations and Administration*,, Harvard University Press

Ayres, R. (1977) 'The Use of Case Studies in Training' in *BACIE Journal*, vol. 31, no. 3 March, pp. 42–44

McLennan, R. (1974) 'How Well Do You Use the Case Method?' in *Industrial Training International*, vol. 9, nos. 10 and 11 pp. 323–4 and 348–50

Simmons, D. D. (1975) 'The Case Method in Management Training' in Taylor, B. and Lippitt, G. L. (eds.) *Management Development and Training Handbook*, London: McGraw-Hill

Towl, A. R. (1969) *The Study of Administration by Cases*, Harvard University Graduate School of Business Administration, Boston

Hayward, G. (1972) 'European Case Development Workhop' in *Industrial and Commercial Training*, vol. 4, no. 11, pp. 544–7

See also: Case history; Personal case history; Critical incident analysis; Incident process method; Active case study

CIRCULATED LECTURE NOTES
This method involves students being provided with a full set of lecture notes together with questions and assignments designed to extend thinking and comprehension. In one version of this approach it was found that possession of the notes by the students did not discourage attendance at the lectures which became occasions for feedback on test performance rather than for reception of information for the first time. It was found that 90 per cent of the students took the tests either always or frequently. In another application, feedback was obtained by contact with seven discussion groups during the first half hour of the lecture period and then by group reports followed by a general discussion.

Several variations of this method are possible. One can circulate notes to students which are not completely full. While they contain enough information to make the basic conceptual structure of the lecture material clear, in order for the student to appreciate them fully, the learner has to extricate various bits of connected detail himself. This approach is most effective with the more able students. A second variation is for a tutor to attend a lecture given by a colleague along with the students. He takes notes which are then made available to the students. This helps students, particularly new ones, to check on the adequacy of their note-taking style, lets them see how meaningful the notes are which they have taken, and illustrates to them another person's perception of the structure of the lecture. In this approach there is no collaboration between the lecturer on the rostrum and the tutor who is sitting in the audience. However, one will usually know of the other's presence. A final approach is to give individual students the responsibility to take notes from a lecture for use by their peers. This may include follow-up work to make sure the notes are clear and comprehensive.

Elton, L. R. B. (1970) 'The Use of Duplicated Notes and Self-Tests in University Teaching', paper read at the 1970 National Conference of the Association for Programmed Learning and Educational Technology

MacManaway, L. A. (1969–70) 'Teaching Methods in Higher Education-Innovation and Research' in *Universities Quarterly*, vol. 24, no. 3, pp. 321–9

MacManaway, L. A. (1967–68) 'Using Lecture Scripts' in *Universities Quarterly*, vol. 22, no. 3 pp. 327–36

See also: Handout; Tutorial-tape-document learning package approach; Personalised system of instruction; Guided study

CLARIFYING EDUCATIONAL ENVIRONMENT

In this approach the lecturer makes use of elements of the 'real world' (people, objects and principles) while carrying out real life activities. The specific elements are dependent on the subject orientation of a learner's particular activity, i.e. they are consciously selected and combined to give a clearly structured environment in which the learner can work on a particular subject and acquire certain skills depending on his own interests. He can do this either alone or in a group. An example of this in management might be the setting up of a microcomputer room in a college, university or training centre where the types of hardware and software that are typically used in business organisations would be displayed.

The experiences within this simplified but real situation should prepare the learner for correspondingly more complex situations in real life. The model must also promote the learner's ability to explore his environment alone, and to use his acquired knowledge actively for subsequent learning. The CEE is so structured as to enable the learner to assume different roles in interaction with other participants. This permits him to reflect upon himself and his relationships with others. It is also structured in such a way as to be free from any physical, psychological or social pressures or indeed any 'extrinsically' influential factors which are not related to the learning. CEE activities should therefore have a purpose within themselves.

The CEE centre is usually organised by a teacher who formulates one of several work places or projects and who provides the materials necessary for their realisation. The learners are informed (by literature, media or verbally) about the organisational aspects of the study centre and about how they might control and structure the learning processes in the centre. Since learners work primarily independently, the learning environment must be clearly structured. Learners interact with their learning environment by carrying out their designated work plans either alone or in a group. Each learner assumes various roles in the process of his studies and in social interaction with his partners. The teacher functions as an organiser in the preparatory phase and as an adviser in helping to solve content-related, technical or group-dynamic problems. The work materials provided are limited to those required for the carrying out of the designated projects. These include structured study guides which inform the learner about the organisation; procedures and subject matter of the learning situation and his place within it and, depending on the subject, material such as technical and experimental equipment and literature.

See also: Vestibule training

CLINIC MEETING

A Clinic Meeting is perhaps best described as a short, intensive, multi-activity, large group learning experience. The emphasis throughout is on the diagnosis, analysis and solving of problems arising out of the participants' fields of experience. Clinic meetings employ a pattern of activities that may include large, general-session type meetings, small discussion groups, planning groups, problem-solving groups, skill practice groups, instructional groups, special interest groups, reading periods, individual consultations and recreational periods. Such meetings may vary in length from one day to several weeks and they are often residential.

See also: Conference meeting; Institute meeting; Colloquy meeting; Forum meeting; Symposium meeting

CLOZURE

This method is derived from Structuralist theories of Semiotics. In essence, students are helped to increase their conceptual comprehension of a basic passage or text related to the subject being studied by being offered a kind of game in which one of every so many words (e.g. 1 in 10) has been omitted. This process of word extraction is done rigorously, irrespective of what kind of word is being removed. The students are then required to supply the missing words in a way that makes sense of the whole text. This can be done in one of two ways. In the first, a sheet of text is provided with the words omitted and students are instructed to 'supply words in this sheet that will make the whole thing read as a piece of coherent argument or description'. An alternative is to provide a list of extracted words, placed in alphabetical order alongside the text. Students are then asked to select from that list which words will go where.

The approach can be used at a variety of levels. At its simplest, it is an exercise in vocabulary training and intelligent reading for staff at supervisor level or for whom English is not their first language. At a more complex level, it can be used to identify the 'gestalt' of a passage and to consider how this gestalt enables one to predict what the particular statements made in the passage will be. By taking the words out at random, one can extract a collection of words which includes key words, as well as others which indicate syntactic relationships. The student is therefore being asked to close the syntax of a passage. He is usually given one paragraph without any omissions in order to provide him with a background against which to do the task. An example of an 'unclosed' paragraph is shown below:

> When a close procedure is ... to reading tasks the ... is asked to fill ... gap with a single word ... has been left out ... the text. To do ... successfully the word must ... to the rules of ..., have the correct meaning, ... be consistent with the ... and language patterns of ... author.

If one wants to make the task more difficult, one merely increases the frequency with which words are taken out. Thus the extraction rate is increased from 1 in 10 to 1 in 5.

Boydell, T. (1981) 'Beauty and the Beast: A Participative Fairy Story' in *Management Education and Development*, vol. 12, no. 2, pp. 81–4

See also: Tests and quizzes

COACHING/COUNSELLING

Coaching and Counselling can be considered as closely related activities and defined as a process in which the manager, through direct discussion, helps a colleague to learn to solve a problem or do a task, using a problem-solving approach. Counselling and coaching can be done between any two managers and is not just relevant to the boss and his subordinate. Coaching/Counselling is problem-oriented and thus involves problem-solving processes. The parties come together and may work through a number of steps such as problem presentation, generation of possible solutions, evaluation and choice of solutions and action planning. The way in which Coaching/Counselling is done can affect its outcomes. The style used by the boss may be directive (i.e. the boss takes the steps for the subordinate and solves the problem) or non-directive (where the junior is helped to take the steps himself and learns to solve the problem himself). The process is conducted through a face-to-face dialogue. It is a purposeful activity and requires a considerable level of skill by the manager doing it and indeed by the person being counselled. Some of the skills needed are listening, reflecting what is said, probing and interpreting. Success depends a great deal on the relationship between the counsellor and the counsellee. This will be affected by relationships in the company as a whole.

Mumford (1980) has argued that acceptance of the coaching role by the boss is problematic. One difficulty concerns the time involved, especially if the boss perceives the activity to be of no direct benefit to him personally. A second has to do with the interpersonal style that some forms of Coaching/Counselling relationships with subordinates can demand. Some managers have it while others do not. Still others may possess it but feel unable to switch in and out of it easily. Mumford went on to identify two coaching roles. These might be labelled intensive and non-intensive respectively. As regards the intensive role, those managers who had the ability and desire to perform it should be encouraged to do so. However, the others should not be forced into adopting a role with which they clearly felt uncomfortable. In what I have called the less intensive coaching role, Mumford saw the boss as working to help the 'manager to recognise and operate on his own weaknesses, and helping him to reflect on and analyse his experience'. This can be achieved by the boss discussing problems with his subordinate, giving him constructive feedback on his written and verbal presentations and discussing with him the reasons underlying certain decisions taken.

Boydell, T. and Pedler, M. (eds) (1981) *Management Self-Development: Concepts and Practices*, Aldershot: Gower

Mumford, A. (1980) *Making Experience Pay*, London: McGraw Hill

Brammer, L. M. (1973) *The Helping Relationship: Process and Skills*, Englewood Cliffs, New Jersey: Prentice-Hall

Singer, E. J. (1979) *Effective Management Coaching*, London: Institute of Personnel Management

Mooreby, E. T. (1975) 'Coaching in Context' in *Personnel Management*, vol. 7, no. 3, pp. 28–30

Mumford, A. (1975) 'Management Development – With or Without the Boss' in *Personnel Management*, vol. 7, no. 6, pp. 26–28

Megginson, D. F. and Pedler, T. H. (1968) *A Guide to Management Coaching*, London: British Association for Commercial and Industrial Education

Ivey, A. E. (1974) 'Counselling Technology: Micro-Counselling and Systematic Approaches to Human Relations Training' in *British Journal of Educational Technology*, vol. 5, no. 2, pp. 15–21

Sperry, L. (1975) *Developing Skills in Contact Counselling – Workbook and Techniques for Developing People in Organisations*, Reading, Mass.: Addison Wesley

See also: Co-counselling; Re-evaluation counselling

CO-COUNSELLING (Re-evaluation Counselling, Reciprocal Counselling, Peer Counselling, Exchange Counselling)

This is a generic term for a group of methods concerned with personal growth and development. They are based on the work of Harvey Jackins and Carl Rogers. The emphasis is on personal problem solving and personal development through awareness. Some of the guiding principles include the equal investment of those involved to help and to seek help; the acceptance of the client's values, views and emotions; non-judgementality and validity. The skills required are based on self awareness and sensitivity to others, empathy, active listening, reflecting and confronting. The emphasis is on mutual aid between individuals and rests on the theory that human beings suffer from restrictions and rigidities of attitude and behaviour which are called 'patterns'. These are said to be caused by the accumulation of undischarged distresses and hurt from the past. Co-counsellors take it in turns to be client and counsellor. The client uses a variety of simple but powerful techniques to discharge the past distresses described, and thereby break up the 'patterns'. The counsellor gives supportive and free attention and makes occasional suggestions about what the client may say or do. Never does he or she interpret, advise, criticise or analyse. The client is basically self regulating and in charge of the process. He is said to spontaneously re-evaluate, i.e. to gain insight into his past experience and its relation to the past. Re-evaluation Counselling is the original and still licensed approach developed by Harvey Jackins of Seattle, USA in the early 1950s. The Re-Evaluation Counselling Communities authorise their own teachers and run training courses in the fundamentals of the technique.

Heron, J. (1974) *Reciprocal Counselling*, Human Potential Research Project, Department of Adult Education, University of Surrey, Guildford.

Watts, A. G. (1977) (ed.) *Counselling at Work*, Bedford Press Square, National Council for Social Service

Handbook on Co-Counselling, London Co-Counselling Community, 1979

Hoare, I. D. (1981) 'Peer Counselling for Personal Development' in *Training*, vol. 7, no. 2, p. 9

Marshall, J. (1980) 'Alternative Methods of Employee Development – Coaching and Counselling' in *Training*, vol. 6, no. 10, pp. 12–15

Smith, P. B. (1980) *Group Processes and Personal Change*, London: Harper and Row, chapter 9

Heap, N. (1980) 'Exchange Counselling' in *Training*, vol. 6, no. 3, pp. 20–21

See also: Re-evaluation counselling; Coaching/counselling

COLLABORATIVELY DESIGNED COURSE

This involves teacher and students together designing a course to be run. An important issue is the extent to which the participants are involved in the course design itself. Such collaboration can be at two levels. Firstly, the decisions involved on the gross design of the course. For example, students might contribute to the choice of content for various sessions in the course and in respect of the methods to be used in the particular sessions. The second level is that of the design of the particular sessions in the course. Members might feed forward to the course teacher the specific questions they want answered, the specific information that they need or the specific demonstrations they would like to see.

Collaboration of this kind can range along a continuum. At one extreme the course organiser interprets the needs of participants in making suggestions for future sessions. Greater involvement is achieved if he consults the course members themselves about what they are particularly interested in and then makes provision for the appropriate sessions to be conducted. A further stage occurs when the organiser facilitates the emergence of a genuine design by the course members of some future sessions by, for example, arranging for small groups to share their concerns and come up with items of content and practice which they would like to have in later sessions. Finally, a Learning Community in which tutors and students collaboratively come to an agreement on what the appropriate course aims are, what content should be covered, what methods are appropriate and how progress might be assessed constitutes the other extreme of the collaborative continuum described.

Boud, D. and Prosser, M. T. (1980) 'Sharing Responsibility – Staff-Student Cooperation in Learning' in *British Journal of Educational Technology*, vol. 11, no. 1, pp. 24–35

Huczynski, A. A. (1981) Self Development Through Formal Qualification' in Boydell, T. and Pedler, M. (eds) *Management Self Development: Concepts and Practices*, Aldershot: Gower

Kilty, J. (1978) *Design for Learning*, London: British Postgraduate Medical Federation, mimeo

See also: Course design as learning; Learning community; Learning organisation

COLLOQUY MEETING

A Colloquy is a type of formal stage presentation to large audiences. It can be considered to be a first cousin to a Panel Discussion in that it includes a greater degree of audience participation. In a Colloquy three or four members of the audience join an equal number of experts on the stage to question them on a given subject. These experts then respond to the audience as a whole. The audience may or may not be permitted to participate in turn. A Colloquy is best used as a technique when discussion hinges around a particular topic or problem. It is a useful way of allowing students the opportunity to understand and explore a specific topic, stimulate their interest in it or help them to identify and clarify the problems or issues involved.

The topic or problem to be discussed may be raised or identified by an audience panel previously. A chairman/moderator keeps the process moving and involves the audience members when he feels it is appropriate. Such a chairman needs to know the basic subject to be dealt with, the goals to be achieved during the session (since it is not a general chat), the amount of time that is available and the background of the students present. This last point is important since it is essential to ensure that he understands the procedures and knows when best to involve them in audience participation. The moderator's job involves explaining the purposes of the Colloquy and the ground rules to be followed regarding audience participation; working to encourage students to participate; relating student questions to Colloquy goals; maintaining pace to ensure the topic is covered and directing all discussions while remaining neutral himself and summarising at the conclusion.

If audience participants are 'planted' ahead of time and briefed, this encourages and generates audience discussion especially when a large audience size may inhibit discussion. Colloquys allow large group participation and can motivate an audience by involving it more in what is going on. Speakers also tend to stay alert when they know that questioners are present. Success however depends heavily on the ability of the moderator. If the students are poorly informed then the consequent participation will also necessarily be poor. If the resource people – experts – are poor, this will lead to inadequate input.

See also: Panel discussion; Interview meeting; Forum meeting; Audience reaction/watchdog team; Brains trust; Interrogation of experts; Clinic meeting; Conference meeting; Institute meeting; Reaction panel; Symposium meeting

COMMITTEE ASSIGNMENT

Managers may be requested to volunteer to serve on company

committees or be nominated to serve on them by their bosses. When a boss receives such an invitation he may decide that in staff development terms it is most valuable to send the junior manager who is most expert in the subject to be discussed, or who may have little direct experience of what is to be discussed but who would greatly benefit from the acquisition of the experience which such committee membership would provide. Where a committee is composed of staff from different departments or levels of seniority, the manager can become aware of the different perceptions and varying attitudes towards the same issue or problem. Through the membership of such committees, he may acquire informal links with organisational staff whom he might not meet in his day-to-day work. There are however drawbacks. In terms of taking action, membership of a committee in which members have basically equal status may be preferable. Committees in practice seldom decide and most often compromise. They have a tendency to become social gatherings with those with the strongest personality doing the deciding. If the conditions are favourable, a Committee Assignment may speed the development of an individual manager. They are perhaps most successful when an individual is assigned a specific area of responsibility and is not just an observer and/or when a committee consists of a number of representatives from different functional groups.

There are of course a range of specific committee skills that can be taught to enable the participant to become a more effective committee chairman or committee member. The imparting of these skills has constituted a major management development activity. People assigned to this form of development must be trained in these skills beforehand. If they are not, one might be doing them harm rather than good in suggesting this form of developmental activity.

Bradford, L. P. (1976) *Making Meetings Work: A Guide for Leaders and Group Members*, Mansfield: University Associates of Europe

Schindler-Rainman, E., Lippitt, R. and Cole, J. (1975) *Taking Your Meetings Out of the Doldrums*, Mansfield: University Associates of Europe

Maude, B. (1975) *Managing Meetings*, London: Business Books

See also: Development assignment; Research assignment; Evaluation assignment; Consulting assignment; Study assignment; Proposal team assignment; Selection board assignment; Staff meeting assignment

COMMUNITY OF ENQUIRY (Liberating Structure Approach)
This approach involves the application of an autonomous learning approach to large classes in a graduating university course. Its originator, William Torbert, has identified what he calls the 'qualities of liberating structures', i.e. the characteristics of the organisation of educational settings which enhance student self-direction. He recognises the paradox of leadership for self direction and consciously adopts what he calls an 'ironic approach'. The qualities identified are recognition that students will, at least initially, view the course differently from the staff and will need to be introduced to a new way of looking at learning; an integration of learning products with the learning processes which involves the setting of tasks that cannot be completed without reference to the processes of learning which are taking place; planned change to the structure of the course as it progresses so that students can take increasing responsibility; the provision of feedback in the course structure and learning tasks so that the process of learning is monitored; the use of the power held by the teacher to support the structure which places increasing responsibility on students; the emphasis on the critical examination of the nature and functioning of the course itself by both teachers and students; teachers being publicly accountable to their students for conducting the course along the lines which have been agreed and committed to seeking and righting any incongruities which may have been identified.

This is a high risk approach to teaching which depends on skilled practice. It has been used by Torbert on a compulsory undergraduate course for 360 students. It aims to educate participants towards a sense of shared purpose, self-direction and quality work. To achieve these goals, an ironic kind of leadership and organisation is required which is simultaneously educative and productive, simultaneously controlling and freeing.

Torbert, W. (1972) 'An Experimental Selection Process' in *Journal of Applied Behavioural Science*, vol. 9, pp. 331–50

Torbert, W. (1978) 'Educating Towards Shared Purpose, Self-Direction and Quality Work: The Theory and Practice of Liberating Structure', in *Journal of Higher Education*, vol. 49, no. 2, pp. 109–35

Torbert, W. (1976) *Creating a Community of Enquiry: Conflict, Collaboration, Transformation*, Chichester: John Wiley and Sons

Torbert, W. and Hackman, J. (1969) 'Taking the Fun Out of Out Foxing the System' in Runkel, P., Harrison, R. and Runkel, M. *The Changing College Classroom*, San Francisco: Jossey Bass

See also: Learning community; Learning organisation; Autonomy lab; Instrumented laboratory

COMPUTER-ASSISTED LEARNING (Computer-assisted Instruction)

Computer-assisted Learning (CAL) refers specifically to the use of the computer as a teaching medium or learning resource. Used as a teaching medium, the computer controls the presentation of instructional material to a learner seated at a terminal on the basis of that individual learner's previous responses. The computer adapts teaching to the individual. The model is derived from Skinner and the programmed learning movement where the computer is a tutorial teaching machine. This use is sometimes referred to as 'Computer as Tutor'. Its second use is as a learning resource. This is based on the research uses of computers and their impact on subject disciplines. The label sometimes used here is 'Computer as Laboratory'. Used in this way, the computer provides a range of facilities for the learner such as modelling, calculation, problem-solving, simulation and data base interrogation. In this application the computer acts as a 'dry laboratory' facility and does not necessarily teach in any direct sense at all. In the USA, the term 'Computer Assisted Instruction' tends to be associated with the use of the computer as a teaching medium. In industry, CAL has developed on other applications of the computer. Thus British Airways has a CAL system added to its existing international airline booking system to train the users of that system. Computer manufacturers are developing CAL courses for the teaching of data processing and computing. It is likely that the Computer as Laboratory type of CAL will grow as the range of disciplines which require computing grow. The 'Computer as Tutor' applications are likely to grow more slowly because the teaching profession is unlikely to accept any significant diversion of resources.

Computer-assisted Learning can take many forms. The work ranges from the use of computer programs that simulate physical systems to drill exercises in learning languages, to problem solving using computer programs. All these approaches involve the student's individual use of interactive computer terminals, sometimes as part of their course and sometimes as an adjunct to it. In all cases, the aim is to exploit the capabilities of computers and interactive terminals in areas of the curricula where (*a*) alternative teaching methods are needed, and (*b*) where CAL is an appropriate alternative.

The two applications mentioned are examples of helping students to learn. It is important to distinguish these two facets of CAL from what has been called Computer-managed Learning or Computer-managed Instruction. Computer-managed Instruction (CMI) involves the use of the computer to manage teaching and learning, particularly where individualised learning systems are favoured. It is not a teaching/learning system itself. Under CMI the computer performs one or more of the following four main tasks: test marking, analysis and production; the 'routing' of students through an individualised course of study where the teaching is done not by computer but by teachers, books, and self-instructional media; the keeping of classroom records and finally the writing of reports – for students, teachers and administrators.

Hooper, R. (1975) *National Development Programme for Computer Assisted Learning*, London: Council for Educational Technology

Laurillard, D. (1978) 'Evaluation of Student Learning in Computer Assisted Learning' in *Computing and Education*, vol. 2, pp. 259–65

Morris, R. (1981) 'Computer Based Learning Systems' in *Training*, vol. 7, no. 1, pp. 2–7

Hooper, R. (1974) 'The National Development Programme for Computer Assisted Learning' in *Programmed Learning and Educational Technology*, vol. 11, no. 2, pp. 59–73

Harding, R. D. (1980) 'Computer Assisted Learning in Higher Education' in *Studies in Higher Education*, vol. 5, no. 1, pp. 101–14

British Journal of Educational Technology, vol. 8, no. 3, 1977. Special issue on Computer Assisted Learning, October

Tawney, D. A. (1979) (ed.) *Learning Through Computers*, London: Macmillan

Edmunds, E. (1980) 'Where Next in Computer Aided Learning?' in *British Journal of Educational Technology*, vol. 11, no. 2, pp. 97–104

See also: Programmed learning

CONCENTRATED STUDY
This is a method for conducting a conventional course over a concentrated period of time. For example, a course of ten hours which is normally taught in one-hour blocks once a week over a ten-week term is concentrated in two days. Concentrated Study is defined as the allocation of a fixed period of time to the study of a particular theme or topic to the virtual exclusion of all other aspects of the programme. This exclusive

concentration on a subject is for a longer period than is normally allowed in a traditional programme. The second key point is that there are no concurrent activities. Its chief aim is to change certain dimensions of undergraduate education, to encourage a more committed approach to studying, to enable closer student/teacher relations and to introduce a wider range of activities than is usually possible.

The main consequences of this method have been found to be an increased effectiveness in the learning, increases in the degree of understanding and the quality of the social interaction and organisational arrangements. As an approach, Concentrated Study is rarely to be found and its advantages over its disadvantages mean the benefits are finely balanced. Some authors propose its selective application in otherwise traditional courses – for example, at the begining of a degree programme as a form of induction to help people become acquainted; for the acquisition of particular skills and basic information, especially if this can be treated as an entity in its own right (e.g. computing or study skills); for the development of social skills, group relations, general morale; where understanding can be increased by bringing together experiences which would otherwise remain dispersed and unrelated; sometimes late in a traditional course as a concentrated integrating experience; or, finally, as a way of stepping up the pace of a course when required.

Parlett, M. R. and King, J. G. (1971) *Concentrated Study: A Pedagogic Innovation Observed*, Guildford, Surrey: Society for Research into Higher Education

Swanton, M. (1976) 'The Tutor Midwife: Concentrated Study in the Humanities' in *Studies in Higher Education*, vol. 1, no. 2, pp. 169–78

Hewton, E. (1977) 'The Curricular Implications of Concentrated Study' in *Studies in Higher Education*, vol. 2, no. 1, pp. 79–87

Gould, F. and Croome, D. (1977) 'The Foundation Course "Carousel" at PCL' in *Studies in Higher Education*, vol. 2, no. 1, pp. 55–68

See also: Workshop; Minicourse; Module; Residential

CONFERENCE MEETING

A Conference is a meeting of people in large or small groups. The Conference may be of the high-powered type where members work well into the night, or it may be a less intensive type of social gathering. Most Conferences have a designation in their title, e.g. personal management

conference, which indicates for whom they are intended. The participants who attend are usually a close-knit group who consult together in a
formal fashion on problems in which they have a serious interest. The
number attending the Conference tends to determine the techniques that
are used. It is usual for a chairman to set the scene, and a keynote speaker
may be asked to address the participants raising some general issues.
Conferences can be divided into two types: the Educational Conference
and the Working Conference. Educational Conferences tend to embrace
a large, or sometimes extremely large, number of people and tend to have
a theme designed to promote an idea. Working Conferences are usually
technical in nature and have a limited number of participants. They may
include a few brief lecture sessions to stimulate participants, but papers
and booklists would have been distributed in advance and the conference
format involves participants working hard in small groups. Conferences
are a way of meeting people from outside of one's work and geographical
environment. Participants frequently value them for the contacts and
acquaintances that they make.

Burke, W. W. and Beckhard, R. (eds.) (1976) *Conference Planning*,
Mansfield: University Associates of Europe, 2nd edition

Humphreys, L. (1980) 'Making It a Success or How to Avoid the Pitfalls'
in *The Training Officer*, vol. 16, no. 11, pp. 294–5

Zelko, H. P. (1957) *Successful Conference and Discussion Techniques*, New
York: McGraw-Hill

See also: Colloquy meeting; Clinic meeting; Forum meeting;
Institute meeting; Symposium meeting

CONFERENCE METHOD
The Conference Method is a training approach in which a group of
between twelve and twenty people pool their ideas, examine facts, test
assumptions and draw conclusions. The Conference is an open
discussion designed to encourage group thinking on a problem, with the
eventual acceptance of the conclusions by the group members. The
instructor and trainees deal with specific, practical job situation
problems. The trainee is a participant in this approach rather than a
spectator. The method has several characteristics. Conference group
members are people who are faced with common problems and have a
common desire to seek a solution to these problems. Usually each group
member brings with him years of practical experience. The subject

discussed is within the group's experience. They are expected to solve the problem by pooling these experiences and by thinking it through together. They meet to learn together and not to be instructed.

The training group gathers in an informal atmosphere to express ideas freely without constraints. The tutor's opening remarks should emphasise informality, the pooling of ideas which together constitute a body of information if all members contribute. The session is begun by asking members simple, easily answerable questions that are of known interest to all participants. The establishment of good working relationships between conference group members is essential. The group must accept the leader as one of themselves, and he in turn must know each of them. The leader gives direct information sparingly, and only if it is not made available by other members. He encourages individuals to talk to the whole group and not just himself. All ideas and comments produced by members are charted irrespective of their perceived value. This allows all the facts and ideas to be put before the group thereby allowing them to consider each point on its merits.

The role of the leader is to stimulate and guide the conference group. He needs to familiarise himself with the personalities in the group and make use of the strong members present. He guards against the monopolisation of discussion by the vocal few and seeks to encourage equal participation. He checks that no useful suggestion is overlooked and gives encouragement with a carefully worded question to an individual when the group appears hesitant to begin discussion. He takes time to state the problem clearly and precisely. He lists the pros and cons of each course of action proposed as well as the possible solutions. If the discussion goes astray he will seek an opportunity to bring it round in the desired direction. Effective leaders know the objectives, and have thought them through in advance of the meeting. They establish good working relations in the group, avoid posing as teachers, stimulate and guide discussion related to objectives, encourage active and constructive thinking on the part of the group and secure or prepare suitable supplementary material for the group.

Busch, H. M. (1949) *Conference Methods in Industry*, New York: Harper Bros

See also: Directed conversation method; Problem-solving cycle

CONFIDENCE-BUILDING TRAINING (RSI method)
This is a method of helping students to increase their self confidence

which can allow them to take a part in and gain greater benefits from all types of independent learning situations. It is based on the belief that traditional educational systems emphasise student dependency which saps people's ability to learn on their own. In consequence, when confronted with more autonomous, self-initiated learning situations, these traditionally educated, dependent students turn off and cannot cope.

Confidence-building Training has three elements or techniques which are relaxation, suggestion and imagery. For this reason it is sometimes referred to as the RSI Method. Between three and four treatment sessions are used. Participants are first asked to relax with the use of deep breathing exercises, counting, the fixation of the eye on a bright object, muscle heaviness or the mental visualisation of a pleasant scene. Once relaxed, the facilitator talks to them quietly, employing a series of positively worded suggestions designed to produce ego enhancement. These pertain to increased energy, improved health, ability to cope with problems, increased calmness, personal well-being, feelings of contentment, increased self confidence and improved concentration. Once relaxed, the critical 'watchdog' facility of the mind reduces and allows acceptance of suggestions which are in accordance with the wishes of the student. People can be helped to gain confidence in their own power to change themselves in directions in which they want to change and to transcend the often unreasoned limits they place upon themselves. The emphasis is upon the way in which the participant's confidence would increase as he realised the power he had to control his own life. This is done through verbal suggestion and to encourage the person to think of himself as he would like to be (imagery).

Stanton, H. E. (1980) 'The Modification of Student Self Concept' in *Studies in Higher Education*, vol. 5, no. 1, pp. 71–6

Stanton, H. E. (1977) 'Self Concept and the Self Enhancement Group' in *Journal of Adult Education*, vol. 17, pp. 2–7

Stanton, H. E. (1979) *The Plus Factor: a guide to a positive life*, Sydney: Collins/Fontana

Stanton, H. (1981) 'Independent Study: A Matter of Confidence' in Boud, D. J. (ed.), *Developing Student Autonomy in Learning*, London: Kogan Page

See also: Assertiveness training; Motivation training

CONFLUENT EDUCATION

Confluent Education involves the deliberate integration of the affective domain (emotions, attitudes, values and senses) with the cognitive domain (thought, intellect, reason) in learning, teaching and everyday practice. A premise of Confluent Education is that people both need and want the opportunity to learn cognitively and affectively – within themselves, in relation to others, and in their relationships with the world. When we learn in this way, we are likely to find ways to be deeply rooted in the skills, values, feelings, senses, thoughts and behaviours which have traditionally been seen as important. Confluent Education has been used in disciplines as far apart as medicine, geology, English and psychology. Curricula have been designed in three broad goal categories: (*a*) to achieve traditional subject matter, (*b*) to achieve non-traditional goals of personal and interpersonal or social development, and (*c*) to learn process skills that will help individuals obtain their own goals.

The ideas underlying Confluent Education were developed by Dr George Brown (University of California, Santa Barbara) who was awarded a grant by the Fund for the Advancement of Education of the Ford Foundation for 'a pilot project to explore ways to adapt approaches in the affective domain to the school curricula'. The term Confluent Education emerged, and refers to the integration or flowing together of the affective and cognitive elements in individual and group learning which is sometimes called humanistic or psychological education. Confluent Education allows for intellectual, emotional and physical learning, and uses the techniques and methodology of Gestalt Therapy as developed by the late Dr Frederick (Fritz) Perls.

Brown, G. I. (1971), *Human Teaching for Human Learning: An Introduction to Confluent Education*, New York: Viking Press

Castillo, G. A. (1974), *Left Handed Teaching*, New York: Praeger Publishers

Thayer, L. (ed.) (1976) *Affective Education: Strategies for Experiential Learning*, Mansfield: University Associates of Europe

Eiben, R. and Milliven, A. (1976) *Educational Change: A Humanistic Approach*, Mansfield: University Associates of Europe

Weinstein, G. and Fantini, M. D. (1970) *Toward Humanistic Education: A Curriculum of Affect*, New York: Praeger Publishers

See also: Gestalt techniques; Values clarification; Appercep-tion-interaction method; Jurisprudential model

CONSCIOUSNESS-RAISING GROUP
The goal of a Consciousness-raising Group is to examine and frequently to change the circumstances of a particular category of person in society, e.g. women in management. The group meets and may focus on a particular topic during a session at which a participant may share his particular experience and take responsibility for running that session. The emphasis tends to be very much on previous life experience sharing, in which similarities and differences are explored. This approach encourages members to see previous adversities or problems not as being caused by their own personal weaknesses, but as inherent in current social structure. This could result in a reduction of member depression and anxiety and an increase in assertiveness and aggression. Changes may be expressed either in terms of changed individual behaviour or political action.

Smith, P. B. (1980) *Group Processes and Personal Change*, London: Harper and Row

Lieberman, M. A. and Bond, G. R. (1976) 'The Problem of Being a Woman: a survey of 1700 women in consciousness raising groups', *Journal of Applied Behavioural Science*, vol. 12, pp. 363–79

See also: Confidence-building training; Self help group; Asser-tiveness training

CONSTRUCT LESSON PLAN
In essence this is an approach towards group instruction but its unique characteristics merit its inclusion as a separate method. The Construct Lesson Plan (CLP) is a way of organising and implementing classroom instruction which seeks to remove the inefficiency and ineffectiveness of much of group instruction. It does this by accounting for, and following through on the preparatory study by students themselves. CLP includes the use of a Diagnostic Pre-Test, a set of Lesson Plan Cards and a Content Outline.
One begins by defining a lesson plan on the basis of learner objectives. These focus on student-teacher interaction and provide a base against

which to organise, implement and evaluate the CLP. These also structure the pre-meeting for students who are given specific reading to do with the objectives to hand. A Diagnostic Pre-Test is then written which measures each of the objectives of the Lesson Plan. Students take this home and complete it after they have done their preparatory study, but just before coming to the class. This test is the link between the student self-study and the classroom instruction which is to follow. The teacher's pre-planned Lesson Plan consists of two elements – the Lesson Plan Cards and the Content Outline. These allow the teacher to plan the lesson in full, but only select those aspects of immediate need to students. This 'on-the-move' decision making is achieved by having a separate Lesson Plan Card written for each objective. The card contains: the objective (organised by topic/sub-topic; answers to pre-test questions measuring the objectives; a space for content reminders/media support to be used etc.). The card gives the flexibility to assemble a lesson in class to the specific and immediate learning needs of the students. The Content Outline is an overview of the lesson built around the major and minor content headings. In the margin each of the objectives of the lesson is listed by the number to which it relates in the lesson. The numbers match the objectives' numbers and the Pre-test questions' numbers. These elements of the CLP come together in the following way.

Students are instructed to do preparatory work. The objectives for the coming lesson are specified, as is the reading which is to be covered in a textbook. They read at home and complete the diagnostic test. At the beginning of the class the teacher quickly goes over the results on a group basis to identify the areas of common group difficulty. During this period, the Lesson Plan Cards are stacked into two piles representing objectives achieved already by students alone and others requiring classroom instruction. A lesson is thus assembled to meet the immediate learning needs of students. The approach does not preclude the use of any other teaching methods or media. If instruction is based only on the objectives not achieved by students working alone the class would be fragmentary and not form a cohesive learning unit. To avoid this the Content Outline is used as a guide. Beginning at the top of the list, any objectives already mastered by students are covered in an overview manner, until an objective needing classroom attention is reached. This keys the teacher to go to the Lesson Plan Card which is in one of the presorted piles. This objective is then dealt with in greater depth.

Langdon, D. G. (1977) 'The Construct Lesson Plan: Taking the Inefficiency Out of Group Classroom Discussion' in *Programmed*

Learning and Educational Technology, vol. 14, no. 3, pp. 199–206

Pedrick, L. and Tarquinio, N. F. (1978) 'The Construct Lesson Plan: Evaluating the Efficiency of a New Approach to Group Classroom Discussion' in *Programmed Learning and Educational Technology*, vol. 15, no. 4, pp. 257–61

See also: Self instructional modules and interactive groups; Data approach method; Guided group problem solving

CONSULTING ASSIGNMENT

In a Consulting Assignment, a manager goes to another department or another plant of his own company or to another company. The development task is to give advice and help the solution of some identified problem. Like any other consultant, he has no formal authority of his own to implement any changes and may have to draw on a different power base if he wishes to get his ideas implemented. Such assignments can aid the establishment of a relationship between staff in the same company and develop the analytical and problem-solving skills of those involved.

There is the problem of re-entry following an extended period of consulting. On re-entry, the manager may need to be supported by staff specialists and line supervisors. In this form of development, the individual needs to be thoroughly prepared for his return as well as supported by a dedicated tutor. This is particularly important when the consulting takes place outside of his own organisation. Large companies sometimes help small independent firms by seconding one of their own executives. Young inexperienced managers may be so loaned on a full-time basis. This gives them contact with a wide range of management problems that they might meet at middle or senior management level within a large company. It allows them to develop their skill and potential quickly and with no risk to the efficiency of their 'home' organisation. It can help to keep the younger managers motivated and decreases the chances of them moving away from a large company which may have stopped growing.

See also: Action learning; Committee assignment; Development assignment; Evaluation assignment; Proposal team assignment; Research assignment; Selection board assignment; Study assignment; Task force assignment

CONTEXT TRAINING

Context Training was an approach developed by the late Hawdon Hague. The idea which underlies the method is that (*a*) managers develop only when they take the initiative, (*b*) they develop only in the real situation and (*c*) that self-development does not just happen, somebody needs to get into the real situation to help self-development along. Thus Context Training is about helping managers to help themselves. The person intervening may be a boss, a tutor, or anyone who acts as a 'catalyst' rather than as a tutor. The catalyst or tutor works on an individual basis, actually teaching on the job and working on whatever blocks to self-development he discovers. This is done by a series of visits, during which suggestions are fed in, progress is checked, and dialogue opened up with the boss. The responsibility for taking decisions is pushed onto the manager himself. In the Context Training approach one can work explicitly on the organisation as a whole and on its climate. This is to remove the constraints, real or imagined, that commonly give managers the feeling that they have neither the room nor the encouragement to change. The tutor helps individuals and organisations to develop themselves by dealing with actual situations as they arise and by carrying out the sort of rethinking exercise normally given to consultants. Project teams are a vehicle of this approach and the company gets major problems tackled by its own executives who get good learning value in the process and are more likely to implement the ideas produced. It is based on the idea that a man's job is his most powerful (work) influence, together with the help and reaction that he gets from his boss. Changing his job or coaching him in it are therefore important ways to train him. Other ways are projects on an individual or group basis. With this approach the trainer makes learning capital out of whatever turns up, or so structures the situation that managers develop themselves.

Hague, H. (1974), *Executive Self-Development*, London: Macmillan

Hague, H. (1979), *Helping Managers to Help Themselves*, Oxford: Context

Hague, H. (1973), *Management Training for Real*, London: Institute of Personnel Management

Hague, H. (1977) 'Getting Self Development To Happen', Part I in *Journal of European Industrial Training*, vol. 1, no. 5, pp. 24–9

Hague, H. (1978) 'Tools for Helping Self Development', *Journal of European Industrial Training*, vol. 2, no. 3, pp. 13–15

Daley, P. and McGivern, C. (1972) 'The On-Going Management Situation as the Training Vehicle' in *Industrial and Commercial Training*, vol. 4, no. 3, pp. 137–41

See also: Coaching/counselling; Self development; Action learning

CONTROLLED DISCUSSION

Points or questions are raised from the lecture floor. The main purpose of this method is the clarification of matters of fact and the development of thought and interest that have been generated. Most teachers use this form of discussion after lectures. Its success depends on how stimulating the lecture was. Since not all members of a large lecture class will be able to contribute, misunderstandings and interesting viewpoints may not be revealed. Some people are more vocal and can dominate. It is difficult to ensure that the points raised permit a balanced consideration of the subject and frequently one fails to get a discussion but a series of one-to-one interactions with different students. A better discussion atmosphere can be created if the teacher does not reply to the points raised but asks for further contributions from the audience. While students may raise the questions or comment, the general direction of the discussion is always under the control of the teacher. It is normally used after a presentation method with a whole class and not just a group.

Improving Teaching in Higher Education, University Teaching Methods Unit, University of London, 1976

Bligh, D. A. (1972) *What's the Use of Lectures*, Harmondsworth: Penguin Books

See also: Guided discussion; Directed conversation method

CONTROLLED PACE NEGOTIATION

This is a form of training used in the teaching of negotiations which can be applied to other spheres. Its purpose is to slow down the pace of negotiation interactions thereby giving time for people to reflect. The trainer divides the class into two groups, *A* and *B*. He puts them in different rooms and presents them with a problem which requires mutual agreement from the groups. For example, there is only a limited amount of beer available in the bar after the session. How can we best share out what there is? The problem can be more work oriented if desired, but it must be genuinely relevant to the parties involved. After the problem is stated, each person in group *A* is given three minutes to write down the message he wishes the trainer to carry to group *B*. When all of group *A* members have finished as individuals, they must choose as a group the individual message the trainer will carry. They are not allowed to write a new, composite group message. The trainer delivers the message to the other group and goes through the same process. A gradual interchange of messages between the groups builds up.

While the trainer is out of the room, the groups can discuss strategy and tactics. Alternatively, the tutor may set the group the task of categorising the messages it sends and those it receives against a simple list, e.g. helpful suggestion, seeking information, etc. Debriefing of the exercise can take place either at the individual level (personal negotiation style), the group level (tactics and strategy of negotiation), or perceptual level (e.g. messages classified by senders as helpful suggestions perceived as attacks by receivers). A variation of this approach can be used by the individual manager in his day-to-day dealings with others, especially those with whom he has a difference of opinion. When discussing a topic with another person, he may decide to discipline himself to fully understand what the other person is saying before putting his own point. He is thus controlling the pace of his own interaction with the other person by taking time to listen objectively to the speaker and summarising his understanding of what he believes the other person has said.

Rackham, N. (1972) 'Controlled Paced Negotiation as a Technique for Developing Negotiation Skills' in *Industrial and Commercial Training*, vol. 4, no. 6, pp. 266–75

Stewart, A. and Stewart, V. (1976) *Tomorrow's Men Today*, London: Institute of Personnel Management, chapter 5

Kennedy, G., Benson, J. and McMillan, J. (1980) *Managing Negotiations*, London: Business Books

See also: Process analysis; Game; Experiential exercise

COOPERATIVE EDUCATION (Cooperative Learning, Sandwich Courses)
Cooperative Education is a type of experiential education whose purpose is to extend the learning process into the workplace. Herman Schneider

has been credited with instituting the first cooperative educational programme at the College of Engineering in the University of Cincinnati in 1906. In Cooperative Education programmes, students alternate academic periods at college with structured work experiences in study or career-related employment outside of the classroom. The employment experiences tend usually to be in business, government or professional organisations. Similar types of programmes, but with a primarily 'service ethic' which emphasises community and national development, is decribed elsewhere under the heading of Study Service. Cooperative Education thus provides the opportunity for students to integrate classroom learning with its application in the workplace. In the United States, students in professional programmes such as engineering or nursing, are employed on study related and frequently well paid jobs. In Britain, the term 'sandwich course' is used to describe the integration of work and study experience. Such programmes are a feature of many polytechnics and of several universities such as Brunel and Bradford.

The aim of Cooperative Education is to complement traditional education. In particular it is designed to help students reinforce and expand their learning, encourage their personal growth and provide them with career direction. Through work experiences, students learn about interpersonal relationships at work, supervision and how to meet responsibilities. They become self-reliant and develop confidence in their decision making. It helps them prepare for their careers, allows them to test tentative career choices, to learn employers' needs, select appropriate future courses and acquire professional level work experience.

Various models of Cooperative Education exist. However, most are characterised by the work experience being productive and considered as an essential part of the overall educative process. The work assignments are related to the students' fields of study and/or students' career interests. Alteration is provided whereby students receive more than one period of supervised employment long enough to permit them to have a full learning experience which is economically and practically feasible for the employer. Minimum performance standards and assessment techniques are integral to the programmes where academic credit is provided or where Cooperative Education is a degree requirement. The work experience should progress in complexity and responsibility matching the student's academic progress.

Programmes differ in the way they integrate work/college experience by virtue of different placement patterns. In a full-time alternating pattern students are divided into two or three cohorts and one group works full time away from the college while the others do full-time study.

With a parallel pattern, students attend classes for part of the day and are on cooperative work assignments for the remainder. Finally, in a field pattern, students leave the campus for a specified period of time at least once during their period of undergraduate study, but no more than once in any given year. Other variations include being with one or several employers, and also the degree to which such work assignments are optional or compulsory.

To provide a link between college and work periods, and to aid assessment, 'learning contracts' and the linking of assignments to college courses have been used. A learning contract is an agreement between the student, tutor and frequently the employer on the learning goals that the student is expected to achieve and on which he will be evaluated. Cooperative educational experiences can be linked to existing college courses to provide a base for student learning on the work assignment. They may be concurrent with or precede the work experience. Evaluation of cooperative experience can be done by student projects/papers, employer evaluations, staff members visiting students on site and student self-evaluation.

Daniel, W. W. and Pugh, H. (1975) *Sandwich Courses in Higher Education*, PEP Report Paper in CNAA Degree in Business Studies, vol. XLI, broadsheet no. 557

Smithers, A. *An Evaluation of Sandwich Courses*, National Foundation for Educational Research

Proceedings of the First World Conference on Cooperative Education, March 1981, National Foundation for Educational Research

Moore, J. P. (1978) 'Sandwich and Co-operative Education' in *Industrial and Commercial Training*, vol. 10, no. 11, pp. 453–4

Joint Working Party on Sandwich Courses, University, Polytechnics and Industry Committee (UPIC) Report, Confederation of British Industry, 1975

Williams, E. and Marsh, P. (1972) 'Sandwich Courses in Management' in *Industrial and Commercial Training*, vol. 4, no. 1, pp. 16–21

Wilson, J. W. (1979) *Summary Report: Co-operative Education – A National Assessment*, Boston: Cooperative Education Research Centre

Wilson, J. W. (1978) 'Patterns of Awarding Degree Credit in Cooperative Education', *Journal of Cooperative Education*, Autumn, pp. 87–92

See also: Study service; Internship; Field project/attachment

CORRESPONDENCE COURSE

In Britain the term Correspondence Course is often used synonymously with Distance Learning. Thus the services offered by accountancy tuition schools through postal exchange of materials, and the Open University service, are all frequently labelled as Correspondence Courses. In fact, such courses are only one small part of the approach which is called Distance Learning. Even in this country, few so-called Correspondence Courses rely on this single medium. In addition to the postal exchange of written materials, most employ some form of short residential facility (e.g. summer school) while others use radio and television. In North America, Distance Learning can involve the use of satellites to facilitate tele-conferences between tutors and students.

See also: Open learning; Directed private study; FlexiStudy; Flexastudy

COURSE DESIGN AS LEARNING

A number of teaching staff who have taken small groups of students over a period of a year have got them to learn about the subject by designing a course on it themselves. The idea is based on the concept that having to teach a subject is the best way to learn it. The class group has to decide on the basic text to be used and the supplementary reading. They decide which topics need to be covered, how they are related to one another and in which order. In practice the learning for the students comes from doing basic reading and critically evaluating it, and through discussion with other course members. The tutor acts as a consultant to the group indicating the implications and consequences of their choices. The finished product of the team is a course brochure which defines the topic, explains how it will be taught and assessed. It also contains a reading list, specifying recommended reading for each session.

Pheysey, D. (1979) 'Spadework as Learning' in *Management Education and Development*, vol. 10, no. 3, pp. 167–71.

See also: Collaboratively designed course; Learning organisation; Learning community

COVERDALE TRAINING

Developed by Ralph Coverdale, Coverdale Training is the practical applied part of his philosophy. In essence this is the belief that in growing organic organisational systems, it is appropriate to analyse the causes of success and look for strengths in order to improve on them, rather than to look for causes of failure to put things right. Coverdale observed that more knowledge exists than is used or applied. What is required are behavioural skills in putting knowledge into practice. In consequence, he devised his own methods of planned behaviour improvement. Such skills can only be acquired through practice and experience, but there must be a system to ensure that men learn from experience. His aim was to develop a cycle of preparation, action and review through which skills could be learned. This itself is a skill and a prerequisite in turning experience into advantage. Coverdale Training is based on this 'cycle of learning' aiming to help men learn from experience and help them practise skills which are relevant in cooperating with others in getting things done. Members work together in small groups carrying out short pieces of work called 'tasks'. Some of these may involve participants going out of the study centre, e.g. to count the cars in the vicinity, while others may require them to produce a report.

The focus of the learning is not on the task itself, but on the interaction it engenders amongst members. Consideration is given to the way in which the groups carry out their tasks, agree on an effective approach, how they plan and combine talents and build on effective team practices. Given the learning cycle which consists of a sequence of differing tasks, participants are encouraged to experiment with different behaviours and group structures. By repeating those which appear effective while discarding those which do not, members acquire a knowledge of human behaviour and habits of good management which they can develop in the future.

The philosophy of Coverdale Training is to enable people to learn from experience. The emphasis is on experiment and discovery. Coverdale techniques are based on trial and experience and help members consider the establishment of aims, working methodically towards them, cooperating and getting cooperation, observing, listening, identifying and making use of others' talents, planning, leadership and authority.

Waterson, J. (1979) 'Coverdale Training' in Babington-Smith, B. and Farrell, B. A. (eds) *Training in Small Groups: A Study of Five Methods*, Oxford: Pergamon Press

Taylor, M. (1979), *Coverdale on Management*, London: Heinemann

Frank, E. and Margerison, C. (1978) 'Training Methods and

Organizational Development', in *Journal of European Industrial Training*, vol. 2, no. 4, pp. 19–22

Smallwood, A. (1976) 'The Basic Philosophy of Coverdale Training' in *Industrial and Commercial Training*, vol. 8, no. 1 pp. 12–16

Roche, S. (1967) 'Coverdale Training – a method for developing managers and the organization' in *Manpower and Applied Psychology*, Cork, Eire: Ergon Press

See also: Action training; Process analysis; Structured social skills seminar

CREATIVE DIALOGUE
In this method the tutor or lecturer writes several questions on the blackboard or flipchart which are intended to encourage group discussion. After doing this he leaves the room. Students then form several groups and discuss the assigned topic and questions under the direction of an assigned spokesman. Towards the end of the hour, the tutor returns and the class reassembles to listen to what the spokesman reports. It has been found that Creative Dialogues help focus the discussion and permit a more open exchange than typically occurs in the normal classroom.

Tighe, M. J. (1971) 'Creative Dialogue: Teaching Students to Teach Themselves' in *New Directions in Teaching*, vol. 2, no. 4

See also: Leaderless group discussion; Associative group discussion; Free discussion method

CREATIVITY TRAINING
Creativity Training is based on the belief that creativity is not a chance characteristic possessed by a handful of people. On the contrary, it is held that every person possesses creative capacity which needs to be developed and brought into the open. Arnold at the Massachusetts Institute of Technology was amongst the first to institute 'creativity training'. His students were given problems which forced them to develop new ways of thinking. For example, they had to design cars and razors for planets with different laws of gravity and with different chemical and physical conditions. Creativity Training is therefore a generic term for a variety of different programme designs which include

within them specific 'techniques' or 'exercises' whose names are frequently as inventive as the type of thinking they attempt to engender.

Such training programmes usually include the creation of a climate of creativity within the organisation, overcoming personal blocks to creativity, setting objectives, problems and challenges. Other tools are used to release the creativity which is deemed to be inherent in all people. Amongst other techniques one would list the Deferred Judgement Method; Bionics; Metaphor and Analogy; Directed Speculation; Selective and Planned Ignorance; Maintaining Forward Motion; Incubation; 'Fooling around to generate ideas'; Brainstorming; Quick Think; the Little Techniques; Systematised Directed Induction and forcing relationships between seemingly unrelated things. Subsequent topics on such courses involve the process of idea evaluation, especially the development of criteria against which to evaluate and how to weigh these in order of importance. Finally the implementation and monitoring of new ideas are considered.

Freeman, J., Butcher, H. J. and Christie, T. (1971) *Creativity: A Selective View of Research*, Guildford, Surrey: Society for Research into Higher Education, 2nd edition

Rickards, T. and Freedman, B. (1979) 'A Reappraisal of Creativity Techniques' in *Journal of European Industrial Training*, vol. 3, no. 1

Parnes, S. J. (1967) *Creative Behaviour Guidebook*, New York: Charles Scribner's Sons

Osborn, A. (1965) *Applied Imagination*, New York: Charles Scribner's Sons, 3rd edition

Rawlinson, J. G. (1980) *Introduction to Creative Thinking and Brainstorming*, London: British Institute of Management

Gordon, W. J. J. (1975) 'Creativity Comes of Age' in Taylor, B. and Lippitt, G. L. (eds) *Management Development and Training Handbook*, London: McGraw Hill

Rickards, T. (1975) *Problem Solving Through Creative Analysis*, Aldershot: Gower

Ryan, T. (1977) 'Creative Thinking: A Training Approach' in *Journal of European Industrial Training*, vol. 1, no. 3, pp. 25–8

Osborn, A. F. (1952) *Wake Up Your Mind*, New York: Charles Scribner's Sons

Osborn, A. F. (1954) *Your Creative Power*, New York: Charles Scribner's Sons

Bosticco, M. (1971) *Creative Techniques for Management*, London: Business Books

See also: Synectics; Lateral thinking; Brainstorming

CRITICAL INCIDENT ANALYSIS

Members form into small groups. Each person spends a few minutes recalling from his personal experience a critical incident in human relations in his organisation. It may be a crisis in communication, decision making or implementation. The group members then share these experiences with one another. One or more such incidents might be taken further through the use of a Role Play and/or the use of the Problem-solving Cycle.

Lacey, J. D. and Licht, N. C. (1980) 'Culminating Experience: A Tool for Management Training' in *Training and Development Journal*, vol. 34, no. 3, p. 88–90

Heron, J. (1973) *Experiential Training Techniques*, Department of Adult Education, University of Surrey, Guildford

See also: Problem-solving cycle; Role play; Sociodrama; Personal case history; Incident process method; Case study method

CROSS OVER GROUP (Square Root Group)

The purpose of Cross Over Groups is to provide a structure whereby the individual ideas and opinions of class members can be quickly shared and exchanged amongst the others. The tutor organises the total class into a number of groups in such a way that the number of people in each group is the square root of the total number participating. Extra students are allotted the role of observers. Each group then discusses a topic or question supplied by the tutor for a given period of time. At the pre-appointed time, one member from each of the groups transfers to another group, and he himself is replaced by an in-coming member. This person carries information on the opinions and ideas from his previous group and shares this with his new group. He in turn is briefed by the participants on what was discussed in the group before his arrival. This process of discussion followed by transfer is repeated until only one person remains in the original group. The technique can be used after a brief question-raising lecture. Cross Over Groups are organised in order to make participants aware of the different views and opinions that exist. Alternatively, they can be used as an ice-breaking activity at the start of a course or conference.

See also: Buzz group; Group discussion

DATA APPROACH METHOD (Data Response Method)

The Data Approach Method (DAM) is a form of guided learning which helps students to deal with aspects of the subject of economics. The general approach, however, has a wider application. Developed by Trotman-Dickenson, DAM can be applied to all areas of studies in which statistics are taught. It is a simple method which requires no prior knowledge of mathematics but which seeks to make students numerate. It is particularly useful for those students who are not mathematically minded and it can serve as an introduction to a quantitative methods course in most subjects. In the field of economics, it can be used to give students a quantitative knowledge of the economy, make them familiar with economic data, develop their skills in selecting relevant material and give them practice in analysing and interpreting figures. Prior to a DAM seminar taking place, the students are given an economic problem and data. A package of DAM materials provides a comprehensive coverage of an economy and international comparisons. The key data which are listed under each discussion question provide a signpost for factual information which should be considered in search of an answer. Once a framework has been constructed by the student on the basis of the indicated tables, he fills in the gaps with data of his own choosing. The completed picture is then presented by one of the students at the seminar itself. This is followed by a general discussion. Other class members may be familiar with the same material but may have arrived at a different conclusion. The problems presented in successive seminars are linked so that by the end of the course the students should have an overall view of the economy. The emphasis in a DAM approach is on the integration of material.

DAM is not just giving references to statistical sources and occasional handouts of economic data. It is a structured method of instruction. Once the students are familiar with the data in tabular form, they are encouraged to present it in different ways which may convey it more effectively for a special purpose. Using DAM, students can be given instructions on the use and construction of bar and pie charts, index numbers, graph drawings and discuss the merits of the various presentations. The teaching materials consist of economic problems and tables of economic data.

Trotman-Dickenson, D. I. (1978) 'The Use of Data Response in the Teaching of Economics' in *British Journal of Educational Technology*, vol. 9, no. 3, pp. 201–4

Trotman-Dickenson, D. I. (1969) *Economic Workbook and Data*, London: Pergamon Press

See also: Tutorial-tape-document learning package approach; Construct lesson plan; Self-instructional modules and interactive groups; Re-writing

DEBATE

In a traditional Debate, the students are assigned to take up specified positions and argue these. Within the context of management education the technique can be used to help students obtain a thorough grasp of some complex theoretical positions, for example the differences between Fox's 'Unitarist' and 'Pluralist' perspectives on organisation and society. These frames of reference can be examined in the context of a Debate. To increase reality, the task can be set in terms of a television Debate. The class is divided into three groups: management, unions and the TV production team. The topic 'Are workers and managers more equal today?' is specified and the management group is asked to argue from a unitarist perspective, while the union members couch their argument in pluralistic terms. The 'production team' plans the seating, questions, question order and appoints a 'Robin Day' type interviewer. Members from each of the other two teams appoint two representatives who have to be ready to respond, from their assigned perspectives, to any question that the interviewer may ask them. During the Debate, the remaining members act as the studio audience.

A modified form of Debate has been used in training supervisors. The tutor obtains some 'problems' in supervisor/employee interaction and from these four or five pro and con statements are derived – e.g. pro: 'As supervisors, we help to increase company profits by getting the production out. We get nothing else from it.' Con: 'As supervisors, we help colleagues achieve their own aims and develop our own skills and abilities in the process.' The pro and con Debate begins with a short presentation of the standpoints by the tutor, who provides any supplementary information required. The members then individually rate the standpoints on a +2, +1, 0, −1, −2 scale, indicating where they stand in their opinion. There is a need to be clear about the meaning of any rating scale being used. For example, if it runs from 'completely true' to 'completely false', a different rating may be obtained than if it runs from 'strongly agree' to 'strongly disagree'. If it is rephrased with the conceptually similar, but affectively different 'just how I feel' to 'not my opinion at all', a third and different rating scale may be obtained.

The individual ratings are collected and presented to the whole group on a flipchart. The group members then divide into two groups, with those mainly with pro-rating making up a pro-group and the others the con-group. Both groups discuss their standpoints before meeting up once again in a plenary session to develop a perspective on the role of the supervisor. The key point of the Debate may be 'What does it mean to be a supervisor?' The debating session can develop role-awareness, and the extremities of the pro and con statements present a challenge to reflect on the situation. It allows participants to develop their own standpoints and defend them in an environment of criticism. The preparation and Debate processes also encourage interaction. The Debate can be videotaped and used for evaluation.

Clyde, C. and Kurtz, H. J. (1979) 'Developing Role Awareness in Safety Observer Training' in *Journal of European Industrial Training*, vol. 3, no. 1 pp. 9–12.

See also: Short talks by students; Jurisprudential model; Visiting lecturer

DECISION TABLE

As a communication strategy, Decision Tables share with Algorithms the fact that they can be used to present complex rules, procedures and instructions in such a way that the selection of a correct solution is guaranteed if the necessary information is accurate. Decision Tables are a simple way of presenting information. The one exemplified in Figure 3.2 is in fact simpler than it appears since only two conditions (rules 2 and 3) disqualify and if these do not apply, all other permutations and decisions must apply. A Decision Table is based on two parameters implicit in all information: that questions have to be asked, and that decisions must be taken on the basis of those answers. They permit search to be carried out serially or sequentially through information, but disregarding particular elements or areas which are

CONDITION STUB	CONDITION ENTRIES					
Q1 Were the contributions paid late?	No	Yes	Yes	Yes	Yes	Yes
Q2 Were the contributions paid before the death of the subject of the claim?	—	No	Yes	Yes	Yes	Yes
Q3 Is the insured person alive?	—	—	No	No	No	Yes
Q4 Were the contributions paid before the insured person died?	—	—	No	No	Yes	—
Q5 Have the contributions already been taken into account for a claim for a widow's or retirement pension?	—	—	No	Yes	—	—
ACTION STUB	ACTION ENTRIES					
Death grant is payable.	★			★	★	★
Death grant is NOT payable.		★	★			
Rules	(1)	(2)	(3)	(4)	(5)	(6)

(A dash in the condition entry column indicates that either a yes or no answer is acceptable. In other words, the answer to the question does not affect the final outcome.)

Figure 3.2   Example of a Decision Table

irrelevant. Decision Tables ensure exposure to every eventuality and minimise possible sources of error due to oversight. They help to define the problem and clarify causal and effectual relationships between conditions and actions. They are one of the few strategies available which allow amendments to the logic of the instruction to be carried out without introducing hidden and undesired consequences.

Grad, B. (1961) 'Tabular Form in Decision Logic' in *Datamation*, vol. 7, no. 7

Magee, J. F. (1964) 'Decision Trees for Decision Makers' in *Harvard Business Review*, July–August

See also: Algorithm; Heuristic; Flowchart

DEMONSTRATION–PERFORMANCE METHOD
(Tell-Show-and-Do Approach)
This is a stage on from the 'Tell-and-Show' approach of the Lecture-Demonstration. The method combines an actual portrayal of procedures or operations with practice by the learner. The individual is shown how to do a particular procedure, and is then given the opportunity to practise himself. In essence it is a tell-show-and-do method which might be alternatively described as an acted out lecture. A well planned demonstration which is skilfully executed is an effective teaching device.

It appeals to all the senses, provides actual practice, stimulates interest and maintains attention. It is effective for groups of 25 or less and beyond that number the groups have to be divided up with a separate leader for each sub-group. The planning of a demonstration involves the breaking up of the skill/activity into the various steps arranged in a logical order. Practice is then usually required by the learner to become familiar with the steps. A summary or review is conducted after all learners have had an opportunity to practise. During the individual performance, the tutor goes around observing, spotting and remedying incorrect techniques before they become established habits.

See also: Lesson-demonstration; Drill and practice session; Mathetics; Discovery method

DEVELOPMENT ASSIGNMENT
This is a generic term for a form of development of which there are many varieties. Development Assignments usually accentuate individual development. In the past these have received bad publicity because they were used as gimmicks and were offered as a cure-for-all. There are two basic prerequisites in their use. Firstly, any required skill training must precede the assignment. If a production manager is to work in the finance department on a Development Assignment, then he must be taught the financial and accounting skills that he will require to fulfil the task. Second, any Development Assignment presumes that one-to-one coaching of the manager undertaking the assignment will be available. Line managers should search their own experience to determine what Development Assignments will be useful to their staff. The company's training specialist can provide guidance in this area.

Daley, P. and McGivern, C. (1972) 'The On-Going Management Situation as a Training Vehicle' in *Industrial and Commercial Training*, vol. 4, no. 3, pp. 137–41

Zeira, Y. (1973) 'Introduction of On-The-Job Management Development' in *Personnel Journal*, vol. 52, December, pp. 1049–55

Honey, P. (1976) 'On-The-Job Management Training' in *Industrial and Commercial Training*, June, vol. 8, no. 6, pp. 229–35

See also: Acting assignment; Assignment attachment; Assignment to community organisation; Assignment to government study group; Assignment to manager with high development skills; Committee assignment; Evaluation/audit assignment; Expanding job assignment; Research assignment; Selection board assignment; Study assignment; Task force assignment; Proposal team assignment; Consulting assignment

DIARY EXERCISE

Diary Exercises are a variation on the self-assessment approach. Using this method, selected members of the department are asked to log their daily work activities over a period of ten to fourteen days. On completion, these are reviewed with the boss and the diary confirms the way in which they are spending their time and approaching their job. The review can be carried out either individually or with a group. The aim is to develop and implement an action plan if the diary shows this to be necessary. The diary frequently provokes interest and can be used outside of the company context by the college lecturer who may ask intending course members to keep a diary for a week before the course starts and bring it with them to the training session.

The data can alternatively be analysed by the company trainer. The focus is on actual performance and on what may be needed to achieve ideal performance. Diaries can be broad and consider a whole range of managers' job content, or they can be more specific to focus on a few training needs in greater depth. Stewart and Stewart (1978) write that in designing a diary, a trainer should go through a series of steps. The first is the pilot investigation to see what are the appropriate training objectives. Second, since the diary shows what demands are being placed on a manager, these should be recorded, e.g. duration of activity. Third, each designated activity is broken into codes, one for the activity itself, another for contacts, etc. The aim here is to make the manager's task of completing the diary as simple as possible. A questionnaire containing the diary is assembled and a statement of its purposes and instructions on how to fill it in is enclosed.

Diaries fail if the purposes of the diary are not made clear to those taking part. Will the data be individually examined or as part of a group? When diaries are completed by members before a course and are brought to the training session, tutors can discuss a particular topic such as communication and the type of interactions managers have and refer to the diaries of participants. Syndicate work is then conducted, based on the diaries the course members have brought with them. While it is used primarily on courses concerned with Time Management, the diary approach has a much wider contribution to make as a teaching tool.

Stewart, R. (1970) *Managers and Their Jobs*, London: Pan

Mumford, A. (1980) *Making Experience Pay*, London: McGraw Hill, chapter 3

Stewart, V. and Stewart, A. (1978) *Managing the Manager's Growth*, Aldershot: Gower

Lane, C. (1980) 'Beating Time to Meet Objectives' in *Personnel Management*, vol. 12, no. 3, pp. 36–9

See also: Critical incident analysis; Instrumented feedback; Logging critical incidents

DIRECTED CONVERSATION METHOD

The Directed Conversation Method is a type of group discussion method which can be used on a one-off basis by a trainer or tutor in a classroom situation. Its distinguishing feature is its informality which is achieved by the timing of its introduction by the tutor into the class session. This approach is particularly useful in encouraging student discussion and suggestions in a situation where it is felt, or where it has been shown, that a more formal approach would inhibit the achievement of such aims. DCM developed from the observation made by teachers that some of their most useful work with students was conducted either before or after the formal class session. After a class, as students dispersed, some would gather around the lecturer and discuss additional points. Similar fruitful discussions may take place before the lesson proper commences. It appears that during formal class discussions, students somehow self-censor their contributions, but that outside of these bounded limits they are often much more prepared to contribute.

DCM involves encouraging learning by the blurring or redefinition of the formal session time boundaries. For example, a tutor may feel that junior staff are not receiving the help and guidance from their bosses which they require for their development. If he were to confront the senior staff with this point, they may react hostilely. If such a group of managers were attending a course on some other topic, the trainer might plan to use DCM to achieve his objective. To do this he arrives before the formal session is scheduled to begin. He engages a couple of participants in conversation, raising the problem and expressing the hope that something can be done. The three of them start to talk and as other course members arrive; they too join in this conversation. During the first half of any time slot, the conversation is continued. The trainer directs the conversation in such a way that the participants themselves suggest some ways in which junior staff might be helped. During the second half of the session, the Conference Method is used to chart, build upon and agree implementation strategies for ideas produced in the first stage.

See also: Informal discussion method; Conference method

DIRECTED PRIVATE STUDY

Directed Private Study (DPS) is the term used to describe the linked courses of oral and postal tuition with continuous tutorial advice. DPS evolved from correspondence education which relies on set reading, exercises and tutor marking. This has recently changed with videotapes, records and audiotapes being added. However, rarely do such courses include the element of face-to-face tuition. The critical feature which distinguishes DPS from correspondence courses is this interactive element. A typical DPS may consist of three stages. In stage one there are two weeks of intensive class contact. In addition to the usual teaching, students are given information about stage two and leave with an understanding of what will be required of them. One of the main aims of this phase is to motivate the students over the long second stage. This may consist of up to 20 months study by correspondence. A specified number of study units each with an estimated worktime allocation may be completed in each month plus written tests. During the third phase there might be a second period of oral tuition of about six weeks' duration. The final week tends to be devoted to examinations.

Jones, L. H. (1968) 'Directed Private Study' in Robinson, J. and Barnes, N. (eds) *New Media and Methods in Industrial Training*, BBC Publications

Jones, L. H. (1977) 'Directed Private Study' in *BACIE Journal*, vol. 31, no. 2, February, pp. 31–2

Eagle, F. H. (1976) 'Directed Private Study in the Docks' in *BACIE Journal*, vol. 30, no. 9, October pp. 166–8

See also: Teaching at a distance; Correspondence course

DISCOVERY METHOD (Discovery Training, Discovery Learning)
The Discovery Method refers to a style of teaching that allows a student

to learn by finding out principles and relationships for himself. It stands in contrast to traditional approaches which tend to emphasise the memorisation of what has been read in books or what the teacher has taught himself. The method has an application in any field of study or level of student. Within the industrial training context, the Discovery Method has been made more explicit and has tended to be applied to the approach originating from programmed instruction. This was refined by Eunice and Meredith Belbin for use in the retraining of British Rail steam locomotive drivers to operate the diesel electric trains. The Discovery Method was used to teach the basic principles of electricity to men who only had a vague theoretical knowledge. Learners were given progressively more complex tasks to work on in pairs. Each task demonstrated a basic principle of electricity theory. Written instructions told them what pieces to assemble, and they were to observe and draw conclusions. The instructor remained in the background and answered any questions. Trainees using Discovery Method attained higher test scores than those who has been traditionally lectured. The success of this approach depends on precisely gauging at what point the student can solve the problem, finding out how much the student can be pressed to look for general patterns and devising a suitable discovery situation.

Belbin, R. M. (1969) *The Discovery Method in Training*, Training Information Paper No. 5, HMSO

Rogers, J. (1977) *Adults Learning*, Milton Keynes: Open University Press, Chapter 9

Clay, M. (1980) 'Discovery Training' in *Training*, vol. 6, no. 3, pp. 17–19

See also: Mathetics; Demonstration–performance method; Lesson–demonstration method

DISCUSSION GUIDE
There are two types of Discussion Guides, one which involves people and will be dealt with here. The other utilises prepared outline questions or statements and will be dealt with under the title Learning Through Discussion. However, either type may be used effectively to facilitate proper direction in a discussion. Individuals may be selected to act as Discussion Guides on the basis of their interest or knowledge of the subject. They are assigned a specific responsibility in the development of

the discussion. To prepare they may be required to read about the subject or obtain information from others. Each guide is given a cue in the progress of the discussion. Three or four individuals may serve as guides in a single discussion meeting. The discussion leader determines the nature and timing of the guides' contribution during a discussion. It is important that group members do not discover that persons are serving as guides since any detected artificiality in the situation may hinder spontaneity in discussion. The chairman should ensure that everybody has a chance to get into the discussion between and following the contributions of the guides.

See also: Learning through discussion; Structuring seminars

DISSERTATION PROPOSAL

In most programmes of study leading to the award of a diploma or degree, some form of research project, assignment or dissertation is necessary. However, as an alternative to this, or a preparation for it, the students may be required to complete a dissertation proposal. In essence, this involves defining the problem to be tackled and specifying how one would go about its solution. The content of a dissertation proposal might include some of the following aspects: specifying the problem, the purpose of the research, how it will contribute to theoretical/practical knowledge, survey of what has previously been done in the field, a research plan indicating the steps that will be taken and a statement of research plan implementation.

Duckworth, D. (1978) 'An Approach to Preparing Research Proposals', *Management Education and Development*, vol. 9, no. 3, pp. 206–7

See also: Research degree; Literature search; Library assignment; Guided reading

DISTANCE LEARNING (Distance Teaching; Teaching at a Distance)

This includes all the types of correspondence courses that are available from Linguaphone to the Open University. Correspondence courses are a form of programmed learning. Students receive units of work on which to do certain exercises which are sent off and returned with comments. The degree of student pacing depends on the particular course. Some have flexible timetables and exams, others are very rigidly timetabled.

Learning alone requires much self discipline and it tends to make anxious students more anxious. Older adult learners tend to be prone to this. Correspondence teaching requires the student to be relatively skilled and reasonably confident in his ability to cope with his own written work and books. Frequently, students experience difficulty in controlling the pace of their work. Many have lost the skill of studying. Attention to the materials used and course organisation can overcome these problems.

In the United Kingdom, the definition of Distance Learning has been very narrow, and frequently limited to the different varieties of correspondence courses defined earlier. By contrast, in North America, the term refers to a more formalised system where there are satellite educational units located hundreds of miles away from the main campus but controlled by it. These units may consist of four or five students who come together at a particular time and are linked with the teacher at the main campus with whom they are able to have a two-way conversation. The British tradition of Distance Learning is primarily, although not exclusively, of individuals working alone on sets of materials provided for them by a central organisation. In such a model, student-teacher interaction is de-emphasised.

Many argue that the key in Distance Learning is to include and emphasise those factors which are important in a face-to-face learning situation. In preparing distance learning materials, teachers have found that they improved their normal teaching materials. In this model of teaching, the quality of the materials prepared by the tutor has to be high. There is a heavy emphasis on objectives, assignments and evaluation. The presentation of the material to the learner also needs careful preparation and monitoring. A crucial element in any distance learning system is the means of communication between teacher and learner. With the available technology, there is no end to where one can start and stop. Post, television and radio are all being used while the use of satellites is also becoming feasible as costs fall. Perhaps the important element in communication is not the technology used but the extent to which the student can control the pace and mode of study.

Amongst management students, a proportion may well have taken their accountancy qualification or professional qualification by the correspondence method. During recent years there has been an increased awareness of the needs of part-time students. The CNAA Diploma in Management Studies has been available in the part-time study mode for a long time. Part-time students may not be able to attend college regularly or may live a long way away. The attractiveness of distance learning systems is their flexibility and cost-effectiveness.

Holmberg, B. (1981) *Status and Trends of Distance Education*, London: Kogan Page Ltd

Holmberg, B. (1977) *Distance Education: A Survey and Bibliography*, London: Kogan Page Ltd

Neil, M. W. (ed.) (1981) *The Education of Adults at a Distance: A Report of the Open University Tenth Anniversary Conference*, London: Kogan Page Ltd

Kaye, A. and Rumble, G. (eds.) (1981) *Distance Teaching for Higher and Adult Education*, Croom Helm

Clarke, J. and Leedham, J. (1979) *Aspects of Educational Technology: Vol X, Educational Technology for Individualised Learning*, London: Kogan Page Ltd

Teaching by Correspondence in the Open University, Bletchley: Open University Press

Nathenson, M. B. (1979) 'Bridging the Gap Between Teaching and Learning at a Distance' in *British Journal of Educational Technology*, vol. 10, no. 2, pp. 100–109

Harrison, B. (1974) 'The Teaching–Learning Relationship in Correspondence Tuition' in *Teaching at a Distance*, no. 1, Open University Press

Teather, D. C. B. and McMechan, J. P., 'Learning From a Distance: A Variety of Models' in Howe, A. and Budgett, R. E. B. (eds) *International Yearbook of Educational and Instructional Technology 1980–81*, New York: Kogan Page, London/Nichols Publishing

See also: Correspondence course; Directed private study; Work-related exercise

DRAMATIC SKIT

This method involves the use of dialogue and action to interpret situations and events. It differs from role playing in that it usually involves a longer period of time and a more fully developed plot. Dramatic skits are rehearsed in advance and usually play more heavily on the emotions of the observers. *Full length plays* may be used for ambitious projects where time is not a limitation. Plays may be original and tailored to the situation. *Situation stagings* or creations may be presented but designed to treat only a segment of the problem. This form of dramatic skit requires orientation in and supplementary discussion or further development at the conclusion using other methods. It lends itself well to the re-enacting of court room dramas, conventions and legislative bodies in session. The *playlet* is a third type of dramatic skit. It involves small-scale productions to treat a small problem area or a small segment of a larger problem. It may be used alone to set the stage for the treatment of a problem using other methods, or a series of playlets may be used together to portray successive stages of the development of the relationship between two or three people. A short dialogue can develop sufficient background to set the stage for a surprise or quick ending. Dramatic skits enable knowledge and experience to be presented in a manner which affects the audience emotionally. Ideas may be placed in situations which are more readily identifiable to the audience. They allow the viewer to place himself alternatively in the shoes of various actors and get an insight into the people's feelings and attitudes. The device permits the converting of abstract concepts and theories into real life situations. It gets people involved and skits can be devised to fit almost any situation.

See also: Monodrama; Sociodrama; Role playing

DRILL AND PRACTICE METHOD

The difference in acquiring knowledge about how an operation should be performed and actually being skilled in its performance has been recognised for a long time. Through problem solving, project execution and trial and error methods, people learn the requirements for the performance of a given activity. Frequently there may be a requirement to perform an act with such speed and accuracy so as to deliberately avoid the necessity for reflection. The act is thus made automatic.

For the execution of such skills, the Drill and Practice Method can be used. The terms Drill and Practice are frequently interchangeable. However, here the term Drill is used to refer to an activity carried out in a step-by-step manner under the immediate and active direction of an instructor (e.g. fire drill). By contrast, Practice refers to an activity in which the trainee engages either under instruction or alone. Practice activity has a larger place than Drill activity in adult learning as applied to business and industrial programmes. The instructor aims to advance the trainees as rapidly as possible to a state when practice is as meaningful as possible. When a trainee can practice an entire procedure, lesson or task, the learning task becomes more meaningful, less arduous and the improvement becomes rapid. Hence the value of using meaningful units for Practice. It is also useful to make periods of instructor dominance as brief as possible and vary their nature as much as possible.

See also: Mathetics; Demonstration-performance method; Discovery method; Lesson–demonstration method

EDUCATIONAL VISIT

The Educational Visit, whether to France or the local museum, has a long history in educational practice. The study of management especially lends itself to the 'trip round the factory'. Visits can provide an opportunity for new experiences and information to be gained; objects and people can be observed in their natural surroundings; students interest and keenness of observation may be stimulated and the opportunity might be provided for learning by doing. Depending on the type of visit, procedures may be observed and experienced which participants may later duplicate in their own work environments. Generally, visits can provide a sense of reality to problems, help in the understanding of ideas and may stimulate members to participate in discussion activities following the visit.

While such advantages may indeed accrue to learners, visits are usually expensive to make, both in terms of money and in amount of travelling time. Some investigations indeed suggest that films, film strips and slide-illustrated lectures appear to be just as effective as visits and considerably cheaper. Nevertheless, visits and excursions do seem to be useful in realising some cognitive, but especially affective objectives. The timing of a visit during a course depends on the lecturer's objectives. It may take place late in the programme and be used to summarise and consolidate material initially presented by more traditional methods, or it can be used early in a course as an introduction to the subject being studied. Whatever use is made of it, a visit requires careful planning, preparation and follow-up. It should be preceded by discussions to identify what is to be learned.

The Educational Visit is best used to provide first-hand knowledge or something which cannot be brought into the classroom. The observation or study on location is particularly suited to helping the student to relate theory to practice by observing the object or action in its natural setting. It is essential for the organiser to be well prepared and have answers to questions such as what is the exact time of arrival on site? When and where do we meet for departure? What will be the total time for the trip? What is the objective of the trip? What are the points to cover or show on the trip? Are all the necessary lunch reservations made? What other resources are needed for the trip? Have the travel plans been checked? Have the students been briefed (objectives, what is expected of them, cost/time of trip, proper clothing, nature of follow up)? The Educational Visit provides first hand experience, can help to create classroom rapport and gives the opportunity for first hand observation. However, it depends on object availability, time to attend, and being clearly related to teaching objectives.

Kefford, C. (1970) *A Programmed Approach to Environmental Studies*, London: Blandford

See also: Studycade; Field trip

ENCOUNTER GROUP

In an Encounter Group participants are encouraged to say what they really feel, and to feel what it is that they are saying or hearing or doing and generally to experience and share their own reality. In normal circumstances this is too risky for most people since they fear rejection. We have aspects of ourselves that we do not want to tell others about. But if we take the risk, and do it properly, we find that we feel much better about ourselves. Such groups are based on the values of total honesty. Encounter Group is a general term which subsumes at least three different sub-types. Two of these have an application in college learning environments: these are basic Encounter or Rogerian Group developed and run by Rogers and his colleagues. The other is Open Encounter as used by Schutz at the Esalen Institute in California. A third, Synanon Encounter, has been used by Dederich in working with drug addicts.

Egan, G. (1970) *Encounter: Group Processes for Interpersonal Growth*, Brooks/Cole Publishing Company

Burton, A. (ed.) (1969) *Encounter: Theory and Practice of Encounter Groups* Social and Behavioural Science Series, Jossey Bass

Siroka, R. W., Siroka, E. K. and Schloss, G. A. (1971) *Sensitivity Training and Group Encounter: An Introduction*, New York : Grosset and Dunlap

See also: Basic encounter; Open encounter; Gestalt therapy

ESSAY

Since Essays are used in term assignments and written during formal examinations, they tend to be considered primarily as tools of student assessment. However, in many subjects they constitute the principal medium of learning for the student. The amount of learning that a student gains in completing his Essay is partly dependent on the degree to which the individual has prepared and organised himself to complete it. It also depends on the nature and detail of the comments, both verbal and written, from the tutor. If Essays are to be used for educational as opposed to assessment purposes, that is for formative rather than summative evaluation, the comments which constitute the feedback to the student, need to be quite detailed. Minimal feedback consists of a grade, and perhaps a short comment at the end ('Quite good'). This tells the student little since he does not know what it was that was 'quite good'. Greater depth is obtained when a grade is accompanied by a series of 'indicators' in the margin which relate to more detailed comments made on a separate sheet. Substantial comments regarding the overall structure of the Essay are provided and the reasons for the particular grade given. The usefulness of this lies in the fact that the comments relate the inclusion or omission of various specified points. The overall structure and organisation of the Essay can be dealt with in the final comments and the reasons for the grade enable students to persevere with the admirable habits and discontinue those which are dubious. Two further levels of sophistication exist. Written comments may indicate what could have been done, compared to what was, and finally the tutor may discuss the Essay as a whole with the student in person.

There are further levels of sophistication beyond those described above. Both occur before the Essay is handed in. First, the tutor can negotiate the actual detailed topic of the Essay with the student concerned. This starts off with the student selecting a preferred area in which he wants to learn something. The next stage is the mutual examination of the student's draft plan for the Essay once he has completed the investigative work but before the Essay is submitted. A second variation involves the student being asked to use the Essay not only as a means of learning something, but also as a way of learning how to learn (e.g. essay planning and essay writing are used to learn about finding and presenting information). A further development of the approach described above involves the student first writing an Essay on a chosen topic in the normal way. In response, the tutor offers a detailed counterpoint to some of the views and ideas expressed in the student's work. This response is usually substantial, running perhaps to two or three pages. This plus the original Essay is returned to the student who is then given the task of responding to the tutor's detailed comments.

Henderson, E. S. (1980) 'The Essay in Continuous Assessment' in *Studies in Higher Education*, vol. 5, no. 2, pp. 197–203

Cockburn, B. and Ross, A. (1978) *Essays,* Teaching in Higher Education Series No. 8, School of Education, University of Lancaster

Nimmo, D. B. (1977) 'The Undergraduate Essay: A Case of Neglect?' in *Studies in Higher Education*, vol. 2, no. 2, pp. 183–9

See also: Assignment attachment; Examination

EVALUATION AUDIT ASSIGNMENT

In this development activity the manager is required to make some sort of a judgement of one kind or another based on information that he has collected. The evaluation may be of an individual, new technology, information system or anything else chosen for him. The individual concerned is allocated time in which to develop criteria for judgement, obtain the necessary data needed for the decision and present a report which details his decision and supports it with evidence.

See also: Committee assignment; Consulting assignment; Development assignment; Proposal team assignment; Research assignment; Selection board assignment; Staff meeting assignment; Study assignment; Task force assignment

EXAMINATION

The formal three-hour written Examination remains an important part of the student assessment system within most colleges and universities which offer graduating programmes in management and related studies. The Examination can be considered as an experiential learning event provided that it is suitably introduced and debriefed. It has been found that students who do well on course assignments which are done in their own time with ample opportunity for reading and reflection often do not perform as well within the time constraints of an examination system. Their performance drops when they are required to respond intelligently, in an understandable and comprehensive manner to a specific question with well defined and frequently tight time limits. This type of exam situation can simulate an aspect of the student's work environment. While it is possible to integrate formal organisational requirements such as exams into a management educational programme, the difference in objectives may cause problems. Degree examination scripts are rarely available for debriefing purposes, but there is no reason why class exam scripts, written under similar constraints, should not be.

Various other approaches have been used to transform what are primarily assessment procedures into learning events. Two are described here. When a formal Examination is to be set by the tutor, consisting of perhaps three compulsory questions, the students can be given the opportunity to devise a list of questions, even where the final decision for their inclusion or exclusion from the end of course exam, rests with the tutor. Halfway through the course this task may be introduced to them. Working as a group, the students agree a list of criteria for a 'good question'. They then individually develop a list of such questions relevant to the course based on the agreed criteria. Each week from then on, part of the class time is devoted to students comparing, revising and refining a group-agreed list of such questions. The final outcome of this exercise is a list of about ten questions, presented by the students to the tutor and ranked in order of preference. It is from this list that the teacher chooses the three compulsory ones. The process of selection, discussion, evaluation and final selection requires students to reflect on and revise the course material. It thereby offers a continuous learning opportunity.

An alternative or additional method is for students to agree, first individually and then in groups, the criteria of what constitutes a good essay answer and allocate marks to the different criteria depending on their importance. The marking scheme is agreed with the tutor. They then carry out a piece of work, the title of which may be chosen by themselves, the tutor or jointly. Having completed it they can use the pre-agreed criteria to mark it themselves, and/or have a fellow student mark it, before comparing their own rating with that of the tutor. These two finally agree a mark based on the criteria.

See also: Peer assessment; Learning contract; Student-planned learning; Essay; Self tests and quizzes

EXHIBIT (Exhibition)

An Exhibit is a stationary display used for the purpose of instruction. A department of mechanical engineering in a college may have a cut-away car or aeroplane engine on display which is used for teaching students. Within medicine, various organs of the body are preserved and can be displayed during a teaching session. The Exhibit as a learning resource has a long history. In management education, a group discussion concerning aspects of plant layout can be helped by the use of a scaled down model.

An Exhibition brings together under a single roof, for a given period of time, a number of Exhibits. It is a public display of art, products, skills or activities. It is a show where the Exhibits themselves are of primary interest and constitute the focus of attention. Exhibitions are educational events in the sense that they seek to inform and acquaint prospective buyers and the public at large with the range and quality of currently available or planned products or services. Thus a manager or management trainee may be sent to an industrial exhibition in order to find out what is going on in the field.

Moss, M. (1974) 'Models as an Aid to Training' in *Industrial and Commercial Training*, vol. 6, no. 7, pp. 314–7

See also: Fair; Festival

EXPANDED JOB ASSIGNMENT

This is a form of managerial job enrichment in which the manager is consciously given added responsibilities to perform. These may be in the form of new areas or products to look after, or he may be given more power, authority and discretion in dealing with his existing job tasks. The employee himself is in the best position to expand his job. Helping him to do so is largely a matter of motivation. Employees must be brought into decision making if they are to assume responsibility for enlarging their jobs. Their opinions must be sought. This involves seniors delegating more authority downwards.

See also: Planned delegation; Acting assignment; Development assignment; Sick leave/holiday replacement assignment

EXPERIENCE-BASED LEARNING

The connotations of the concept of Experience-based Learning are so varied that many of the writers who seek to discuss it use the task of definition as the basis of their description (Boydell, 1976; Anderson, Boud and McLeod, 1980). A very inadequate definition might be to regard experiential learning as that which arises from the first hand experiences of the learner. It is this key feature which distinguishes it from other forms of learning. Defined in this way, it is clear that experiential learning is not a specialised teaching approach as such, but one which is contained in a variety of methods such as Action Learning, Coverdale Training, workshop activities, educational visits and internship programmes and a host of otherwise dissimilar approaches.

Boydell, T. H. (1976) *Experiential Learning*, Manchester Monographs No. 5, Department of Adult Education, University of Manchester

Roskin, R. (1976) 'Learning by Experience' in *Journal of European Training*, vol. 5, no. 4, pp. 181–212

Anderson, B., Boud, D. and McLeod, G. (1980) *Experience based Learning – How and Why?* Australian Consortium on Experiential Education

Allner, D. and Tiere, J. (1976) 'Experiential Learning: A View from the Inside' in *Industrial and Commercial Training*, part 1 in vol. 8, no. 1, pp. 27–35; part 2 in vol. 8, no. 2, pp. 73–8 and part 3 in vol. 8, no. 3, pp. 114–9

Keeton, M. T. and Associates (1976) *Experiential Learning: Rationale, Characteristics and Assessment*, San Francisco: Jossey-Bass

Keeton, M. T. and Tate, P. J. (eds.) (1978) *Learning by Experience – What, Why and How?* New Directions in Experiential Education No. 1, San Francisco: Jossey Bass

Boud, D. J. and Pascoe, J. (1978) *Experiential Learning: Developments in Australian Post-Secondary Education*, Sydney: Australian Consortium on Experiential Education

Ayal, H. and Segev, E. (1976) 'Integrating the Didactic and Experiential Approaches in Management Education' in *Journal of European Training*, vol. 5, no. 5, pp. 276–83

Kemp, B. (1979) 'A Local Government Experience with Experiential Learning' in *Personnel Management*, vol. 11, no. 6, pp. 37–41

See also: Experiential exercise; Cooperative education; Action learning; Coverdale training

EXPERIENTIAL EXERCISE (Substitute Task Exercise)

In a structured Experiential Exercise, the learner is put into a situation of accelerated experience. These experiences usually contain what are called 'substitute' tasks, e.g. building a Lego man, ranking a number of items. The focus here is not so much on what is done as on how it is done. Stress is laid upon the process and so the tasks are made simple or childlike so that they do not distract too much from the process. Observation by half the group as the other half engages in the task is essential. To obtain high quality observation, participants and observers need to have been given some form of conceptual framework or background. This may be a model, e.g. of decision-making styles, or a list of functions, e.g. Fayol's Management Functions. As much time needs to be given to planning and organising the observation and the post task debriefing as to the stage management of the task itself.

Experiential Exercises involve activity of a short specified length (½ to 3 hours). Their goals tend to be specific and well defined while outcomes tend to be predictable and uniform. They are structured in pre-planned steps and are run by following a timetable. Exercises are a way in which theories or principles can be made to influence practice or experience. They put the flesh onto theories. To be effective the tutor needs to have a good grasp of the theories and principles involved and be clear about what the exercises selected will contribute to the session and to the course as a whole. It is helpful, although not essential, for the tutor to have had previous experience of the exercise he is going to use. In recent years there has been a dramatic increase in the number of such exercises developed and these are now readily available in book form from the major publishing houses.

Boydell, T. H. (1976) *Experiential Learning*, Manchester Monograph No. 5, Department of Adult Education, University of Manchester

Pfeiffer, J. W. and Jones, J. G. (eds.) *A Handbook of Structured Experiences for Human Relations Training*, vols. I–VII, Mansfield: University Associates of Europe

Kolb, D. A., Rubin, I. M. and McIntyre, J. M. (1974) *Organizational Psychology: An Experiential Approach*, Englewood Cliffs, New Jersey: Prentice Hall

Beatty, R. W. and Schneider, C. E. (1977) *Personnel Administration: An Experiential Skills Building Approach*, Reading, Mass.: Addison-Wesley

Harvey, D. F. and Brown, D. R. (1976) *An Experiential Approach to Organizational Development*, Englewood Cliffs, New Jersey: Prentice-Hall

Kast, F. E. and Rosenzweig, J. E. (1976) *Experiential Exercises and Cases in Management*, New York: McGraw-Hill

Knudson, H. R., Woodworth, R. T. and Bell, C. H. (1973) *Management: An Experiential Approach*, Irwin Dorsey

Glueck, W. F. and Jauch, L. R. (1977) *The Managerial Experience: Cases, Exercises and Readings*, New York: Holt, Rinehart and Winston

Finch, F. E., Jones, H. R. and Litterer, J. A. (1976) *Managing For Organizational Effectiveness: An Experiential Approach*, Maidenhead: McGraw-Hill

Lau, J. B. (1976) *Behaviour in Organizations: An Experiential Approach*, Irwin Dorsey

Bradford, D. and Eoyang, C. (1976) 'The Use and Misuse of Structured Exercises' in Cooper, C. L. (ed.) *Developing Social Skills in Managers: Advances in Group Training*, London: Macmillan

See also: Experience-based learning; Programmed simulation; Action maze; Non-verbal exercise; Tape stop exercise

EXPOSURE TO UPPER MANAGEMENT

A manager may be assigned to work for a period of time either with a single member of senior management or perhaps a group. The individual is engaged on work and in decisions which have not previously been in his scope. He is able to see the way in which senior management works, and in particular the decisions it makes. Thus a committee of senior managers who are reviewing an aspect of company policy, may include in their number a person from a department who is not necessarily the most knowledgeable about the topic to be discussed, but who can potentially learn a lot from being involved in this kind of activity.

Another aspect of this same approach is to send a subordinate to represent a manager before his superiors. This can be an effective training device. He can present a programme, answer questions and generally act in the manager's stead. It is essential that the subordinate is thoroughly coached beforehand. Two effects of this approach are that the junior is seen to the best advantage by his seniors and secondly he learns something about the people to whom his boss reports and how these people think and act. A word of caution. Usually there is more than a single subordinate who may benefit from this form of training. The boss should not let one man's success or failure blind him to the needs of the other staff who report to him.

See also: Assignment to manager with high development skills;

Job rotation; Job swop; Manager exchange; Manager shadowing; Sick leave/holiday replacement assignment

FAIR

A Fair is a non-sequential mixture of exhibits and activities. Originally the word 'Fair' was applied to a travelling entertainment with sideshows which visited the same place each year. Buyers and sellers gathered at these set times for the purposes of trade. From the point of view of the organisers, a Fair may be an effective format for reaching people who do not read publications, listen to broadcasts or attend meetings or courses. At the present time, the purpose can be to create interest, promote standards of excellence, show the results of activities, enlist community support, demonstrate a process or get new members for organisations. As a learning situation, a Fair is too transitory to achieve educational objectives in much depth, but it is probably one of the most effective formats for arousing interest.

See also: Festival; Exhibit

FEEDBACK CLASSROOM

This is an audio-visual support system which is capable of being added to a traditional lecture room which, when used in association with the large lecture, significantly alters the learning context. The nearest analogy is that of the 'clapometer' used on a popular British television talent contest. The term Feedback Classroom has been used to refer both to the physical location in which a particular type of teaching takes place, e.g. a specially equipped lecture room, and to the teaching machine itself which is used in this teaching situation. As used here, the label applies to the entire learning situation being created through the use of this equipment. The machine itself can be used either by the teacher as an aid or as an operator-controlled teaching or examining machine. One version of it was designed for 18 students and was arranged to use multiple choice questions. Each student was provided with a response unit which was connected to a master console controlled by the teacher or operator. The classroom itself employs a slide projector with a remote control facility which presents multiple choice questions to the group. The questions can also be presented by the teacher using a blackboard or overhead projector transparency. The presentation device can be separate from the response/feedback machine. The system permits up to six alternative answers with each student response unit having six switches.

After studying the projected question, the student indicates his choice of answer by pressing the appropriate switch on his unit. If the response is correct, the student is rewarded by a green light and a similar light appears on the tutor's master console. Selection of an incorrect response results in the display of red lights. In addition, a large scale meter displays to the whole class the overall percentage correct response. It can also be used to show the percentage of the class choosing each alternative answer.

Used as a teaching aid, a lesson can be prepared in the form of linear programmed instruction with clearly defined objectives. Test slides are prepared to test students' understanding of each item of the instruction given. Failure to obtain an adequate percentage correct response to any part of the lesson is immediately apparent to the teacher and further instruction can be given before proceeding with the planned lesson. This helps to monitor continually the efficiency of teaching. Since it is also possible to determine which of the alternative answers has been selected by each student, learners with problems can be identified and can be offered tutorial assistance. Lessons can be arranged with the instructional material as well as the test questions available on slides. This makes it possible for the class to be conducted and results recorded by a non-teacher, manual operator. This is a form of group tape/slide with programmed learning. An added spin-off is that it makes lecturers structure their work more systematically so that questions can be included.

Finally, the Feedback Classroom can be used as an examination machine. It eliminates the need for marking and provides immediate feedback to students and teachers. The speed of operation allows it to cover the whole breadth of syllabus. It can also be used diagnostically to assess a student's suitability for a course. As a form of group programmed learning, the Feedback Classroom shares the advantages and disadvantages of the Skinnarian system upon which it is based. It offers increased teaching efficiency by claiming to provide better test results, by reducing the time taken to cover a given teaching programme while at the same time allowing a teacher to handle larger classes. It claims to increase student motivation by encouraging active student involvement in learning; to offer better selection of students for courses and to improve teacher training while reducing the educational cost per student.

Twelker, P. A. (1967) 'The Teaching Research Automated Classroom (TRAC): a facility for innovative change' in *Programmed Learning and Educational Technology*, vol. 4, pp. 316–23

Holling, K. (1964) 'Feedback Classroom' in *Programmed Learning*, vol. 1, no. 1, pp. 17–20

See also: Programmed learning; Construct lesson plan; Assignment attachment; Self-tests and quizzes

FESTIVAL

A Festival is a day or period of time which is set aside for celebration or feasting. The term is applied to any occasion for celebration especially one which commemorates an anniversary or some other significant event. It consists of a programme of public festivity which frequently includes an organised series of special events and performances which usually take place in a single geographical location.

See also: Fair, Exhibit

FIELD PROJECT/ATTACHMENT

This is a general term for a situation in which an individual, usually a college student, spends a period of time 'attached' to a department or unit in a private company or public enterprise in which he carries out some task or project. The chosen activity should involve personal learning which has a full and proper function within the course and which is undertaken at a time when it can be performed effectively. It is important that the host institution should be one from which the trainee can learn, and which can provide expert supervision for this task since this will not be available in the college or training department. Field Attachments of real value seem to depend on the availability of institutions of sufficient size and challenge; a density of manning which allows time to be given to the project, a provision of expert supervision and the availability of sufficient time for a worthwhile piece of work to be concluded. Field projects of a modest size are possible within the context of a full-time one-year course.

See also: Cooperative education; Internship; Overseas project; Real life project; Industrial project

FIELD TRIP (Study Visit)

Field Trips by students of geology or geography are a common feature of many such courses. Unlike Educational Visits which tend to be brief, perhaps lasting a single day or at most two, a Field Trip involves a longer period of time away from the classroom. Because the purpose of such a visit is to obtain first hand information about the phenomena being studied, the Field Trip can be considered as an aspect of Experience-based Learning or the Laboratory method. In the field of business, groups of British managers regularly go on Study (or Field) Visits to look at Japanese and German factories. The purpose of these is to allow members to learn about the organisation of the factories and compare their own methods and approaches with those being visited.

See also: Educational visit; Studycade

FILM

Management training films tend to be synonymous with the training films that are produced for sale or hire by the major companies in the field such as Guild Sound and Vision, Video Arts and Rank. These can be used either as a supplement to other training methods, or as the main vehicle of learning. Increasingly, the tutor's notes which accompany the films include suggested role-plays and associated case studies. Suessmuth (1978) distinguished four different types of management training films. The first he called the Didactic Film which emphasised facts, and which could also be called a 'message film'. It aimed to communicate specific points to the audience on, for example, how to run a meeting, or how to approach a customer. The Point of View Film took a particular viewpoint on a subject and provided evidence to support this perspective, for example, that the interests of management and the workforce are the same. The Attitude Shaping Film was described by Suessmuth as one in which a preconceived idea was taken and then was either strengthened or modified in the minds of the audience. Finally, there was the Open Ended Film which was a type of filmed case study which often had an abrupt ending.

An organisation may choose to make its own film for a special purpose and may be deciding between using 16 mm film or video. What are the advantages of each medium? Both Video and Film give a series of pictures. Films can be shown anywhere since film sizes have been universally standardised for a long time and a 16 mm film can be shown on any 16 mm projector. The same is not true of Video. Slowing down and speeding up time is a much more common and flexible facility in film equipment. Film pictures can be projected on to a large screen with clearer definition than is possible with video. Films can be successfully recorded on to videotape for viewing on a television set while transfer the other way is less successful. Film sequences can easily be cut to an accuracy of 1/24 of a second; a time of one second is usual for videotape. For the tutor, these factors will determine the choice of one or the other. Film companies offering management films for sale or hire regularly hold previews several times a year. An advantage claimed for Film is that it motivates students, extends their range of experiences, aids the poor and slow reader, is valuable for introducing new material, can clarify processes and procedures, increases the amount of material learned within a specified time, strengthens retention, clarifies perceptions, concepts and understanding, encourages further reading and study, produces more and better group discussions, reinforces other methods of learning and can encourage desirable attitudes and behaviour.

Teather, D. C. B. and Marchant, H. (1974) 'Learning from film with particular reference to the effects of cueing, questioning and knowledge of results' in *Programmed Learning and Educational Technology*, vol. 11, no. 6, pp. 317–27

Teather, D. C. B. (1974) 'Learning from film: a significant difference between the effectiveness of different projection methods in *Programmed Learning and Educational Technology*, vol. 11, no. 6, pp. 328–34

Marchant, H. (1977) 'Increasing the Effectiveness of Educational Films: a selected review of research' in *British Journal of Educational Technology*, vol. 8, no. 2, pp. 86–96

Suessmuth, P. (1978) *Ideas for Training Managers and Supervisors: Useful Suggestions, Activities and Instruments*, Mansfield: University Associates of Europe, chapter 27

Nolan, J. (1980) 'The Use and Misuse of Films in Management Training' in *Training and Development Journal*, vol. 34, no. 3, pp. 84–5

Unwin, D. (1979) 'Production and Audience Variables in Film and Television: A Second Selected Bibliography' in *Programmed Learning and Educational Technology*, vol. 16, no. 3, pp. 232–9

See also: Television; Trigger film

FISHBOWL EXERCISE

Half the class members sit in an inner circle and hold a discussion while the remaining members sit on the outside and observe the interaction. A general discussion follows in which the 'outside' observers comment on what they saw happening within the observed group. A further sophistication of this technique is possible in which, not only do the fishbowl observers comment on what they saw happening within the observed group, but in addition, the observed group states what it saw happening to itself. These two reports may highlight perceptual and affective discrepancies thereby producing a lot of useful understanding of the subjective nature of perception.

See also; Group with ground rules; Process analysis

FLEXASTUDY (Learning by Appointment, Learning on Demand)
Flexastudy is a college-based Open Learning system in which the student buys blocks of time to use the facilities of the college or of the tutor. It is an individualised learning system. With Flexastudy the course is organised in such a way that students progress through their studies at a greater or lesser speed depending on their length of attendance at college. The approach has been used to prepare students for the examinations of bodies such as the Association of Certified Accountants, Institute of Bankers and the Institute of Purchasing and Supply. In a Flexastudy scheme there are no lectures and the course is not synonymous with the class. Students have a wide range of choice over when and for how long they wish to join a class. Written work schemes are used to structure the student's learning and to provide information. Tutorial supervision and assistance are provided to reinforce the students' motivation and to ease their learning difficulties. Although the emphasis is on individual tuition, facilities are usually provided for tutors to arrange group learning in a seminar situation.

Students enrol and choose a particular course they wish to follow from a range which is offered. They also select the level of the examination for which they want to study, the date on which they wish to begin attendance and the number of weeks they want to attend. Having enrolled, the full-time student arrives at a Flexastudy centre on his first day and sits in an open-plan room which may have forty or so desks. He is allocated a desk which he will use for the duration of his course and supplied with a timetable. The timetable is a normal weekly one divided into set time periods which are allocated to subjects (with tutors' names) or to private study. Each student can progress through his course at a greater or lesser speed depending on the length of time he attends. During a subject period the student is visited by his tutor. At their first meeting, the tutor gives him a suitable scheme of work for his course and they agree a date for completion of the first topic. On that date, he will set the student a work assignment to test his understanding. After this work has been completed and assessed, the next topic is tackled and so on. During the intervening period, the tutor checks if the student is having any problems. A similar procedure is followed by the tutor in each subject.

The Flexastudy system is self-pacing with the learning being dependent on the individual student's aptitude and motivation. Reinforcement is through work schemes and individual tutorial supervision and assistance. A bank of work schemes needs to be built up for each subject. To do this a course is divided up into modules each of which has a written set of instructions which the student receives from the tutor. Topic areas make up a module and instructions indicate what needs to be done to cover each topic. Student progress is monitored through the work schemes. With student agreement, the pace of study may be altered by varying the time period spent on particular topics. Where difficulties are experienced by a number of students, a general seminar may be held.

Morris, J. H. (1978) 'Flexastudy' in *Industrial and Commercial Training*, vol. 10, no. 7, pp. 288–90

Albrecht, A. and Spencer, D. C. (1976) *Flexastudy: The Professional Tutorial System Operated at Redditch College*, Coombe Lodge Case Study, Information Bank No. 1119

See also: Learning contracts; FlexiStudy; Directed private study; Open learning

FLEXISTUDY

FlexiStudy is a locally-based Open Learning system and can be distinguished from Flexastudy which is college-based. The student works at home and has regular contacts with the college through seminars and tutorials. It was originally designed for mature students who did not wish to follow degree-level courses. Its aim is frequently stated to be an analogue of the Open University and it shares many of the approaches and ideas of that organisation. It developed out of the need felt by correspondence students for face-to-face contacts both with each other and with teaching staff. The desire was to combine distance learning with local learning. Traditional college-based courses tend to offer little flexibility in terms of their time length, the attendance that is required of students and the times of admission to the course. Also there are frequently problems associated with minimum enrolment figures and course drop-out. FlexiStudy attempts to overcome these problems by combining study at home by the learner with occasional tutorials held in college. The correspondence material the student receives is carefully structured and referenced and may be preceded by helping the learner to develop his study skills. The study scheme attempts to provide the maximum amount of feedback to the student and makes the best use of the resources that are available in the local college. The college tutorials and individual learner-communication systems are together intended to provide the learner with the best and fastest advice on both his study approach and on the subject matter. The FlexiStudy system is now being operated from a number of local colleges throughout the country.

Sacks, H. (1980) 'FlexiStudy – An Open Learning System for Further and Adult Education' in *British Journal of Educational Technology*, vol. 11, no. 2, pp. 85–95

FlexiStudy: a manual for local colleges, National Extension College Reports, Series 2, no. 4, Cambridge: National Extension College, 1978

Davies, T. C. (1977) *Open Learning Systems for Mature Students*, Working Paper 14, London: Council for Educational Technology

See also: Open learning; Flexastudy; Directed private study

FLOWCHART

In an instructional design, Flowcharts are a means of representing choices or actions in a systematic or diagrammatic form. They are often used to describe tasks, or as aids to the instruction and teaching of a task. A college room which houses microcomputers can have scattered around it Flowcharts which indicate the steps any new user needs to take in order to activate a terminal, insert a programme from a cassette recorder and use it. Such a Flowchart eliminates the need for the continual presence of an instructor since the chart teaches the user the stages. An example of a Flowchart indicating the stages in the production of a tape-slide programme is shown in Figure 3.3.

FORUM MEETING

A Forum is a stage presentation in which the opportunity is given to members of the audience to ask questions and make comments. These usually come after the lecturer or symposium members have given their

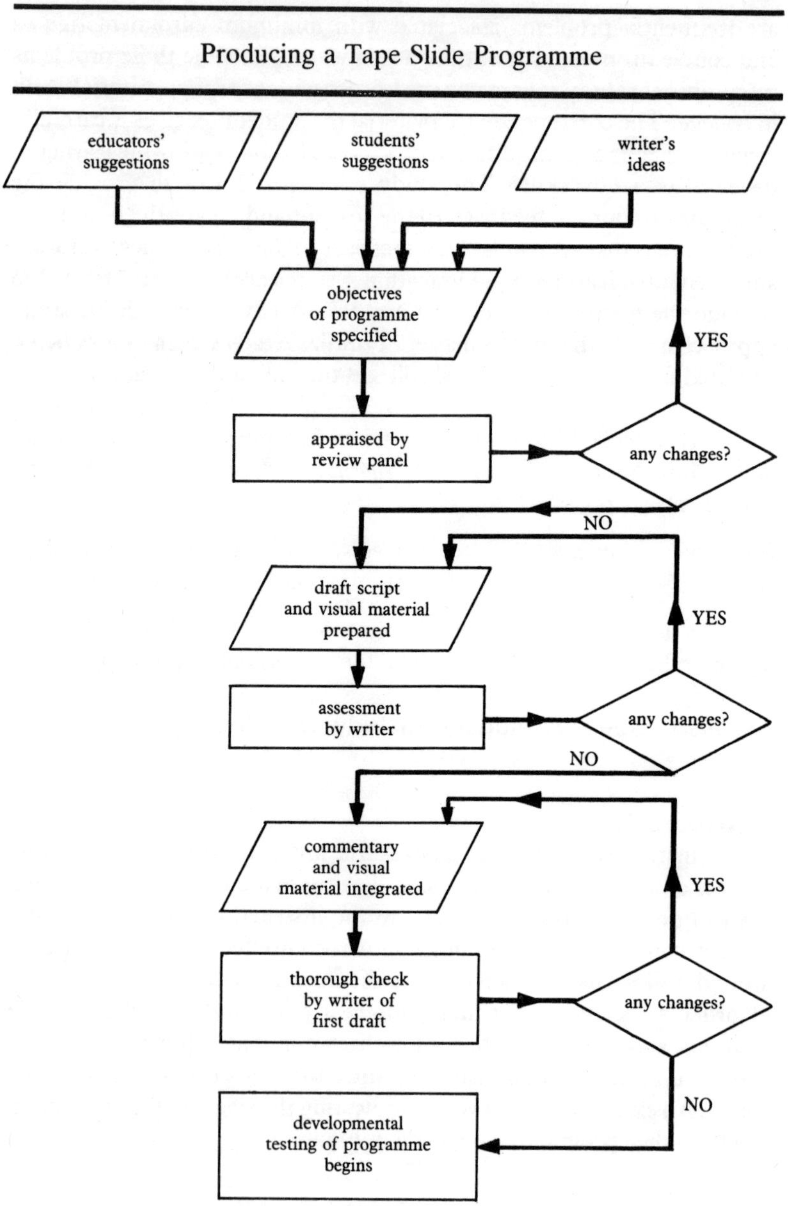

Producing a Tape Slide Programme

Figure 3.3   Example of a Flowchart

presentations. The key to a successful Forum Meeting is the chairman who encourages the audience to participate. Every member of the audience should be fully aware before the formal presentation begins that he will have the opportunity to ask questions or make responses. If the audience is large (over 100), a few planted questioners can help. If the forum concept is brought into the formal stage presentation, the name given to the presentation should be Lecture Forum, Symposium Forum or Panel Forum. The advantage of this method is that it permits a lot of information to be given out which can stimulate audience members to think. This is especially so when they have the opportunity for further clarification through questions.

See also: Listening team; Colloquy meeting; Brains trust; Reaction panel; Audience reaction/watchdog team; Panel discussion; Symposium meeting

FREE DISCUSSION METHOD

The Free Discussion Method is a learning situation in which the topic and direction of the discussion are controlled by the student group while the teacher observes and very occasionally comments on the process. It can be used to encourage changes in attitudes and feelings. One can distinguish its use in the training context from that in the university/college setting. Barber reported the use of Free Discussion Method with supervisors. Groups of a dozen supervisors met to apply a problem-solving approach. It was preceded by Job Analysis and followed by this Free Discussion Method which was the main training vehicle. Before the course there was a briefing session when the purpose of the training was explained. Supervisors were given a list of questions relevant to their daily work. These were based on interviews carried out on the job by training staff and senior management. The supervisors were invited to choose which questions they wanted discussed, and were asked to submit any additional questions of their own. Examples of questions included: 'To what extent is a supervisor free to deal with a shopfloor labour problem on his own?' and 'What advice and assistance does the Personnel Department give a supervisor in taking on a new man?' At the briefing session, the topics chosen for discussion are revealed and participants are asked to be frank and free with their comments during the forthcoming course. The role of the training officer is to ensure effective and purposeful discussion. He is there as a neutral person who must know about the firm in detail and be a competent discussion leader.

The approach requires the trainer to establish quickly a lively and informal atmosphere. A way of doing this is to ask participants to introduce themselves and state what they find to be most satisfying and least satisfying about their job. The comments with group permission can be noted and communicated to senior management emphasising that it is interested in improvements. A distinguishing aspect of this approach is that a member of senior management takes the chair for the rest of the day which has been vacated by the trainer following his opening remarks. However, the trainer does not leave, but his role changes to that of catalyst in discussions and the maintenance of an atmosphere of openness. The senior manager meanwhile presents the problem or question and asks for comments and ideas while at the same time resisting the desire to put forward his own personal viewpoint. His task is to listen to the comments of the supervisors and report them to his colleagues. The chairman's role may be taken by another member of senior management on the following day. The discussion group may choose to formalise its suggestions by presenting a written summary of its ideas and conclusions.

Within this training context, this approach may be integrated with Conference Method and the Problem-solving Cycle. Its key difference lies in the way in which the discussion topics and questions are raised and the nature of the involvement of senior management. It is based on the idea that to participate effectively is to learn. Such a view has been challenged by those who consider group work of any kind to be of doubtful value. Nevertheless, the method is practical and specific. It can help to develop more effective teamwork and can assist in the improvement of communications between different organisational levels.

Barber, J. W. (1968) 'Free Group Discussion Method in the Training of Supervisors' in Robinson, J. and Barnes, N. (eds.) *New Media and Methods in Industrial Training*, London: BBC Publications

Barnett, S. A. (1958) 'An Experiment with Free Discussion Groups' in *Universities Quarterly*, vol. 12, pp. 175–80

Abercrombie, M.L.J. (1960) *The Anatomy of Judgement*, Harmondsworth: Penguin Books

Abercrombie, M.L.J. (1974) *Aims and Techniques of Small Group Teaching*, Society for Research into Higher Education, 3rd edition

Johnson, M.L. (1952) 'Teaching by Free Group Discussion' in *Universities Quarterly*, vol. 6, pp. 290–5

See also: Conference method; Small group teaching; Directed conversation method; Problem-solving cycle; Leaderless group discussion; Group discussion; Associative group discussion

GAME

Business games have been described as case studies with feedback and a time dimension. They also contain elements of role playing which promote the acquisition of technical competence. Games are characterised by a competitive element; some form of time relation; a representation of an actual or typical business situation which has been simplified and which provides feedback to learners on the consequences of their decisions and permits them to take account of their experience. These games can be played by two or more teams consisting of between five and a dozen players. The teams represent the business enterprises which are in competition with each other. Individual members of each team are designated to play specific company roles, e.g. managing director, sales manager, production manager. Each team is presented with information which they have to consider and are then required to make a decision. During a Game, each team makes a great number of decisions which affect its continuing operation, e.g. decisions on raw materials' purchase, hiring and firing personnel, marketing of the product etc. Individual team decisions may be fed into a computer programmed to respond to them in terms of a dynamic situation and to determine the outcome of each specific decision for the well being of each company engaged in the exercise. The impact of the decisions is then fed back to students in the form of statements about their assets or the consequences for the total enterprise. The teams are required to make further decisions on the basis of the information provided. The final objective of each team is to survive and if possible to beat the opposition on some specified criteria, e.g. return on capital employed, dividend payment, achieved market share, stability of employment etc. Simpler business games are non-interactive with the decisions of one team not affecting the outcomes of the others. Decision analysis and feedback may be done manually by the tutor.

Each business game uses a model of a business situation designed by its creator. A Game frequently uses a model with a set of mathematical relationships built in. It is difficult to make a hard and fast distinction between a Game on the one hand and a Simulation. It has been argued that a Game *compresses* time so that an entire year or even five years in a company's existence may be shortened into a few hours, whereas a Simulation operates in real time. However, there are examples of Simulations also compressing time. Equally, it is sometimes said that a Game has rules, players and competition, whereas a Simulation represents reality. Once again one can argue that the quality of a business game is judged by the extent to which it represents reality, and that competition and rules are part of that same reality.

In educational terms such Games have been found useful in the teaching of concepts in business decisions, giving students experience in relating elements together into a complex whole and allowing them to make judgements and test assumptions about a business model. Pedagogically, participants experience a high degree of involvement in the learning situation and the immediate feedback process gives them direct information about the adequacy of their own decisions without the tutor having to be involved. The skills of data and logical assessment of a situation are stressed. Skills illustrated by the Game tend to be easily assimilated and become readily transferred into the trainee's work situation. It closely approximates to the process that the learners must go through in arriving at on-the-job judgements and decisions.

Meurs, F. and Choffray, J. M. (1975) 'Business Games: Their Role in Training and Development' in *Journal of European Training*, vol. 4, no. 2, pp. 81–112

Kibbee, J. M. et al. (1961) *Management Games*, New York: Holt Rinehart

Elgood, C. (1976) *Handbook of Management Games*, Aldershot: Gower

Lovelock, C. (1975) 'The Construction, Operation and Evaluation of Management Games' in Taylor, B. and Lippitt, G. L. (eds.) *Management Development and Training Handbook*, London: McGraw-Hill

Lloyd, D. C. F. (1978) 'An Introduction to Business Games' in *Industrial and Commercial Training*, vol. 10, no. 1, pp. 11-18

Sleet, D. A. (1981) *Guide to Health Instruction: Simulations, Games and Related Activities*, Irvine, California: Human Behaviour Research Group Inc.

Elgood, C. (1975) 'Designing a Business Game' in *Journal of European Training*, vol. 4, no. 1, pp. 15–24

See also: Simulation; Programmed simulation; Action maze

GESTALT THERAPY (Gestalt Techniques)

Gestalt Therapy was formulated by Frederick 'Fritz' Perls. Gestalt in German means an organised whole and the gestalt approach considers man as a total organism functioning as a whole rather than as a set of fragmented parts. Gestalt Therapy has been used in clinical and general educational settings and its influence within management training can be traced back to the 1970s. The approach contains three basic elements: emphasis on the present (the 'here and now'); self-awareness and self regulation and the integration of new insights plus acceptance of how one is, thereby leading to the possibility of personal change. Gestalt Therapy methods underlie Encounter Groups and Confluent Education. They have also been used in organisational development activities.

Smith, P. B. (1980) *Group Processes and Personal Change*, London: Harper and Row, Chapter 8

'A Gestalt Primer' in *Self and Society Special Issue*, vol. 4, no. 2, February/March, 1980

Perls, F., Hefferline, R. F. and Goodman, P. (1976) *Gestalt Therapy*, Harmondsworth: Penguin Books

Perls, F. S. (1974) *Gestalt Therapy Verbatim*, New York: Bantam Books

Stevens, J. O. (1978) *Gestalt Is*, New York: Bantam Books

Passons, W. R. (1975) *Gestalt Approaches in Counselling*, New York: Holt, Rinehart and Winston

See also: Confluent education; Values clarification, Illuminative incident analysis; Encounter group

GRID TRAINING (Managerial Grid Training)

Developed by Robert Blake and Jane Mouton, the Managerial Grid provides a framework which managers can use to help them to understand their own and other managers' behaviour, thereby leading to the development of more appropriate behaviour patterns for individuals and groups in the organisation. The Grid itself is a chart on which the horizontal axis represents concern for production and the vertical aspect concern for people. The point on the Grid where a manager's concern for people meets his concern for production indicates his 'managerial style'. In this approach, management style is indicated by numbers. Thus a '9.9 manager' is said to accomplish work from committed people and have a common stake in organisational purposes leading to relationships of trust and respect.

Although the application of the Grid has taken many forms, its use usually follows a pattern where managers, first individually and then in teams, are presented with a number of problems to solve. In the process of handling the problems each manager learns about the effectiveness of teams and has the opportunity to analyse his own management style and that of the other group members. The Grid has six parts or phases:

phase 1 focuses on personal and interpersonal development; phase 2 on team development; phase 3 on intergroup interface development; phases 4–6 focus on total organisational system development.

Blake, R. R. and Mouton, J. S. (1979) *The New Managerial Grid*, Houston: Gulf Publishing, 3rd edition

Blake, R. R. and Mouton, J. S. (1975) 'Managerial Grid in Practice' in Taylor, B. and Lippitt, G. L. (eds.) *Management Development and Training Handbook*, London: McGraw Hill

Blake, R. R., Mouton, J. S., Barnes, L. B. and Greiner, L. E. (1964) 'Breakthrough in Organisational Development' in *Harvard Business Review*, November–December

Blake, R. R. and Mouton, J. S. (1968), *Corporate Excellence Through Grid Organization Development*, Houston: Gulf Publishing Company.

Smith, P. B. and Honour, T. F. (1969) 'The Impact of Phase 1, Managerial Grid Training' in *Journal of Management Studies*, vol. 6, pp. 318–30.

Williams, A. P. O. (1971) 'The Managerial Grid: Phase 2, Case Study of a Top Management Team' in *Occupational Psychology*, vol. 45, nos. 3 and 4, pp. 253–72

Hart, H. A. (1974) 'Grid Appraised- Phase 1 and 2' in *Personnel*, vol. 51, September, pp. 44–59

See also: Action-centred leadership; 3-D Organisational effectiveness training

GROUP DISCUSSION
This strategy is always student centred. The situation can range from a large unstructured one in which the teacher plays a non-committed, neutral role to a largely structured one where the teacher adopts a strict or autocratic manner. Regardless of the form, discussion usually centres around a specific problem and some agenda has usually been agreed beforehand. Research suggests that most people work harder when they work together and that groups are superior over individuals in some problem-solving tasks. Individuals have been found to learn more rapidly in groups and group experiences transfer back into individual work, in that students learn more efficiently when alone. Superior students have not been found to benefit from group learning and the

group social process actually inhibits their learning. While discussion methods can transmit knowledge, their main advantage has been found to be in the changes that are brought about in motivation, emotions and attitudes. Changes in interpersonal relationships have also been attributed to the group experience. However, Group Discussion is not optimal for realising lower order cognitive objectives, its superiority is in the achievement of higher order cognitive objectives as well as affective ones. In order to increase effectiveness, it is sometimes useful to put all the low contributors in one group and all the high contributors in another. If individuals are divided into groups, sufficient time should be allocated so as to allow the groups to reassemble into a plenary session, and to share ideas under the guidance of the lecturer who ensures that all groups get an equal share of time.

Varieties of Group Discussion in University Teaching, London University Institute of Education, University Teaching Methods Unit, 1972

Debenham, A. I. S. (1976) *A Trainer's Guide to Discussion Leading*, London: British Association for Commercial and Industrial Education (BACIE)

Davis, R. H., Fry, J. P. and Alexander, L. T. (1977) *The Discussion Method*, Guides for the Improvement of Instruction in Higher Education No. 6, East Lansing, Michigan State University

Hyman, R. T. (1980) *Improving Discussion Leadership*, Teachers College Press

Andrews, D. J. W. (1980) 'The Verbal Structure of Teacher Questions: Its Impact on Class Discussions' in *Professional and Organizational Development Quarterly*, nos. 2, 3 and 4, pp. 129–63

See also: Small group teaching; Free group discussion; Problem-centred group; Syndicate group method

GROUP DYNAMICS LABORATORY

The primary focus of this form of training is on the *group* as a unit rather than on the individual, interpersonal or organisational determinants of behaviour. The approach is intended to help the participant to diagnose and intervene in group processes. Exercises can be used to explore group decision making, group problem solving and the way in which group cultures and structures develop. Additionally, participants examine how group norms change and how a group might organise itself to accomplish specific tasks. The focus is the study of the developing structure of the group and the ways in which that character can be analysed, i.e. through process analysis, and changed through the actions of group members.

See also: Process analysis; Tavistock conference method; Laboratory method; Human relations laboratory; Organisational laboratory; Personal development laboratory; Power laboratory; Team laboratory; Sensitivity (T-group) training

GROUP WITH GROUND RULES

This is a form of small group discussion in which the participants with the aid of a facilitator establish certain 'ground rules' which direct the nature of the learning task. Frequently rules include group members speaking in the first person singular ('I was amazed when you...' rather than 'It was surprising...'). Another rule may be that members categorise each comment they make (e.g. proposal, summary, request, etc). Rules can be used to make participants more aware of certain aspects of their interactional styles.

Heron, J. (1973) *Experiential Training Techniques*, Department of Adult Education, University of Surrey, Guildford

See also; Fishbowl exercise; Process analysis; Buberian dialogue; Think and listen session; Interpersonal skills training

GUIDED DISCUSSION

This method combines private learning with group development and criticism. The emphasis is on the common exploration and discovery based upon strenuous cooperation and personal contribution. It is one of the most varied, flexible and effective teaching methods available. Effectively conducted it can meet cognitive, interpersonal and role requirements to a high degree and lends itself to the development and reinforcement of values. It is an efficient instrument for making the full use of the experience, knowledge and expertise that there is in the group. The tutor plans and directs the work of the group on the basis of his superior knowledge and experience. This is focused upon a scheme of work. The value of the discussion depends largely on the students' prior knowledge of the material to be discussed. Each meeting of the group is a point in time in which personal study and experience are pooled, shaped and then refocused on the next stage of individual work which will be similarly treated at the next meeting. Learning comes from the members' and tutor's comments, although the latter's should be limited and where possible aimed at encouraging students' contributions along the lines of the structure agreed. Twelve to fifteen is the optimum size for a Guided Discussion group. To be effective, the group needs the individual member's commitment as well as meticulous preparation by the tutor. The work of the group needs also to be continuously recorded by and circulated amongst group members so that progress can be measured against the agreed scheme. In this way participants are provided with feedback material and receive a permanent record of what they are achieving. The sense in which the discussion is guided is not by the interventions of the tutor while the discussions are taking place, indeed discussions may be held by students in the absence of the tutor altogether, it is guided by the self-feedback mechanism and by the fact that the group members know that they have to work to a specific time scale and a specific ground plan.

See also: Controlled discussion; Construct lesson plan; Self instructional module and interactive groups; Tutorial-tape-document learning package approach

GUIDED GROUP PROBLEM SOLVING

This is a non-traditional teaching strategy developed at Purdue University whose full title is the 'Purdue Three Stage Model for Course Design'. Stage 2 concerns the teaching and learning strategies that take place in classroom settings and are designed to help students attain three major goals: (*a*) learning basic knowledge and theory of a discipline, (*b*) learning problem-solving skills for applying knowledge to the solution of realistic problems, and (*c*) learning the social skills necessary for working effectively in small task-oriented, decision-making groups.

The Purdue Three Stage Model helps students to learn basic concepts, principles and theories and generally to foster the development of higher order cognitive abilities. Stage 1 involves the achievement of the basic subject matter. Knowledge and comprehension is the focus. Facts, terms, concepts and principles are acquired and the student is helped to become a self-directed learner. The knowledge-comprehension objectives for each content unit must be mastered by students prior to the beginning of the in-class activities related to a given unit. Readings for this stage are directed by a Self-Instruction Guide (SIG) that aids students in preparing for the mastery quiz. Mastery quizzes of subject-based content are necessary for making significant contributions to the in-class discussions involved in stage 2, and the individual work in stage 3. Stage 1 activities may include programmed instruction, audio-tutorials, units, taped and live lectures. Stage 2 involves the application of the basic knowledge to realistic questions which require students to develop high-order cognitive abilities and interpersonal skills. All the instruction is carried out by students working in small groups within the class setting. Occasionally, a group will have to meet outside of class time to do a project. For a given task the group is directed by a Group Instruction Guide (GIG) that presents an introduction to a given task, states objectives and delineates the task/product to be completed. Stage 3 requires students to demonstrate their ability to use the knowledge and skills developed during the first two stages in order to solve realistic problems on their own. These activities are guided by a set of instructions called Procedures for Individual Projects. Each stage of the Purdue model is based upon different theoretical concepts and instructional approaches. Stage 1 is related to Keller's Personalised System of Instruction; Stage 2 on Wales and Stager's Guided Design approach, small group dynamics theory and problem-solving concepts. Stage 3 emphasises critical thinking and individual problem-solving concepts.

Feldhusen, J. F., Linden K. W. and Ames, R. (1975) 'Using Instructional Theory and Educational Technology in Designing College and University Courses: A Three Stage Model' in *Improving College and University Teaching Yearbook 1975*, Cornvallis, Oregon: Oregon State University Press, pp. 64–9

Ames, R., Linden, K. W. and Feldhusen, J. F. (1977); 'Guided Group Problem Solving in The Purdue Three Stage Model of Instruction' in *Educational Technology*, vol. 17, no. 8, pp. 12–16

Ames, R. and Linden, K. W. (1978) *Small Group Problem Solving Activities for Applied Educational Psychology: A Three Stage Model Approach*, Prospect Heights, Illinois: Waveland Press Inc.

See also: Instrumented team learning; Construct lesson plan; Self instructional module and interactive groups; Personalised system of instruction; Autonomous group learning

GUIDED STUDY

Guided Study arose from the unsatisfactory conditions and results of home study and so often emphasises the development of study skills. It is usually combined with various other methods. Specific provision is made for study periods under the guidance of the tutor who demonstrates analytical thinking, active reading, outlining and other key study skills. Guided Study offers an unusual opportunity to provide for both the bright and the slow student. The tutor can modify assignments to fit the needs of these different students. Problems may be studied or drill and review sessions proposed as necessary. In terms of actual tutor tasks, Guided Study consists of lecturers producing annotated booklists and then developing these into a programme of assignments. In these, the learning requirements and a date for completion are clearly specified and precise references to books and other sources of information are spelt out. The materials may be given in the form of a study pack, or the student may seek references for himself. Often the lecturer produces notes on points of difficulty or confusion and sets some practical or written work to be completed by a target date. The lecturer's classroom role is to review briefly the material to be covered and to expand and develop the subject and encourage group discussion.

Baum, T. (1980) 'Reference Lists for Students' in *Programmed Learning and Educational Technology*,. vol. 17, no. 3, pp. 175–6

Keen, T. and Reid, F. (1977) 'Guided Learning: A Discussion' in *Programmed Learning and Educational Technology*, vol. 14, no. 1, pp. 26–32

Collier, K. C. (1968) *New Dimensions in Higher Education*, London: Longman

Fowler, R. L. and Barker, A. S. (1974) 'Effectiveness of Highlighting for the Retention of Text Material' in *Journal of Applied Psychology*, vol. 59, no. 3, pp. 358–64

See also: Tutorial-tape-document learning package approach; Text; Handout; Block method

HANDOUT

The provision of Handouts by the lecturer and the taking of notes by the students can be seen as opposite sides of the same coin. Lecturers often ask students at a lecture to 'just listen as all the necessary information is in the handout being circulated'. Handouts may be used to give factual information before a lecture and thus act as a 'leveller' to ensure a common basic background in the subject among students before a topic is further elaborated or developed. They are thus a means of teaching more detail than could normally be absorbed in a lecture and thereby permit the building of complex concepts upon more simple ones which would have been unfamiliar without the Handout. The presentation of information before a lecture period can release time for discussion or other activity, or relieve the pressure of a crammed syllabus. Handouts can also be used to prepare students for problem-solving lectures. Their function here is to relieve students of the need to absorb new information and thus free them to think about application, validity or relation to other topics. To be most effective, this form of Handout must be distributed a week in advance. The use of headings and subheadings provides the clarity needed for the new information to be absorbed.

There are a number of other types of Handout. A Teaching Objectives Handout given before the first lecture lists the objectives of the course, and sensitises students to what is to be learned. The Lecture Guide Handout seeks to guide students through a difficult lecture enabling them to see the whole topic before any single part is considered. It should be given out well in advance and contain blank spaces for students to insert their own notes. It enables the least able student to carry away an accurate record of the major points. Note-taking Handouts summarise lectures so as to discourage note taking and are useful when it is difficult to take notes, e.g. during a tape/slide programme. Thinking Handouts contain questions, tests or theoretical issues designed to stimulate thought.

Reading Handouts are aimed at stimulating and guiding reading and can be issued in advance. It is possible to have a carefully structured programme of Reading Handouts in the course of a set of lectures which are intended to teach the student, by practical experience, that lectures are only one of many sources of information that are available to the learner. By structuring the Reading Handouts so that initially one offers the student very precise reading references (chapters, paragraphs, page numbers) related to very precise parts of the lecture course, then gradually the reading references become more and more outlined until eventually the student is given a reading list of books with the instruction to 'choose from among these'. By this means one is training students in the use of books.

MacManaway, L. A. (1967–8) 'Using Lecture Scripts' in *Universities Quarterly*, vol. 22, no. 3, pp. 327–36

Hartley, J. (1976) 'Lecture Handouts and Student Note Taking' in *Programmed Learning and Educational Technology*, vol. 13, no. 2, pp. 58–64

Hartley, J. and Davies, I. K. (1978) 'Note Taking: A Critical Review' in *Programmed Learning and Educational Technology*, vol. 15, no. 3, pp. 207–24

McDougall, I. R., Gray, H. W. and McNicol, G. P. (1972) 'The Effect of Timing of Distribution of Handouts on Improvement of Student Performance' in *British Journal of Medical Education*, vol. 6, pp. 155–7

Helweg-Larsen, B. (1979) 'Teaching the Technique of Patterned Note Taking' in *British Journal of Guidance and Counselling*, vol. 7, pp. 107–13

Howe, M. J. A. and Singer, L. (1975) 'Presentation and Students' Activities in Meaningful Learning' in *British Journal of Educational Psychology*, vol. 45, pp. 52–61

See also: Circulated lecture notes; Tutorial-tape-document learning package approach; Personalised system of instruction; Guided study; Text

HEURISTIC

Heuristics are a communication strategy that can be used to present complex rules, procedures and instructions. However, unlike algorithms or decision tables, a Heuristic does not guarantee that a correct solution will be selected. Heuristics involve trial and error discovery learning. Miller and Galanter (1960) have defined a Heuristic thus: 'If we try to short cut the systematic plan (plan here meaning a hierarchy of instructions which control the order in which a series of operations are to be carried out) by guessing, asking for help, trying to remember when we last saw it, etc. the plan we are following is a heuristic'. A systematic plan, when it is possible, is sure to work, but it may take too long, or cost too much. A Heuristic plan may be cheap and quick but may sometimes fail to produce the intended result. When our motor car fails to start in the morning we tend to implement a Heuristic fault-finding plan.

When a large number of alternatives are involved, a heuristic strategy becomes the only practicable method of realising a task. Any other strategy would involve a systematic search through an enormous number of alternatives until the correct one had been identified. Thus a computer may be given some 'tips' or Heuristics to avoid searches through billions of possibilities. A heuristic strategy is effective and efficient when the number of possible outcomes is very large, when the number of possible interactions is very large and when the relationships are complex. Also when the underlying structure of the task is unknown and the risks following an incorrect solution can be accepted.

Landa, L. (1976) *Instructional Regulation and Control: Cybernetics, Algorithmization and Heuristics in Education*, Englewood Cliffs, New Jersey: Educational Technology Publications

Miller, G. A., Galanter, E. and Pribram, K. H. (1960) *Plans and Structure of Behaviour*, New York: Henry Holt

See also: Algorithm; Decision table; Flowchart

HISTORICAL ANALYSIS

Many subjects utilise an analysis of history as a means of learning. For example, there are courses on the history of psychology and sociology which trace the development of themes within the subject. The approach involves the study of either primary or secondary source material. It examines the ideas prevalent, the political and economic causes of actions and the role of key figures and their influence on events. Texts suitable for this form of study exist both in the history of industries and of individual organisations. Biographies and autobiographies of numerous managers exist. Many management theorists, e.g. Frederick Winslow Taylor and Elton Mayo, have expounded their philosophy of management which could be used for historical analysis purposes.

The fairly recent development of the History of Ideas as a specific area of study has had two important implications for Historical Analysis. It has provided students with a series of explicit methodologies for dealing with Historical Analysis and has highlighted the pitfalls which conventional Historical Analysis courses rarely consider. Second, the History of Ideas as a subject area is essentially interdisciplinary, whereas many Historical Analysis courses are only single or double discipline.

See also: Process analysis

HUMAN RELATIONS LABORATORY

Laboratory learning is a term used to describe the process of learning about oneself and others, and the groups and organisations to which one belongs. This is done through the direct experience of participating in groups which have been formed specifically for this purpose. An effort has been made in this direction to specify the focus of the learning in each different type of laboratory. Thus a Human Relations Laboratory focuses on the exploration and understanding of interpersonal or between-people relationships. One may contrast this with the Group Dynamics and Power Laboratories where the primary focus is on the group and organisational issues respectively. In a Human Relations Laboratory, participants are given opportunities for the generation of interpersonal data, diagnosis of the interpersonal situation and for the development of skills for enhancing communication, creating interpersonal rapport, providing help in interpersonal problem solving and in resolving interpersonal conflict.

Participants in these types of labs can be from 'stranger' populations, i.e. members who have never previously met one another, or from the same organisation or department of an organisation. Such training has increased in popularity within companies as a way of both increasing the interpersonal competence of managers and of building interpersonal ties among people who have some working relationship. Such training designs can involve a diagonal or horizontal slice of an organisation being selected to undergo this form of training. In neither case does the training group include participants who are in direct superior-subordinate relationships.

Harrison, K. and Cooper, C. L. (1979) 'Design and Training Issues in Human Relations Groups' in Pettman, O. and Margerison, C. (eds.) *European Insights in Personnel and Training*, Bradford: MCB Publications

Cooper, C. L. (1979) *Learning from Others in Groups*, Associated Business Press

Smith, P. B. (1980) *Personal Change and Group Processes*, London: Harper and Row

See also: Group dynamics laboratory; Organisational laboratory; Personal development laboratory; Team laboratory; Micro-lab; Mini-society; Sensitivity (T-group) training; Laboratory method

ILLUMINATIVE INCIDENT ANALYSIS

This is a method of team appraisal and personnel training originally developed by Diana Cortazzi and Susan Roote for use with care staff (e.g. doctors, nurses, social workers). However, the approach has equal relevance to the field of management development and training. The focus of the technique is upon the common crises that such groups experience. Using IIA, a group of staff who work together as a team, or whose work depends on the contribution of others, select an incident from their work in which they have all been personally involved. They then clarify it with a drawing. This helps the group to reach the deeper human and emotional issues involved, as well as the conflicts, tensions and misperceptions that lie behind any crisis in team work. The approach stresses the visual representation of cognitive and affective aspects. The authors argue that such representation is more direct and offers less opportunity for the avoidance of key issues by the blocking of emotions. Operationally, IIA involves each person in the incident representing their own view of it with a drawing. Pin/matchstick men are used to depict the sequence of events. The 'drawer' then puts him or herself in the shoes of each person of the team in turn and examines the attitudes and roles of those involved by exaggerating the initial drawing – frequently to the extent of caricature. For example, the manager might represent himself as being on a treadmill, or as lying on the ground under attack from superiors and junior staff. Such drawings can reveal a great deal about how people see themselves and the people with whom and for whom they work. Additionally, the drawings may indicate how such incidents may be prevented and the team strengthened and developed.

Cortazzi, D. and Roote, S. (1975) *Illuminative Incident Analysis*, London: McGraw-Hill

See also: Gestalt techniques; Monodrama; Psychodrama; Case conference; Sociodrama; Team development; Team laboratory; Action learning

IN-BASKET EXERCISE (In-tray Exercise)

An In-basket Exercise presents the learner with samples of administrative work in the form of a manager's in-basket or post box. The various items in the post require judgement as to appropriate action. In-baskets were first developed by the Educational Testing Service, Princeton, New Jersey as a test to be used in selecting air force officers. In addition to being used in the assessment of people, or for research into management decision making, in-baskets are a useful management training tool. Used in that way they are non-interactive. Each trainee works alone for a period of about an hour on his own material, handling a similar set of items. After the specified time, each basket item is discussed in turn by the class as a whole and the 'best' action for it is determined. In-basket Exercises tend to interest learners and involve them if the problems posed are realistic to them. Trainers can modify items from existing basket exercises or design their own. Baskets also offer a means of obtaining a sample of the learner's stated behaviour on a selected range of problems. They can be chosen to reflect the problems that a particular group is having and be built to fit the time available. Course members receive feedback as to the possible consequences of their actions if they discuss their proposed solutions with others.

A typical In-basket tells the participant to imagine that he has just been promoted to a certain position in an imaginary company. He comes into his new office for the first time on a Sunday morning. He is in a rush because he has to leave in one-and-a-half hours to catch a plane to New York or Birmingham where he will be at a conference for the next week and will thus be unavailable. Because it is Sunday there is no one else in the office and as the switchboard is not manned he cannot talk to anyone outside. In his in-tray he finds a pile of papers which are contained in the packet the tutor hands him. His task is to work through the items as if he were the manager described in the introduction. He then deals with each item as best he can within the set constraints. In-baskets vary according to the job to be done and the skills exercised. Stewart and Stewart (1976) described some of the contents of typical baskets. They could include management information (e.g. manager's manual, day-to-day planner, organisation chart, welcome note from predecessor giving thumbnail sketch of the incoming manager's team, budget statement, etc.); queries demanding an immediate answer (e.g. request to substitute one staff member for another on a sales trip, secretary requesting a day off); queries he must see the need to delegate (e.g. request for him to do something next Monday) and items he should not bother with (e.g. golf club nomination form).

In-baskets can vary in their degree of difficulty. The more complex ones expect the manager to see the hidden implications of an apparently innocuous memo; or put several pieces of information together to reveal a more serious problem, or a greater opportunity than is apparent from looking at any one item individually. Technical, administrative, financial and interpersonal skills can all be exercised depending on how the items are written. The manager himself can help to provide a list of 'good' and 'bad' items. There is some evidence that custom-written in-baskets, designed specifically for the organisational staff being trained are more effective. Each member of the class is given his or her personal packet of in-basket materials and has between one and one-and-a-half hours to sort it out. Once everyone has completed the task individually, the class, led by the tutor, goes through it together. If the In-basket is

137

done as an individual development exercise, then the trainee needs to have a follow-up interview with his boss or the training officer and have a chance to discuss his answers. The In-basket Exercise, since it is conducted in real time, can be considered a type of Simulation.

Zoll, A. A. (1969) *Dynamic Management Education*, Reading, Mass.: Addison-Wesley, chapters 9 and 10

Stewart, V. (1981) 'Training for Managerial Effectiveness, Core Skills 2' in *Journal of European Industrial Training*, vol. 5, no. 1, pp. v–viii

Stewart, A. and Stewart, V. (1976) *Tomorrow's Men Today*, London: Institute of Personnel Management, chapter 5

Meyer, H H. (1970) 'The Validity of the In-basket Exercise as a Measure of Managerial Performance' in *Personnel Psychology*, vol. 23, pp. 297–307

See also: Programmed simulation; Game; Action maze; Simulation

INCIDENT PROCESS METHOD (Incident Process Case Study)

The Incident Process Method was developed to overcome a major disadvantage of the case study which was the impression it gave that management problem solving consisted of finding answers to neatly formulated questions. Management problem solving involves, first, the definition of the problem with the manager obtaining all the information necessary or available. Real world factors tend to prevent the presentation of an objective or clear case history. Second, it requires consideration of all the facts and the formulation and implementation of a solution. Traditional case studies focus only on the latter while the Incident Process Method trains the students in the former.

The method involves six stages. First, the tutor presents the group with a very short account of an incident. It may be verbal or consist of handing out of a memo or some other document which might say, for example, that the workers refuse to operate a new machine. A questioning session then follows where members individually ask any question of the tutor they feel will help clarify the incident to them and provide the background needed. Questions of opinion are however prohibited. The tutor must ensure that he has previously briefed himself on every possible circumstance surrounding the incident, and be in a position to give direct answers to any relevant question of fact raised. It is essential to avoid inconsistencies creeping in. He must supply only the information asked for by the students. In a training session, the manager who was actually involved in the incident may be invited to answer questions. A time limit of half an hour is suggested for this phase and should be made known to students beforehand. At this point there is a choice of ways to proceed. Each student can be asked to note down *individually* his views on what he thinks should be done to solve the problem. Individuals' papers are then collected and the replies charted by the tutor on the board indicating how many associated themselves with a particular line of action. Syndicates of like-minded students are then formed to discuss the matter further. An alternative approach is to issue each student with a voting slip on which two possible but opposed decision options are listed, each of which is workable. Students vote on their choices and syndicates form on this basis. The syndicates formed by whichever method, consider in detail their choice of decision and prepare a report on the reasons favouring it and how it might be implemented. The penultimate stage is the plenary session where reports are presented by each group in turn with opposing syndicates cross examining each other. Finally, the tutor comments on the reports, extracting more information, drawing attention to any inconsistencies in their presentation and any information which failed to be obtained or assumptions taken for granted upon which decisions were taken. The Incident Process Method aims to promote analytical thinking and reasoned judgement.

Pigors, P. and Pigors, F. (1955) *The Incident Process: Case Studies in Management Development*, The Bureau of National Affairs Inc., Washington D.C.

Boyd, B. B. (1980); 'Developing Case Studies' in *Training and Development Journal*, vol. 34, no. 6

Binsted, D., Stuart, R. and Long, G. (1980) 'Promoting Useful Management Learning: Problems of Transition and Transfer' in Beck, J. and Cox, C. (eds), *Advances in Management Education*, Chichester: John Wiley and Sons

See also: Case study method; Personal case history; Case history; Active case study

INDEPENDENT STUDY (Independent Learning, Autonomous Learning)

This is a term which is difficult to define. The Nuffield Group on the subject noted that '... some teachers regard it (independent learning) solely as a method of learning whilst others see it as a situation in which students are responsible for major decisions concerning their own education'. In general terms one can say that whenever there is an attempt to lessen the *direct* influence of the teacher on the immediate learning situation, then some form of independent learning is being attempted. Cornwall amongst others has attempted to identify a hierarchy of steps in independent learning. These are the choices in learning in terms of aspects of the curriculum. Going from bottom to top also reflects an increasing difficulty of institutions to give up control. Thus, starting at the bottom there is a decision to enrol; choice over pace of study; choice over mode of study; involvement in deciding about objectives; participation in assessment and at the highest level, involvement in establishing criteria by which to judge success.

Boud, D. (ed.) (1981) *Developing Student Autonomy in Learning*, London: Kogan Page Ltd

Cornwall, M. (1981) 'Putting It into Practice: Promoting Independent Learning in a Traditional Institution' in Boud, ibid.

Percy, K. and Ramsen, P. (1980) *Independent Study: Two Examples from English Higher Education*, Guildford, Surrey: Society for Research into Higher Eudcation

Nuffield Foundation Group for Research and Innovation in Higher Education (1974) *Towards Independence in Learning*

Dressel, P. L. and Thomson, M. M. (1973) *Independent Study*, San Francisco: Jossey-Bass

Atherton, C. (1972) 'Lecture, Discussion and Independent Study: Instructional Methods Revisited' in *Journal of Experimental Education*, vol. 40, no. 4, pp. 24–8

Hills, P. J. (1976) *The Self Teaching Process in Higher Education*, London: Croom Helm

Cunningham, I. (1979) 'Educational Change and the N.E.L.P. Dip.H.E.', *Educational Change and Development*, vol. 1, no. 3, pp. 26–36

See also: Student planned learning; Learning contracts; Autonomous learning group; Instrumented team learning; Media-activated learning group; Paid educational leave

INDUSTRIAL PROJECT (Line Project)

This term is used to describe a type of project in which a full-time student or more usually a group of students work on a project *for* a company. The company may have defined the aims and objectives of the project and therefore takes a major role in evaluating the finished product. For example, a company may supply a group of final year marketing students with a product which it wishes to launch. The group project involves the production of a marketing plan. The project element gives the students the opportunity to bring together the diverse skills and knowledge of their subject which they have acquired over the course and affords them the opportunity to apply it in a real life situation. The company also gains. For little or no cost, it obtains the fresh ideas and new approaches of young minds as well as a practical assessment of the work of a group of students some of whom it may wish to employ.

See also: Project method; Overseas project; Field project/attachment; Real life project; Project-based management development; Project orientation

INFO BANK

Because libraries contain such a vast amount of information, they can confuse and intimidate potential users. To overcome this problem, the Info Bank has been developed which, in essence, is a highly selective reference library. Its three key elements are subject coverage, material presentation and the nature of student support. The literature contained in an Info Bank is highly specific to a topic. For example, there may be Info Banks on industrial relations topics, or on teaching reading in primary schools. The materials on a given topic are more structured, and greater attention has been paid to guiding the student around them, than would be the case in a traditional library. Part of the reason for this is that the learner is expected to make use of the Info Bank primarily on his own. Assistance is, however, available should he require it.

To use an Info Bank, the student has to clarify exactly what it is he wants to learn, and needs to have some awareness of his own particular learning style. Does he, for example, prefer tape/slide programmes and book summaries to journal articles? He is supported in his choice by specially prepared catalogues, guides, info-papers and summaries. While acting as an individual decision-maker in his learning, he does have access to fellow students and to tutor consultations. Success in using the Info Bank rests with the learner's ability to manage his learning process and to make use of his adviser who directs the learner to the relevant material and helps him achieve his goals. The Info Bank method involves the tutor(s) in collecting relevant materials, writing study guides and producing info-papers. Once established, the staff introduce students to the approach and stress the need for learners to clarify their own learning objectives. The individual student work is supplemented by regular group meetings at which learners can compare their experiences and exchange ideas about the information they have obtained. The group can act as a support and spur to further work. The Info Bank approach draws upon certain key concepts and philosophies. First, it assumes that learners have different learning needs and that they each have a unique learning style. The definition of the learning goal and the way in which it will be achieved will reflect the individual characteristics of the learner. Second, it emphasises the need to place responsibility for learning on the student himself. Hence the stress on goal setting. Finally, it views the role of the tutor as a learning facilitator who, through the medium of counselling, helps the learner to specify and achieve his goals. In addition, it places responsibility on the tutor for the preparation and updating of the support material contained in the Info Bank.

See also: Resource centre; Audio tutorial method; Language laboratory

INSTITUTE MEETING

The term institute usually refers to a department or a division of a college or university. Here it is used to distinguish a particular type of training meeting. Those who come together in an Institute are interested in a specific field. During the Institute new material is presented to add to the knowledge which participants already possess on a subject. The Institute may be a series of one-day meetings or be of several days' duration. It is expected that the information, instruction, problem identification and problem solving will be evident. It is one of the most frequently used forms of adult education. It fosters intensive learning over a short period of time. Informality may be introduced by the use of buzz sessions, group projects, and open discussion as well as formal stage-audience presentations. An Institute presupposes a well organised programme with a keynote address by a speaker who defines the issues, sets the stage and tempo and inspires participants to move towards solutions of the problems at hand. Following the opening address, the group breaks up into small discussion sections with a leader in charge of each. The small groups may reassemble periodically to hear further addresses or summaries of progress. The emphasis in an Institute is on the development of knowledge and skill in a specialised area of concern or practice.

See also: Conference meeting; Clinic meeting; Colloquy meeting; Forum meeting; Symposium meeting

INSTRUMENTED FEEDBACK

This is the general term applied to the distribution to students of questionnaires (or 'inventories') which they fill in and which are then collected by the tutor and marked by him. Such inventories relate to specific managerial and social theories, e.g. McGregor's Theory X and Theory Y, Berne's 'Adult', 'Child' and 'Parent'. The group scores are then reproduced so that individuals can compare their individual rating with that of either the group as a whole or another data base provided by the tutor. Depending on the length and complexity of the questionnaire, students may be asked to mark their own in the classroom.

The method encourages active participation through personal involvement. A wide variety of instruments are used in management training for different purposes. They include: forming groups to control for homogeneity in composition; providing feedback to individual learners; assisting a group to diagnose its own functioning and development; generating sensing data through surveys for organisational diagnosis; teaching various human relations' concepts through self diagnosis and researching the outcomes of education and training designs. Many 'classroom questionnaires' are modified versions of those used in management research. However, when used for teaching purposes, the reliability and validity of such measurement is rarely sufficient to place accuracy on the responses of a given person. Moreover, the term inventory is reserved for the application of theoretically based instruments as defined earlier. It is therefore necessary to caution group members not to overinterpret their scores. Instruments allow learners to become more involved (more than in a case study but less than in a T-group) since they are working with information about themselves. This approach can give a participant an early opportunity to understand the theories involved and give him some constructs and terminology that can be used to categorise and describe his and other people's behaviour, attitudes, values, etc. The feedback received by the learner is low threat and allows him to see himself as he compares himself with others. Inventories are commercially available on all the major management teaching topics, e.g. leadership style, motivation, communication, organisational climate etc.

One of several ways of using such inventories is to create deliberately cognitive dissonance in students to facilitate learning. This is done in the following way. If the subject being examined is group interaction skills, the tutor asks the class members to fill in a questionnaire in which they state the behaviours they feel they usually exhibit during group meetings (e.g. summarising, asking others' views etc.). A group task is performed and half the class observes and scores each individual on the basis of the behaviours they see him exhibiting. During the de-briefing session, the individual compares his own predicted behaviour as indicated by his own completed questionnaire, with the scores produced by the observers. Comparison of the two profiles forms the basis of the subsequent group discussion.

Pfeiffer, J. W., Heslin, R. and Jones, J. E. (1976) *Instrumentation in Human Relations Training*, Mansfield: University Associates of Europe, 2nd Edition

Heller, F. A. (1970) 'Group Analysis Applied to Training' in *Journal of Management Studies*, vol. 7, pp. 335–45

Sykes, P. (1980) 'Guide to the Use of Instruments' in *The Training Officer*, vol. 16, no. 1, pp. 22–4

'In Person: Jay Hall', in *Training*, vol. 6, no. 6, pp. 2–5, August 1980

See also: Instrumented laboratory; Learning community; Process analysis; Autonomy lab; Self appraisal

INSTRUMENTED LABORATORY

The Instrumented Laboratory derives its name from the intensive use of 'instruments' such as questionnaires, tapes, video-recordings and so on which are used to generate data and facilitate the learning process in participants. Instrumented Laboratories can be conducted with or without the presence of a trainer or facilitator. The emphasis is very much on experimentation and on the 'quantitative' representation of group processes. Participants are encouraged to play the role of subjects, observers, analysts, interpreters and consultants. The trainer may play a role in providing instruction in the methods of both generating data and interpreting it. He can demonstrate the theoretical basis of the analytical techniques.

The use of instruments provides the basis for analysing the progress of a group. Quantitative data obtained from such instruments may be used in detecting those more subtle aspects of group behaviour which may go unrecognised in unstructured groups. Organisations may benefit from the instrumented approach since there are certain economies associated with the method. These include the requirement for fewer trainers, the company's own people can be trained using the instruments and fewer training sessions may be required. Instrumented Laboratories are often less anxiety producing in format. Moreover, the data gathered and analysed can be used in the design of management training sessions.

Blake, R. R. and Mouton J. S. (1962) 'The Instrumented Training Laboratory' in Weschler, I. R. and Schein, E. H. (eds) *Issues in Training, Selected Readings Series 5*, National Training Laboratories, pp. 61–76

Cox, C. (1974) 'An EGROM workshop—what is it?' in *Industrial Training International*, vol. 9, no. 9, pp. 277–9

Bass, B. M. (1966) 'A Plan to Use Programmed Group Exercises to Study Cultural Differences in Management Behaviour' in *International Journal of Psychology*, vol. 1, no. 4

See also: Instrumented team learning; Instrumented feedback; Tape assisted learning programme; Autonomous learning group; Media activated learning group

INSTRUMENTED TEAM LEARNING

When introducing student-centred learning two major problems tend to arise. First, how does one direct the learning of the students in the most profitable way without at the same time assuming responsibility for it? Second, how does one encourage the development of task-oriented teamwork and not just of socially pleasant group work? This latter distinction emphasises a team working together in a task-oriented manner and not merely socialising. An approach called Instrumented Team Learning has been developed by Mouton and Blake which aims to overcome some of the issues described. The problem of responsibility for learning is dealt with by the provision of a set of learning instruments and learning directions which have the effect of structuring what is to be acquired by the students. To encourage teamwork, each ITL team is given explicit goals and objectives, tasks, procedures and a way of measuring the operational outcomes of its effectiveness. The ITL method claims to offer expert guidance through the 'teacher-in-absence' influence created by the instruments and learning designs. In team action, the essential structure is provided, yet the control of the actions rests with the students themselves.

ITL is therefore based on principles of student-centred learning as opposed to tutor-centred, but is nevertheless a structured approach. It makes use of the strength of the team rather than individual work. Four instruments or designs are currently available. The 'Clarifying Attitudes Design (CAD)' focuses on attitudes and can be used where interdepartmental relationships are involved or to clarify attitudes to work performance, legislation or training. It has been applied in sales, training, customer service and among employees generally. 'Team Effectiveness Design (TED)' considers team performance and has been used to introduce theoretical concepts in electronics and ventilation as well as new legislation and systems. 'Team Member Teaching Design' (TMTD) is used anywhere where theory, facts or concepts need to be learned. Finally, 'Performance Judging Design (PJD)' is used in areas requiring skill development.

Mouton, J. S. and Blake, R. R. (1975) *Instrumented Team Learning*, Austin, Texas: Scientific Methods Inc.

Mouton, J. S. and Blake, R. R. (1976) 'Instrumented Team Learning' in *Industrial Training International*, vol. 11, no. 2, pp. 53–5

'In Person: Robert Blake and Jane Mouton' in *Training*, vol. 6, no. 1, pp. 8–11, March 1980

Clifford, D. M. (1979) 'Instrumented Team Learning – The British Gas Experience' in *BACIE Journal*, vol. 33, no. 5, May, pp. 79–81

See also: Learning through discussion; Agenda method; Instrumented laboratory; Tape-assisted learning programme; Autonomous learning group; Community of enquiry

INTERACTION MANAGEMENT (Interaction Modelling Training)

Interaction Management is the name of a training package developed and sold by Development Dimensions International. It is based on learning principles taken from both Behaviour Modelling and Behaviour Modification. It has been defined as 'A supervisory skills system, utilising behaviour modelling, which enables first and second level supervisors to manage critical situations (discussions) with subordinates in a manner satisfactory both to the organization and the employee'. IM is offered as an integrated system and as such sits very much on the fence between being a training package and an organisational development intervention strategy. The IM system consists of six elements which allow the trainer to adapt it to specific company needs. The elements are 'Needs Analysis', 'Interaction Management Programme for Supervisors', 'Management Reinforcement Workshop', 'Instructor/Programme Director Certification', 'Implementation of Action Plan' and 'Evaluation'.

As the title suggests, the Needs Analysis component involves the use of instruments to collect, analyse and interpret the supervisors' training needs. This is followed by the selection of the relevant IM module of which there are some 45. Module titles include, 'Improving Work Habits', 'Handling Customer Complaints', 'Informing the Union of a Change' etc. In the second phase, supervisors are trained in groups of six and are instructed in the 'critical steps' for handling each situation. A behavioural description of 'effective supervisory action' is presented to learners by the use of a film. Each member then has the chance to practise the skill described in a similar situation and gets feedback from fellow participants as well as from the tutor. Each such module lasts three-and-a-half hours. Not only are students provided with skills but are also helped to develop confidence in their use.

The 'Management Reinforcement Workshop' is designed not for managers but for their bosses. It is based on the behaviourist view that there is a need to reinforce classroom learning on the job, otherwise such learning will not be applied. The MRW teaches the managers how to provide reinforcement of the skills of the supervisory staff beneath them. Once again, a positive model of what constitutes 'effective reinforcement behaviour' is provided and participants have the chance to practise the relevant skills. IM programmes involve the company managers being trained in the techniques and principles, and then taking on the training role themselves. For this reason, the 'Instructor/Programme Director Certification Workshops' are aimed at helping to develop the skills of the instructor. 'Implementation Plan of Action' concerns implementing a plan of action to initiate the Interaction Management Training System. Finally, the 'Evaluation' component involves using instruments to evaluate the package as a whole.

Robinson, J. C. and Robinson, L. E. (1979) 'How to Make Sure Your Supervisors Do On-the-job What You Taught Them in the Classroom' in *Training* (USA), September

Byham, W. and Robinson, J. (1976) 'Interaction Modelling: A New Concept in Supervisory Training' in *Training and Development Journal*, vol. 30, no. 2, pp. 20–33

Byham, W. C., Adams, D. and Kiggins, A. (1976) 'Transfer of Modelling

Training to the Job' in *Personnel Psychology*, vol. 29, no. 3, pp. 345–9

Byham, W. C. and Robinson, J. C. (1976) 'Interaction Management: Supervisory Training That Changes Job Performance' in *Personnel Administrator*, vol. 21, no. 2, pp. 16–19

See also: Behaviour modification; Behaviour modelling; Managing effective relationships; 3-D Organisational effectiveness training

INTERACTIVE SKILLS TRAINING

The aim of this method is to develop interactive skills. These are defined as the skills used to achieve objectives in face-to-face discussion. They are used to control the discussions and steer them towards successful conclusions. Face-to-face situations include formal meetings, informal chats, negotiation situations and selection and appraisal interviews. IST considers behaviour analysis, non-verbal behaviour, leadership style, person and self-perception, Transactional Analysis and behaviour modification.

It aims to create an awareness in participants of their own behaviour and other peoples', and to develop the skills which will increase the probability of success in all interactive situations. These basic skills can be defined as: analysis of the situation in terms of the task and people involved in it; the definition of the objectives to be achieved in this situation; planning in detail how to behave in order to achieve the objectives; monitoring behaviour in the situation in order to respond to the unexpected. The focus is on learning by doing within an environment which encourages experimentation and provides feedback before further experimentation. Underlying the approach are a number of assumptions. These are that a manager's behaviour influences the behaviour of those he interacts with. This behaviour is shaped more by his perception of external environmental factors than by the relatively unchanging 'internal' factors. There is no single correct behaviour style and to change people's behaviour at all is difficult. Making inferences about people's behaviour needs to be based on careful observations of overt behaviour in the belief that behaviour is capable of being planned and controlled by the individual. The approach consists of analysing behaviour using carefully defined behaviour categories; feeding back to participants information about their behaviour and using behavioural data to create a supportive learning environment, e.g. by using it to mix work groups.

The IST approach can be used either on managerial behaviour in groups or in a more individually oriented way which sets out to help each manager to become better able to pinpoint the most important variables in his own behaviour. Following the analysis, the manager and consultant jointly decide which objectives are to be achieved in the handling of the situation, and in the light of these, plan in detail how to behave in order to maximise the probability that they will be achieved. The emphasis is on the monitoring of one's own behaviour in interaction as well as other people's. One will thus be in a position to make conscious adjustments and apply behavioural antidotes as necessary.

Phillips, K. and Fraser, T. (1980) 'Interaction Training in Management Training' in *The Training Officer*, vol. 16, no. 12, pp. 324–8

Phillips, K. and Fraser, T. (1980) 'Approaches to Social Skills Training' in *Industrial and Commercial Training*, vol. 12, no. 4, pp. 158–63

Fraser, T. and Phillips, K. (1980) 'Feedback in Social Skills Training' in *Industrial and Commercial Training*, vol. 12, no. 5, pp. 196–202

Fraser, T. and Phillips K. (1980) 'The Qualities and Responsibilities of the Social Skills Trainer' in *Industrial and Commercial Training*, vol. 12, no. 6, pp. 242–7

Rackham, N. and Morgan, T. (1977) *Behaviour Analysis in Training*, London: McGraw Hill

Brewster, C. J. and Connoch, S. L. (1977) 'Interactive Skills of Industrial Relations' in *Industrial and Commercial Training*, vol. 9, no. 9, pp. 377–81

Beckett, R. T., Jones, R. A. and King, S. H. (1975) 'Two Person Skills Training' in *Industrial and Commercial Training*, vol. 7, no. 5, pp. 205–9

Honey, P. (1976) *Face to Face*, London: Institute of Personnel Management

Morgan, T., Rackham, N. and Hudson, H. (1974) 'DIS – Three Years On' in *Industrial and Commercial Training*, Part 1 in vol. 6, no. 6, pp. 248–57, Part 2 in vol. 6, no. 7, pp. 318–28

Rackham, N., Honey, P. and Colbert, M. (1971) *Developing Interactive Skills*, Peterborough: Wellens Publishing

Frank, E. and Margerison, C. (1978) 'Training Methods and Organisational Development' in *Journal of European Industrial Training*, vol. 2, no. 4, pp. 11–13

See also: Controlled pace negotiation; Coverdale training; Managing effective relationships; Process analysis

INTERNSHIP

An Internship Programme is a period of supervised work experience. It may be undergone by persons after they have completed their studies and examinations but before they are finally awarded their qualifications and/or are licensed to practise. Alternatively, it can take place during one's period of study as part of a Cooperative Education programme. The exact procedure will depend on the profession or occupation concerned and will vary a great deal. For example, in medical education which represents the most developed form of this approach, Internships are required and are paid in the USA. In fact staff undergoing this form of training are called Interns. However, a similar procedure exists in other professional groups. For example, students of pharmacy in the United Kingdom, once they have received their degree undergo a form of Internship within a pharmaceutical company, hospital or retail pharmacy before they are admitted to the British Pharmaceutical Society with their licence to practice. Internship as a form of training developed from the concern of professional schools with the application of knowledge and analytical skills to the job situation. It was argued that if students were to receive a well rounded professional education in fields such as medicine, pharmacy, accountancy etc., then application-oriented experiences must complement the classroom teaching received. This is another facet of the debate of balancing theory with practice.

Internships are only a single, but nevertheless important aspect of the Cooperative Education approach. Antony (1981) has described the key objectives, benefits and disadvantages associated with Internship programmes. The primary aim of this form of training is to allow students to begin to develop the particular technical skills which are relevant to their field of work and do so while being exposed to the normal political and administrative processes within the organisations in which they work. This latter dimension, which emphasises the context in which experience is gained, seems to be the crucial element. In terms of the time involved, an Internship usually lasts a minimum of one year, although the student may be permitted to choose two locations at which he will spend six months. This long time period allows the intern to gain familiarity with the objectives and working procedures of the organisation he joins and this increased level of familiarity usually leads him to being given increasing responsibilities.

As with other forms of non-permanent work experience programmes, the success of an Internship programme depends on the amount of advance planning and organising that precedes the setting up of a programme. It has been argued that it is the higher degree of such planning which distinguishes an Internship programme from a sandwich course placement. Other variables influencing Internship success are the selection of individuals, choice of the organisation, type of job provided for the intern and the degree of academic work-learning experience integration which exists.

Antony (1981) summarised the advantages and disadvantages he saw as accruing to the parties involved in an Internship programme – the student, his college and the host institution. The positive outcomes for the student include the opportunity to develop a sense of responsibility in his chosen work area by having the chance to perform his work duties satisfactorily and meet the various organisational demands put upon him. His career prospects are enhanced through the work experiences thus gained which, in addition, provide him with a broader base for making choices about career options. The college gains an additional learning setting for its students; keeps abreast of what is happening in professional practice outside of its four walls and is able to establish a continuing dialogue between its students, staff and the surrounding community. The host institution in its turn gains a source of employees which can help it surmount a work peak, has access to new ideas and a pool of potential new employees from which it can recruit.

There are of course also disadvantages. The student's graduation or licensing is delayed and his immersion in the hurley burley of organisational life and the demands these make may lead him to develop negative attitudes towards academic work. There is the danger that because of lack of adequate planning, or due to unforeseen circumstances, the intern learns little of value and finds that he has wasted his time. For the college, an Internship programme represents unstructured learning and its initiation, maintenance and monitoring involves staff time diverted from their academic duties. There may also be the problem of relating classroom teaching and intern experience. A problem in this area has characterised the training of nurses in Britain. Finally, for the host institution to accept interns may involve a disruption of their normal work environment through the need to induct these new arrivals.

Antony, W. P. (1981) 'Using Internships for Action Learning' in *Journal of European Industrial Training*, vol. 5, no. 1, pp. 11–16

Handbook for Professional and Administrative Internships, Resource Development Internship Project, Bloomington, Indiana, March 1972

Huhlman, C. (1971) *Internship Concepts and Applications: A Report to the Centre for Urban Affairs*, Indiana University, November

Abrahamsson, K., Kim, L. and Rubenson, K. (1980) *The Value of Work Experience in Higher Education*, Stockholm: Stockholm Institute of Education

See also: Cooperative education; Study service; Sitting by Nellie; Assignment to manager with high development skills; Manager shadowing; Apprenticeship; Field project/attachment

INTERPERSONAL PROCESS RECALL

This technique seeks to contribute to the improvement of the way in which people relate to each other and attempts to provide a reliable method of teaching them to live with each other without inflicting pain or destruction on each other. The method was developed by Professor Norman Kagan and his colleagues at Michigan State University. He observed that if a person is videorecorded as he relates to another person and is shown the recording immediately afterwards, then the person is able to recall his detailed thoughts and feelings in depth. The video (or audio) playback is used as a trigger to help learners 'relive' their experiences during an interaction. Self evaluation is a usual accompaniment of the intricate account of how the participant felt affected by the other person. The approach is underpinned by a learning by discovery model with the learner being in total control of his/her learning. Participants are provided with a remote control switch and are encouraged to stop and start the playback as they choose. This leads to a verbalisation of a multitude of underlying thoughts, feelings and motives. This method was found to work more reliably when a trained facilitator or 'Inquirer' encouraged the viewer to verbalise perceptions and elaborate upon them. This second individual needs to be trained in this special role to help the learner explore the experience and in particular his/her unspoken thoughts and feelings. The Inquirer's task is neither to teach nor to give feedback but to facilitate in self discovery, exploration and insight.

Kagen, N. (1980) 'Influencing Human Interaction – Eighteen Years with IPR' in Hess, A. K. *Psychotherapy Supervision: Theory, Research and Practice*, John Wiley

Kagen, N. and Schauble, P. G. (1969) 'Affect Simulation in Interpersonal

Process Recall', *Journal of Counselling Psychology*, vol. 16, 309–313

See also: Trigger film; Video confrontation; Co-counselling; Confluent education

INTERROGATION OF EXPERTS

Within the learning process the asking of good questions by both students and teachers is one of the skills. This approach combines the development of question-asking skills in students with a library assignment and the innovative use of expert guest visitors. There are three stages in this method. In the first phase, several sessions are run by the tutor on the topic of questioning. Students are helped to become aware of the purposes that are served by questions. Among these one might include stimulating reflective thought, developing understanding, encouraging the emergence of new concepts, applying information, developing appreciations and attitudes, developing the power and habit of evaluation, changing beliefs or attitudes, focusing attention on cause-and-effect relationships, determining informational background, creating interest and so on.

Following this, students are helped to determine the criteria for distinguishing between good and bad questions. For example, in good questions the objective of the question is clear and precise. 'What do you think about' questions are avoided as are leading and catch ones. A good question is directed at attainable objectives. Some questions, while clearly stated, call for answers which are either not available or which can only be guessed. Some questions have puzzled the best thinkers we have. Questions such as 'When shall we get industrial peace in Britain?' are clearly permissible when it is understood that the objective is to stimulate discussion. The wording of questions should be precise and direct. One should avoid digressions and involved statements, ambiguity, asking the question two or more ways in the same statement and calling for more than one unified reaction at a time. Finally, the wording should be precise and direct; the vocabulary used should be within the comprehension of the person being questioned.

At the conclusion of the first stage students acquire an understanding of the characteristics of a good question. They are then informed that in perhaps two weeks time they will be visited by Mr X or Mrs Y who is an expert in a certain field. The choice of expert will depend on the lecturer's subject. They are further told that this person has not been asked to make any formal presentation but only to respond to the questions asked by class members. It may be necessary to provide students with information about the expert's present job, past posts, interests, etc.

In the second phase students work either individually or in groups to prepare a set of questions to ask the visiting expert. They use the library to obtain background information and their criteria of what constitutes a good question. On the appointed day the visitor comes, the questions are asked and the replies given. The session can usefully be audio- or video-taped. In the third and final phase, the previous session is reviewed. The lists of questions produced by students are circulated and evaluated. The responses they elicited from the expert are also analysed.

Andrews, J. D. W. (1980) 'The Verbal Structure of Teacher Questions: Its Impact on Class Discussion', *Professional and Organizational Development Quarterly*, vol. 2, nos. 3 & 4, Fall/Winter

Sanders, N. M. (1966) *Classroom Questions: What Kind?* New York: Harper and Row

Carin, A. A. and Sund, R. B. (1971) *Developing Questioning Techniques*, Columbus Ohio: Charles E. Merrill

Burton, W. H. (1962) 'Improvement in the Use of Questions', *The Guidance of Learning Activities*, Appleton-Century-Crofts, pp. 436–447

See also: Socratic enquiry; Socratic questioning; Questioning; Invitation to discover; Reaction panel

INTERVIEW MEETING
The term is used here to refer to large group meetings in which an audience is present. There is a main speaker located on a stage and that person introduces a second participant on to the stage. If additional people are introduced on to the platform, then the interview may become a Symposium (i.e. a series of statements), a Panel Discussion or a Group Interview. In all these cases, the interaction is only between platform members. The audience plays no active role but only listens to what is happening on the platform or stage. Late night television 'chat shows' with a resident compère and invited guests use this format.

See also: Colloquy meeting; Listening team; Panel discussion; Symposium meeting; Forum meeting; Brains trust; Clinic meeting; Conference meeting; Institute meeting

INTERVISITATION

Course members can benefit from watching other members as they work in their own job situations. To be feasible, the course concerned must be run over a number of training sessions and participants need to be geographically near. Members arrange visits to one another's companies, plants or departments and these can help to clarify the nature of job problems, extend the diagnosis of a job group's difficulties or illustrate how a method or technique introduced on the course can be used on the job. If a feedback period is included, this can help to make the job situation into an extension of the course.

A course group may address the question of running effective meetings and study the steps and procedures necessary. A participant may then invite some of his fellow course members to attend the next company meeting he runs, and observe it and offer him feedback on his performance. Planning for Intervisitation needs to take into account the probable effects of visitors or observers at a meeting or similar event. The method appears most useful when the person visited has clearly expressed his need, when the purposes and procedures of the visit are clarified by all concerned and when the follow up discussion of the experience is a normal part of the procedure.

Miles, M. B. (1959) *Learning to Work in Groups: A Program Guide for Educational Leaders*, Bureau of Publications, Teachers College, Columbia University, New York

Huczynski, A. A. (1978) 'Problems of Learning Transfer' in *Journal of European Industrial Training*, vol. 2, no. 1, pp. 26–29

See also: Training transfer training

INVITATION TO DISCOVER

An Invitation to Discover is a discussion method which is designed with the specific intention of helping students to learn discovery techniques such as critical thinking procedures. The primary aim is not to teach subject matter but to involve students in learning how they can best use their minds to make discoveries. However, invitations tend to be designed to match the subject of the study, e.g. industrial relations, marketing. In a typical invitation, a problem is presented to the student, and by carefully designed questions he is invited to devise a method to solve it, make hypotheses, draw conclusions from data and interpret data or identify factors involved in the problem. Invitations may be presented in a written form to individual students, for them to read and respond to, or they may be given to small or large groups.

Carin, A. A. and Sund, R. B. (1971) *Developing Questioning Techniques*, Charles E. Merrill Publishing Company.

See also: Interrogation of experts; Questioning; Socratic questioning; Socratic enquiry; Creativity training

JOB ENRICHMENT

Job Enrichment refers to the deliberate redesigning of jobs and the way they are performed in order to make the content of the work more challenging for the employee. Planning, evaluating and doing are no longer separated and the employee does each of these functions himself. The concept has traditionally been applied to routine, semi- or unskilled jobs. However, since the objective of Job Enrichment is the provision of meaningful and interesting work which gives the employee the opportunity for growth, recognition, challenge and achievement, the general concepts involved can equally well be applied to the 'enrichment' of many managerial jobs. In this sense therefore, Job Enrichment can be considered as a staff development technique.

Job Enrichment is a general term indicating an objective. It can be achieved through the selection of one of several different approaches or through the use of a number of approaches together. One of these is *job enlargement* which can be either vertical, horizontal or both. Applied to managerial work, if a manager's job were expanded so that he was doing a greater number of tasks, his job would have been enlarged horizontally. For example, he might be made responsible for new groups of staff in addition to those already under him, or he may be given the additional responsibility for a new unit which is being set up in the organisation. Alternatively or additionally, he may be given a greater degree of autonomy with regard to assigning staff to tasks, whereas before he may have had to check with his superior. He may represent his boss at committees or conferences, or attend meetings for which he previously only supplied information. All of these would be examples of vertical job enlargement. Survey evidence suggests that a policy of Job Enrichment for managers is possible. Many managers, especially at the lower and middle organisational levels find their present jobs lacking in challenge. Respondents report that they want to feel they are making a contribution. To do this they want tasks which are meaningful and clearly important in the context of their organisations' objectives.

Mansfield, B. (1980) 'The Superior's Share of Job Enrichment' in *Personnel Management*, vol. 12, no. 4, pp. 40–44

Guerrier, Y. and MacMillan K. (1978) 'Developing Managers in a Low Growth Organization' in *Personnel Management*, vol. 10, no. 12, pp. 34–8

Buchanan, D. A. (1979) *The Development of Job Design Theories and Techniques*, Aldershot: Gower

Buttriss, M. (1971) *Job Enrichment and Employee Participation: A Study*, London: Institute of Personnel Management

Cooper, R. (1974) *Job Motivation and Job Design*, London: Institute of Personnel Management

Paul, W. J. and Robertson, K. B. (1970) *Job Enrichment and Employee Motivation*, Aldershot: Gower

Taylor, L. K. (1980) *Not for Bread Alone: An Appreciation of Job Enrichment*, London: Business books, 3rd edition

See also: Expanding job assignment; Planned delegation

JOB ROTATION

Properly carried out, planned Job Rotation enables employees to develop new skills and thereby broaden their skill base. Job Rotation differs from Manager Exchange in that participants do not necessarily go back to their 'old job' after a period of time. The aim of Job Rotation may be to develop a range of skills and knowledge in a number of individuals so that each could take over the job of another. It is most suitable for a small number of people and as a deliberate preparation for general management rather than as a scheme to give a large number of people experience of more than one department. Used selectively it is an economical, sound method of learning and a good basis for assessing the potential of staff for general management. It presumes that the training needs of the manager to be rotated have previously been identified and that the skills and knowledge needed for the future post the manager will occupy have also been taken into account. Jobs in different departments, regions or countries can be chosen as helping to meet such training needs. For example, a production manager might be put in a service function post in order to broaden his experience of the company's operations. Frequent in-company job changes are a feature of many large companies and may not necessarily be carried out for developmental reasons. Most job changes are straightforward promotions, but people are also moved sideways into another function or to another factory/office. Any new job tends to stretch a manager until he learns how to cope and make positive achievements. Cynicism may however develop about ritual organisational 'musical chairs'.

Guerrier, Y. and Philpot, N. (1978) *The British Manager: Careers and Mobility*, Management Survey Report No. 39, British Institute of Management Foundation

Hague, H. (1976) 'Job Rotation Beats Stagnation' in *Industrial Management*, April, pp. 11–12

Hill, R. (1974) 'Exxon Plays Global Chess With Its Managers' in *International Management*, vol. 29, September, pp. 14–18

Lord, D. (1972) 'Uniroyal Trains its Managers by Moving Them Around' in *International Management*, April, pp. 59–62

Wren, W. H. (1970) 'Management Development Through Planned Job Transfer' in *Factory Management*, vol. 8, no. 10, October, pp. 4–6

Zeira, Y. (1974) 'Job Rotation for Management Development' in *Personnel*, vol. 51, July, pp. 25–35

See also: Rotation training; Job swop; Manager exchange; Acting assignment

JOB SWOP (Secondment)

This term is reserved for a project that a manager from one firm might carry out in a different firm. Operationally, a manager from company *A* will swop with one in company *B* for a specified period of time to carry out a specific task. The details of the temporary exchange will be defined by the participating companies. Whatever procedure is used, it is essential that the managers concerned will have received the prior training in skills and knowledge that they will need to carry out the Job Swop project. Additionally, they will need someone with whom to discuss progress and problems. This may be either a senior manager or training officer at one or other of the companies concerned. The 'swopee' must ensure that the training objectives are kept in sight and these are not swamped by the demands of the job and the glamour of the development programme in which he is taking part. The manager works in a new environment and the host organisation gains from the fresh perspective on problems provided by someone new from the outside. There is a danger that the experience gained by the secondees may be considered by them to be less than satisfactory and in the process they may fear being forgotten or missing opportunities in their organisations while they are away. Indeed while Secondment is favourably considered as a way of helping individuals appreciate other people's viewpoints, there are many practical difficulties which prevent it being applied on a wide scale. The assimilation of secondees back into their home organisations is not costless and may require considerable effort especially on the part of staff specialists and line supervisors. Another problem is that a company may feel unable to make any promises about what will happen to the returning manager in terms of career and promotion.

Mumford, A. (1980) *Making Experience Pay*, London: McGraw Hill

Preen, D. W. (1970–71) 'Exchanging Roles' in *Universities Quarterly*, vol. 25, pp. 17–19

See also: Consultancy assignment; Action learning; Rotation training; Manager exchange; Assignment to community organisation; Assignment to customer as representative; Assignment to government study group

JOINT DEVELOPMENT ACTIVITIES

The term was coined by staff at the Manchester Business School to refer to a form of management development activity which jointly involves a company, a number of their managers and MBS staff. JDAs have been described as a declaration of intent rather than a programme or a standard package. It would therefore be more correct to use the title as a generic term to indicate the way in which the MBS works with a client organisation. As a form of work problem-based learning activity, the JDA represents an attempt to break away from the traditional didactic, course-oriented, education-centre located, general problem approach to management education development. A JDA consists of the establishment of a link between the senior management of a firm, and the members of the business school who together act as a steering group to guide the project group of managers. In a JDA, one works on a real organisational issue which is the main vehicle for learning. A group of managers from the client organisation work in conjunction with staff of the university who become available to the project group as a resource. The educational institution provides an understanding of development needs and mechanisms of development, as well as the resources to assist with the process through which development takes place. The underlying theory of JDAs is linked with the concept of 'resourceful managers' (those who are self-developed) and development functions within organisations (those concerned with developing new patterns of activity, adapting existing ones). JDA projects tend to focus on identifying or creating new ideas or opportunities for the organisation.

Morris, J. 'Joint Development Activities: From Practice to Theory', in Beck, J. and Cox, C. (eds.) (1980) *Advances in Management Education*, Chichester: John Wiley and Sons

Lupton, T., Berry, A. J. and Warmington, A. (1976) The Contribution of a Business School to a Joint Development Activity, *Management Education and Development*, vol. 7, no. 1, pp. 2–12

Morris, J. (1974) 'Joint Development Activities', *Management Review and Digest*, vol. 1, no. 1.

Morris, J. F. and Burgoyne, J. G. (1975), *Developing Resourceful Managers*, London: Institute of Personnel Management

See also: Action learning; Project-based management development

JURISPRUDENTIAL MODEL

This is a way of using controversial topics as a basis for discussion. The tutor arranges for a discussion to take place which deals with a conflict of values. For example, 'The interests of the working man' might be one value and 'The interests of the country as a whole' might be another. A situation where the two come into conflict would be the topic of the discussion. Resolving the conflict requires members to clarify principles, establish the facts and define the words used in the discussion. Having to handle all three provides a general strategy or a 'jurisprudential framework'.

Eight intellectual operations are involved which have been specified by Joyce and Weil (1980):

1 Abstracting general rules from concrete situations – thus what are the values involved in 'management's right'?
2 Using general value concepts as dimensional constructs – Are there degrees of 'workers' rights' or is it an all-or-nothing thing?
3 Identifying conflicts between value constructs – explaining how the two values identified in step 1 conflict with each other.

4 Identifying classes of value conflict situations – what are the differences between 'management's rights' and 'management's privilege'?

5 Developing analogies to the problem under consideration.

6 Working towards a general qualified position.

7 Testing the factual assumptions behind a qualified position.

8 Testing the relevance of statements

In applying this structure it is important for the tutor to remind students which point they have reached and to where they are about to move. Students can be given the job of making the summaries and transitional statements.

Oliver, D. W. and Shaver, J. P. (1966) *Teaching Public Issues in High School*, Boston: Houghton Miffin

Joyce, B. and Weil, M. (1980) *Models of Teaching*, Englewood Cliffs, New Jersey: Prentice Hall, 2nd edition

See also: Values clarification; Debate; Appraisal

KEPNER–TREGOE APPROACH

This approach focuses on managerial problem solving and decision making. Following research, Charles Kepner and Benjamin Tregoe developed a technique of making these processes more rational and more effective. Defining a problem as a deviation between what should be and what is actually happening, caused by some changes, Kepner and Tregoe divide problem solving into three stages – problem analysis, decision making and potential problem analysis. These are then divided into a series of steps which must be gone through. Since, in their view, managers were unaware of the thought processes they used and the assumptions they made when trying to solve problems, Kepner and Tregoe analysed and formalised the essential steps into a systematic approach in order that each problem could be approached in a logical and systematic fashion.

At the problem-analysis stage, there are seven steps: (*a*) an awareness of what should be done, (*b*) recognition of a deviation from this standard, (*c*) precise definition of this deviation, (*d*) the search for other recent changes restricted to what had been affected by the deviation, (*e*) inspection of these changes to find out which are relevant, (*f*) deduction from this of possible causes, (*g*) discovery of the real cause by identifying which of the possible causes explains all the facts. Having found the problem, the manager must make a decision about what, if anything, must be done. Once again the manager goes through a series of logical steps to ensure that his decision will meet his objective and is the best possible alternative in the circumstances considering its advantages and the probability and seriousness of possible adverse effects. His decision made, the manager must again consider these possible adverse effects, i.e. he must engage in potential problem analysis, with a view to preventing or minimising the likelihood of occurrence of these effects and, where necessary, make plans to deal with them if they occur. In the training programme devised by Kepner and Tregoe, managers are given, in a one-week course, opportunities to put into practice the ideas and concepts presented as they participate in solving the problems in an imaginary organisation. Feedback on performance is provided so that managers see where and why they are not being as effective as they might be.

Kepner, C. H. and Tregoe, B. B. (1980), *The New Rational Manager*, John Martin Publishing

O'Neill, H. (1976) 'Back to Training – with Kepner–Tregoe' in *Industrial Training International*, vol. 11, no. 2, pp. 60–1

See also: Creativity training; Lateral thinking; Problem-solving groups; Problem-solving cycle; Problem pack

LABORATORY METHOD (Practical Work)
Laboratory Methods can be employed in any academic discipline where practical experience is related to theoretical formulations. Such methods need not be confined to 'the laboratory'. The term can be applied more broadly to include field trips, interviews, visits to real-life situations, companies etc. Laboratory Methods are instructional procedures through which the cause, effect or properties of a phenomenon can be explored by actual manipulation or experience, under controlled conditions or in the field. Laboratory Methods frequently benefit from being combined with other instructional approaches. Students can be prepared for their 'laboratory experience' by lectures, assignments or individual instruction. Similarly, the laboratory experience can be followed by a lecture summary, a debriefing session or a general discussion.

Within the field of management education and development, the term 'laboratory' is most frequently associated with Sensitivity (T-Group) Training. The original design was developed by Kurt Lewin in 1946 and came to be known as human relations laboratories. The term continues to be applied in the field of group dynamics training. There are now a wide variety of different types of 'labs', each distinguished by its title which is intended to emphasise the focus, e.g. Power Lab, Organisational Lab, Interpersonal Relationships Lab. In each of these, groups of individuals come together for a period of time to examine the causes and effects of phenomena such as intimacy, perception, affiliation, control and authority.

The Laboratory, Guides for the Improvement of Instruction in Higher Education No. 9, East Lansing: Michigan State University

Bolman, L. (1970) 'Laboratory Versus Lecture in Training Executives' in *Journal of Applied Behavioural Science*, vol. 6, pp. 323–36

Lippitt, G. L. and This, L. E. (1980) 'Leaders for Laboratory Training' in *Training and Development Journal*, vol. 34, no. 6, pp. 56–67

See also: Sensitivity (T-group) training; Power laboratory; Human relations laboratory; Group dynamics laboratory; Micro-lab; Mini-society; Organisational laboratory; Personal development laboratory; Team laboratory

LANGUAGE LABORATORY

The conventional title of Language Laboratory is misleading as it limits the possibilities of the machines or the resources provided. Learning Laboratory would be a better title. Anything which is worth putting on to tape and which can be listened to can be prepared and placed in a learning laboratory. In such cases the audio tapes are frequently supported with worksheets and one may thus have the beginnings of an Info Bank or Resource Centre. However, when a management department wishes to introduce some form of student self-paced study system, the audio cassette and worksheet often provide the simplest and frequently most effective form of self instruction. However, if these learning resources are to be used 'on campus' rather than sent through the post for the student to work on at home, then a student self-learning area needs to be provided. While a library may go some way in meeting this need, it may need to be specially equipped. For this reason the Language Laboratory, usually located in the languages department, can provide an alternative and ready-to-use facility.

In the traditional learning laboratory situation, each trainee works alone in a soundproof booth. The tutor can monitor each one's progress and can intervene through headphones to correct grammar or pronunciation. Alternatively, the student can come in on his own, take a cassette, and work through the programme individually with the tape exercises being so designed that the student gets feedback on his grammar and pronunciation. The Language Laboratory principle is useful for speech skills in cases where a number of managers need to be trained or refreshed in a foreign language. Many continental business schools and an increasing number of British ones now incorporate language training in their courses for managers and several have developed a full Language Laboratory facility. There are at least two further sophistications possible. Although the Language Laboratory basically teaches speech, it is perfectly possible to include the teaching of some written skills. Indeed there exist in various further education institutions what are called Writing Centres which specialise in helping students to develop skills in the written form of communication. Within a Language Laboratory it is possible to provide directed self-study using laboratory facilities without any intervention of the tutor.

See also: Re-writing; Audio tutorial method; Laboratory method; Resource centre; Info bank

LARGE GROUPS AS SMALL GROUPS

Various strategies have been developed which aim to apply small group learning methods to large, usually lecture type, classes. Moss and McMillan described one approach to develop problem-solving skills in a 100 student class. The content concerned was international relations although the method employed has much wider applicability. Students were divided into four large independent groups of 25 and told that each group was to tackle a set problem and produce a set of coherent policies to present to a plenary session of all students in four weeks time. Groups consisted of mature students as well as school leavers. Six timetabled one-hour sessions were set aside for group meetings in a large seminar room. The design was based on room availability and on research which indicated both that less able students benefited from group problem-solving situations, and that groups modified the risk-taking aspects of individual decision making. The group organisation lent itself to creativity exercises such as buzz groups and brainstorming. Each student was supplied with an extensive reading list and basic articles. All the reference material was made available in the library.

Two keynote lectures were given at the start as 'advance organisers'. Four tutors worked with each group of 25 students although it was found, in retrospect, that such a large number was not necessary. A student-centred approach was suggested using a five-stage model. To begin, the large group examined the problem presented and utilised buzz group/brainstorming techniques with subgroups of 4–6 to identify how the overall problem might be subdivided into component parts. The large group then evaluated subgroup suggestions and identified several areas for further study. These were remitted to a subgroup for further analysis, i.e. problem defined, analysed and further redefined. In stage two, the first-stage process was repeated until each individual subgroup member had identified and defined a relevant topic area for his own research. Stage three consisted of individuals researching on their own with cross referencing of findings and ideas at small group meetings. The output was a series of related individual policy recommendations. In the fourth stage, the individual contributions were evaluated by the subgroup as a whole to produce an interrelated policy statement for presentation to the large group of 25. The fifth and final stage involved the large group reconvening to evaluate the proposals of the small groups and to synthesise these into an overall proposal to report to the plenary session at which the entire class of 100 was present. This is only one of several strategies which attempts to overcome the constraints imposed by large group teaching and the references below refer to some other approaches being tried out.

Moss, G. D. and McMillan, D. (1980) 'A Strategy for Developing Problem-Solving Skills in Large Undergraduate Classes' in *Studies in Higher Education*, vol. 5, no. 2, pp. 161–71

Goldschmid, M. L. (1970) 'Instructional Options: Adapting the Large University Course to Individual Differences' in *Learning and Development*, vol. 1, no. 5, pp. 1–2

Cowan, J., McConnell, S. G. and Bolton, A. (1969) *Learner Directed Group Work for Large Classes*, Department of Civil Engineering, Heriot-Watt University, Edinburgh

Cotsonas, N. T., Kaiser, R. J. and Dowling, H. F. (1958) 'Adapting The Group Discussion Technique For Use With Large Classes' in *Journal of Medical Education*, vol. 33, pp. 152–62

Northcraft, G. B. and Jernstedt, G. C. (1975) 'Comparison of Four Teaching Methodologies for Large Lecture Classes' in *Psychological Reports*, vol. 36, pp. 599–606

See also: Buzz groups; Community of enquiry; Learning cell

LATERAL THINKING

Lateral Thinking is claimed to be a new way of thinking rather than just another creativity technique or training device. It was developed by Edward de Bono who, in his book *Mechanisms of the Mind*, identified four different ways of thinking. These were natural, logical, mathematical and lateral. Natural thinking was seen as flowing along established patterns while logical thinking was seen as being the result of training which attempted to restrain the excesses of natural thinking. In contrast, mathematical thinking was concerned with translating materials into symbols which were then processed according to previously established rules. All of these, in different ways, stressed previously acquired knowledge and approaches. Lateral Thinking had been developed to counteract the errors of natural and mathematical thinking. De Bono considered problems as being the difference between what one had and what one wanted. He divided them into three basic types. There were those which required the processing of available information or the collection of additional information; situations in which there were 'no problems', where one just had to accept the existing state of affairs; and problems which could be solved by re-organising information which had already been formed into a particular type of pattern. Lateral Thinking was particularly suited to the last type of problem, while logical and mathematical thinking was suitable for the others.

Like Creativity Training, Lateral Thinking uses a variety of techniques or tools which go against the rules of logical thinking. These techniques can be roughly grouped under four headings which constitute the principles of this thinking approach. These are the recognition of dominant or polarising ideas which involves first the recognition, and then the abandonment of old ideas which may inhibit new thinking. The search for different ways of looking at things involves deliberately seeking out varying viewpoints. This may involve generating a fixed number of different problem approaches prior to pursuing any of them. Relaxing rigid control on thinking is the third principle. Vertical or logical thinking in de Bono's view neither produces new ideas, nor encourages their production. Because logical thinking needs to be right at every stage, it can act as a hindrance to new ideas. By contrast, Lateral Thinking assumes that everything is possible and does not require correctness at every stage. It does not tackle every problem head on, nor does it immediately freeze phenomena by labelling and classifying them. Finally, Lateral Thinking involves the use of chance. Many past innovations have been based on chance and therefore Lateral Thinking techniques are designed deliberately to allow chance to occur. While Lateral Thinking was developed by de Bono in Britain, a similar approach labelled Neologics or 'Oblique Thinking' was being used in the United States by Theodore Cheney. Neologics claims to be a new way of thinking as well and shares certain common elements with Lateral Thinking. It encourages participants to think obliquely and stimulates innovation by getting them to engage in perfectly reasonable illogical thinking.

de Bono, E. (1970) *Lateral Thinking*, Harmondsworth: Penguin books

de Bono, E. (1975) *The Uses of Lateral Thinking*, Harmondsworth: Penguin books

de Bono, E. (1976) *The Mechanisms of the Mind*, Harmondsworth: Penguin books

de Bono, E. (1978) *Teaching Thinking*, Harmondsworth: Penguin books

See also: Creativity training; Synectics

LEADERLESS GROUP DISCUSSION

The original purpose of Leaderless Group Discussion was not as a learning method but as a measurement or assessment tool. Its claimed originator was J. B. Rieffert who directed German military psychology between 1920–31. The German Army used LGD until about 1939 and the German Navy employed it well into the Second World War. After 1945, it was being used by the British Civil Service and by industry to screen job applicants. Used as an assessment method, it involves asking a group of examinees to carry on a discussion on one or more job-relevant topics for a given period of time. There is no appointed leader or structure given for the interaction. Due to this lack of structure, one or more leaders must emerge to give the structure and guidance to the discussion in order for it to achieve the objectives set out for it at the start. The examiners who are in the room do not take part but rate the performance of each examinee. Leaderless Group Discussion has been used to assess candidates for many professions and occupations.

Used as a learning method, its main aim is to encourage students to solve problems on their own through mutual participation, criticism and correction. The group is leaderless because the teacher's presence would not help the realisation of learning objectives. Many teachers and instructors are reluctant to employ the technique despite the fact that there is evidence of its educational value. It is well known that participation in small groups offers learners educational and psychological advantages such as reduction of anxiety; increased understanding and appreciation of arguments due to increased possibility of feedback. There is an absence of authority which might compel the acceptance of otherwise unsupported statements and opinions; there is greater freedom, so that emotional feelings, which can block problem solving can be fully expressed, and there is an increased opportunity for practising a whole variety of intellectual and social skills. Without the teacher, it is claimed that these processes can develop without hindrance and constraint, and middle-order cognitive and affective objectives can be realised. It is argued, however, that worthwhile discussion might not develop in the absence of a teacher's stimulus and students may not be able to perceive and challenge fallacious arguments and errors. Research suggests that these objections might be ill founded. However, it is useless to assign students to leaderless groups and tell them to discuss. Careful preparatory detailed briefing and concrete outcomes are all essential if the learning objectives are to be realised. Within this model the teacher is not redundant. He acts as a resource and adviser but only when invited in by the students themselves and only to meet clearly pre-specified objectives.

Powell, J. P. (1981) 'Reducing Teacher Control' in Boud, D. J. (ed.), *Developing Student Autonomy in Learning*, London: Kogan Page Ltd

Ansbacher, H. L. (1951) 'The History of the Leaderless Group Discussion Technique' in *Psychological Bulletin*, vol. 48, pp. 383–91

Powell, J. P. and Jackson, P. (1963) 'Learning Through Unsupervised Discussion' in *Hermathena*, vol. 107, pp. 99–105.

Bass, B. M. (1949) 'An Analysis of Leaderless Group Discussion', in *Journal of Applied Psychology*, vol. 33, pp. 527–33

Bass, B. M. (1950) 'The Leaderless Group Discussion Technique' in *Personnel Psychology*, vol. 3, pp. 17–32

Powell, J. P. (1964) 'Tutorials without Tutors' in *Vestes*, vol. 7, pp. 207–10

Bass, B. M. and Norton, F. T. M. (1951) 'Group Size and Leaderless Discussion' in *Journal of Applied Psychology*, vol. 35, no. 6, pp. 397–400

Bass, B. M. (1954) 'The Leaderless Group Discussion' in *Psychological Bulletin*, vol. 51, no. 5, pp. 465–92

Jaffee, C. L. (1967) 'The Partial Validation of a Leaderless Group Discussion for the Selection of Supervisory Personnel' in *Occupational*

Psychology, vol. 41, no. 4, pp. 245–8

See also: Instrumented team learning; Learning through discussion; Tape-assisted learning programme; Media-activated learning group; Creative dialogue

LEARNING CELL

The Learning Cell is a form of cooperative learning enterprise which takes place between pairs of students. In each pair, students are asked to take turns in asking and answering questions on prepared materials. Each 'cell' must have its learning task highly structured. To prepare for a Learning Cell, the students in the class read an assigned piece of work and write questions dealing with the major points that are in the reading itself or related materials. When the class begins students are assigned randomly to pairs and one dyad member begins by asking his partner a question. Once the second person has answered the question, which he may have corrected or given additional information on, he then asks his first question and receives an answer. While the pairs are working together, the tutor goes from group to group and both answers and asks questions. A variation on this method involves each student reading or preparing different material. In such cases one student 'teaches' the other the essentials of his reading, then asks prepared questions. Students then change roles.

Goldschmid, M.L. and Shore, B.M. (1974) 'The Learning Cell: A Field Test of an Educational Innovation' in Verreck, W. A. (ed.) *Methodological Problems in Research and Development in Higher Education*, Amsterdam: Swets and Zeitlinger, B. C., pp. 218–36

Goldschmid, M.L. (1971) 'The Learning Cell: An Instructional Innovation' in *Learning and Development*, vol. 2, no. 5, pp. 1–6

Goldschmid, B. and Goldschmid, M.L. 'Peer Teaching in Higher Education: A Review' in *Higher Education*, vol. 5, pp. 29–33

See also: Peer teaching; Short talks by students; Co-counselling; Instrumented team learning; Learning through discussion; Parrainage; One-to-one learning

LEARNING COMMUNITY (Peer Learning Community)

Learning Community is a general term to describe a learning situation where a group of people come together to meet specific and unique learning needs and to share resources and skills. It is based on the principle of each individual being responsible for the identification and achievement of his own learning needs, and in taking responsibility for helping others meet their own needs and offering himself as a resource for all community members. As an approach, the Learning Community is used to achieve what Carl Rogers described as 'significant learning'. It also encourages autonomous learning which has been defined as a situation in which the learner is able to identify his own learning needs, use the available resources to meet them and be able to evaluate the degree of his own learning. Learning Communities emphasise student-centredness and the development of the ability to learn how to learn. The Learning Community approach stresses the responsibility of both students and tutors for the planning and implementation of all the learning within the community; the expression of the affective dimension of learning; acknowledges the individual needs of learners and emphasises the range of learning resources available to community members. A Learning Community can be described in terms of the stages through which the participants, including the leader/facilitator, usually pass. The first of these is the setting of a climate within which all members can learn. This involves establishing openness between members in terms of what they say, a degree of mutual trust, mutual interdependence and equality of status. In the next two stages the needs of members and the resources available in the group are identified. Following on from this, programme planning and execution takes place which allows all members to meet their individual needs.

Heron, J. (1974) *The Concept of a Peer Learning Community*, Human Potential Research Project, Department of Adult Education, University of Surrey, Guildford

Megginson, D. F. and Pedler, M. (1976) 'Developing Structures and Technology for the Learning Community' in *Journal of European Training*, vol. 5, no. 5, pp. 262–75

Pedler, M. (1974) 'Learning in Management Education' in *Journal of European Training*, vol. 3, no. 3, pp. 182–4

Pedler, M. (1981) 'Developing the Learning Community' in Boydell, T. and Pedler, M. (eds.) *Management Self-Development: Concepts and Practices*, Aldershot: Gower

Turner, I. (1976) 'A Course Without a Structure' in *Studies in Higher Education*, vol. 2, no. 1, pp. 21–32

See also: Learning organisation; Community of enquiry; Autonomy lab; Instrumented laboratory

LEARNING CONTRACT (Contract Learning)

A Learning Contract has been defined as a document drawn up by a student and his instructor or adviser which specifies what the student will learn, how this will be accomplished, within what time period and what the criteria of evaluation will be. Ideally the contract or agreement is written and contains a clearly understood set of specific learning objectives, a number of learning activities and a description of how achievement will be evaluated. The major advantage of this method is that each student can have a different contract, thereby individualising the course. The contract is usually designed as a joint student–teacher effort, but in some cases, the teacher may offer a contract to the entire class, specifying clearly the amount of work and types of activities required for different grades. Students are then asked to indicate what grade they want to work towards.

The use of a Learning Contract changes the relationship between staff and students. The role of the former changes from subject content expert to learning facilitator. Teachers become learners alongside their students. Such interdependence helps to develop mutual discovery and decision making. Staff find they need to know more about the characteristics of the adult learner and the implications of this for teaching and learning; an understanding of the steps of contract learning; how to apply course standards to individual Learning Contracts; how to develop a Learning Contract and an appreciation of the role of the teacher as a learning facilitator. Its historical antecedents go back to when it was called the Dalton Plan. Often, but not with entire accuracy, it was called the contract method. It was originated by Helen Parkhurst at Dalton in Massachusetts in 1919 and was designed to provide for varying rates of individual achievement. Each student was supplied with an assignment called a 'contract' in which detailed information was given concerning topics, projects, exercises, memory work and other requirements. As soon as the student completed the assignment, he would be given another contract. Students worked as long as they cared to on a particular assignment. Occasionally student group conferences would take place. Each student advanced as rapidly as his ability and inclination permitted. The instructor was available for help and guidance. Graph cards were used to record the extent and quality of student achievement. Contract Learning allows students to advance in accordance with their own abilities and promotes the development of individual initiative.

Knowles, M. S. (1975) *Self-Directed Learning: A Guide for Learners and Teachers*, New York: Association Press

Knowles, M. S. (1970) *The Modern Practice of Adult Education*, New York: Association Press

Buzzell, M. and Romen, O. (1981) 'Preparing for Contract Learning' in Boud, D. (ed.) *Developing Student Autonomy in Learning*, London: Kogan Page Ltd

Donald, J. (1976) *Annotated Bibliography on Contract Learning*, Ontario Universities Programme for Instructional Development, McGill University

Berte, N. R. (1975) (ed.) 'Individualising Learning by Learning Contracts' in *New Directions in Higher Education*, San Francisco: Jossey Bass

Stuart, R. (1978) 'Contracting to Learn' in *Management Education and Development*, vol. 9, no. 2, pp. 75–84

Donald, J.G. (1976) 'Contracting for Learning' in *Learning and Development*, vol. 7, no. 5

Barlow, R. M. (1974) 'An Experiment with Learning Contracts' in *Journal of Higher Education*, vol. 45, pp. 441–9, June

Esbensen, T. (1978) *Student Contracts*, Guides for the Improvement of Instruction in Higher Education No. 17, Englewood Cliffs, New Jersey: Educational Techniques Publications

Christen, W. (1976) 'Contracts for Student Learning' in *Educational Technology*, vol. 16, pp. 24–8

See also: One-to-one learning; Parrainage; Learning cell; Learning on Demand; FlexiStudy; Block method

LEARNING CONVERSATION

The Learning Conversation approach aims to develop 'learning to learn' skills in managers by assisting them to become self-organised learners. The techniques used are designed to enable them to converse with themselves about the process of learning. The methods employed consist of content-free heuristics. Learning to learn is defined as the ability to converse with oneself about the process of learning. It involves observation, search, analysis, formulation, review, judgement, decision and action on the basis of personal outcomes. A 'Conversational

Repertory Grid' and 'structuring of meaning procedures' are used to elicit, display and reflect upon personal systems of meanings.

Harri-Augstein, E S. and Thomas, L. F. (1978) 'Learning Conversations: A Person Centred Approach to Self-Organised Learning' in *British Journal of Guidance and Counselling*, July.

Harri-Augstein, E. S. and Thomas, L. F. (1981) 'Learning Conversations' in Boydell, T. and Pedler, M. (eds) *Management Self-Development: Concepts and Practices*, Aldershot: Gower

Thomas, L. F. (1976) 'The Self-Organised Learner at Work' in *Personnel Management*, vol. 8, no. 6, pp. 32–5

Thomas, L. F. and Harri-Augstein, E. S. (1977) 'Learning to Learn: the personal constructs and exchange of meaning' in Howe, M. (ed.) *Adult Learning*, Chichester: John Wiley and Sons

See also: Repertory grid training; Reflective learning

LEARNING ORGANISATION

A Learning Organisation can best be described as a more structured version of a Learning Community. It was designed primarily to achieve the same goals, but to do so within the framework of a part-time, graduating university course. The way in which such aims are achieved is through the giving of responsibility to students for the selection of subject content and course process goals; the timing and sequencing of the content to be addressed and the selection of learning methods used. In the short term the assessment procedures are largely outside the control of either the students or the tutors. Among the key differences between a full-time course and a part-time one is that in the latter there is a need to structure the class contact time more efficiently. To do this, the available time is divided into subject blocks, to each of which are assigned a number of students who compose the 'block team'. The team approach is an attempt to encourage participants to take responsibility for their own learning and to contribute to the learning of all course members. Within the model, the tutor plays a slightly larger role than the facilitator in a Learning Community, but his involvement is as an equal member of the Organisation and his contributions and interventions take place in response to, and/or with the approval of, all the members of the Organisation. In essence, the tutor provides the structure and continuity which the part-time course demands. Having direct access to the resources of the educational institution, he helps to promote the achievement of the objectives specified by participants.

Huczynski, A. A. and Boddy, D. (1979) 'Learning Organization' in *Studies in Higher Education*, vol. 4, no. 2, pp. 211–22

Gourlay, R. (1975) 'A Process Orientated Leadership Workshop' in *Industrial Training International*, vol. 10, no. 6, pp. 183–5

Reynolds, M. (1976;) 'Experience-Based Designs in Organizational Development' in Cooper, C.L. (ed.) *Developing Social Skills in Managers: Advances in Group Training*, London: Macmillan

Farnes, N. (1976) 'An Educational Technologist Looks at Student Centred Learning' in *British Journal of Educational Technology*, vol. 7, no. 1, pp. 61–5

See also; Learning community; Community of enquiry; Instrumented laboratory; Autonomy lab

LEARNING THROUGH DISCUSSION

Learning Through Discussion (LTD) is a method which helps a learning group to deal with any book, paper or journal. It assists a group to structure the group discussion process by providing a Cognitive Map. This 'map' contains a guide through the logical process of discussion, a list of group roles and member skills and a lot of criteria against which to judge group discussion performance. One of the main advantages of LTD is that it allows small groups to work without tutor-leaders on appointed texts. Kitchener and Hurst's *Student Manual for Education Through Student Interaction* is similar to the LTD, but requires additional questionnaires to be filled in by every group member. One questionnaire is to be filled in advance of each session, while the other, which is completed at the end of the session, asks for an assessment of the group's proceedings, and provides both group and teacher with information on the group's progress. With the guidance provided by ETSI, leaderless groups may be run without risk.

Hill, W. F. (1975), *Learning Thru Discussion*, London: Sage Publications

Kitchener, K.H. and Hurst, J.C. (1972) *The Student Manual for Education Through Student Interactions*, Fort Collins (Colorado), Rocky Mountains Behavioural Sciences Institute

Fineman, S. and Hamblin, A. C. (1978) 'Teaching Organisational
Behaviour Through Discussion Groups' in *Studies in Higher Education*,
vol. 3, no. 1, pp. 46–62

Northedge, A. (1975) 'Learning Through Discussion in the Open
University' in *Teaching at a Distance*, no. 2, pp. 10–19

Diamond, M. J. (1972) 'Improving the Undergraduate Lecture Class by
Use of Student Led Discussion Groups' in *American Psychologist*,
vol. 27, pp. 978–81

See also: Leaderless group discussion; Audio tutorial method;
Instrumented team learning; Tape-assisted learning programme; Media-activated learning group; Creative dialogue

LECTURE METHOD

A lecture can be defined as an organised oral presentation of subject
matter on a definite topic prepared for a specific purpose by the
instructor. To be effective, the literature advises that one should lecture
only when the occasion calls for it; have a specific purpose which is
known and acceptable to trainees; rarely use it in its pure form but make
provision for additional methods, e.g. buzz groups, question and answer
interludes; organise it according to a definite plan geared towards
students' interests which will cause them to think and enable them to
learn; include material pertaining to the subject and serving learner
objectives; avoid talking over the heads of the group; prepare to alter
lecture plans according to the requirements of the situation and be as
brief as possible before turning to other methods.

The Lecture Method is still widely used in some form or another in the
teaching of management students especially in the polytechnics and
universities. Comparisons of the effectiveness of the Lecture Method
with other methods suggest that it can be used efficiently to convey
information, but it cannot be used effectively on its own to either
promote thought or else to change or develop attitudes in listeners.
Research suggests that a lecturer's technique is as important as his
selection of an appropriate method. In terms of 'cost effective' teaching
the lecture has distinct advantages. Lecturing to a massed audience can
bump up any department's staff-student contact hours ratio. However,
it is clear that the lecture should be reserved for lower level cognitive
objectives. Other studies show that student recall of lecture material
immediately after the conclusion of the lecture is rarely higher than 40
per cent, and drops to 20 per cent within seven days. Where some

complex or controversial topic is being dealt with, a series of lectures can be given on a single theme by different lecturers who express different points of view. These are known as Ring Lectures. They can be followed by a dialogue or even an argument between the lecturers expressing different points of view. While a lecture is useful for giving information, it can also be used to give information about information, i.e. to give the student an example of how an argument in an academic field can be structured. The lecture itself will contain such an argument structured in such a way. For this method to work, the student has to be directed to the fact that there is this second layer involved and be asked to watch out for it. Time at the end of the lecture has to be made available not only to summarise conclusions reached, but also the steps by which those conclusions were reached.

Bligh, D. (1972) *What's the Use of Lectures?* Harmondsworth: Penguin Books

McLeish, J. (1968) *The Lecture Method*, Cambridge Monographs on Teaching Methods, no. 1, Cambridge Institute of Education

McLennan, R. (1975) 'Lectures, Learning and Information Transmission' in *Journal of European Training*, vol. 4, no. 1, pp. 56–66

Gregory, I.D. (1975) 'A New Look at the Lecture Method' in *British Journal of Educational Technology*, vol. 6, no. 1, pp. 55–62

Black, P. J. (1976) 'Aims, Processes and the Engineering of Teaching' in *Studies in Higher Education*, vol. 1, no. 2

Brown, G. and Tomlinson, D. (1979) 'How to Improve Lecturing' in *Medical Teacher*, vol. 1, no. 3, pp. 128–35

Borrell, P. (1977) *Lecturing*, Keele: Keele University Library

Brown, G. (1978) *Lecturing and Explaining*, London: Methuen

Brown, G. (1979) *Learning from Lectures*, Nottingham: University of Nottingham.

Powell, L.P. (1970) *Lecturing to Large Groups*, London: BACIE, 3rd edition

See also: Lesson–demonstration method; Demonstration–performance method; Talk

LESSON–DEMONSTRATION METHOD (Tell-and-Show
Method)
The Lesson–Demonstration is a traditional method, and variations of it
may be found in industrial training departments. As a technique it is less
autocratic than a lecture, but less permissive than a discussion. It
consists of three phases: an introduction or brief lecture in which the aim
is stated; a development phase, which usually features a good deal of
question and answer and other class activity; and a consolidation period
in which the material is rehearsed, revised and tested. Variation is used
for achieving both cognitive and psycho-motor skill objectives. Being
located somewhere between the lecture and the discussion, it is difficult
to pin down the approach for evaluation purposes. It can be said that the
classical Lesson–Demonstration is an optimal teaching strategy for
average and below-average students with an untrained or inexperienced
teacher. Only lower-order affective objectives are likely to be realised,
although both lower and middle-order cognitive objectives can be
achieved in skilled hands. The main advantage is the support given to the
teacher since the successive phases and subphases of lesson development – all of which are readily laid out in basic textbooks – supply a
model of what is expected of him as an instructor.

The Demonstration is a planned presentation that shows the students
how to perform an act, skill or procedure. Usually it is accompanied by
an appropriate visual presentation, student questions and student
involvement. Its prime use is to show learners how to perform an act,
develop a skill or use new equipment/machinery/products. It builds
their confidence in performing in these circumstances. Its advantages are
that it is easier to visualise steps than to have them presented orally or in
writing. It gives the learner an opportunity to test his learning under
guidance and to build his confidence in performing under these
circumstances. It also assists in relating the steps in the process. Its
disadvantages are that the equipment may not be readily available or
easily moved. It may be difficult to get the audience to the equipment
site, e.g. management students to the college computer centre. There
may be problems of student opportunity to practise because of class size
and the approach is limited to practical problems only. This method
provides additional student interest when used in association with the
Lecture Method. Learning comes from the observation of the subject
matter functioning in action and thereby duplicating, to an extent, a
job-like situation. A basic principle of adult education is that a mature
learner wants to see the thing he is studying in action just as he will use it
outside. The practice obtained through 'hands on' experience with the

microcomputer by managers would be an example.

Ayres, R. (1977) 'Strategies in Giving Group Instruction' in *BACIE Journal*, vol. 31, no. 7, July, pp. 118–20

Ayres, R. (1977) *A Trainer's Guide to Group Instruction*, London: British Association for Commercial and Industrial Training

See also: Vestibule training; Lecture method

LIBRARY ASSIGNMENT

A Library Assignment is an example of individual work. Students are given a series of questions to which they are required to find answers from books and other resources located in the library. The complexity and sophistication of the approach will vary with the objectives that the tutor may have. For example, it may be organised as an initiative test/speed trial in which members have to use their ingenuity to obtain the correct answers to the questions in the shortest possible time. Alternatively, the aim may be to compare the availability and intelligibility of different data sources in which case a particular type of instruction and time scale will be provided.

Howard, M. (1968) *Library Assignments*, London: Edward Arnold

See also: Re-writing; Data approach method; Literature search; Guided reading; Book reviewing; Worksheet

LISTENING TEAM

Listening Teams can be used in large group discussions. The teams may be designated listeners who take notes and question a formal lecturer or symposium participants, or they may listen, evaluate and question a group participating in informal discussion. Each member of a Listening Team keeps a record of the most important ideas presented by the speaker(s). He identifies the issues, questions, problems and opinions developed by the participants. The use of the Listening Team varies in group discussions. The team may be required to summarise what has been said and to point out concepts and problems which are significant to the group. Alternatively, it may be asked to summarise the problems or concepts presented by a speaker, panel or symposium. Listening Teams need to include individuals who are well informed on the subject under consideration, yet have no bias and are alert and able to interpret the presentation or discussion. Normally Listening Team members do not enter the discussion until the chairman calls them. They may assist a discussion leader in starting the discussion, or in helping the group to decide the objectives/aims it wishes to accomplish. Most Listening Teams are comprised of two or three people but up to five can be used when a large group is involved.

See also: Brains trust; Audience reaction/watchdog team; Panel discussion; Reaction panel; Interrogation of experts

LITERATURE SEARCH
The Literature Search is in many ways the reverse of guided reading. The aim here is to get students to become aware of the range of literature that is available in a subject area by using their initiative to seek it out, classify it and critically evaluate it. The degree of guidance given by the lecturer will depend on his objectives. Students may be given only minimal instructions, e.g. the library floor to go to, and the subject to be investigated. Alternatively a reading list can be issued and specific questions asked, e.g. evaluate the book on the following criteria. It is probably advisable to precede any set of Literature Search exercises by some sort of training in how to be systematic in conducting a Literature Search. This is the sort of training which is given by library staff on introductory courses concerned with the use of resources.

See also: Guided study; Book reviewing; Reading; Reading parties; Library assignment; Dissertation proposal; Research degree

LOGGING CRITICAL INCIDENTS
With this approach, individuals log, each day, the one incident in their job that has caused them to experience greatest difficulty. After a suitable interval, the incidents are jointly reviewed by the individual and his boss and any necessary training plans are agreed and put into action. By using the Critical Incident Logging technique, a manager can restrict his training activity to 'training by exception'. Attention is thereby concentrated on those aspects of the job that are causing employees actual difficulty. Alternatively, a manager or trainer can interview managers asking them to tell him about the most difficult problem they have had to deal with during a given period of time. The period of time considered is related to the manager's reporting cycle on the basis of one-and-a-half times his reporting cycle. Thus for a manager for whom

one week is similar to another, he is questioned about his most difficult problem during the last ten days. For a senior manager the period may be three or four months. The questioner asks: 'Can you tell me about the incident in the last six months which has caused you the greatest difficulty?' He then goes on to ask probing questions, such as: 'When did this happen? Was it a one-off problem? Why? Was it your problem or someone else's? What caused it? What was the cost? Will it happen again? How was it solved? Any long term effects?'

Mumford, A. (1980) *Making Experience Pay*, London: McGraw-Hill

Flanagan, J. C. (1951) 'The Use of Comprehensive Rationales in Test Development' in *Educational Psychological Measurement*, vol. 11, pp. 151–5

Flanagan, J. C. (1949) 'Critical Requirements: A New Approach to Employee Evaluation' in *Personnel Psychology*, vol. 2, pp. 419–25

See also: Diary exercise; Critical incident analysis

MANAGEMENT AUDIT

A Management Audit is a methodical review of the whole range of managerial activity in an organisation by reference to defined criteria of good management. Unlike management techniques such as O & M, work study, network analysis or operational research which are concerned with the examination of specific procedures, processes and problems, Management Audit looks at broader issues. For example it asks whether the authority structure, communications systems and the practices of all those with management responsibility produce a dynamic and well integrated organisation capable of responding rapidly to a changing situation and of getting the best out of every individual working in it. Audit looks broadly at the whole range of management activity. The audit document itself is similar to some types of staff appraisal forms except that it focuses on organisational and managerial behaviour stated in input terms. It consists of sets of statements, grouped under the topic area covered, e.g. organisational structure, communications, public relations, health and safety, personnel management etc. A typical statement might include: 'The managing director has regular meetings, both formal and informal, with departmental heads'. A series of such questions are posed to which the responding manager might be asked to reply: Yes, No or Not Sure and offer comments. The audit poses a number of such questions which are based on a previously agreed statement of what constitutes good management practice in the company concerned. Such a checklist provides a framework for the critical examination of organisational functioning and allows a regular review of existing practices to be carried out. The audit exercise can of course be related to staff appraisal systems. There are a number of ways in which a Management Audit can be carried out within a company. For example, an internal or external management auditor can be appointed. However, when used primarily as a staff development activity it is more likely that the individual manager and his boss will complete the audit independently and discuss their individual answers together.

Rose, T. G. (1961) *The Management Audit*, Gee

Management Audit, British Institute of Management, London, 1975

Dale, A. G. (1973) 'Management Audit' in *British Hospital Journal and Social Service Review*, 26 September

Leonard, W. P. (1962) *The Management Audit: An Appraisal of Management Methods and Performance*, Englewood Cliffs, New Jersey: Prentice Hall

Santocki, J. (1974) 'Management Audit – Chance, Challenge or Lost Opportunity?' in *The Accountant*, 3 January

See also: Self appraisal; Performance review; Instrumented feedback; Logging critical incidents; Self criticism

MANAGER EXCHANGE
In this form of staff development activity, a manager exchanges his position with another in his own company for a specified period of time. He then returns to his original post. Such exchanges may take place within the same plant or between managers from different plants of the same company. They may also take the form of staff-to-line or line-to-staff exchanges. In this latter case, the objective may be to overcome the misunderstandings and conflicts that can arise betwen these departments.

See also: Development assignment; Job swop; Acting assignment; Manager shadowing; Sick leave/holiday replacement assignment; Action learning; Job rotation

MANAGER SHADOWING
Manager Shadowing is a less formal type of development than

apprenticeship. Here there is no necessary requirement that the newcomer will take over the job of the person he is shadowing. Equally, the shadowed manager need not be senior in the organisation. The key learning point for the person doing the shadowing is to discover what jobs/tasks are performed and how these are done. The trainee can act as an 'assistant to' the manager being shadowed. The idea underlying this approach is that a man can best learn how to handle a job by observing and assisting a man who is experienced in it. These assignments are however fraught with pitfalls, for it is easy for an assistant to become little more than a caddy. If he is aggressive and seeks to assume line responsibility, he can cause serious troubles for his senior. To be useful, this assistant role needs to be clearly defined and the occupant given the preparatory training/experience necessary to carry it out. If the superior uses him properly, a great deal of development can take place. The boss should give the assistant substantial freedom to gather facts and interpret them while exercising care to reserve all active direction and coordination of other subordinates to himself. The assistant can then become a positive contribution through the proper exercise of his role which is a supporting one. The method assumes that one can learn managerial techniques and practices by observing a model manager in action. The problem for the trainee is to judge the relative importance of what he observes. The approach might usefully be combined with training in observation, including guidance to the trainee in clarifying the different situations and types of problems the manager is solving, and the types of strategies and solutions used by the manager who is involved. Observation without a system is seldom systematic. It is subject to bias and is not likely to be an efficient or effective learning method.

Taylor, C. (1977) 'Shadowing: The Creative Approach to Supervisory Training' in *Management*, vol. 24, no. 8, pp. 14–15

See also: Sitting by Nellie; Development assignment; Job swop; Acting assignment; Manager exchange; Sick leave/holiday replacement assignment; Job rotation

MANAGING EFFECTIVE RELATIONSHIPS (MER Training)

This form of training is aimed at helping participants to increase their knowledge and competence in using strategic interpersonal skills. The application of these, it is claimed, enables them to have productive and satisfying relationships. The method was developed by Helen Clinard and the model on which it is based is called the 'MER Lens'. Its purpose is to help people choose the most appropriate interpersonal style to use in any given situation. The most important skills suggested by the model are presented in behavioural terms and their uses are demonstrated in situations relevant to participants. Six basic skills are considered.

Appreciation Messages are concerned with commenting on the behaviours of others whom you like in a way that leaves the other person feeling appreciated and motivated. Facilitative Listening is listening in a way that demonstrates understanding, respect and empathy and which allows the other person to ventilate feelings and to get to the bottom of problems and find solutions. Constructive Confrontation is confronting another person with a behaviour which causes you a problem in such a way that it leaves the other person feeling cooperative and thereby avoids resentment, resistance or the lowering of the other person's self-esteem. Mutual Problem Solving is a process for finding solutions to problems or conflicts of needs in such a way that leaves everybody involved feeling respected, cooperative and motivated to make the proposed solution work. Unsolicited Consultation involves using persuasion or selling skills to give advice when it has not been asked for in such a way that the other person wants to hear and consider what the speaker says. Solicited Consultation is the using of influencing, counselling or helping skills when the other person wants help with their problem solving. To be effective in applying the skills described, participants must know what the skills are and how to use them; develop confidence in putting the skills to use and appreciate the value and benefit of applying the skills and therefore feeling motivated to understand, develop and use them.

Clinard, H. (1978) 'Managing Effective Relationships' in *BACIE Journal*, vol. 32, no. 3, pp. 51–4

Clinard, H. (1981) 'Developing Higher Levels of Interpersonal Communication Skills' in *BACIE Journal*, vol. 35, no. 4, pp. 77–8

See also: Interactive skills training; Coverdale training; Interaction management

MATHETICS
Mathetics is an approach to the teaching of skills which breaks down the task into a number of stages, e.g. the teaching of a person to fold a paper origami figure. The usual way of instruction is to start with a blank piece of paper, tell him how to make the first fold, then the second and so on until the figure is complete. A second piece of blank paper is produced and the trainee is asked to do it himself. But under these conditions how

much of the instruction can he remember? When does he get lost? How many times does he have to be reminded? To evaluate one's instruction using this method one can count the number of trials it takes for the trainee to get it right alone. Teaching the same procedure the Mathetics way, the trainee is handed the origami figure almost completely folded but with the last fold missing. The trainer then tells the student how this last step is done. He then hands him a second almost completed figure but this time the last two stages are omitted. Again he is instructed on the last two steps and goes on to complete the figure. A figure complete except for the last three stages is provided for completion and so on until the trainee starts with a blank sheet. It has been found that the Mathetics method can reduce the number of trials needed to learn a given procedure and that its use reduces forgetting. The reason for this is the satisfaction produced by successful completion. The fact that one learns one new step at a time and rehearses all the others means that practice is achieved. Thomas Gilbert is accredited with this behavioural analysis called Mathetics. The approach is relevant whenever objectives involve the learning of sequences, e.g. testing a hypothesis, constructing a profit and loss account. Irrespective of whether the sequence chains are simple or complex, Gilbert stressed the motivational value of 'backward chaining'. Research has found that not all chains are necessarily best taught backwards, but it nevertheless demonstrates that in teaching, the obvious sequences may not always necessarily be the best ones.

Gilbert, T. F. (1962) 'Mathetics: The Technology of Education' in *Journal of Mathetics*, vol. 1, pp. 1–73

Mager, R. F. (1961) 'On the Sequencing of Instructional Content' in *Psychological Reports*, vol. 9, pp. 405–13

See also: Lesson–demonstration method; Demonstration–performance method; Drill and practice session; Discovery method

MEDIA-ACTIVATED LEARNING GROUP
This is an audio visual programme consisting of slides and audio cassettes which is produced by the tutor and which serves to orientate and structure the activities of the students who meet without a tutor or teacher. There may be an optional phase in which individualised study for a preview and review of material takes place. There are six phases of group work in this approach: (*a*) Orientation Phase – objectives outlined, assignments read, oral introduction; (*b*) Stimulus Phase – mini-lecture, presentation of problem requiring group response;

(*c*) Response Phase – evaluation of solution alone or in groups; (*d*) Confirmation Phase – audio visual presentation of teacher's solution; (*e*) Validation Phase – programme deficiencies are referred to teacher for revision; (*f*) Review Phase With Teacher Present – analysis of group's comprehension and interpretation. Information about the use of the MALG reveals that where there is a dependence in the programme on a text, plus group pressure, this means that students read most of the set text before attending the group session. This tends to overcome the major problem of learner-centred groups, which is that students do not do the set reading.

Berman, A. I. (1974) 'Field Studies of Small Media-Activated Learning Groups' in Verreck, W. (ed.) *Methodological Problems in Research and Development in Higher Education*, Amsterdam: Swets and Zeitlinger, B. V.

See also: Agenda method; Instrumented team learning; Learning through discussion; Leaderless group discussion; Tape-assisted learning programme; Autonomous learning group

MICRO-LAB

The Micro-lab is a planned selection of activities from amongst the many possibilities that exist within laboratory learning, e.g. T-group. The aim of these methods has been to help people to learn about themselves, their relationships with other individuals, with other groups and the organisations to which they belong. Such learning comes from the members' direct participation in groups formed specifically to achieve this purpose. A Micro-lab samples what might occur in a T-group, encounter group or human relations group. Micro-lab groups are usually small, consisting of between three and six people. A number of groups can be run in parallel. The time limit mitigates against larger sized groups since it prevents group members from sharing. Unless the groups which are running in parallel are of roughly equal size, then they may get out of phase with one another as each group moves from activity to activity.

At the outset of a Micro-lab, members are asked to just go along with the activities, to participate in them fully and not to judge their worth until later. They are further asked to stay with the topics suggested and not to digress into small talk. Since some activities involve giving feedback to others. members are asked at the start to avoid advising others but rather to listen to them, learn from them and share their own feelings and thoughts. The directions for the activities in which Micro-lab group members engage can either be given by a leader/facilitator or by a member of the group itself. Typical Micro-lab activities may include:

1 Share your first impressions of each other, both positive and negative (5 minutes).

2 Tell each other the one thing you would most like other members of the group to know about you (6 minutes).

An entire Micro-lab may contain 10–12 of such activities and will last an hour.

See also: Sensitivity (T-group) training; Encounter group; Tape-assisted learning programme; Group dynamics laboratory; Human relations laboratory; Organisational laboratory; Personal development laboratory; Power laboratory; Team laboratory; Laboratory method; Mini-society

MICRO TEACHING

Micro Teaching is used primarily in teacher education but has a wider applicability. A learner-teacher takes a group of three or four students on a specific subject for five minutes. This lesson is videotaped. When it is over, a supervisor who has been operating the camera, gives the students who have been given the teaching by the trainee a questionnaire to fill in. They do this quickly and leave the room. The supervisor and learner teacher then discuss the lesson, review any notes the supervisor took, consider the student feedback forms and view part of the videotape. After a short break the process is repeated with a new group of three or four students. The key elements of the Micro Teaching approach are that above all it is real. The participant engages in real teaching. Secondly, the Micro Teaching lessons have the complexities of normal classroom teaching, but other variables such as class size, time and scope of concept have all been reduced. The approach focuses on training for the accomplishment of specific tasks, e.g. practice of instructional skills, techniques of teaching, mastery of curriculum materials. It permits increased control over practice. Time, student and feedback variables can all be manipulated and it expands the normal knowledge of results or feedback dimension.

Perrott, E. (1977) *Micro-teaching in Higher Education: Research, Development and Practice*, Guildford, Surrey: Society for Research into Higher Education

Falus, I. and McAlleese, W.R. (1975) 'A Bibliography of Microteaching, in *Programmed Learning and Educational Technology*, vol. 12, no. 1, pp. 34–53

Jesson, C.K. (1974) 'An Economic Use of Micro-Teaching Techniques to Achieve Objectives for a Basic Course in Learning Resources' in *Programmed Learning and Educational Technology*, vol. 11, no. 2, pp. 87–96

Titmar, H-G., Hargie, O.D.W. and Dickson, D.A. (1977) 'Social Skills Training at Ulster College' in *Programmed Learning and Educational Technology*, vol. 14, no. 4, pp. 300–4

Allen, D. and Ryan, K. (1969) *Micro-Teaching*, Reading, Mass.: Addison-Wesley

Perlberg, A. (1970) 'Microteaching: a new approach to improving teaching and training' in *Journal of Educational Technology*, vol. 1, no. 1, pp. 35–43

See also: Video confrontation; Interpersonal process recall; Surrogate clients

MINICOURSE

A Minicourse is an independent miniature course and is different from the type of module which may go towards making up a unit of some extended programme. In fact it differs from a module, modular course, audio-tutorial package, unit box or learning activity package in a number of important ways. Above all it is a fully self-contained, flexible miniature course for individuals and groups which is based upon an educational technology model and involves a variety of media and strategies appropriate for adult learners. A Minicourse has clearly defined objectives which are achievable in a short time span, usually a few days or less. It is not packaged for independent study, as it depends extensively on the dynamics of small group interaction. A Minicourse will usually have a manual associated with it, but it depends basically for its coordination on the presence of a course leader and on group work. It exists as an entity only during the hours of its presentation.

Minicourses are based on a systems approach to curriculum development which uses behavioural theory concepts. Meyer described how each Minicourse is based on precisely defined stimulus–response chains in which reinforcement to students is provided at the end of each response phase. These stimulus–response chains are organised as linear sequences of input-process-output (IPO) cycles which in turn are aggregated into 'super-cycles' and go to form a single Minicourse. Each Minicourse is designed to optimise some twenty-four conditions which have been shown in the research literature as being likely to lead to effective learning. These include active participation; immediacy of application; clarity of objectives; provision for reinforcement and feedback; democratic leadership; effective group work; logical step-by-step structuring; variety of methods and media; modelling, contiguity of elements and so on.

Meyer, C.R. (1979) 'The Development of Minicourses (with a Basis in Educational Technology) for the In-Service Education of Teachers and Trainers' in *Programmed Learning and Educational Technology*, vol. 16, no. 1, pp. 23–37

Meyer, C.R. and Jenkins, C. (1979) 'Preliminary Studies of the Effectiveness of Minicourses for In-Service Education of Teachers and Trainers' in *Programmed Learning and Educational Technology*, vol. 16, no. 3, pp. 210–8

Brandt, D., Ansell, M. and Cryer, N.B. (1974) 'Minicourses in a first year physics laboratory' in *Physics Education*, vol. 1, pp. 23–6

See also: Concentrated study; Workshop; Module; Residential

MINI-LEARNING EVENT

Developed by staff at the Centre for the Study of Management Learning, University of Lancaster, a Mini-learning Event has been described as a technique which allows course participants to take their jobs to the learning. As described by Binsted, Stuart and Long (1980), a Mini-learning Event consists of four sequential stages which are carried out by a group of some five people working together. The stages are those of Diagnosis, Design, Implementation and Review. In the Diagnosis phase, members identify a work problem and analyse it to distil its essential aspects. This is then followed by each person designing a learning event, lasting no longer than thirty minutes, which can help to examine the problem identified. The time constraint means that the distilled problem has to be 'miniaturised' so as to be capable of being tackled within the time limits. Next, the individual implements his design with other group members and it is a condition of the exercise that they should learn something as well as the experimenter. The event concludes with a review when the designer of the event obtains feedback from fellow group members.

Binsted, D., Stuart, R. and Long, G. (1980) 'Promoting Useful Management Learning: Problems of Translation and Transfer' in Beck, J. and Cox, C. (eds) *Advances in Management Education*, Chichester: John Wiley and Sons

Binsted, D. and Stuart, R. (1979) 'Designing Reality into Management Learning Events, 1, Towards Some Working Models' in *Personnel Review*, vol. 8, no. 3, pp. 12–19

See also: Training transfer training; Sociodrama; Role playing

MINI-SOCIETY

Developed in Scandinavia, the Mini-society comprises a fairly large population in a laboratory-type setting which, as far as possible, contains a wide cross section of society as a whole. The procedure is group based, but on groups whose members are sociologically similar. The interaction of these groups living together over time produces a good deal of insight on the dynamics by which society as a whole operates. Participants in Mini-societies also tend to find, act out and become aware of the preoccupations of the larger society that they bring in with them. In a Mini-society that was run in the United Kingdom, a deep concern was discovered by groups with the problem of the distribution of power in society, particularly with the dominant élites. Members became preoccupied with this issue. In another, it was discovered that there was a widespread disbelief in normal processes, particularly the political ones by which we traditionally achieve our public objectives in society today. Members of a Mini-society discover such issues by themselves through their own intergroup and personnel relationships.

Hjelholt, G. (1973) 'Group Training in Understanding Society: Mini-Society' in Cooper, C. L. (ed.) *Group Training for Individual and Organizational Development*, Basle: S. Karger, pp. 140–52

See also: Laboratory method; Sensitivity (T-group) training; Group dynamics laboratory; Human relations laboratory; Organisational laboratory; Personal development laboratory;

Team laboratory; Micro-lab; Tavistock conference method; Power lab

MODULE (Modular Instruction)

The term Module has been used loosely in many areas of education and it has been applied to a course which may have little relation to others taken by the student as part of his diploma or degree programme. In this context the term is used to refer to a self-contained cluster of concepts which are presented to the learner through instructional channels which are appropriate to the 'nature' of the knowledge contained therein. Thus a Module may be a semi-programmed and self-paced unit. In all cases it tends to be designed to achieve highly specific objectives in a short time of several days. It can be packaged for use as an independent learning resource and may or may not be a unit of some extended course. The basic idea of modular instruction is to offer individual units that cover the major content areas of the course. Where Modules are designed for self study they frequently employ audio or visual media. A set of units may be completed in sequence, or students may choose from several Modules at any one time. Time limits may be set for the completion of each Module or students may be permitted to complete the units at their own pace. The task of the instructor is to develop the Modules, monitor their use and evaluate them as well as student achievement.

Goldschmid, B. and Goldschmid, M.L. (1972) 'Modular Instruction in Higher Education: A Review' in *Higher Education*, February, pp. 15–32

Russell, J.D. (1974) *Modular Instruction – A Guide to the Design, Selection, Utilization and Evaluation of Modular Materials*, Burgess Publishing Company

Church, C. (1975) 'Modular Courses in British Higher Education: A Critical Assessment' in *Higher Education Bulletin*, vol. 3, no. 3, pp. 165–84

Owens, G. (1970–71) 'The Module' in *Universities Quarterly*, vol. 25, pp. 20–27

See also: Concentrated study; Minicourse; Workshop; Residential

MONODRAMA

Monodrama needs to be distinguished from several related approaches.

Its distinguishing feature is that the subject enacts the entire 'drama' alone, guided only by the facilitator. In Psychodrama, other members of the group are invited to take roles, while Sociodrama examines interpersonal rather than intrapersonal issues. In a Monodrama, the subject sits in a chair with several other chairs being available. Each such chair is there to symbolise a different aspect of the self, e.g. ambition, indecision, greed. He first identifies the different aspects, assigning a chair to each of them. He then 'writes a script' between the aspects moving from chair to chair. In each chair he speaks in the first person and identifies fully with the aspect which that chair represents. The facilitator encourages the subject to move quickly from chair to chair and to keep the script going spontaneously without inhibitory contemplation. The approach can be used in a group when a person wants to explore the conflicts and relative claims among for example his professional role, domestic role and other social and recreational roles. The foregoing was an example of an intrapersonal use of Monodrama. It can also be used interpersonally. The subject acts out a dialogue between himself and some other person or persons. In a professional group this might be between his professional role and someone in a counterpartial role, e.g. secretary, client, boss. Again the subject will move from chair to chair as he identifies with himself and with the other role. The purpose is to help the member develop empathy with respect to the other role occupant and gain some insight into the dynamic of the interaction between himself and the other. Thus it is best if he re-enacts a real life, problematic situation with a problematic person.

Heron, J. (1973) *Experiential Training Techniques*, Department of Adult Education, University of Surrey, Guildford

See also: Dramatic skit; Sociodrama; Psychodrama; Role playing

MOTIVATION TRAINING

Can group interaction and support be helpful in the development of the entrepreneurial spirit? In studying 'high achievers' McClelland designed a pilot training programme to test methods of promoting high motivation and entrepreneurial behaviour. The key variable in these studies was found to be the 'need to achieve'. Group strategies based on McClelland's approach are the foundation of Motivation Training. Its aims are:

(*a*) to teach participants how to think, talk and act like persons with a high need to achieve;

(*b*) to stimulate participants to set for themselves high, but carefully planned, goals over a specific period of time;

(*c*) to increase participants' knowledge about themselves;

(*d*) to create a group spirit among participants – from learning about each others hopes, fears, successes, failures, and from sharing an emotional experience in a retreat setting.

Group interaction is guided in such a way that participants reinforce each others striving towards individual goals. The group thus constitutes one element in an ever-widening network that supports the individual need to achieve. Change in individual behaviour, however, takes place essentially through introspective processes: each member must examine his own motives, values, attitudes, fantasies, and aspirations and involve himself in creative problem-solving and risk-taking experiences. The group acting as a mirror, provides feedback and help to individual members in examining their own behaviour and in increasing their effectiveness in attaining the goals they set for themselves. Motivation Training has been used in the training of rural leaders in a UNESCO project in Honduras.

McClelland, D.C. and Steele, R.S. (1972) *Motivation Workshops: A Student Workbook for Experiential Learning in Human Motivation*, New York: General Learning Press

Reynolds P.M. (1971) 'Achievement Motivation Training in the U.K.' in *Industrial Training International*, vol 6, no. 9, p. 266

Aronoff, J. and Litwin, G.H. (1971) 'Achievement Motivation Training and Executive Advancement' in *Journal of Applied Behavioural Science*, vol. 2, March, pp. 215–29

Alschuler, A.S. (1972) 'Psychological Education' in Purpel, D.E. and Belanger, M. (eds) *Curriculum and the Cultural Revolution*, McCutchan, Berkeley, California

See also; Assertiveness training; Confidence-building training; Career life planning

NETWORK

People often enter social relationships on the basis of a common interest in order to deal more easily with their own lives and to improve its quality through learning together. This may take place in organised forms, from loosely structured groups to highly structured clubs or associations. This kind of mutual learning comes from the direct exchange of practical ideas. To help people to communicate regularly with others who share the same interests or problems, independent clubs or associations can be established for reciprocal help in specific subject areas. A Network is an institutional model or an 'organisational principle' which might be described as consisting of several 'threads' or relationships of communication held together by 'knots', or individuals, who learn from and help one another, while they solve specific problems. Networks are particularly suitable when an objective is not easily achieved by a single central institution or group or where regional variations mean that differing groups and forms are best suited to meet local needs and circumstances. For example, in the Netherlands where the Open School Project aims to provide recurrent and remedial adult education, it is organised through a Network which links educational centres, womens' groups, ethnic community centres and literacy organisations all of whom are providing a similar service. The Dutch government funds a Network information centre which keeps these diverse groups in touch with one another and thereby ensures that they are aware of what each is doing.

Fordham, P., Poulton, G. and Randle, L. (1979) *Learning Networks in Adult Education*, London: Routledge and Kegan Paul

Henderson, A. (1972) 'Private Network' in *Management Education and Development*, vol. 2, no. 3, pp. 117–27

Illich, I. (1973) *Deschooling Society*, Harmondsworth: Penguin Books, chapter 6

See also: Concentrated study; Flexastudy; FlexiStudy

NON-VERBAL EXERCISE

Non-verbal Exercises rely on a variety of other modalities to produce learning. These often include using gestures to communicate, paper and crayons for pictorial representation, dance and movement, sensory awareness exercises and individual or group fantasies. Although this last one may involve verbal description, the basic medium is pictorial. The idea underlying the use of this approach is that words can both block and facilitate communication since verbal responses are more under a person's control than is his behaviour. Non-verbal Exercises, being more direct, convey the communication message in bold relief. Like rough woodcuts rather than delicate pastels, they communicate feelings.Intellectualisation can serve as a defence against fully experiencing feelings. Since words can easily keep people in a rational state, the constraint of silence can heighten the awareness of feeling. The very advantage of Non-verbal Exercises can produce problems. Because they are so unfamiliar to people, these activities can prove unsettling. Most people have little experience of this method, so they feel less in control of what they do. Some may feel so threatened that they cannot get into the experience and this can block meaningful learning for them. Such difficulties are not unique to this method. Sensitivity training and indeed any approach which involves the learner affectively, is capable of producing similar effects. It is important that the intending user should seek the assistance of an experienced colleague and have had firsthand experience of the use of this method himself.

Watson, G. (1972) 'Non Verbal Activities: Why? When? How?' in Dyer, W.G. (ed.) *Modern Theory and Method in Group Training*, New York: Van Nostrand Reinholt Company

See also: Trust exercise; Experiential exercise; Gestalt techniques; Tape stop exercise; Illuminative incident analysis

ONE-TO-ONE LEARNING (One-to-one Discussion)

Related to Co-counselling, this approach is not used as a one-off method, or as a bit of a course. It is used as a complete programme of study. A course is run which uses student one-to-one methods only. There are no lectures or group work. It is based on several principles and ideas. First, the one-to-one talk periods are brief and varied; the wording of all questions to be discussed, even academic ones, is open ended. For example: 'What is inflation?' is preferred to 'What are the causes of inflation?'. Closed questions are avoided; the open-ended ones are preferred to allow students the opportunity to work from limited information. Activities are included which build self-confidence, self-knowledge and group identity. These are considered as steps and not objectives. One-to-one Learning courses are usually ungraded. Both attendance and a given amount of written work are required to be presented. Students are asked to produce a weekly written statement or 'journal' on their experiences. Its purpose is to help them consolidate learning, develop writing skills and to give feedback to tutors.

The method works in the following way. A student group of 16 or so students divides into one-to-one partnerships. A programme is presented in which a series of discussion questions are set, e.g. 'What is a fact?' Person 1 has three minutes to speak, then person 2, then person 1 again, and then person 2 once more. Each person in the duo speaks twice for an uninterrupted period of three minutes. A series of other questions are subsequently presented. These student–student discussions are supplemented by readings. The questions chosen by the tutor are broad enough to allow students either to do the reading as set or else to develop their own lines of enquiry and find their own reading. A variation of the method involves mixing the one-to-one work with a short lecture. A question is presented, one-to-one discussion takes place, and this is followed by a five-minute lecture by the tutor to remind students of basic content and to raise problems or suggest various perspectives. Following the lecture, the class returns to one-to-one discussion.

Potts, D. (1981) 'One to One Learning' in Boud, D. J. (ed.) *Developing Student Autonomy in Learning*, London: Kogan Page Ltd

See also: Buzz groups; Peer teaching; Socratic enquiry; Co-counselling: Coaching/counselling; Learning cell

OPEN ENCOUNTER
The Open Encounter approach was developed by Will Schutz and others at the Esalen Institute in California. It differs from Carl Rogers' Basic Encounter method in several ways. First, it is more body orientated and emphasises that people interact with their bodies even though they may not mean to. Thus chairs are not used, sitting is on the floor with the shoes removed, frequently there is an emphasis on breathing. A second difference is in the role of the leader. Here he or she is more active. The facilitator may start the group with some breathing exercises and take responsibility for setting the group's basic norms and generally get the group moving. This makes Open Encounter a more intensive experience, since the norms are set higher by the leader than they would be by the group as happens in Basic Encounter. There is an emphasis on energy throughout. It is not the words or actions that are held to matter but the energy behind them. There is a general adoption of the outlook of Gestalt Therapy.

Schutz, W.C. (1967) *Joy: Expanding Awareness*, New York: Grove Press

Schutz, W.C. (1973) *Elements of Encounter*, Joy Press

Smith, P.B. (1980) *Group Processes and Personnel Change*, London:

Harper and Row, chapter 8

See also: Encounter group; Basic encounter; Gestalt techniques

OPEN LEARNING (Distance Learning, Teaching at a Distance)

Open Learning is an umbrella term which is used to refer to a wide range of different learning systems which have the characteristics of being generally both student centered in terms of their learning focus, and flexible in the way in which the students can use them. At present, three distinct types of Open Learning system are in operation. The first and perhaps best known is the one called Distance Learning. Here, the work that the student has to do is sent through the post and is supported by a tutorial facility at either the local or regional level. The form of study offered by the Open University is an example of a distance learning system. Second, there are Locally Based Systems, where students are able to work at home while receiving contact with the college through regular college tutorials. Examples of this system are described in the entry on FlexiStudy. Finally there are various College Based Systems with names such as 'Flexastudy', 'Learning on Demand' and 'Learning by Appointment'. Here the student uses college facilities (e.g. books, self-learning programmes) and receives tutorial support from staff, based on his individual learning needs.

While Open Learning refers to these different flexible learning systems, there are a number of important similarities between them. First of all, the systems allow the learner a measure of freedom as to the nature of his study. He can choose when to study and where to study, but has no immediate access to a tutor. However, although the student is separated from his teacher, he nevertheless obtains a benefit from the tutorial organisations which supply him with tuition, planning and guidance with respect to his studies. The system overcomes a number of traditional obstacles to learning. The learner may be unable to attend the centre at usual times, he may live too far away, he may be handicapped in some way, or his interests may be so unique that they make a 'viable class size' impossible.

Holmberg, B. (1981) *Status and Trends of Distance Education*, London: Kogan Page Ltd

Holmberg, B. (1977) *Distance Education: A Survey and Bibliography*, London: Kogan Page Ltd

Neil, M.W. (1981) (ed.) *The Education of Adults at a Distance: A Report of the Open University Tenth Anniversary Conference*, London: Kogan Page Ltd

Kaye, A. and Rumble, G. (eds.) (1981) *Distance Teaching for Higher and Adult Education*, Croom Helm

Clarke, J. and Leedham, J. (1979) *Aspects of Educational Technology: Vol X, Educational Technology for Individualised Learning*, London: Kogan Page Ltd

Teaching by Correspondence in the Open University, Milton Keynes: Open University Press

Nathenson, M.B. (1979) 'Bridging the Gap Between Teaching and Learning at a Distance' in *British Journal of Educational Technology*, vol. 10, no. 2, pp. 100–9

Harrison, B. (1974) 'The teaching-learning relationship in correspondence tuition' in *Teaching at a Distance*, No. 1, Open University Press.

Teather, D.C.B. and McMechan, J.P. 'Learning From a Distance: A Variety of Models' in Howe, A. and Budgett, R.E.B. (eds) *International Yearbook of Educational and Instructional Technology 1980–81*, New York: Kogan Page, London/Nichols Publishing

See also: Correspondence course; Directed private study; Work-related exercise; Distance learning; FlexiStudy; Flexastudy

ORGANISATION LABORATORY
An Organisation Laboratory is an approach designed to deal with larger organisational systems. The content focus for laboratories of this type is on inter-group relationships and the causes and resolution of organisational conflict. An Organisation Laboratory can involve up to a hundred people depending on its objectives and design. It can stimulate a variety of organisational configurations and analyse the consequences of each form of design. In common with laboratory forms of education, time can be spent on both theory building to help understand emerging phenomena, and on individual and group skill development in coping with the problems of the simulated organisation. Laboratories of this kind have been successfully used in organisational settings. For example, as a learning exercise to prepare members for an organisational merger. It is not of course essential to run such a lab with such a large number of people. Organisation Laboratories can be used with

15–20 students where the focus is on the understanding of issues concerned with organisational role, status, structure and the individual.

Handy, C. (1974) 'Putting an Organization into the Classroom', *Journal of European Training*, vol. 3, no. 2, pp. 85–96

Reynolds M. (1976) 'Experience-Based Designs in Organisational Development' in Cooper, C.L. (ed.) *Developing Social Skills in Managers: Advances in Group Training*, London: Macmillan

Boydell, T. and Pedlar, M. (1976) 'An Organizational Laboratory in Ghana' in *Industrial and Commercial Training*, vol. 8, no. 5, pp. 187–92

Walker, H. (1975) 'Organizational Simulation in Management Training' in *Industrial and Commercial Training*, vol. 7, no. 3, pp. 118–20

See also: Laboratory method; Power laboratory; Tavistock conference method; Group dynamics laboratory; Human relations laboratory; Personal development laboratory; Micro-lab; Mini-society; Sensitivity (T-group) training; Team laboratory

ORGANISATIONAL ROLE ANALYSIS

Orgnisational Role Analysis (ORA) assumes that there are significant differences between: (*a*) what the manager is supposed to do in his work (normative version of role); (*b*) his experience of what actually happens (an existential role), and (*c*) his role as a phenomenon observable by others (a phenomenological role). Out of this the manager distils his 'role idea', his idea or statement about his relationship to work, which helps him to determine and regulate his behaviour. The approach was developed by Bruce Reed and his colleagues at the Grubb Institute. Their concept was that although role analysis represents a self-limiting device in relation to particular work, far from limiting the individual's power, it provides him with a way of preserving what power he has, both inside and outside of his immediate work. While classic consultancy approaches attempt to move people from where they appear to be to where they should be, ORA attempts to interpret why they are where they are, and what the outcomes of attempts to change are likely to be. As the consultation proceeds, so does the capacity of both client and consultant to predict the likely outcomes of contemplated action. A major advance in ORA is when the manager recognises that he is describing his map of his organisation which mirrors his own assumptions, beliefs and feelings. In attempting to describe the organisation, he is at least in part describing himself. The objective of ORA is to enable an individual to identify the basic role idea which can direct and regulate his behaviour for the performance of the task for which he is employed; to relate his basic role idea to his other role ideas; to trace out the systems and groups which indicate the connections between his role idea(s) and other members of the enterprise, and to check what skills, beliefs, capacities and resources can be marshalled by the role idea for task performance.

Reed, B. 'Organizational Role Analysis' in Cooper, C. L. (ed.) (1976) *Developing Social Skills in Managers: Advances in Group Training*, London: Macmillan

Mant, A. (1976) 'How to Analyse Management' in *Management Today*, October

McGivering, I. 'Facilitating Re-Entry Through Role Analysis' in Beck, J. and Cox, C. (eds.) (1980) *Advances in Management Education*, Chichester: John Wiley and Sons

See also: Role prescription

OUTSIDE SPEAKERS

Outside or 'guest' Speakers are a regular part of most management education and training programmes. The members of an in-company training programme which has been discussing organisational problems may invite an academic, consultant or some other 'outsider' to make a contribution which can rise above the detail discussed hitherto, and thereby provide a theory, model or framework which can help clarify, put in context or explain the issues which the managers have been talking about. Alternatively, on a college or university course, the invited Outside Speaker may frequently be a 'practitioner' of some description, usually a manager. Here the purpose may be to link some of the abstract or theoretical ideas suggested by research and assess their validity or suitability in relation to real-life managerial situations. Frequently the difficulty is one of how best to use the speaker and how to integrate him into the course programme as a whole. It is essential to brief the prospective guest in detail about the course as a whole and on which topics students have already covered and those they will go on to deal with. Failure to do this may result in the all too common student response, 'Yes it was interesting, but I'm not sure how it fits into the course'. Guest speakers are not lecturers. Some have little or no experience of this but are, nevertheless, keen to make a good showing and frequently spend a lot of time in preparation.

See also: Interrogation of experts; Interview meeting; Brains trust; Panel discussion; Visiting lecturer

OUTWARD BOUND TRAINING (Adventure Training, Development Training)

In contrast to the more traditional classroom bound, or even company-oriented forms of management development, Outward Bound focuses on giving participants experience in leadership (and followership) roles in small groups working on physical tasks of some severity. The approach owes much to the military tradition of officer training where participants have to cross a river using limited aids, or have to canoe or camp, or scale rocks. Debriefing sessions precede or follow these activities and give conceptual guides and interpretations of the experiences gained. Outward Bound programmes are run on an intensive residential format and members are totally preoccupied by the events, and the total experience is disconnected from the outside world. Members remain in their groups continuously and the activities in which they take part tend to produce a high degree of physical tiredness. The approach is based on the belief that leadership or man-management is the key to effective management in general. During the programmes, the stress is on growth in confidence, awareness of strengths and weaknesses and discovery of latent resources. Development of self is emphasised by the stress put on self-reliance and shifting responsibility onto partici-pants. Such programmes are run by the Leadership Trust, and the John Ridgeway Adventure Centre. They have been supported by a number of major British companies.

Radcliffe, P. J. and Keslake, P. S. (1981) 'Outward Bound?' in Boydell, T. and Pedler, M. (eds) *Management Self-Development: Concepts and Practices*, Aldershot: Gower

Keslake, P. S. and Radcliffe, P. J. in 'Inward Bound – A New Direction for Outward Bound: Towards a Holistic Approach to Management Development' in Beck, J. and Cox, C. (eds) (1980) *Advances in Management Education*, John Wiley and Sons

Parsons, A. G. (1980) 'How to Train Managers to Lead the "Leadership Trust" Way' in *Training*, vol. 6, no. 8, pp. 5–7

Williams, D. H. (1980) 'Adventure With a Purpose' in *The Training Officer*, vol. 16, no. 10, pp. 259–61

Krouwell, B. (1980) 'Management Development Using the Outdoors' in *The Training Officer*, vol. 16, no. 10, pp. 262–5

Kenton, L. (1976) 'Management's Toughest Course' in *Industrial Management*, November

See also: Studycade; Educational visit; Field trip

OVERSEAS PROJECT

The key aspect of any form of Overseas Project or Assignment is that the student or manager conducts a study or carries out a job task in a country or culture with which he is not familiar. An Overseas Project can be conducted as part of a manager's in-company development as when he is sent abroad for a period of time to a foreign plant of the company. The task involves the manager learning about the host country in terms of its economic, political and social institutions before going on to consider specific problems or issues which may be the focus of the project itself. In the case of full-time students, the 'year abroad' has been a compulsory aspect of nearly all undergraduate language degrees as well as some others. With the development of larger world economic units, a new species, the 'Euromanager' has been born. The need to prepare management students for the international dimension of their work has meant that a number of business schools now have exchange arrangements with their counterparts in Europe and the United States. Thus there is an increasing two-way traffic of management students visiting other countries, frequently as part of their Masters degree programmes.

See also: Project method; Field project/attachment; Real life project

PAID EDUCATIONAL LEAVE (Sabbaticals)

Educational Leave does not have a single meaning. For youth movements it means the possibility that youngsters will obtain certain adjustments in working hours to enable them to follow training courses. For trade union organisations it means the time trade union members and leaders are allowed to devote, during working hours, to the completion of their trade union or civic training. For apprentices it means the theoretical and practical instruction provided to complement the vocational training received in the firm or workshop. For workers already in occupations who wish to improve their knowledge, the adult education system in many countries provides an opportunity through which to achieve social advancement. Educational Leave can be defined as the paid or unpaid leave that is granted under legal provisions, collective agreements, arrangements with firms or by individual authorisation to workers in industrial, commercial or agricultural enterprises and employees of public services to enable them to attend educational or trade union, civic, or vocational lectures, courses or seminars. A recent Scottish research project defined it as 'The granting of leave by employers with adequate financial support provided by them or by others, to allow adult employees to attend educational or training courses primarily during working hours, and to retain normal employment rights'.

Educational Leave is not based on any specific training need. When a manager is seen as stretched and as needing time to think and ponder, or if he has been under pressure for some time, this method may be appropriate. A Sabbatical is seen as a length of time spent in a learning environment without formal pressure. It may involve a trip abroad visiting other plants in different countries, or time spent in a library among experts and other managers but not attending other courses. It may involve time on courses which have no immediate relevance to the work at hand. Several firms have asked universities to put on short summer courses on topics which have nothing to do with management, e.g. archeology, English literature. These are attended by managers who have 'run too hard for too long' and who need time to reflect and to get back into the habit of learning. Sabbaticals have very specific objectives and should not be seen merely as holidays. In recent years, Paid Educational Leave has begun to be considered in broader terms. With increasing unemployment, it has been suggested that employees should be granted paid leave funded by the Government in order to temporarily and voluntarily withdraw from the labour market and take the opportunity to retrain and develop new skills and acquire new knowledge.

Hill, R. E. (1976) *The Management Sabbatical and Psychological Development*, Division of Research, Graduate School of Business Administration, University of Michigan, Working Paper No. 136

Casper, P. (1979) 'Paid Educational Leave in France' in Sculler, T. and Megarry, J. (eds) *World Yearbook of Education: Recurrent Education and Lifelong Learning*, London: Kogan Page Ltd

Crummenerl, R. and Dermine, G. (1969) *Educational Leave, A Key Factor of Permanent Education and Social Advancement*, Council of Europe

Mackmurdo, R. (1978) *Time Off*, New Commercial Publishing Company

Bryant, I. (1980) Paid Educational Leave in Scotland, *Scottish Journal of Adult Education*, vol. 5, no. 1, pp. 17–21

See also: Research degree; Independent study

PANEL DISCUSSION
A Panel Discussion is defined as a small group of persons, between four and six, who sit around a table in the presence of an audience and discuss a topic of which they have a special knowledge. The number of panel members allows a topic to be discussed more thoroughly. A skilled panel leader can extract points from the panel and develop an informal atmosphere, which can add to audience knowledge and appreciation. Administratively the technique is simple but it is necessary to ensure that the platform or stage used by the panel is raised above the audience and that microphones are used if the audience is large. A danger is that a vocal panel member can dominate discussion. Success depends on the panel members' discussion skills. Frequently, each discussant is left on his own to develop the discussion theme as he sees fit with no thought of coordination, integration or summarisation in evidence. This tends to confuse the audience and the organiser needs to ask if the Panel Discussion is the best way to achieve the learning objective, i.e. will the audience gain the most knowledge or inspiration from a Panel Discussion or will some other technique be more successful. There is no audience participation at all. All communication is one-way from stage to audience. The Panel Discussion has the advantage that it is possible to assemble a group of experts for a single meeting. A diverse group offers different views on a topic as well as an informal approach. However, the value is reduced if the panel lacks qualified members, has a poor moderator who cannot control and where the audience fails to understand or respond to the experts on the panel. The panel technique is often employed to help clarify or identify problems or issues, to present several different points of view on a given topic or to stimulate interest in a topic for the students' benefit.

See also: Brains trust; Colloquy meeting; Forum meeting;

Interview meeting; Symposium meeting; Clinic meeting; Conference meeting; Institute meeting

PARRAINAGE (Peer Counselling)

This is an example of peer teaching which takes place outside of the context of course work. Each senior student (parrains) is assigned four or five entering students (filleuls) in the same department. The former act as counsellors and tutors and help the freshmen adapt to and succeed in the new environment. Separate meetings at the beginning and end of the programme with first and fourth-year students serve to explain the purpose and procedures of the 'Parrainage'. Subsequently, the professors in charge of the project meet regularly with the parrains in order to guide them and to deal with problems beyond the students' competence. Early meetings between parrains and filleuls are designed to assist the latter to solve problems such as using the library, organising study time and so on. Later, issues such as note taking and curriculum are discussed. Formal groups at a set hour are followed by informal (often individual) encounters requested by filleuls. This method has been found to meet the needs of new students and has helped them to solve problems. The faculty-parrain meetings become a valuable feedback channel with respect to general course problems. While developed within the context of formal university/college courses, Parrainage offers valuable ideas for the organisation of company induction programmes and employee-counselling systems. The Austrian Union of Students operates a version of this method which is systematic, i.e. the Parrainage groups are also learning groups and the senior students are given group dynamics training during the long vacation before they take up their responsibilities as parrains.

Goldschmidt, M. (1981) 'Parrainage – Students Helping Each Other' in Boud, D. (ed.) *Developing Student Autonomy in Learning*, London: Kogan Page Ltd

Goldschmidt, B. and Goldschmidt, M. L. (1976) 'Peer Teaching in Higher Education: A Review' in *Higher Education*, vol. 5, pp. 9–33

Gentry, N. O. (1974) 'Three Models of Training and Utilization' in *Professional Psychology*, vol. 5, pp. 207–14

Wrenn, R. L. and Mencke, R. (1972) 'Students Who Counsel Students' in *Personnel and Guidance Journal*, vol. 50, pp. 687–9

See also; Sitting by Nellie; Apprenticeship programme; Assignment to manager with high development skills; Peer teaching; Teaching as learning; One-to-one learning

PEER TEACHING

This label is applied to a variety of practices which involve students teaching and helping other students of approximately the same age and educational experience. Activities would include discussion groups led by fellow students and autonomous study groups using the teachers as consultants. Peer Teaching methods have the advantage of encouraging active learning by facilitating social relations between students, developing their social skills and improving the efficacy of teaching. In one of the techniques used, the students are divided into several small groups and each student in a group is assigned a topic to teach the other members of his group. Once a topic is completed, each group leader summarises for the entire class how he or she taught the topic, sharing with others the major points that were covered. The instructor may sit in on the groups or be available to answer particularly difficult questions. To ensure high quality teaching, the instructor must closely monitor the work of peer teachers.

Research indicates that both 'student teachers' and 'student learners' benefit from Peer Teaching both cognitively and affectively, especially if students alternate between roles. Learning by teaching is significant for the student tutor because it is closely connected with his own social and instructional activities. He can recognise its immediate practical effects rather than merely hoping that what he learns will be of value in the future. This experience can motivate him and lends significant value to what he learns, namely being able to help others in their learning process. Furthermore, learning becomes meaningful if the learner works with subject matter which is important, or which he thinks is important, in dealing with the problems in his own life. By planning and organising learning processes for others, the student tutor assumes the role of a consciously acting subject as opposed to a 'receptive' object. Student tutors have been found to become more autonomous, self-reliant, and self-confident when they assume the role of both student and teacher. They feel more able to take responsibility for their own learning processes. Finally, a variation of this method is Peer Revision. Here a group of students comes together in order to revise information or a technique.

Collier, K. G. (1980) 'Peer Group Learning in Higher Education: the development of higher order skills' in *Studies in Higher Education*, vol. 5, no. 1, pp. 55–62

Boud, D. J. and Prosser, M. T. (1980) 'Sharing Responsibility: staff-student cooperation in learning' in *British Journal of Educational Technology*, vol. 11, pp. 24–35

Schmerhorn, S. (1973) 'Peer Teaching' in *Learning and Development*, vol. 5, no. 3, Nov/Dec.

Goldschmidt, B. and Goldschmidt, M. L. (1976), 'Peer teaching in Higher Education, A Review' in *Higher Education*, vol. 5, pp. 9–33

Klaus, D. J. (1975) *Patterns of Peer Tutoring*, National Institute of Education Project No. 4–0945, Washington, D.C.: American Institute of Research

See also: Course design as learning; Learning organisation; Learning community; Collaboratively designed course; Learning cell; Tutorium; Proctor model; Self-directed student learning group; Media-activated learning group; Teaching as learning

PERFORMANCE REVIEW (Staff Appraisal, Job Performance Review)

The term 'appraisal' came to Britain from the United States. Even there it was probably not used much before the Second World War. Since that time it has largely superceded the term Merit Rating. The need for some kind of systematic evaluation or assessment of personnel occurred at the turn of the century. Employee appraisal is the systematic evaluation of the individual with respect to his performance on the job and his potential for development. It usually takes place within the context of a formal company staff appraisal system which frequently prescribes the structure of the discussion between an employee and his boss and the timing of that meeting during the year. The purpose is to develop the individual and to improve his performance on the job. During the appraisal interview the boss and his subordinate mutually set goals for the latter to achieve, review critical incidents in the job, and set performance standards for the future. After such an interview, the boss may stimulate the employee to analyse his own performance and to set his own objectives in line with job requirements. The superior acts in a helping and counselling role. From a learning viewpoint, and depending on the way in which it is carried out, Staff Appraisal can offer the employee feedback on his performance. For such information to be of value; it must be reliable; the assessment must be related to a common standard; in its final form the information must be usable and the whole scheme must be taken seriously by all concerned. Most importantly, each employee must feel that he is being treated as an individual (despite the formal and all-embracing nature of most staff appraisal schemes), and he should receive sufficient feedback to enable him to know where he stands and be able to give his own view before major decisions are made regarding his career.

The Staff Appraisal scheme can be divided into three elements; the 'reward review' which relates pay, power, status and self-fulfilment of the employee; the 'potential review' which predicts the level and type of work the individual will be capable of doing in the future and how long he will take to achieve this; and the performance review itself which relates the need to improve job performance of staff in their present jobs. There is a strong argument for carrying out these three reviews separately. While staff appraisal discussions contain the potential for learning, Mumford (1980) felt that it was only under unique circumstances that significant learning resulted from them. He suggested five things that a boss could do in an appraisal to increase its learning possibilities for the junior. First, the boss needed to ensure that the feedback which he was providing about the junior's performance was related to standards and criteria that had been defined earlier and which were specific. He needed to assess how the staff member was likely to react to the appraisal discussion, and in particular, to that part of the interview which dealt with his needs for further development. As the boss carried on the discussion, he needed to assess the impact that it was having on the subordinate. Was it an attack–defend interchange, or a mutual problem-solving discussion? What depth of discussion was appropriate? Was it a matter of the boss suggesting useful training courses, or could the two openly discuss the failure of the subordinate to accept increased responsibility in the job? Finally, suggested Mumford, the boss might wish to discuss the possibility of agreeing with the subordinate issues which would not be recorded on the appraisal form.

Randell, G. A., Packard, P. M. A., Shaw, R. L. and Slater, A. J. (1972) *Staff Appraisal*, London: Institute of Personnel Management

Taylor, D. S. (1976) *Performance Reviews*, London: Institute of Personnel Management

Mumford, A. (1980) *Making Experience Pay*, London: McGraw Hill, chapter 3

Adams, R. (1973) 'Performance Appraisal and Counselling' in Torrington, D. P. and Sutton, D. F. (eds) *Handbook of Management Development*, Aldershot: Gower, pp. 219–60

See also: Management audit; Self appraisal; Instrumented feedback; Logging critical incidents; Self criticism

PERSONAL CASE HISTORY

Personal Case Histories are a method of management training in which course members' own contributions, either in the form of actual experience, mental maps or models, are regularly used. They consist of reports on the management activities of participants who are willing to discuss and analyse their cases with teachers and other course members. These reports may concern the situation of the specific organisational unit for which the participant is responsible or the situation in the organisation to which he belongs. The subject of the case history may cover a short or long time period. As a training method the PCH aims to transfer specialised knowledge and to help managers develop special skills. A PCH teaching session may last three or four days. It begins with a statement of objectives by the tutor who explains that the focus of study will be on real situations occurring within companies. Participants work in groups with each one preparing an analysis and diagnosis of situations described in order to suggest possible action. Personal Case Histories are offered and the most suitable selected. The 'owners' of these form work groups. The next stage is the historical analysis which consists of a step-by-step case reconstruction. The most significant events are analysed. Following this, groups are required to make a diagnosis of the present condition of the system being studied, and finally to make a set of suggestions for that system and any improvements. A major feature of this approach is the stress on the application of the methodological patterns and conceptual frames of reference previously dealt with by the students. The PCH, like the case method, develops skills in the analysis of complex situations and events in organisations, but offers a real case derived from the members' own experience instead of a situation especially built for the analysis of an organisational problem.

Quaglino, G. P. and Testa, G. (1979) 'The Use of Personal Case Histories as a Tool of Management Education' in *Management Education and Development*, vol. 10, no. 2, pp. 112–23

See also: Case study method; Critical incident analysis; Active case study; Case history

PERSONAL DEVELOPMENT LABORATORY

The content of the learning is aimed at providing individuals with an opportunity to become more aware of their own behaviour. The focus is primarily personal with the self being the focus of attention. The laboratory design permits an exploration and diagnosis of behaviour via feedback from others. The purpose is for each individual to understand more fully what he or she is doing, how they are doing it and thereby encourage options for behaviour change. Exercises in which the individual can engage, either alone or with others, are often used in Personal Development Laboratories in order to facilitate learning. Training experiences of this kind are usually designed for 'strangers', i.e. people who do not normally have relationships with each other outside of the laboratory setting.

Mill, C. R. (1976) 'Recent Developments in Experiential Group Methods: the USA' in Cooper, C. L. *Developing Social Skills in Managers: Advances in Group Training*, London: Macmillan

Wilson, J. E., Mullen, D. P. and Morton, R. B. (1968) 'Sensitivity Training for Individual Growth' in *Training Development Journal*, vol. 22, pp. 47–54

See also: Laboratory method; Human relations laboratory; Sensitivity (T) group training; Micro-lab; Mini-society; Group dynamics laboratory; Organisational laboratory; Power laboratory; Team laboratory; Tavistock conference method

PERSONALISED REFLECTION (Reflective Recall)

The oldest discussion on reflection appears in Dewey's book *How We Think* and is considered by many to be the best. Dewey defined reflective thought as the 'active, persistent and careful consideration of any belief or supplied form of knowledge in the light of the grounds that support it and the further conclusions to which it tends'. This type of reflection offers a managerial learning opportunity on the job. It is carried out by the manager individually and involves the application of Kolb and Fry's Learning Cycle. The circular learning pattern begins with having some Concrete Experience such as interviewing a job applicant. One then tries to Observe what happens and Reflect upon it. For example you may notice that all the questions you asked the job applicant were answered by a 'yes' or 'no', whereas the questions of a colleague launched the interviewee into a long reply which revealed a lot of things about him.

From this you then develop some Abstract Concepts and Generalisations; that, for example, your colleague asks 'better' questions which require the applicant to think divergently and which are straightforward and structured. Having done this, you test the implications by thinking up some similar high quality questions yourself and testing your ideas in the next Concrete Experience you have of selection interviewing. The method requires the manager to discipline himself to reflect on his actions so that unsuccessful outcomes do not continue to be repeated.

Kolb, D. A. and Fry, R. (1975) 'Towards An Applied Theory of Experiential Learning' in Cooper, C. L. (ed.)) *Theories of Group Process*, Chichester: John Wiley and Sons

Dewey, J. (1909) *How We Think*, Boston: Heath

Bayes, E. E. (1960) *Democratic Educational Theory*, New York: Harper and Row, chapter 12

Bayes, E. E. (1950) *Theory and Practice of Teaching*, New York: Harper and Row

Burton, W. H., Kimball, R. B. and Wing, R. L. (1960) *Education for Effective Thinking*, New York: Appleton-Century-Crofts

Hunt, M. P. and Metcalf, L. E. (1968) *Teaching High School Social Studies*, New York: Harper and Row, 2nd edition, chapters 3 and 8

See also: Process analysis; Reflective learning

PERSONALISED SYSTEM OF INSTRUCTION (Keller Plan, Self-paced Study)

Personalised System of Instruction (PSI) is a self-paced form of guided study. The work is broken down into specially prepared modules or assignments based on existing published materials. The tutor devises a variety of tests to assess 'mastery' of the subject (which means attaining 80 per cent plus on a test). Such tests are taken by the student as and when he feels ready for them. They are marked immediately by the tutor in the presence of the student. A specific example of PSI is the Keller Plan, a type of independent learning originally developed by F. S. Keller, at Columbia University. Students work largely on their own and at their own pace, from written materials, each unit representing about a week's work. The aims of each unit are set out as clearly as possible, together with suggested ways of achieving them. Students may, for example, be advised to read specified pages of a textbook, together with specially prepared discussion notes and then to work on certain practice questions. They are encouraged to cooperate and help each other with problems. When a student feels he has mastered a given unit, he presents himself for a short test which he must pass before he is permitted to go on to the next unit. After the test (which carries no penalties for failure other than the need to resit) the student discusses with the tutor any problems that have arisen either in working through the unit or tackling the test itself. Keller Plan in the United Kingdom is characteristically different from the American version because of the way in which education works. PSI is defined more strictly in the US and must contain five separate elements before it can be called a PSI course. The British are more flexible with the only required criterion being that the course should be self-paced. The Americans insist on the use of student proctors. The Keller Plan is an individualised, self-paced, mastery-oriented instructional design. Printed study guides are used as the primary teaching devices although a few lectures may be given by the instructor. A student entering a Keller course finds the course work divided into closely defined topics or units. In a simple design, the content of a unit may correspond to a chapter in a textbook. Study guides are used to introduce the unit, suggest study procedures and list study questions. The student must demonstrate mastery of the first unit by achieving a 'mastery level' of performance on a short examination. The actual percentage score is set by the teacher and tends to be high. The student requests the exam when he/she feels prepared. Each unit must be passed before moving on to subsequent units. The emphasis is on achieving competence rather than studying for a certain amount of time such as a term. The instructor's role is to select and organise materials used in the course, write study guides and construct examinations. A few optional lectures or demonstrations may be given during the course, but typically the lectures are not compulsory and examinations are not based on them. Undergraduate tutors (often advanced students in the field) who have already done well in the course may grade tests and offer support and encouragement.

Boud, D. J., Bridge, W. A. and Willoughby, L. (1975) 'PSI Now – A Review of Problems and Progress' in *British Journal of Educational Technology*, vol. 6, no. 2, pp. 15–34

Keller, F. S. and Sherman, J. G. (1974) *Keller Plan Handbook*, Menlo Park, California: W. A. Benjamin

Sherman, J. G. (eds) (1974) *PSI – Forty One Germinal Papers: A Selection of Readings on the Keller Plan*, Menlo Park, California;

W. A. Benjamin

Keller, F. S. (1968) 'Goodbye, Teacher ...' in *Journal of Applied Behavioural Analysis*, vol. 1, no. 1

Programmed Learning and Educational Technology, vol. 13, no. 1, 1976. Special issue on Individualisation of Learning in Higher Education

MacKenzie, M. K. (1979) *Deciding to Individualise Learning: A Study of the Process*, London: Council for Educational Technology

Daley, D. and Robertson, S. (1978) *Keller Plan in the Classroom*, Glasgow: Scottish Council for Educational Technology

See also: Programmed learning; Audio tutorial method; Autonomous learning group; Proctor method; Tutorial-tape-document learning package approach; Self-instructional modules and interactive groups; Guided group problem solving

PHILLIPS 66 TECHNIQUE

Developed by J. Donald Phillips, the 'Phillips 66' technique can be used with groups of 10–20 or large groups of several hundred. In this system the large group is asked to form into smaller groups of six persons with as little movement of chairs as possible. In a lecture hall with fixed seating, a group of three will turn to face the three people in the row above them. Each such group is then encouraged to take a minute or two to get acquainted and select a chairman or secretary. At the end of the getting acquainted and organisation period, a clear and concise statement of a problem or issue is given and should be so worded as to encourage specific single-statement answers. A time limit of six minutes for discussion is then started. The chairman of each group attempts to get the viewpoint of each member of his group and they try to come to an agreement as to the best answer. When each person in the group has expressed his opinion which has been recorded by the secretary, the group selects the best one or two answers for group report. At the end of the six minutes, the tutor reconvenes the class and calls for reports from the secretaries of the groups if there are ten or fewer groups. The Phillips 66 Technique is designed to obtain a quick mass of ideas, suggestions, attitudes or recommendations. It may serve as an interest provoking starter when opening a meeting but is not intended to be a meeting in its own right. It is used to supplement other group discussion methods. The nature of the questions asked of the groups is crucial in this form of exercise.

Andrews, J. D. W. (1980) 'The Verbal Structure of Teacher Questions: Its Impact on Class Discussion' in *Professional and Organizational Development Quarterly*, vol. 2, nos. 3 and 4, pp. 129–63

See also: Buzz group; Group discussion

PLANNED DELEGATION

This is one of the most immediate forms of training and development a manager can give his staff. A log of daily activity is kept. It is reviewed and a list prepared of those activities that can be delegated. A delegation timetable is made up with dates against each responsibility it is intended to delegate. For example, who can be sent in the place of the boss to meetings, outplant exercises etc? A review of staff performance on delegated assignments is carried out as soon as possible after their completion. Planned Delegation involves the provision of a task which stretches a man or woman beyond their previous capacity and gives them an opportunity to learn and practise new skills. The manager who is delegating must think about providing a subordinate with the skills and knowledge required for his new responsibility. By doing this he ensures that the subordinate will benefit from the exercise of responsibility himself. Temporary delegation opportunities occur when the manager concerned is absent or on a course, but they are rarely used as staff development opportunities. Delegation can be seen as a stage of training after coaching and may require a return to the techniques involved in coaching, especially the skills of listening and observing.

Mumford, A. (1980) *Making Experience Pay*, London: McGraw Hill

Forrest, A. (1971) *Delegation*, London: Industrial Society

Mumford, A. (1971) *The Manager and Training*, London: Pitman Publishing

Holroyde, G. (1970) *How to Delegate: A Practical Guide*, Rugby: Mantec Publications

See also: Acting assignment; Coaching/counselling; Sick leave/holiday replacement assignment; Job enrichment; Expanding job assignment

POST-COURSE FOLLOW-UP

When a subordinate returns from a course, the superior asks him to submit a report outlining what benefits he believes he obtained from the course and what plans he has for applying his learning to improve his performance on the job. To do this successfully, the boss must ensure that he knows about the course material, that it is relevant and that he is in sympathy with it. Following the presentation of the report by the subordinate, both meet to establish an action plan for implementation of the ideas that have been agreed as feasible. The superior then monitors performance in the usual way. This technique can be effective in improving performance. It relates theory to action in terms of an agreed plan of action and demonstrates to the subordinate that his superior is interested and involved in his development.

O'Neill, H. and Loew, H. (1975) 'The Anatomy of a Problem: Follow Up Training in Analytical Trouble Shooting' in *Industrial and Commercial Training*, February, vol. 7, no. 1, pp. 27–31

Farnsworth, T. (1968) 'After the Course is Over – Dynamism or Despair?' in *Personnel and Training Management*, February, pp. 26–8

Weiss, E., Huczynski, A. and Lewis, J. (1980) 'The Superior's Role in Learning Transfer' in *Journal of European Industrial Training*, vol. 4, no. 4, pp. 17–20

See also; Application discussion group; Training transfer training; Interaction management

POWER LABORATORY
This is a design for learning based on a theory of power dynamics developed by Oshry. Upon arrival at the course participants are divided into two groups labelled 'Haves' and 'Have nots'. Each group contains powerful 'Ins' and other powerful members. All the group resources, including food, shelter, clothing, transportation and access to communications, are unevenly distributed, grossly in favour of the Haves. Moreover, the Haves are not allowed to give up their power. In a five-day programme, about half the time is devoted to processing the dynamics which come into play under these circumstances. Participants report significant changes in their feelings of potency and ability to cope with the influence of forces in their lives.

Oshry, B. (1972) 'Power and the Power Lab' in Burke, W. W. (ed.) *Contemporary Organizational Development: Conceptual Orientations and Interventions*, Washington, D. C.: NTL Institute, pp. 242–54

See also: Laboratory method; Mini-society; Micro-lab; Tavistock conference method; Group dynamics laboratory; Human relations laboratory; Organisational laboratory; Personal development laboratory; Team laboratory

PRE-COURSE LEARNING

The term Pre-course Learning is used to refer to a set of activities which a tutor may require or request an intending student to engage in before the course or programme *officially* begins. Since such activities are designed to aid student learning, they can be considered as an aspect of the learning methods employed. In most cases, such material is sent to the student in the post, and he is expected to consider it either at work or at home. Its primary purpose is to stimulate the student's thinking prior to the course. Such material can come in one of several forms.

Perhaps the most popular and well known form of Pre-course Learning material is the set of *Course Objectives*. These define what the course is trying to achieve. While they can focus the student's mind, they contain disadvantages. Objectives can, for example, be ambiguous and fail to communicate the teacher's intentions. There may be more than one path through a body of knowledge, and lists of 'what the student should be able to do' at the conclusion of the course, may not reflect the structure of the knowledge being presented. Learners may react against Objectives, either in terms of the formal language in which they are frequently couched, or else because the Objectives are the 'teacher's' and are not necessarily shared by the students. In order to overcome some of these problems, a number of alternative Pre-course Learning techniques have been developed.

Amongst these is the *Pre-Test* which is a set of related questions which are given to learners before any formal teaching or instruction takes place. The items included in the test may be related to an intended post-test. Learners are asked either to answer the questions or only to study them. The purpose of the questions is to focus the attention of students on key concepts and material, or to serve as a model of what will ultimately be accomplished. Pre-tests have also been found to teach. They increase the learner's sensitivity to the learning situation, alert learners to the issues, problems and events to follow and help in evaluating the learning task in terms of its apparent relevancy and meaning. Pre-test questions have an alerting and orienting function both towards the character and content of the teaching that is to follow. A second alternative to Objectives is the *Overview*. This is a short summary of what is to be accomplished. In general, Overviews use a continuous prose (unlike Objectives or Pre-tests) and their purpose is to introduce learners to new material by familiarising them with the central arguments being presented. Overviews may be used to emphasise key points, introduce technical terms or prepare students for the general structure of the material to be covered. They are useful in establishing a mental set in the student and acting as introductions to the teaching that is to follow. Unlike Pre-tests which serve to alert learners, Overviews seek to prepare them for the learning ahead. They are written in the same style as the material which is to follow, and at the same level of detail and inclusiveness. The best Overviews are those which emphasise the salient points, and select and condense the material.

Finally there are the *Advance Organisers*. While Pre-tests alert learners, and Overviews prepare them, Advance Organisers clarify the learning task ahead. While the other pre-instruction categories described are content oriented, Advance Organisers are process oriented. They are frequently pitched at a higher level of abstraction, generality and inclusiveness which provides a broad framework rather than a limited, narrow and highly specific outline. The expository Advance Organisers are used when the new material is likely to be completely unfamiliar. It provides a framework or foundation for this new material, and includes knowledge already possessed by learners. Comparative Advance Organisers by contrast, are used when the material is not new and thus the emphasis is on the way in which the new material is both similar to and different from that already known.

Davies, I. K. (1976) *Objectives in Curriculum Design*, London: McGraw-Hill, chapter 10

Hartley, J. and Davies, I. K. (1976) 'Introducing new materials: the role of pre-tests, behavioural objectives, overviews and advance organisers as pre-instructional strategies' in *Review of Educational Research*, vol. 46, no. 2.

McDonald-Ross, M. (1973) 'Behavioural Objectives – a critical review' in *Instructional Science*, vol. 2, no. 1, pp. 1–52

Hartley, J. (1973) 'The Effect of Pre-Testing on Post-Test Performance' in *Instructional Science*, vol. 2, no. 4, pp. 193–213.

Ausubel, D. P. (1965) *Educational Psychology: A Cognitive View*, New York: Holt, Rinehart and Winston

See also: Text

PROBLEM PACK (P4)
This is a generic term for problem-solving exercises which are presented on packs of cards with the students/trainees working through them on an individual basis. They are given a problem and are asked how they are going to solve it. This is a sophisticated development of a branching form of programmed text. It is used with a well defined problem situation. It can be used for technical problems and has been applied in the training of doctors in diagnosis, e.g. in what tests to apply. These students are given the results of the tests which they requested and they then go on to make more decisions. Problem Packs can also be used for assessment purposes. Students are given a pack and are scored on whether they get through it with the minimum number of decisions.

See also: Action maze; Programmed simulation; Programmed learning; Work cards

PROBLEM-CENTRED GROUP
The purpose of a Problem-centred Group is to encourage students to think analytically or creatively. They can do this by focusing on a given problem supplied by the teacher and in solving it they may need to evaluate information or else apply some previously agreed criteria to its solution. Operationally, a PCG consists of about six students and it can be used either during a lecture session by the simple expedient of joining up two Buzz Groups, or during a small group discussion session. Whenever it is used, the problem focus of the group discussion provides the tutor with information on how well students are able to apply the material that has been presented in the lectures or prescribed reading. As they work on the task, the teacher is available to answer points of clarification. Bligh has suggested five different types of problem that can be set for a PCG:

1 Selection and organisation of the literature – to teach facts, how to find out, how to use available subject literature. Groups may go to the library to look for sources or 100 books may be brought into the classroom. The set problems can be answered by using these references.
2 Problems that have a correct solution, e.g. identifying the cause of some phenomenon. The aim here is to consolidate knowledge of general principles; to teach their application by students; and to assist learners to relate facts to principles.
3 Problems – with a number of possible solutions – to encourage students to be aware of, and understand different viewpoints.

217

4 Problems requiring judgement – e.g. they may be asked to evaluate a theory.

5 Revision and preparation for examination.

Bligh, D. A. (1972) *What's the Use of Lectures?*, Harmondsworth: Penguin Books, p. 192

Miles, M. B. (1959) *Learning to Work in Groups*, Bureau of Publications, Teachers College, Columbia University, New York

See also: Problem pack; Problem-solving group; Problem-solving cycle; Conference method; Literature search; Skills session

PROBLEM-SOLVING CYCLE

A Problem-solving Cycle involves participants forming into groups of four or five. A facilitator then takes the groups through a set of stages as a way of examining, for example, a critical incident that highlights some behavioural problem in a company. Each of the following stages is given a time allocation: (*a*) clarify the symptoms and distinguish between these and the underlying causes; (*b*) discriminate all possible causes; (*c*) isolate relevant causes; (*d*) generate a wide range of alternative solutions without pausing to evaluate any of them (Brainstorming); (*e*) evaluate and test the solutions and select the most viable. If the groups have all been working on the same problem, gather them together into a plenary group and collate the task group solutions.

Ackoff, R. L. (1980) *The Art of Problem Solving*, Chichester: John Wiley and Sons

Koberg, D. and Bagnall, J. (1976) *The Universal Traveller: A Soft System Guide to Creativity, Problem Solving and the Problem of Reaching Goals*, Los Altos, California: Wm. Kaufmann Inc.

Heron, J. (1973) *Experiential Training Techniques*, Department of Adult Education, University of Surrey, Guildford

Zoll, A. A. (1974) *Explorations in Managing*, Reading, Mass.: Addison-Wesley, Chapter 14

Kaufman, R. (1979) *Identifying and Solving Problems: A Systems Approach*, University Associates of Europe, 2nd edition

See also: Critical incident analysis; Brainstorming; Kepner–Tregoe approach; Problem pack; Problem-solving group

PROBLEM-SOLVING GROUP

A problem is any situation that presents a difficulty facing the trainee. It may be a decision to be made, a thought provoking question to be answered, a choice of different ways of performing an act to be made, a conclusion or inference to be drawn, an analysis to be made, a solution to be found or a relativity to be determined. If a situation can be successfully met without reflective thought, e.g. by the use of an algorithm, then no problem is presented. In the teaching/learning situation, problems may be planned, that is presented by the teacher, or they may originate from work. The application of the Problem-solving Method is not a unique technique. All instructional procedures should be orientated towards problem solutions. Problems can also be formulated so that the trainee applies the conceptual steps of the scientific method. These include: (*a*) observing a chosen phenomenon; (*b*) accumulating facts; (*c*) noting any patterns arising from these; (*d*) finding a plausible explanation of the pattern with the facts, i.e. hypothesis construction; (*e*) making new predictions on the basis of explanations; (*f*) checking predictions with experimentation.

Staff can be guided to identify the key issues in a problem and helped to generate alternative solutions; this is as important as selecting a particular alternative. Sometimes, the generation of alternative actions can uncover a huge number of choices. With the tutor's help, the students can be helped to discriminate between alternatives and will exclude those which are unsuitable. In choosing between alternatives, three bases of selection can be used; experience, experimentation and research and analysis. The experience view emphasises that one's mistakes and successes provide an infallible guide to the future. The problem is that it is rare for us to recognise the underlying reasons for our mistakes. The lessons of our experience may be unsuited to new problems. Experience, if analysed and not blindly followed, can aid problem solving. Experimental problem solving involves trying out to see what happens, but may be expensive in terms of time and money. Research and analysis is most effective. Data is gathered and analysed in the light of the problem identified. The problem is broken down into its components and the various tangible and intangible factors are studied. The approach involves a search for the factor that may limit or set parameters. Research and analysis is cheaper than experimentation and can be applied in a training context. The tutor may present the subject matter in a non-problematic but informative way to a group of students or trainees. He may give the facts and show the way, or he may choose to present the topic as a definite problem, difficulty or question in order to provoke thought on the part of the group. This may foster either a partial or complete solution on the part of the trainees themselves. The approach can also be used as an individual development technique when the manager throws his subordinate an immediate or long-term issue and asks him to prepare a solution. Problem presentation may be through talking or more deliberately by asking for comments in writing. The intention is to help the manager solve the problem, encourage the subordinate to think on a wider plane and test the quality of such thinking.

Gillespie, R. J. (1972) *Developing Creative Problem Solving Talent*, London: InComTec

Jackson, K. F. (1975) *The Art of Solving Problems,*. London: Heinemann

Rickards, T. (1975) *Problem Solving Through Creativity Analysis*, Aldershot: Gower

Tarr, G. (1973) *The Management of Problem Solving*, London: Macmillan

Tuma, D. T. and Reif, F. (1980) *Problem Solving and Education: Issues in Teaching and Research*, New Jersey: Lawrence Erlbaum Associates

See also: Problem-centred group; Problem pack; Problem-solving cycle

PROCESS ANALYSIS (Behaviour Analysis)
This involves taking any content-focused activity such as a lecture, discussion, business game or staff meeting and allocating time to consider *how* problems are being solved and roles allocated. During this period the group discusses the suitability of the method they have for resolving differences of view, whether individuals are dominating the conversation, whether the meeting is being well handled etc. The purpose is to help the group overcome the limitations of exclusive task orientation. It aims to help them to cultivate process awareness and process skills. By discussing ways in which group members react to one another, members can gain an increased insight into their own behaviour and that of others. It can also help them to relate more effectively to others. Process Analysis can be applied to the lecture situation as well as small group work, as when the teacher reviews the structure and approach of the lecture.

Schein, E. (1969) *Process Consultation: Its Role in Organizational Development*, Reading, Mass.: Addison-Wesley

Rackham, N., Honey, P. and Colbert, M. (1970) *Developing Interactive Skills*, Northampton: Wellens Publishing Company

Rackham, N. and Morgan, T. (1977) *Behaviour Analysis in Training*, London: McGraw-Hill

Mumford, A. (1976) 'Management Development and the Powers of Observation' in *Personnel Management*, vol. 8, no. 10, pp. 26–9

See also: Controlled pace negotiation; Coverdale training; Interactive skills training

PROCTOR METHOD

The Proctor is an essential element in the Keller plan (Personalised System of Instruction). In the context of peer teaching by students, the student Proctor has the skills and necessary knowledge to help a student complete a specified unit of work. Proctors work individually with students and thus differ in role from the student teacher in the Tutorium. The Proctor Method is capable of application outside the Keller Plan system. It involves helping the students to master course material that has been specified by the teacher. The Proctor administers tests to the students who have worked on individual units and he gives constructive feedback on results. The Proctor works in association with the course lecturer. In helping each student perform well, the Proctor provides the lecturer with feedback on his performance, progress of students and aspects of the course which are presenting difficulties. Proctors practise and rehearse skills learnt in studying in the past and help to overcome the problem of impersonality while helping all students to gain subject mastery.

Born, D. G. (1971) *Instructor Manual for the Development of a Personalised Instruction Course*, University of Utah: Centre to Improvement Learning and Instruction

See also: Tutorium; Peer teaching; Personalised system of instruction; Teaching as learning

PROGRAMMED LEARNING (Automated Teaching, Individualised Programme Instruction)

Programmed Learning is a self-teaching approach which has been used in the learning of facts, techniques, principles and ideas. The approach is based on B. F. Skinner's behaviourist theories. It has tended to be used in the acquisition of knowledge, i.e. cognitive learning. In this method the trainee is (*a*) active and doing what he is to learn; (*b*) successful, e.g. making the minimum number of errors; (*c*) informed at all times of the adequacy of his actions, i.e. he receives immediate knowledge of results, and, (*d*) self-pacing, i.e. progressing at his own speed. This enables the learner to control his own learning process to a certain degree. He chooses the programme that corresponds most closely to his needs and interests, decides on the time and duration of his studies, chooses between the different 'branches' of a programme, evaluates his own learning process and takes advantage of work groups or the help of advisers. The designation of the learning steps in the programme is in the control of the programme designer. It is this person who defines the learning goals and puts them into operation; divides the learning into single steps, each of which follows the pattern of present material – learner reacts – direct feedback. Thus the source of control is the programme writer.

Two kinds of programme exist. There is the linear programme, in which each student works through the same material in a set sequence, and the branching programme, which has a common path for quick learners and 'branch lines' of remedial material for the less able trainees. A third method called Mathetics attempts to reduce the study time by careful analysis of the learning situation. Some writers argue that PL is well suited to imparting factual information on subjects which have clearly recognised procedures and 'correct' answers, but that it is difficult to write programmes in areas where the subject matter is not, or perhaps cannot be, clearly defined. Other experts regret that PL has tended to be used primarily for the achievement of lower order cognitive objectives. Commercially produced materials can be purchased to teach basic facts and formulae. It has been argued that such programmes are boring and uninspiring and have led to the fallacious belief that PL can only be used in this way. In fact successful programmes have been written for medical diagnosis, art and poetry appreciation and good listening. The full potential of PL has not yet been achieved and it is capable of realising middle order cognitive and affective objectives, especially when integrated with flexible approaches such as Computer Assisted Learning (CAL).

It should be stressed that the major PL materials are presented in printed form (usually a book) for the learner to read. The reading is active in that the learner has to answer questions, do tasks or make other responses to the material at frequent intervals. The immediate feedback on performance is claimed to guarantee subject mastery. The programmed material can be presented in a number of ways: by texts, teaching machines or increasingly by computer or micro-computer. One can even produce a Programmed Learning pack which is multi-media, involving a range of stimuli. Irrespective of how it is presented, the key aspect of Programmed Learning is the programme itself, i.e. *the sequencing and organisation of the units of information and instruction leading to the required terminal behaviour or performance*. Comparative research suggests that human teachers are seldom more effective than programmed materials and frequently no difference in effectiveness is found. PL takes less training or learning time. In training, PL can be made available to large numbers of trainees at a low cost; can be sent to geographically dispersed trainees; has standardised procedures; gives all trainees the same method of instruction and provides immediate training for an irregular intake.

Markle, S. (1969) *Good Frames and Bad*, Chichester: John Wiley and Sons

Neale, M. H., Toye, M. and Belbiner, C. (1968) 'Adult Training: the use of programmed instruction' in *Occupational Psychology*, vol. 42, no. 1, pp. 23–31

Hudson, H. (1976) 'The Resurgence of Programmed Instruction' in *BACIE Journal*, June

Dodd, B. (1967) *Programmed Instruction for Industrial Training*, London: Heinemann

Shirley-Smith, K. (1973) *Guide to Programmed Techniques in Industrial Training*, Aldershot: Gower

See also: Computer-assisted learning; Tutorial-tape-document learning package approach; Programmed simulation; Mathetics

PROGRAMMED SIMULATION

A Programmed Simulation, as the name suggests, is a combination of programmed learning and simulation. It is devised for initial individual work which is then followed by group discussion. This form of simulation frequently focuses on decision making. Each member of the class is given a booklet containing a number of individual 'mini-cases', each of which requires a decision. Usually a number of possible options are offered from which a choice is to be made. The class breaks up into groups of about four. In each stage of the case study, the individual first makes his own decision and then goes on to agree a group decision with the other members. From the booklet the participants receive information regarding the suitability/appropriateness of their decision choice. Each case consists of seven or eight stages or episodes, each of which requires an individual and a group choice. Unlike the Action Maze, the choice made does not affect the outcome of a future stage.

Elgood, C. (1980) 'The Use of Business Games in Management Training' in *The Training Officer*, vol. 16, no. 12, pp. 332–4

See also: Action maze; Programmed learning; Simulation; In-basket exercise

PROJECT METHOD

A Project is the term used to describe an integrated programme of work built around a central situation or idea. Projects involve the solution of a problem often, though not necessarily, set by the student himself. They involve initiative taking by the student and necessarily involve him in a variety of educational activities which result in an end product, e.g. report, design, computer programme. The work can cover a considerable length of time (one day to two years) and teaching staff are involved in an advisory rather than a didactic role, at any or all of the stages. A central characteristic of the Project is that students are responsible for taking the decisions which affect them. Project Methods make learning active. They provide a vehicle for combining knowledge from different disciplines and permit and encourage inventiveness and originality. Group projects may involve students from the same course or from different courses. The project allows a learner to look more deeply into a subject field and offers a flexibility that acknowledges the different speeds at which students work and learn. A project should generate involvement, develop skills for independent study and group work, provide feedback to the student on his performance and on his ability to communicate. However, not all learners flourish in a state of individualised learning and many may need tutor or group support in order to sustain their interest and develop their ideas.

Harding, A. G. (1973) 'The Objectives and Structure of Undergraduate Projects – I' in *British Journal of Educational Technology*, vol. 4, no. 2

Harding, A. G. (1973) 'The Project: Its Place in the Learning Situation' in *British Journal of Educational Technology*, vol. 4, no. 3, pp. 216–32

Adelie, K. et al. (1976) *The Use of Project Methods in Higher Education*, Guildford, Surrey: Society for Research into Higher Education

Rees, F. M. and Watson, M. J. (1976) 'Project Based Teaching of Market Research Techniques' in *Journal of European Training*, vol. 5, no. 5, pp. 228–33

Abercrombie, M. L. J. (1981) 'Changing Basic Assumptions About Teaching and Learning' in Boud, D. J. (ed.) *Developing Autonomy in Student Learning*, London: Kogan Page Ltd

Casey, D. (1978); 'Project Training for Managers' in *Journal of European Industrial Training*, vol. 2, no. 5, pp. 3–6

Garrett, R. (1971) 'Project Based Education and Development' in *Management Education and Development*, vol. 2, no. 1, pp. 40–49

Goodlad, S. (ed.) (1975) *The Use of Project Methods in Higher Education*, Guildford, Surrey: Society for Research into Higher Education

See also: Project orientation; Industrial project; Overseas project; Field project-attachment; Project-based management development; Real life project

PROJECT ORIENTATION (Action Project)

This is to be distinguished from the Project Method which may form the teaching approach for a part or whole of a degree or diploma course. Project Orientation, in the way it has been used in countries such as Denmark, Holland and West Germany, refers to an approach which focuses on the solution of real life problems as the basis of the entire programme. At the Roskilda University Centre in Denmark, the two-year basic course is organised completely around a project or problem-centred approach. The central concept is that the subject studied and the skills acquired by any student are determined almost entirely by the demands of a real interdisciplinary problem – 'the project'. No formally prescribed, or even advised, syllabus exists. The studies are anchored in problems and the activities thrown up by the project. The curriculum thus created relates strongly to students' own interests and motivations. Formal lecture courses are almost non-existent, although 'teacher-guided' courses are provided in reponse to requirements expressed by students and arising from project work. The learning approach fits into this and reflects a form of democratic institutional organisation which does not exist in UK colleges or universities. Students work in groups of four to ten on a project. There are no schools or departments, only three interdisciplinary faculties (humanities, natural sciences and social sciences) which are divided into social and study units called 'houses'. Each house provides a work centre for seventy people, seven of whom are teachers. The house is allocated a budget of which half goes directly to the teachers and the remainder is controlled by an overall house finance committee. The choice of projects in each house differs. A whole house can decide on a single project and divide it up. Alternatively, a 'house theme' may be agreed but projects proceed independently while relating to this theme. Another approach is for each group to select a project independently. In Bremen in West Germany, 'house project' ideas were used. A theme can be, for example, the influence of lead pollution or the implications of a nuclear power station development. Projects need to have social and political importance which is a necessary condition for their acceptance.

Cornwall, M. (1974) 'Authority v. Experience in Higher Education – Project Orientation in Some Continental Universities' in *Universities Quarterly*, vol. 29, pp. 272–98

Cornwall, M. G., Schmithals, F. and Jacques, D. (1977) *Project Orientation in Higher Education*, London: Brighton Polytechnic and the University of London Teaching Methods Unit

Brown D. and Goodlad, S. (1975) 'Community based – Related Project Work in Engineering' in Goodlad, S. (ed.) *Education and Social Action*, London: Allen and Unwin

Cornwall, M. G. (1978) 'A New Approach to Higher Education: Project Orientation' in *Journal of Further and Higher Education*, vol. 2, no. 3, pp. 43–57

See also: Project method; Action learning; Overseas project; Real life project; Industrial project; Project-based management development

PROJECT-BASED MANAGEMENT DEVELOPMENT

As a form of in-house, management development activity, Project-based Management Development (PBMD) is located within the same philosophical school as Joint Development Activities and Action Learning. Indeed, it shares many aspects of design and method. Essentially, PBMD is a part-time training activity which involves regular meetings of participant managers (who constitute the project team), and trainers (who act as the staff team). Presentations are made to senior managers (the advisory group). A real company problem is the vehicle for learning and all aspects of the approach are based on this. The participating managers of a company form a project team to make recommendations on the problem to the senior managers. Their ideas are scrutinised by this advisory group of senior staff and the staff team act as resources to the participants, giving them the knowledge and skills which allow them to progress in their project. PBMD aims to ensure that the learning received by participants is relevant to the organisation's needs in terms of the required managerial skills, knowledge and attitudes. The design allows senior managers to take a more direct and active involvement in the development of their staff. They regularly hear about and comment on the progress of participants. The problem of the lone individual attending an external course is thus overcome by teams of company staff working together.

Ashton, D. and Easterby-Smith M. (1979) *Management Development in the Organization*, London: Macmillan, chapter 6

Ashton, D. (1974) 'Project Based Management Development' in *Education and Training*, July–August, pp. 203–5

Ashton, D. (1974) 'Project Based Management Development' in *Personnel Management*, vol. 6, no. 7, pp. 26–8

Ashton, D. (1974) 'The Trainer's Role in Project Based Management Development' in *Journal of European Training*, vol. 3, no. 3, pp. 206–13

See also: Joint development activities; Action learning; Project orientation

PROMPT LIST
A Prompt List consists of a number of questions that are relevant to an issue or problem at hand. Taking any subject that the learner may wish to study, the tutor can specify a number of key questions. For example, on the topic of the organisation of training, questions may include: How is training organised in this company? Who is primarily responsible for it? How are the needs and priorities defined? A question Prompt List can be used in different ways. In a job attachment, the short-term visitor can be helped to do the job. He is left to find the answers to the questions posed. It can help him in discussions and in the establishment of improved relationships with the job holder by demonstrating an informed interest. It can be used as a development aid in that each question is a potential project for an individual. Once a learner's strengths have been identified

in appraisal, it is possible to discuss with him the appropriate questions which link with those strengths.

The Prompt List provides an 'action learning' approach if it takes the individual into another job area. It can assist in decisions about moving people from job to job or adding new areas to existing jobs. It can be used in team-building activities, acting as a starter for any group feedback analysis session. It has also been used as a stimulus for coaching. It uses the 'discovery learning' method since the list sets out the parameters of the job, but does not provide any answers. The trainee has to discover these for himself. Some management training staff have used Prompt Lists as a substitute for lengthy course notes and their course handouts now come in plastic wallets of the type used to hold credit cards.

Barrington, H. and Beanland, D. (1978) 'The Prompt List in Training' in *BACIE Journal*, vol. 32, no. 1, January, pp. 6–7

See also: Work-related exercise; Work cards

PROPOSAL TEAM ASSIGNMENT (Junior Board)

In reviewing current working methods and future approaches, a company may establish a number of Proposal Teams, consisting of middle or junior management (rather than top management). These teams have the remit of reviewing existing operating procedures and policies, and of making recommendations on changes and improvements. Junior membership on these has been favoured since this group is held to have a higher motivation to introduce improvements, whereas senior staff may be more satisfied with existing practices and less critical of them. The team may be composed of staff from different departments within the same organisation and such a working party may be required to study, for example, the application of a computer data system or the introduction of a Flexitime system. A related approach has sometimes been labelled 'Junior Board'. This is a participative technique designed specifically to teach more junior executives to grapple with broad gauge problems extending beyond the confines of a single function. Here a group of managers meet together to consider some problem that may have been submitted to the main board of the company. This Junior Board may be either a permanent group of senior managers, perhaps those at the level just below the main board, or it may consist of quite junior managers who rotate. In both forms the benefits include learning about senior management problems, and thereby extending their knowledge of the company, and considering answers. However, the methods do have a disadvantage. Since the group meeting rarely has the power to act on the proposals themselves or to take responsibility for them, it may consider that it is working on an unreal task. This might be overcome to some extent if the role of the Junior Board were defined as being advisory. The decisions could be presented to the board of directors before it decided on the issue under study.

Lazorko, L. (1972) 'Junior Boards Train Managers' in *International Management*, January, pp. 40–2

Mumford, A. (1971) *The Manager and Training*, London: Pitman Publishing, chapter 8

See also: Development assignment; Committee assignment; Selection board assignment; Staff meeting assignment; Task force assignment

PSYCHODRAMA

In the literature, the term Psychodrama is used in at least two different ways. In one, it is applied as an all-embracing term which includes sociodrama, role playing and other 'active' methods. Its second usage is more specific and closer to the idea of Moreno who developed the technique; that is, a form of psychotherapy in which the patient or subject enacts his conflicts instead of talking about them. Usually it is conducted in a group setting with other group members playing roles in the person's private drama. This process is called 'alter ego-ing'. The therapist or trainer becomes the director. The problem considered is one in which he/she is personally involved.

In the first phase of a Psychodrama which is called *realisation*, the person (or 'actor') begins by acting out the situation from his everyday life. The scenes portrayed may be entirely realistic or consist largely of fantasies. The second phase is the period of *replacement*. Trained staff assume the necessary reciprocal roles in the drama. They may be real persons drawn from the actor's life, or those imagined in his fantasy. The final phase is that of *clarification*, when analysis and feedback takes place. The Psychodrama as developed by Moreno requires a fairly large and well trained staff. Above all it requires a 'director' who has an active role and is expected to act as producer, social analyst and therapist, although assisted by a trained auxiliary staff. Moreno also developed the technique of Soliloquy. Following the completion of the action in a Psychodrama, the participants are asked to re-enact the scene as it happened, but also to act out those feelings they failed to express. These previously unspoken feelings are often delivered in a softer voice – in soliloquy. Psychodrama differs from Monodrama in that the latter is acted by the subject playing the different parts himself. Sociodrama by contrast, considers interactive situations which focus on the collective aspects of a problem, e.g. the hierarchical structure of an organisational department. Also, in Role Playing, the individual can look at ways of dealing with his own specific problem, e.g. getting a job. Psychodrama has been used in a variety of settings from therapy to superficial game-playing exercises.

Moreno, J. L. (1946) *Psychodrama*, New York: Beacon Press

Moreno, J. L. (1953) *Who Shall Survive?*, New York: Beacon Press, 2nd edition

Moreno, J. L. (1946) 'Psychodrama and Group Psychodrama' in *Sociometry*, vol. 9, nos 2 and 3, pp. 249–53

Blatner, H. A. (1973) *Psychodrama, Role Playing and Action Methods*, Beacon House

Smith, P. B. (1980) *Group Processes and Personal Change*, London: Harper and Row

Yablonsky, L. and Enneis, J. (1956) 'Psychodrama, Theory and Practice' in Fromm-Reichmann, F. and Moreno, J. L. (eds) *Progress in Psychotherapy Volume 1*, Arune and Stratten Inc.

Yablonsky, L. (1981) *Psychodrama: Resolving Emotional Problems Through Role Playing*, Gardner Press

See also: Monodrama; Sociodrama; Role playing; Role reversal

QUESTIONING

At some point in most learning/teaching events questions are asked. Students may ask for points of clarification, but tutors need to be more versatile in their questioning approaches and recognise their value as learning aids. Andrews (1980) conducted research into the effects of different types of Questioning. Questions can be divided according to their types. Bloom's hierarchy of objectives in the cognitive domain provides one such listing. Questions may be 'low level' requiring only memorisation, comprehension or application, or 'high level' requiring the student to demonstrate analysis, synthesis or evaluation. Teachers defined a 'good discussion' as one in which, as each point was raised, a number of different responses were elicited from students; in which the majority of students were actively involved; and students continued to interact for a time without the need for further tutor contribution. The term 'mileage' was applied to refer to this overall level of student response. Andrews found that the most useful questions called for divergent thinking from students were of the 'high level' type and were straightforward and structured. He went on to produce a question 'species typology' presented in decreasing order of mileage. Three high-mileage and eight low-mileage questions were identified. The former will be emphasised here. The Playground Question ('Let's see if it is possible to make any generalisations about the problem described in this case study') was found to have the highest mileage. The tutor delineated a specific intellectual sphere and students were given wide latitude in the way in which they approached the question. In Andrews' terms, this was an invitation for the student to explore and allowed him to choose the theme, concept or category he wanted to use in responding to it. Other Playground Question openings included: 'How do you interpret. ...?', 'What can you draw from. ...?' and 'What are the possible meanings of ...?' The Brainstorm Question ('Suggest as many different ways as possible of how the manager in this case could get himself out of his current predicament') was second highest on mileage. Like the creativity-encouraging technique of Brainstorming, the teacher seeks a wide range of ideas and suggestions to his specific problem or question. In this type of question the subject matter is less tightly focused with all aspects of the case description being within the scope of the question. However, the issue to be addressed ('getting out of the predicament') is specific. The third type of question Andrews discovered was the Focal Question. It was centred on or around an issue which required a decision ('Which is the better choice, to raise equity capital or secure a bank loan?'). A number of alternatives are posed, usually between three and five. Students make a choice and defend it in argument with others. Andrews wrote that when students take a stand on a particular decision and then defend it, this demands from them high order thinking and the marshalling of information which supports their view. He found that when different stands are taken by students on the same issue, each tries to persuade the other and an inter-student debate follows. The Focal Question poses alternatives, yet is still open by virtue of the fact that students select from their own information base to support their choices. These three high-mileage questions were of the structured, divergent type. Others of low mileage were found to be either too mechanical, open, narrow or vague. These were the General Invitation (What did you think about the case?), the Low Level

Divergent Question ('What are the names of some of the other motivation theorists?'), the Analytical Convergent Question ('What was the most important reason that Rolls-Royce went bust?') and the Quiz Show Question ('He developed a five-level hierarchy of human needs. What was his name?'). Andrews also discussed the Single Question, the Multiple Consistent Question, the Shotgun Question and the Funnel Question. These too were all low mileage.

Questioning forms an essential element in all student–teacher and student–student interactions. Some teaching methods, for example, the Case Study Method, Tutorial and Seminar, rely nearly exclusively on Questioning. Training oneself to ask good questions and training one's students to do the same, forms the basis for the successful execution of many teaching and learning methods. Good questions do not come in a flash of inspiration. Questions need to be prepared in advance. Success in using questions involves waiting, asking someone, listening, then reviewing, reinforcing and repeating.

Andrews, J. D. W. (1980) 'The Verbal Structure of Teacher Questions: Its Impact on Class Discussion' in *Professional and Organizational Development Quarterly*, vol. 2, nos. 3 and 4, Fall-Winter, pp. 129–63

Suessmuth, P. (1978) *Ideas for Training Managers and Supervisors*, Mansfield: University Associates of Europe, chapter 18

Hunkins, F. P. (1976) *Involving Students in Questioning*, Boston: Allyn and Bacon

Carin, A. A. and Sund, R. B. (1971) *Developing Questioning Techniques*, Columbus, Ohio: Charles E. Merrill

Sanders, N. M. (1966) *Classroom Questions: What Kind?* New York: Harper and Row

See also: Socratic enquiry; Socratic questioning; Invitation to discover; Interrogation of experts

REACTION PANEL

In a Symposium or Forum Meeting where the number of participants is so large that it would not be practicable to run a question and answer session with the speaker(s) on the stage, a Reaction Panel may provide a suitable alternative. In this format, a group of four to six members come from the audience and sit on the stage and listen to the presentations.

They then give their reactions to what has been said and may question the speakers further, as if on behalf of the large audience.

See also: Interrogation of experts; Audience/reaction watchdog team; Listening team

READING

Despite their forecast demise, books (and journals) continue to be the primary source of information for the majority of students. For many learners independent study in the traditional manner (making intelligent use of libraries, stimulated and assisted by the lecturer's advice) can be one of the most fruitful forms of learning. The mature management student, frequently needs help and advice on what to read, what the relevant priorities are and which books ought to be bought. Students prefer booklists which distinguish core reading from supplementary material. Large, unannotated bibliographies often threaten and confuse students. Many student problems related to reading can be overcome by the lecturer with a little forethought. Apart from producing reading lists that are broken down into categories, e.g. introductory text, advanced reading, the tutor can assist by providing full information about the author, title date and library catalogue number. If the book is to be purchased, he needs to ensure that he has ordered it for the bookshop. The management of books and the ability to skim read are important in this context. One can look for key words and then read in depth when one gets to them. The technique of reading the first sentence in each paragraph, which is usually the topic sentence, is useful in providing a resumé until a passage is reached where there is either an apparant hiatus, which means one needs to read something else in that paragraph or the preceding one, or the topic indicates that one ought to read more closely. The emphasis here is not on speed reading which tends to be stressed in some study courses, but on reading with a purpose. Another facet of reading is the use of novels as the basis of class discussion. While many case studies are characterised by the fact that they are based on real situations, the fictional story provides an alternative stimulus for thought and learning.

Perry, W. (1959) 'Students' Use and Misuse of Reading Skills' in *Harvard Educational Review*, vol. 29. Also included in Gibbs, G. (1977) *Learning to Study: A Guide to Running Group Sessions*, Open University

Mann, P. (1973) *Books and Students*, National Book League

Forster, G. C. F. (1968) 'Books in University Teaching' in Layton, D. (ed.) *University Teaching in Transition*, Edinburgh: Oliver and Boyd

Guillet de Monthoux, P. (1979/80) 'A "Novel" Approach to Management' in *Journal of General Management*, vol. 5, no. 2, pp. 42–52

Egger, R. (1959) 'The Administrative Novel' in *American Political Science Review*, vol. LIII

Kroll, M. (1965) 'Administrative Fiction and Credibility' in *Public Administration Review*, vol. 25

See also: Reading party; Book reviewing; Literature search; Guided reading; Re-writing; Historical analysis

READING PARTY

Reading Parties involve a tutor or group of tutors spending a number of days at a 'retreat' with their students. The focus of the activity may be some problem or topic, and it is expected that before arriving the participants will have done preparatory work in the form of specified reading or else would have prepared papers for discussion. It is not usually expected that the participants will necessarily have done the same reading and indeed the unique contributions of members in terms of their ideas and knowledge plays an important part in the event as a whole. Reading Parties offer participants the opportunity to discuss in depth, over a concentrated period of time, a topic that is relevant to all of them. The party may consist of a lecturer and students discussing Marxist writings, or the staff of a management department coming together to discuss future policy.

See also; Book reviewing; Literature search; Guided reading; Re-writing

REAL LIFE PROJECT

In the context of management and business studies, a more accurate title for this approach might be Real Life Entrepreneurial Project. The method can however be applied to the education and training of students in planning, law and other subjects. The key element is that student activity parallels as exactly as possible, the real life situation. It is perhaps easiest to illustrate this first by the example of a business management project of this type. Students work in groups on this type of project rather than individually. They may be asked to develop, produce and market some service or product with the intention of making a profit on it. The project parallels the development of a small business in which those taking part have a financial stake. In this sense the project is a real one in the way that a business game is not. The scale of the project is less important than the fact that students should have the opportunity to take part in the various stages that go towards the development of a business. A project may involve, for example, the production of handmade birthday cards. Depending on the level of reality being sought, the local bank manager can be asked to take part and might be interviewed by students seeking a capital loan. Market research surveys in the street may be conducted to test market demand. Students from other disciplines have also been involved in this type of approach. For example, students studying planning at a college go to another area and spend a week negotiating planning permission with real local authority officials. Law students have set up local community law clinics to give free advice to citizens.

A separate approach, but one which can share the same title, involves managers rather than college students and can be considered a form of in-company development activity. The middle managers of a large company which is no longer expanding may, in order to be further developed, be invited to give advice to a newly formed, independent company to help it prepare grant applications to financial institutions, undertake market appraisals and test and refine product prototypes. A similar approach might involve the manager concerned coming up with an idea for a new small business which he might personally help develop and take an equity stake in. This would provide added job satisfaction as well as the development of new skills and expertise. However, as with other forms of development activity, it is necessary for the company concerned to show how this form of manager development is likely to benefit it in addition to helping the small company concerned.

See also: Project method; Project orientation; Field project/attachment; Industrial project; Overseas project; Project-based management development.

RE-EVALUATION COUNSELLING
This is the original and licensed form of what has now become known as Co-counselling. It was developed by Harvey Jackins of Seattle, USA during the 1950s. The Re-evaluation Counselling Communities train and license Re-evaluation Counsellors. The focus of the method is on

autonomy. People are helped to become responsive to their environment and to have the ability to make creative and unique responses to situations as they arise, rather than patterned and stereotyped responses from their past.

Foundations of Co-Counselling Manual, Elementary Counsellor's Manual, Seattle: Rational Island Publishers

Jackins, H. (1965) *The Human Side of Human Beings,* Seattle: Rational Island Publishers

Jackins, H. (1970) *Elementary Counsellor's Manual,* Seattle: Rational Island Publishers

Jackins, H. (1973) *The Human Situation,* Seattle: Rational Island Publishers

See also: Co-counselling; Coaching/counselling

REFLECTIVE LEARNING

While there is a great deal of emphasis on learning from experience, that which actually helps us to learn from our experience, i.e. what it is that helps us discover new and personal meanings, is the process of reflection. Reflection is defined as the process of searching for meaning in our past experience. John Dewey, the philosopher and educationalist, included in his definition of reflection, a consideration of the grounds or bases that support one's beliefs and knowledge. The 'experience' that is being reflected on may be departmental meetings held in a company or experiential exercises run by the lecturer in the classroom. The Reflective Learning method was developed by Philip Boxer and Richard Boot and involves the use of reflective techniques or tools which can assist and support individuals as they think over, and try to learn from, their past. At the macro-level, Reflective Learning methods may refer to any form of such assistance. For example, certain forms of co-counselling can fulfil this need. However, in current writings, the Reflective Learning method has been associated with more formal, and indeed computer-based techniques. One of these, known as NIPPER, can be used with individuals or groups to provide a form of feedback which encourages the process of learning from reflection.

Descriptions of the approach demonstrate how closely it is built around the principles of Kelly's Personal Construct theory. RL offers a content-free structure that can be used to reflect on any kind of subject matter. The use of the Nipper facility, which with the use of a computer asks questions of the individual and feeds back quickly the patterns of reflections, also puts one in mind of certain aspects of Socratic Enquiry. The use of the computer is not an indispensable element of RL, but where it is available it has the potential of providing rapid feedback to participants on the emerging pattern of their reflections. As a facilitative device, RL neither draws conclusions, nor interprets the data fed in. These activities are the responsibility of its user. In applying the method, the user has first to clarify his own thoughts in terms of 'elements' and 'concepts'. This parallels exactly the Repertory Grid technique. An element is a specific example of a chosen subject area, e.g. meetings, decisions made, people worked with. Concepts express the subjective evaluations and feelings which describe how individuals react to the elements. For example, in the case of meetings, concepts may include brevity, decision quality, decision acceptance. The next step is to reflect on the extent to which each concept applies to each of the elements. The user can thus clarify to himself the concepts being used. Once entered into the computer, the computer programme feeds back the pattern of reflections which can be represented on a diagrammatic tree or 'dendrogram'. This can, for example, cluster the different types of meetings into 'families' based on some common theme such as satisfactoriness. One would then reflect on these family clusters to check their meaningfulness. It is also possible to search for further underlying concepts.

Boot, R. L. (1978) 'The Aims and Methods of the Management Learning Project' in *Journal of H.P. General Systems*, vol. 2, no. 2

Boxer, P. J. (1978) 'Developing the Quality of Judgement' in *Personnel Review*, vol. 7, no. 2, pp. 36–9

Boot, R. L. (1979) 'The Management Learning Project' in *Industrial and Commercial Training*, vol. 11, no. 1, pp. 8–11

Boot, R. and Boxer, P. (1980) 'Reflective Learning' in Beck, J. and Cox, C. (eds) *Advances in Management Education*, Chichester: John Wiley and Sons

Boxer, P. (1981) 'Learning as a Subversive Activity' in Boydell, T. and Pedler, M. (eds) *Management Self Development: Concepts and Practices*, Aldershot: Gower

See also: Personalised reflection; Learning conversation; Repertory grid

REPERTORY GRID

The Repertory Grid is based upon Kelly's Theory of Personal Constructs which sees man 'as a scientist' who explores his environment and constructs an 'individual map' of the world. These maps are then used to guide individual behaviour. Reportory Grid technique is the research method which is used to discover what an individual's map consists of. It has been used in clinical settings for over twenty years, and has become popular in management training and development during the last decade.

The rationale for its use in training is that if we can identify a person's 'map' we have more chance of predicting his behaviour and may use training to alter the map, and thereby his behaviour. Construct theory conceives of individual maps as containing elements (which are the objects of thought such as people, words etc.) and constructs which are the qualities we use to describe the elements. Repertory Grid is therefore a method of obtaining the elements and constructs of an individual and then analysing them statistically in an effort to produce a quantifiable, individual 'map'. In management training and development, Repertory Grids have been used for this purpose. Students work in threes and elicit constructs relevant to a particular topic, e.g. productivity bargaining, women in management. These are then used either as a discussion device or as an aid to the group to consider a problem. Grids can thus be used in this interactive way with results fed back to subjects in order to help self-development, team building or general organisational development interventions. Other applications of Repertory Grid include job analysis and career counselling.

Easterby-Smith, M. (1980) 'How to Use Repertory Grids in HRD' in *Journal of European Industrial Training/International Journal of HRD*, Monograph, vol. 4, no. 2, MCB Publications

Beck, J. E. 'Changing a Manager's Construction of Reality' in Beck, J. and Cox, C. (eds) (1980) *Advances in Management Education*, Chichester: John Wiley and Sons

Smith, M. 'Applications and Use of Repertory Grids in Management Education' in Beck, J. and Cox, C. (eds) (1980) *Advances in Management Education*, Chichester: John Wiley and Sons

Honey, P. (1979) 'Repertory Grid in Action' in *Industrial and Commercial Training*, Part 1 in vol. 11, no. 9, pp. 358–69; Part 2 in vol. 11, no. 10, pp. 407–14 and Part 3 in vol. 11, no. 11, pp. 452–9

Easterby-Smith, M. P. V. (1977) 'The Repertory Grid as a Personnel

Tool' in *Management Decision*, vol. 14, no. 5, pp. 239–47

Smith, M. and Ashton, D. (1975) 'Using Repertory Grid to Evaluate Management Training' in *Personnel Review*, vol. 4, no. 4, pp. 15–21

Drake, J. (1980) 'What is Repertory Grid?' in *Leadership and Organizational Development Journal*, vol. 1, no. 1, pp. 33–6

See also; Learning conversation; Personalised reflection; Reflective learning

RESEARCH ASSIGNMENT

A Research Assignment within a company tends to have a different purpose from one carried out as part of a degree or diploma programme in a college or university. The research topic for the person may be specified by senior staff and have an induction purpose (to help the individual learn about a part of a company) or a problem-solving purpose (to get an outsider to look at a departmental problem). A manager may be released for a period of time, e.g. one week, to make a study and present a verbal or written report. Some preparatory training will be necessary in how to plan and carry out research if the manager has had no previous experience of this.

See also: Development assignment; Library assignment; Evaluation assignment; Consulting assignment

RESEARCH DEGREE

The carrying out of research, whether for a project, dissertation or thesis is a form of independent learning which can develop in the student unique skills, knowledge and experience. Research always involves a degree of uncertainty and risk. The researcher never knows if all the necessary information will be available, or what it will show. Research has to be self initiated, self structured and self programmed. The learner has to manage the research process himself. This involves planning, organising, controlling and communicating. He sets out to solve a problem, having to contend with possible failure or uncertain outcome. In planning the research a structure must be imposed on the problem and a solution applied. He needs to develop the ability to set realistic goals, plan a systematic programme of work, establish a personal, structured approach to problem identification and solution, identify and analyse problems with confidence and personal initiative and be self reliant and work independently. The research process develops the analytic and creative abilities. He has to manage efficiently the resources of time and material. The analysis of data encourages the ability to reason in a rational, logical and systematic way. In the written report, the argument has to be presented clearly and precisely. From this decription it is clear that, while research is frequently considered an 'ivory tower' activity by many, it does in fact tend to encourage and develop exactly those skills necessary for successful management.

Buchanan, D. (1980) 'Gaining Management Skills Through Research Work' in *Personnel Management*, vol. 12, no. 4, April, pp. 45–8

Pearson, R. W. (1980) 'Higher Degrees as Management Training' in *Journal of European Industrial Training*, vol. 4, no. 1, pp. 17–21

Knibbs, J. R. (1980) 'Part Time Research Degrees and Management Development in the U.K.' in *Journal of European Industrial Training*, vol. 4, no. 7, pp. vi–viii

See also: Dissertation proposal; Independent study; Paid educational leave

RESIDENTIAL
A Residential is a specified period of time in which the student works intensively with other course members on some specified task. In management education, Residentials are required for part-time diplomas in management studies and some personnel management diploma courses. Residentials tends to be a feature of part-time forms of education. While there may be nothing to prevent the residential time of 2–4 days being devoted to lectures, seminars or other forms of similar study, there has been a tendency to use these periods for more intensive and interactive forms of learning. Thus Residentials frequently consist of a major role-playing exercise, e.g. management–trade union negotiations, or a business game.

Cole, G. A. (1980) 'The Pros and Cons of Residential Weekends' in *The Training Officer*, vol. 16, no. 9, pp. 242–5

See also: Concentrated study; Module; Minicourse; Workshop

RESOURCE CENTRE (Multi-media Study Centre, Learning Resource Centre)

Resource Centres are based on the idea of providing learners with various media which they can use independently to help them in their studies. They frequently include introductory guides to the 'media library' which provide information about materials available and chart out a network of possible learning directions for the learner. Resource Centres consist of a physically distinct geographical area which contains within it books, pamphlets, handouts, tape-slide programmes, book illustrations, films, videos etc. The learner himself decides upon the time and duration of learning, as well as what information he will make use of according to his interests and needs. Since the learner has so much choice, this tends to put the responsibility for learning on him. It is important to ensure that students have the necessary skills to exercise this responsibility, or else conditions are created in which such responsibility can be developed. This kind of decision making is held to promote the development of an autonomous self-reliant personality and can also provide a more effective form of learning. The materials in a Resource Centre are organised with the single learner in mind. The underlying premise is that if provided with adequate study materials, the single learner can learn more effectively alone than in a classroom environment. He can follow his interests unhindered and can pace his own learning process. In management training Resource Centres offer a valuable mode of learning which can be used either as the main thrust or, more usually, as a support or back-up to more traditional forms of teaching. This approach can be usefully combined with the tutorial method where the tutor acts as a 'learning planner', i.e. the tutor starts off the resource utilisation process by helping the student to clarify his own ideas of what he wants to do and how he wants to do it.

Lopez, M. and Elton, L. (1980) 'A Course Taught Through a Learning Centre: An Evaluation' in *Studies in Higher Education*, vol. 5, no. 1, pp. 91–9

Noble, P. (1981) *Resource Based Learning in Post Compulsory Education*, London: Kogan Page Ltd

Walton, J. (1975) 'The Initiation and Development of a Regional Resource Centre' in *Programmed Learning and Educational Technology*, vol. 12, no. 3, pp. 141–50

Fothergill, R. (1973) *Resource Centres in Colleges of Education*, London: Council for Educational Technology

Davies, K. and Needham, M. (1975) 'Running a Resource Centre Facility for Individuals' in *Programmed Learning and Educational Technology*, vol. 12, no. 3, pp. 181–5

A Resource Centre is a State of Mind, Glasgow: Scottish Council for Educational Technology

Malcolm, A. H. (1977) *Setting Up a Resource Centre: Basic Ideas*, Glasgow: Scottish Council for Educational Technology

Tucker, R. N. (1976) *Setting Up a Resource Centre: Planning and Staffing*, Glasgow: Scottish Council for Educational Technology

Malcolm, A. H. (1976) *Setting Up a Resource Centre: Retrieval Systems*, Glasgow: Scottish Council for Educational Technology

See also: Info bank; Language laboratory

RE-WRITING

Students are asked to take a subject relevant to the course. Possible subjects might include quality control, case teaching, staff appraisal problems etc. They are then asked to write a report on it. The next stage involves re-writing their original report for various different kinds of audiences. For example, the original report is written and then is adapted for oral presentation as a conference paper to a large audience or to the board of directors or the top management team. The two presentation situations are different and the task involves not merely re-writing but also assessing the suitability of the product for the audience concerned. Oral presentations can perhaps be role-played to check on problems. Re-writing possibilities are endless. A technical report on some product can be taken and re-written as a press release to the company's customers; as a specification to go into a catalogue, or as a product description.

The original piece of writing may be some form of technical report that might be produced within a company. The student is asked how this report might be changed for publication in the firm's in-house newspaper. Specific recommendations are required from the student. What changes would you make? Why would you make them? They are then required to produce the amended version. A further refinement is to have students swop around the material they each produce. They are asked to imagine that they are the editors of the mythical in-house newspaper. They have to decide if they would accept the contribution received and what editorial changes they would make. This in turn raises another problem. How do they communicate their editorial changes to the writer without offending him? Many people feel that they have invested a tremendous amount of emotional capital in their writing and it is possible for perfectly valid criticisms, expressed in the wrong way, to provoke a strong negative reaction. By re-writing material for different audiences it is possible to demonstrate how the perceptions of the validity of something are judged by the style in which it is delivered. A tutor can write or collect examples of 'spoof' articles written in the style of a learned academic journal. A good example of this is provided by Blackmore et al. (1972). Alternatively, he can have 'pop' versions of well researched and substantiated theory.

Stewart, V. and Stewart, A. (1978) *Managing the Manager's Growth*, Aldershot: Gower

Stewart, A. and Stewart, V. (1976) *Tomorrow's Men Today*, London: Institute of Personnel Management

Stewart, V. (1980) 'Training for Managerial Effectiveness: Core Skills' in *Journal of European Industrial Training*, vol. 4, no. 7, pp. iv–vi

Blackmore, D. K., Owen, D. G. and Young, C. M. (1972) 'Some Observations on the Diseases of Branus edwardii (species nova)' in *Veterinary Record*, vol. 90, pp. 382–5. Also reprinted in Heal's Books and Prints, Andersford, Glos.: Whittington Press

See also: Book reviewing; Reading; Reading parties; Literature search

ROLE PLAYING

Role Playing is a technique used to rehearse cognitive skills which have been acquired by other methods and to bring about changes in attitudes. In order to make simulated experience real, trainees take on some of the feelings and attitudes associated with a role. The technique is concerned essentially with problem solving. Instead of talking about the problem students seek to 'play out' solutions. Role Playing has been widely used in management education and training to achieve a range of objectives: for example, to permit the practice of a skill (e.g. grievance handling); to demonstrate a situation for discussion (e.g. this is what happened to me last week); to try out proposed or intended action (e.g. you be the boss, and react to my suggestion), or to make concrete an abstract idea or process. In management training Role Playing can be either spontaneous or highly structured, depending on the tutor's objectives. Descriptions of Role Playing usually insist that a person must obviously be playing a role, and not be himself, so that he is 'protected'. A spontaneous role play may emerge when a student describes an interaction between himself and another organisation member. The tutor may suggest that it might be helpful if a course member plays the other person and the scene is re-enacted. A structured role play may involve the teacher setting up a situation to illustrate a particular point and providing each member with a typed handout describing his or her 'role brief'. Role Playing focuses on real life, continuing problems that involve the participants themselves. The emphasis is as much on feelings as on facts. In terms of aims, Role Playing is primarily concerned with lower-and middle-order classes of knowledge, and also with comprehension and application.

Towers, J. M. (1969) *Role Playing for Supervisors*, Oxford: Pergammon

McGuinness, N. F. (1980) 'Using Closed Circuit Television for Visual Role Plays' in *The Training Officer*, vol. 16, no. 4, pp. 108–9

Bollens, J. C. and Marshall, D. R. (1973) *A Guide to Participation: field work, role playing, cases and other forms*, Englewood Cliffs, New Jersey: Prentice Hall

Maier, N. R. F., Solem, A. R. and Maier, A. A. (1975) *The Role Play Techniques*, Mansfield: University Associates of Europe Ltd

Zoll, A. A., (1969) *Dynamic Management Education*, Reading, Mass.: Addison-Wesley, chapters 5–8

BACIE Journal (1976) 'Role Play', vol. 30, no. 11, December, p. 203

See also: Monodrama; Sociodrama; Psychodrama; Dramatic skit; Surrogate client

ROLE PRESCRIPTION (Role Clarification, Direct Role Training, Role Negotiation)
This is a technique derived from George Kelly's 'Fixed Role Therapy'. Role Prescription is a practical way to arrive at a mutually agreed definition of expectations for a manager's behaviour. It involves collaborative effort by the manager and the 'significant others' in his 'role set'. Persons concerned with the manager's everyday role performance are involved. This helps to produce a realistic appraisal of role requirements as well as ensuring future cooperation and commitment to

the prescription devised for the manager from these others. The manager and his 'role reciprocals' meet in conference. These participants act as consultants to the manager concerned. They assist him in arriving at a mutually satisfactory prescription for his behaviour. Each member of the group is asked to list the characteristics which he would like to see in the manager's performance in a given position in the organisation. The manager generates a list of statements which characterise the way he would like to be while the panel does the same. The two lists serve as a stimulus for discussion. Unrealistic expectations are discarded and compromises are arrived at between the manager and role reciprocals until a provisional Role Prescription is arrived at. A period of role playing then ensues in which the manager attempts to perform the role as prescribed. This is followed by an analysis of all concerned on how well the provisional prescription worked. The manager comments on those aspects of it that seemed awkward or uncomfortable for him. A second cycle of rehearsal, analysis and modification takes place. Several such cycles may be necessary before all concerned are satisfied. The process is not complete until an empirical assessment in the everyday life of the manager and his role reciprocals has taken place to check that the agreed prescription is actually being carried out in the work situation. After a period of time, a further meeting may take place at which the viability of the role, the adequacy of role performance and the need for training for role-relevant skills are all considered.

McGivering, I. (1980) 'Facilitating Re-Entry Through Role Analysis' in Beck, J. and Cox, C. (eds) *Advances in Management Education*, Chichester: John Wiley and Sons

Kelly, G. A. (1955) *Psychology of Personal Constructs, volume 2,* W. W. Norton

Harrison, R. (1972) 'Role Negotiation: A Tough Minded Approach to Team Development' in Berger, M. L. and Berger, P. J. (eds) *Group Training Techniques*, Aldershot: Gower

See also: Team development; Behaviour modification; Organisational role analysis; Role reversal

ROLE REVERSAL

Two real-life protagonists are invited to work through a confrontation with each other: for example, two professionals in some kind of working relationship, between whom there is conflict, tension, misunderstanding, or mistrust. However, the technique need not necessarily be applied where there is conflict. It can equally be used to gain a deeper appreciation of each other's position by those who already have some positive regard for each other. The two sit opposite each other and spend some time in face-to-face discussion in which they outline their differences or develop their distinctive points of view. They then switch chairs and become each other, continuing the same discussion but *A* is now developing *B*'s point of view and *B* is developing *A*'s. Each speaks as the other in the first person. When this starts to run dry, they revert back to themselves and their original chairs and continue the discussion in the light of having got under the other's skin for a while. The trainer will encourage this to develop into a feedback session between the two, in which they share with each other the impact of the exercise upon their attitudes to each other and discuss the accuracy and fairness of their portrayals of each other. They can then be invited to listen *without comment* to feedback from members of the group who have been observing. Role Reversals become an aspect of Role Play when the subject's real-life antagonist is played by a member of the participating group. If used as a training exercise to gain insight into role conflicts within the organisation, both parts may be role played.

Heron, J. (1973) *Experiential Training Techniques*, Department of Adult Education, University of Surrey, Guildford

Muney, B. F. and Deutsch, M. (1968) 'The Effects of Role Reversal During Discussion of Opposing Viewpoints' in *Journal of Conflict Resolution*, vol. 12, no. 3, pp. 345–6

See also: Role play; Role prescription; Monodrama; Psychodrama; Sociodrama; Buberian dialogue

ROTATION TRAINING
This is a formal planned approach to on-the-job training of supervisors from presupervisory to executive level. An established supervisor who needs development in some particular function may be assigned to work with another man who is experienced in that function and who has the time and ability to transmit his superiority to others. In the past this has been used as a method of orienting supervisors to the operations of the entire organisation. Although it is widely used, the technique requires thorough planning. There is a need for a definite assignment of responsibility for the training of the men who are being rotated. Where

the responsibility has been assigned, and the department head given the job of teaching, he must be given assistance in the development of teaching skills and aids. To be effective, a programme of Rotation Training must (*a*) have a definite scheduling of assignments, controlled by the training department, designed to meet the particular needs of each trainee; (*b*) have a pattern of progression that avoids the piling up of trainees in any single company department; (*c*) give a guarantee to the departmental officials responsible for the training of trainees that they will be provided with sufficient time for their teaching and also be given assistance to prepare teaching materials and aids, and (*d*) provide an opportunity in the company for the absorption of trainees into the organisation. The creation of a large pool of trained supervisors for whom there are no opportunities can only lead to low morale. The exposure of the individual through rotation may involve him in different roles. The assignment may be purely observational, or he may have a specific job assignment in each role. The amount of learning gained will be determined by the amount of responsibility given. That is, if he is fully accountable for results, the chances of learning occurring are high. Otherwise, he may merely learn the technical language. He must become personally involved in operations as he moves from one assignment to the next. It is easiest to assign him a functional responsibility.

See also: Development assignment; Assignment to manager with high development skills; Manager shadowing; Job rotation; Manager exchange

SELECTION BOARD ASSIGNMENT

A manager may be assigned to take part in a selection board responsible for making an appointment to a company post. The procedural steps involved in making a satisfactory appointment, e.g. knowledge of job, advertising, shortlisting, interviewing and appointment decision, have a wider relevance to day-to-day managerial functions and can thus broaden the manager's experience.

See also: Development assignment; Committee assignment; Consulting assignment; Evaluation assignment; Proposal team assignment; Staff meeting assignment; Study assignment

SELF APPRAISAL (Peer Assessment)

In its more formal approach, self assessment procedures involve self monitoring of one's experience, reflection upon performance, assessment of performance, determination of the causes of success and failure, the setting of realistic targets for personal development, the determination of the practical means for the achievement of the targets, and the implementation of these means for experimenting with, or learning, new behaviour. Self and peer assessment methods have been used with different occupational groups such as doctors, dentists, teachers, students, nurses, counsellors, managers and health education officers. In general they have been used to assist professional development. The aim is to develop a self-directing and self-monitoring person who does not delude himself about his skill and deceive himself when he assesses his performance. An assessment workshop involves a number of stages. Firstly, participants select an area of practice to assess and go on to agree the criteria of competent practice. They develop ways to assess the quality of practice and conduct an informal/private assessment. Self-monitoring then takes place in daily practice and the practice is revised in the light of the assessment. They report on the application of the audit, on the effectiveness of the audit itself and disclose details about the self assessments. They receive critical questions and amplify their doubts as well as positive impressions of colleagues. Finally, the criteria and methods are reviewed and peer and self accreditation awarded.

Heron, J. (1981) 'Peer and Self Assessment' in Boydell, T. and Pedler, M. (eds), *Management Self-Development: Concepts and Practices*, Aldershot: Gower

Heron, J. (1977) Behavioural Analysis in Education and Training, Department of Adult Education, University of Surrey, Guildford

Mumford, A. (1980) *Making Experience Pay*, London: McGraw Hill

Boud, D. (1980) 'Self Appraisal in Professional Development for Tertiary Teachers' in *Research and Development in Higher Education*

Boud, D. (1980) *Self and Peer Assessment in Higher and Continuing Education*, Tertiary Education Research Centre, University of New South Wales

See also: Management audit; Performance review; Instrumented feedback; Self criticism

SELF CRITICISM (Public Self Criticism)
Self Criticism is most frequently associated with totalitarian Communist

societies where one stands up and criticises oneself in public. At first sight this may appear to be completely foreign to most people's experience. However, in practice the procedure is not that unusual and involves two key elements. The first is private reflection on one's own decisions and activities, and the assessment of its appropriateness and efficacy as judged against some standard or criteria. Such 'personalised reflection' can produce personal learning. In addition, it is possible to make that learning available to others by discussing one's own mistakes in a group. One can learn as much from one's errors as from one's successes. Forms of Self Criticism are an aspect of many existing teaching approaches. In a Problem-solving Group or in a Personal Case History presentation, the manager may describe a problem which he has attempted to solve but has failed. He may ask others for advice. When running an experiential exercise, the tutor may ask participants to comment on why they failed to achieve the task set before he asks the observers to report. Using the Video Confrontation technique and/or the role of Inquirer in the Interpersonal Process Recall method, the facilitator may ask individuals to comment on their own behaviour. In all these cases, the opportunity is offered for the individual to criticise his performance in the presence of others.

See also: Video confrontation; Interpersonal process recall; Personalised reflection

SELF DEVELOPMENT

Self Development is a very broad concept and one which is not easily defined. While the general idea is not new, in recent years it has received a renewed impetus from the work of Tom Boydell, Mike Pedler and John Burgoyne. The trainer or tutor who is introduced to it, through one of the many 'resource' books which are currently available on the subject, may be excused for believing that Self Development is merely a self-teaching package approach to the study of traditional management subjects. These resource packs consist typically of a training needs analysis questionnaire and a series of activities or 'exercises' which the manager can complete either alone, with a colleague or subordinate, or in a group. Considered in these narrow terms, Self Development might incorrectly be thought of as a new application of the self-teaching method. However, it would be erroneous to equate some of the 'technology' of the approach with the much broader concept of Self Development. It is this concept which can guide the design of both individual learning events and educational systems. In their writings, Boydell, Pedler and Burgoyne distinguish between 'development by self' and 'development of self'. The former refers to Self Development as a process, while the latter conceives it as a goal. In 'by self' forms of development, the student controls his own learning in terms of choices about the pace of study, method of learning, nature of the subject content etc. Learning approaches which support this form of development include Learning Communities, Action Learning, and Autonomy Labs. The 'of self' forms view Self Development as a goal rather than as a process. Maslow's 'self actualised man' constitutes the goal striven for. It is believed that within organisations, such individuals demonstrate greater competency and effectiveness in their work. However, the use of specific learning approaches cannot guarantee the attainment of objectives. Pedler and Boydell have argued that 'development is a function of the individual interacting with some part of his environment, either actually or symbolically – there is no development without a developer. ... If the individual is able to find significance and personal meaning in the event, then that is a self development experience'. The problem is the unpredictability of the learning. The manager may not find any personal meaning in an expensive Action Learning Programme but may do so while tinkering with his car on Sunday morning.

Burgoyne, J., Boydell, T. and Pedler, M. (1978) *Self-development: Theory and Applications for Practitioners*, London: Association of Teachers of Management

Pedler, M., Burgoyne J. and Boydell, T. (1978) *A Manager's Guide to Self-Development*, London: McGraw-Hill

Boydell, T. and Pedler, M. (1979) *Self-Development Bibliography*, Bradford: MCB Publications

Boydell, T. and Pedler, M. (1981) *Management Self-Development: Concepts and Practice*, Aldershot: Gower

See also: Self improvement programme; Instrumented feedback; Tape-assisted learning programme; Student-planned learning

SELF HELP GROUP
The key charcteristic of a Self Help Group is mutual learning from members. While leaders, teachers or facilitators may structure the initial

learning environment, the actual learning occurs primarily between group members themselves. The use of such groups reflects an increased preparedness of participants to take responsibility for their own learning, recognise their own potential as learning resources to others and an increased scepticism about the role and utility of 'experts'. Smith (1980) divided Self Help groups into two broad types: those which were intended for a broad range of people, but which were structured in a way which allowed them to be used without direct professional assistance (he put Co-counselling into this category); and those, exemplified by Alcoholics Anonymous and Consciousness Raising groups, which were designed for categories of people who were homogeneous. In terms of the actual methods and approaches used in Self help groups, these vary from the highly structured to the very open.

Smith P. B. (1980) *Group Processes and Personal Change*, London: Harper and Row, chapter 9

Lieberman, M. A. and Borman, L. D. (1979) *Self Help Groups*, San Francisco: Jossey Bass

Emrick, C. D., Lassen, C. L. and Edwards M. T. (1977) 'Non-professional Peers as Therapeutic Agents' in Gurman, A. S. and Razin, A. M. (eds) *Effective Psychotherapy: A Handbook of Research*, Oxford: Pergamon

Messier, G. and Saint Jacques, N. (1975) 'Multi-Media: Three Years; Three Phases' in *Programmed Learning and Educational Technology*, vol. 12, no. 5, pp. 278–86

Griffin, H. and Houston, A. (1980) 'Self-Development for Managers in Making the Most of Existing Resources' in *Personnel Management*, vol. 12, no. 9, pp. 46–8

See also: Co-counselling; Consciousness-raising group; Network; Learning community

SELF IMPROVEMENT PROGRAMME

Not every employee responds to a training programme devised and directed by someone else. For such people, self-initated improvement programmes can often generate a higher level of commitment. Bearing this in mind, a manager might find it useful to ask selected members of his department to consider, on their own account, the following questions:

Where am I going – careerwise?
Where do I intend to go?
What progress have I made to date in terms of skills I have acquired?
What additional skills do I now need to acquire?

The objective of asking such questions is to stimulate some thought and reflection on longer term personal needs. Self-assessment questionnaires can be distributed to members of a department whom the manager thinks will benefit from such an approach. When the questionnaire has been completed, the manager can then jointly review and discuss its contents with the subordinate and agree a suitable programme of specific developmental projects.

Bitton, S. (1981) *This Learning Business: Assignments for Pre-Vocational Courses,* London: McGraw-Hill

See also: Career life planning; Self development

SELF SERVICE EXPERIMENT
This is a version of a programmed text which deals with practical situations. When you want to deal with a topic of study, you take a Self Service Experiment which consists of a programmed text and a practical activity which combine together and produce certain ends.

O'Connell, S., Penton, S. J. and Boud, D. J. (1974) *A Rationally Designed Self Service Laboratory Minicourse,* Institute for Educational Technology, University of Surrey, Guildford

O'Connell, S., Penton, S. J. and Boud, D. J. (1977) 'A Rationally Designed Self-Service Minicourse' in *Programmed Learning and Educational Technology,* vol. 14, no. 2, pp. 154–61

SELF TESTS (Quizzes)
This method involves the provision of regular tests and questions that trainees can use to assess their own progress. These can help them assess their training needs and give the trainer feedback on performance. Personnel staff may receive a quiz in which a question might be: 'How long must a woman have worked for an employer before being entitled to maternity leave?' Questions and quizzes can be used to start a discussion or introduce a topic, or summarise and reinforce past learning. It can also help to put people in a better frame of mind to take advantage of training.

Trainees receive feedback of results by marking their own answer scripts. They are thus helped to become aware of their areas of ignorance and are motivated to do something about it. When used as a starter, the themes can be repeated at the end of a course using different questions. This can help evaluate the training and reward trainees with the sight of their increased knowledge. Quizzes need to be fair. Tutors should clearly state the ground to be covered and reflect the objectives of the course. The degree of openness of the questions should be decided upon and 'what would you do?' questions avoided.

Stewart, A. and Stewart, V. (1976) *Tomorrow's Men Today*, London: Institute of Personnel Management, chapter 5

Elton, L. R. B. (1969) 'Student Feedback to Self-Testing' in *Innovations and Experiments in University Teaching Methods*, Proceedings of the Third Conference, University of London Teaching Methods Unit, April 1968

Carver, R. P. (1975) 'Comparing the Reading-Storage Test to the Paraphrase Test as Measures of the Primary Effects of Prose Reading' in *Journal of Educational Psychology*, vol. 67, no. 2, pp. 274–84

See also: Instrumented feedback; Process analysis; Pre-course learning

SELF-DIRECTED STUDENT LEARNING GROUP

This is a generic term for a variety of approaches which have in common the fact that during the main learning task, the group(s) do not have an instructor or tutor present. Research suggests that independent student group work encourages a more positive attitude towards a continuation of learning beyond the course, increases critical thinking, encourages the search for applications and implications of learning and develops group interaction skills among the learners. Factors which affect group performance and which inhibit the approach have been found to include a preoccupation with one's own knowledge or viewpoint and the inability to lead another to a new insight.

Beach, L. R. (1974) 'Self-Directed Student Groups and College Learning' in *Higher Education*, vol. 3, pp. 187–200

Ferrier, B., Marrin, M. and Seidman, J. (1981) 'Student Autonomy in Learning Medicine' in Boud, D. J. (ed.) *Developing Autonomy in Student Learning*, London: Kogan Page Ltd

Collier, K. G. (1980) 'Peer Group Learning in Higher Education: the development of higher order skills' in *Studies in Higher Education*, vol. 5, pp. 55–62

Todd, F. and Todd, R. C. (1979) 'Talking and Learning: towards effective structuring of student directed learning groups' in *Journal of Further and Higher Education*, vol. 3, no. 2, pp. 52–66

Todd, F. (1981) 'Developing Teaching Skills for Collaborative Learning' in *Studies in Higher Education*, vol. 6, no. 1, pp. 91–6

See also: Tutorium; Learning through discussion; Creative dialogue; Media-activated learning group; Instrumented team learning; Independent learning; Autonomous learning group

SELF-INSTRUCTIONAL MODULES AND INTERACTIVE GROUPS

The aim of this approach is to develop the problem-solving skills of students working in small interactive groups. These groups meet regularly following a prior input of factual material through an independent study module. This is a highly structured method which concentrates on the transfer of knowledge and solution of problems. In essence it involves the use of two teaching methods consecutively, either of which can be used alone. Other combinations of methods are also possible. The original Postlethwaite model of Audio Tutorial included interactive groups as well. Designed for self-paced individual study, the modules provide an input of basic information. There are no separate lectures or laboratory classes. For a given course there may be one module a week over a period of perhaps ten weeks. The objectives and means for the self assessment for each module are clearly communicated to the student. Students work in a multi-media learning centre, principally in carrels, where an audiotape, plus study guides and textbooks, integrate theory and practice. The method has been used in the teaching of biology and similar subjects. Elsewhere in the learning centre there will be tape/slide programmes, demonstrations and additional literature. Part of the approach is based on the Audio Tutorial Laboratory system of learning. In interactive groups, eight to ten students meet weekly with a tutor for between one and two hours. They examine systematically the objective of each module studied during the previous week by the students. Each student has a quiz paper containing questions requiring brief answers. This written answer of two to three lines provides the framework around which discussion takes place. Most questions are based on module objectives and, in the case of a subject like biology, may be accompanied by slides which provide information or clues necessary for the answer. Group members write their answers to one item at a time, or several closely related items. This takes a few minutes and is followed immediately by a group discussion of the answers. In this exchange of opinions, conceptual difficulties are exposed and resolved. As soon as there is consensus in the group about an acceptable answer, the discussion is closed. Individuals then mark their own answers with a symbol (' X ?). The immediate feedback provides an effective learning experience. At the end, student papers are handed to the tutor for review and they are returned the following week.

Brewer, I. M. (1977) 'SIMIG: a case study of an innovative method of teaching and learning' in *Studies in Higher Education*, vol. 2, no. 1, pp. 33–54

Brewer, I. M. (1979)) 'Group Teaching Strategies for Promoting Individual Skills in Problem Solving' in *Programmed Learning and Educational Technology*, vol. 16, no. 2, pp. 111–28

Brewer, I. M. and Tomlinson, J. D. (1981) 'SIMIG: the effect of time on performance with modular instruction' in *Programmed Learning and Educational Technology*, vol. 18, no. 2, pp. 72–85

Brewer, I. M. (1974) 'Recall, Comprehension and Problem Solving: an evaluation of audio-visual method of learning plant anatomy' in *Journal of Biological Education*, vol. 8, pp. 101–12

See also: Audio tutorial method; Autonomous learning group; Construct lesson plan; Data approach method; Tutorial-tape-document learning package approach; Guided discussion; Guided group problem solving

SEMINAR

The Seminar is a form of small group discussion which frequently involves between eight and twelve students. It is a small group situation in which the tutor is present. A Seminar often includes a guest expert. There are conflicting student attitudes to small group teaching in general. A report on university teaching in 1964 suggested that there was a strong demand by students for tutorial and seminar work. Strong reaction is sometimes evident, and comments are made about boring sessions. It seems that this is a 'high risk' form of teaching. It demands a great deal from the teacher and if he or she does not do well, they tend to go very badly wrong. Research studies report how Seminars have turned into lectures given by the tutor, or else students 'vote with their feet' and do not turn up. Learning in groups can be both productive and satisfying, but it is also highly threatening to many individuals. Skill is required by the tutor to weld the individuals into a cohesive group which is likely to be emotionally satisfying as well as task productive.

Abercrombie, M. L. J. (1979) *Aims and Techniques of Group Teaching*, Guildford, Surrey: Society for Research into Higher Education, 4th edition

Abercrombie, M. L. J. and Terry, P. M. (1978) *Talking to Learn: Improving Learning and Teaching in Small Groups*, Guildford, Surrey: Society for Research into Higher Education

Wilson, A. (1980) 'Structuring Seminars: a technique to allow students to participate in the structuring of small group discussions' in *Studies in Higher Education*, vol. 5, no. 1, pp. 81–4

Ruddock, J. (1978) *Learning Through Small Group Discussion: A Study of Seminar Work in Higher Education*, Guildford, Surrey: Society for Research into Higher Education

Broady, M. (1969–70) 'The Conduct of Seminars' in *Universities Quarterly*, vol. 24, no. 3, pp. 273–84

Bogardus, E. S. (1947) 'The Seminar as a Research Institution' in *Sociological and Social Research*, vol. 31, pp. 389–95

Watt, I. (1964) 'The Seminar' in *Universities Quarterly*, vol. 18, pp. 369–89

Thompson, J. T. (1947) 'Seminars Can Be Fun' in *Journal of Engineering Education*, vol. 37, pp. 736–8

See also: Advanced seminar; Group discussion; Small group teaching; Tutorial; Structuring seminars; Tutorium

SENSITIVITY (T-GROUP) TRAINING (Group Relations Training)

Sensitivity Training is difficult to define because it has become a generic term embracing a wide variety of techniques. The strategy used by the small group trainer has three main goals: (*a*) to increase the ability of members to appreciate how others react to their own behaviour; (*b*) to increase the ability to gauge the state of relationships between others; and (c) to increase the ability to carry out skilfully the behaviour required by the situation. Groups meet on a full-time or weekly basis over a period. There is no fixed agenda for discussion and events and issues arise spontaneously from the interactions of group members and are influenced by individual needs, responses and behaviour. The trainer does not take part in the discussion; his role is to point out what is happening in the group. By withdrawing his leadership, and taking the role of interpreter, members are encouraged to develop their own mini society with its agreed procedures, norms and processes. In essence, this technique employs group participation in such a way as to help participants become aware of how they affect others and how others affect their behaviour. While the label 'unstructured' is frequently applied to such groups, it is mainly applicable to the agenda or task that is worked on. In another sense, there is a high degree of predictability on the issues that are raised by members. These include those of identity. (How am I seen in this group?), power and influence (How much influence do I have?), goals and needs (What are my needs, will they be met?) and acceptance and intimacy (How close and intimate will I be expected to be?). The research on Sensitivity Training has been decribed as a large checkerboard, incomplete and uneven. One study found that T-group participants had a better diagnostic understanding of self and others in the groups, as well as in group process; had greater openness, receptivity and tolerance of differences and had acquired operational skill in interpersonal relationships and a greater capacity for cooperation. Findings in this field are, however, inconclusive.

Benne (1964) traced the birth of the T-group to a workshop held on the campus of the State Teachers College in New Britain, Connecticut in the summer of 1946. In addition to Benne, other training staff there included Leland Bradford and Ronald Lippitt. A team of researchers was led by Kurt Lewin. The workshop used mainly discussion groups and a researcher attended each discussion meeting. After each day's sessions, the trainers and researchers would meet to compare notes and discuss what had occurred. Some workshop participants who were staying on campus asked if they too could attend. On hearing the descriptions of their behaviour and the accompanying interpretation of it by the training and research staff, the participants present commented on and challenged these interpretations. In this process, the basic method of the T-group was born.

Bradford, L. P., Gibb, J. R. and Berne, K. D. (1964) *T-Group Theory and Laboratory Method*, New York: John Wiley

Blumberg, A. and Golembiewski, R. T. (1976) *Learning and Change in Groups*, Harmondsworth: Penguin Books

Lippitt, G. L. (1975) 'Guides for the Use of Sensitivity Training in Management Development' in Taylor, B. and Lippitt, G. L. (eds) *Management Development and Training Handbook*, London: McGraw Hill

Cohen, A. M. and Smith, R. D. (1976) *The Critical Incident in Growth Groups: Theory and Technique*, Mansfield: University Associates of Europe Limited (Textbook and Manual)

Smith, P. B. (1980) *Group Processes and Personal Change*, London: Harper and Row

See also: Laboratory method; Mini-society; Micro-lab; Group dynamics laboratory; Human relations laboratory; Organisational laboratory; Personal development laboratory; Power laboratory; Team laboratory; Tavistock conference method

SERVICE IN PROFESSIONAL ASSOCIATIONS

Local branches of organisations such as the British Institute of Management, Institute of Personnel Management, legal groups and accounting institutions offer managers the opportunity to keep in touch with current ideas and thinking. A company may judge an individual's commitment to his work by the degree to which he appears to be interested in new developments. Managers may take an active role in such associations by offering to stand for committee membership or a less active one by attending meetings as a participant. Such membership also offers the opportunity to meet professional colleagues working in different organisations.

See also: Accepting positions of responsibility in community organisations

SHORT TALKS BY STUDENTS

This is useful technique when students need to develop general verbal communication skills or where vivas form part of the assessment. It is equally important when a manager needs to develop the skill of presenting his ideas either formally or informally in front of others. Once accepted by students talks tend to go satisfactorily, but they require careful introduction or else they can flop. Initial training can come in the form of syndicate groups nominating one of their number to report back to the class as a whole. Any 'trauma' experienced by the students can be minimised by asking for only a two-minute presentation and making the occasion informal. Usually over-preparation and speaking too long are the problems. On occasions the objective is to encourage a climate in which students want to learn from each other. Some feedback received indicated that student presentations were bad, they learnt little new and had come to learn from the tutor. Choice of topic is crucial. Each talk requires follow-up class discussion in which the good points of the talk are reinforced. Mumford (1980) has suggested informal boss coaching in presentation skills. He recommends that a manager be asked by his boss to summarise for him the main elements of each written report he presents to him. Once confidence is gained, such presentations can be attempted in front of a group of listeners. At a later stage, he may choose to make a regular contribution as a speaker on in-company or extra-organisational management courses.

Mumford, A. (1980) *Making Experience Pay*, London: McGraw Hill

Stewart, A. and Stewart, V. (1976) *Tomorrow's Men Today*, London: Institute of Personnel Management, chapter 5

Henderson, N. K. (1970) *University Teaching*, Oxford: Oxford University Press

See also: Debate; Jurisprudential model; Visiting lecturer; Teaching as learning; Confidence-building training

SICK-LEAVE/HOLIDAY REPLACEMENT ASSIGNMENT
(Fill-in Assignment)
A company may have a conscious policy of assigning managerial staff to take over temporarily the jobs of others who are suddenly absent because of illness or who are away on holiday. 'Taking over the reins' may involve the individual in finding out quickly the key aspects of the job involved, making decisions about the ability of new departmental subordinates and generally drawing on the type of personal resources that other forms of development can rarely provide. The manager may be given little notice of the impending temporary transfer. In any company, training a manager to fill any job other than his own is difficult because everyone is needed on the job. The programming of specific job training for promotion or transfer at all levels in the organisation can be accomplished by this method in a way that enhances the training function and improves overall efficiency.

Essentially it involves employees filling in for their bosses when the latter are required to be away. Where no reporting relationship exists between two people, a man may take over at the next highest job classification level in the absence of the incumbent. The employee is actually allowed to function on the job he is trying to learn. If he is given guidance and support during these periods, he will have the greatest opportunity to learn the job. He will be challenged, motivated and involved – the keys to faster more efficient learning. Having one person fill in on another job, can set off a series of learning opportunities. He leaves a vacancy that someone at a lower level can in turn fill during the same period. This not only develops a wide base of experience, but also provides for continuous operations with the least possible interruption. The trainees must however be prepared for this type of development. If they do not undertand its purposes or advantages, they may view it negatively. Internal jealousies, fears and tensions can all build up, when people below are learning a higher-level job. Emphasis needs to be put on the advantages of the scheme to all involved. Some managers may see subordinates as a threat and the development method can aggravate this attitude if the people concerned are not properly prepared. The procedure should be planned well in advance to take advantage of any foreseeable absences.

See also: Development assignment; Acting assignment; Job rotation; Job swop; Rotation training

SIMULATION

Here the approach is to reproduce the real world in a controlled fashion. Devices can include mock jury situations, a complex political situation, an economic system or a ghetto environment. The students are asked to play different roles and problems typical to the situation are introduced for them to solve. The emphasis in a Simulation is the application of the subject content learned earlier through reading and studying in a structured fashion. Simulation materials are available commercially or can be designed by the instructor. Simulation therefore attempts to recreate the job environment in a controlled fashion. In its simplest form it can be an extension of an In-basket Exercise with participants sitting at desks, receiving their information, processing it and passing it on in the same way that they might do in an actual job environment. They can also be provided with a telephone to communicate with others or with 'control'. Demands are made on them over the phone or in person by other participants or by the instructor controller. In more complex situations, e.g. the building of an aircraft simulator, the physical environment may need to be restructured. Here the link trainer is used to instruct pilots in instrument flying. This is amongst the best known examples of Simulation. There are two key aspects of Simulation; the replication of the actual working environment, and the ability to control that environment to bring about the conditions under which the responses are elicited. Such control may be by humans who put additional correspondence into the students' 'mail', or by computer as in the case of the flying Simulation. The trainee receives direct feedback based on his responses. Stimuli presented after each response can be further controlled to reinforce correct ones and extinguish incorrect ones. Simulation requires 'real time', i.e. it takes place in a period of time commensurate with the time it would take to carry out the same process in a real job. This is the major difference between Simulation and the Game. The latter nearly always collapses time with months or years of a company's life being represented by game hours.

Gibb, G. I. (1974) *Handbook of Games and Simulation Exercises*, London: E. and F. N. Spon Ltd

Saynor, J. and Ryan, M. (1979) 'Management Development: A Context Learning Programme' in *Journal of European Industrial Training*, vol. 3, no. 6, pp. 2–6

Industrial Training International,(1976) 'Simulation in Training', vol. 11, nos. 3, 5, 6, 7, 9, 10 and 11

Walter, H. (1975) 'Organizational Simulation in Management Training' in *Industrial and Commercial Training*, vol. 7, no. 3, pp. 118–20

Programmed Learning and Educational Technology: Journal of APLET, vol. 13, no. 3, July, 1976. Special Issue on Simulation

Zuckerman, D. W. and Horn, R. F. (1978) *The Guide to Simulation for Education and Training*, 2nd Edition, New York: Western Publishing Company

Atthill, C. R. A. and Dowdeswell, W. H. (1978) 'Simulation in Decision-making: An Experiment in Industrial Education' in *British Journal of Educational Technology*, vol. 9, no. 3, pp. 217–26

McCormick, J. (1972) 'Simulation and Gaming as a Teaching Method' in *Programmed Learning and Educational Technology*, vol. 9, no. 4, pp. 198–205

Taylor, J. L. and Walford, R. (1978) *Learning and the Simulation Game*, Milton Keynes: Open University Press

Jones, K. (1980) *Simulations: A Handbook for Teachers*, London: Kogan Page Ltd

Stammers, R. B. (1981) 'Theory and Practice in the Design of Training Simulations' in *Programmed Learning and Educational Technology*, vol. 18, no. 2, pp. 67–71

Parry, S. B. (1980) 'The Name of the Game is Simulation' in *Training and Development Journal*, vol. 34, no. 6, pp. 99–105

See also: Game; In-basket exercise; Programmed simulation; Surrogate client

SITTING BY NELLIE

Quantitatively, this is probably the most widespread training technique used in industry. One just sits next to and observes someone else doing a job. There are certain conditions which have to be stipulated for SBN to be useful. The most important of these is that Nellie has to be comprehensible, i.e. be able to explain to the person sitting next to her, when necessary, what she is doing and why. In the case of the manager working with a subordinate, he may either lack the time or the ability to explain the reasoning behind a particular course of action that he has taken. The managerial version of SBN may involve the attachment of a trainee to a particular company department or specific manager. Mumford has argued that it is important for the manager to whom the trainee is attached to plan and control what occurs. He recommends that another staff member, at a junior position in the company, should be asked to 'look after' the new trainee.

Mumford, A. (1971) *The Manager and Training*, London: Pitman Publishing

See also: Apprenticeship; Parrainage; One-to-one learning; Manager shadowing; Behaviour modelling

SKILL PRACTICE SESSION

This term is used precisely to describe a training approach which enables people to improve through practice some specific and defined behaviour. For example on a course a student may describe how, in a management meeting, one member may continually react negatively to all ideas and suggestions. The course members may suggest that the formal leader should confront that individual. However, members may be reluctant to engage in this behaviour, perhaps feeling anxious about how the confronted member may react. This may be the occasion on which to organise a Skill Practice Session. To be effective it is essential that the situation should contain specific provision for the following practice process: (*a*) isolating and defining a desired behaviour (intention); (*b*) trying out the behaviour (action); (*c*) collecting evidence on how the tryout worked (feedback of results); (*d*) noting discrepancies from the original intention (desired behaviour), as a basis for further refinement and correction of behaviour. The focus is on *how* an agreed goal can be most effectively reached.

See also; Intervisitation; Sociodrama; Role playing; Interactive skills training

SKILL SESSION

A special type of small group seminar was devised by Black which aimed to develop certain scientific skills (hence the name). Its purpose is to supplement lectures and problem-solving classes or even replace them. In a Skill Session, a 'menu' of problems is offered to the participants, who form groups of four to six and work on one of the problems. The groups are left to themselves for an appointed time of twenty to thirty minutes. A teacher may or may not be available on demand, or he may visit the groups to make sure that none get stuck. After the appointed time the groups reunite, to present, substantiate and discuss their solutions and approaches and arguments used. Thus every group learns something beyond its 'own' problem. In plenary discussion the teacher indicates neglected aspects and implicitly made assumptions.

In designing the menu of problems, the teacher has to consider the pre-knowledge level of the participants, directions of interest and the time available. Open-ended or closed questions are acceptable. Reference books may be made available for use. To allow for the different time needed for different groups, additional supplementary questions are provided for groups finishing well in advance. Black's questions aimed to give students a familiarity with orders of magnitude, giving them the ability to estimate the various influences on a given process and developing a sense for what may be neglected and what not. Questions included 'Estimate the total daily income of a town bus'. Other Skill Sessions may include translation of information between a table, a formula and a verbal description. Skill Sessions may be offered as a whole course or used occasionally to supplement lectures. They increase the student's problem handling and solving ability, develop his ability to express and substantiate ideas, to argue, to speak fluently and understand and judge other people's reasoning.

Black, P. J., Griffith, J. A. R. and Powell, W. B. (1974) 'Skill Sessions' in *Physics Education*, vol. 9, pp. 18–22

Black, P. et al. (1968) 'Group Studies' in *Physics Education*, vol. 3, p. 289

See also: Problem-centred group; Block method

SMALL GROUP TEACHING

In most handbooks and textbooks on teaching methods, there is a reference to Small Group Teaching methods. These are used to distinguish a class of interaction strategies that are separate from those encompassed under the title 'Lecture Method'. Beyond this very basic distinction, it is necessary to define in greater detail the objectives and numbers of learners which Small Group Teaching serves.

Bligh, D. (1975) *Teaching Students*, Exeter University Teaching Services

Abercrombie, M. L. J. (1969) *The Anatomy of Judgement*, Harmondsworth: Penguin Books

Abercrombie, M. L. J. (1979) *Aims and Techniques of Group Teaching*, Guildford, Surrey: Society for Research into Higher Education, 4th edition

Babbington-Smith, B. and Farrell, B. A. (1979) *Training in Small Groups: A Study of Five Methods*, Oxford: Pergamon Press

Abercrombie, M. L. J. and Terry, P. M. *Talking to Learn: improving teaching and learning in small groups*, Guildford, Surrey: Society for Research into Higher Education

Cockburn, B. and Ross, A. (1978) 'Working Together', 'Participatory Discussion', 'A Kind of Learning', 'Patterns and Procedures', Teaching in Higher Education Series, nos. 1–4, University of Lancaster

Lewis, H. A. (1979) 'The Anatomy of Small Groups' in *Studies in Higher Education*, vol. 4, no. 2, pp. 269–77

Wood, A. E. (1979) 'Experiences with Small Group Tutorials' in *Studies in*

Higher Education. vol. 4, no. 2, pp. 203–9

Webb, G. (1981) 'An Evaluation of Techniques for Analysing Small Group Work' in *Programmed Learning and Educational Technology*, vol. 18, no. 2, pp. 64–6

See also: Group discussion

SOCIODRAMA (Dramatisation Method)
A Sociodrama has no script, involves several participants and its outcome is not determined in advance. It can be seen as a combination of demonstration and discussion with individuals from the group doing the demonstrating. While it is an unplanned demonstration, there are nevertheless certain guidelines provided for the participants involved. Sociodrama or dramatisation involves the acting out by individuals, without script or rehearsal, the job techniques needed for specific situations. The participants are told by the tutor what the situation and the desired outcomes are, and in general terms, how each actor should move towards accomplishing the desired outcome. The method can be used to stimulate the group to take a new look at a familiar job technique, or to help it develop the confidence and necessary skills which are new to them.

Dramatisation works best when the members of the group are at ease with each other; a friendly, cooperative atmosphere exists, so that no one will ridicule the actors or 'ham up' the acting; where a number of individuals are willing to participate without rehearsal; and where the trainer is completely familiar with the technique. One must be prepared for an individual becoming embarrassed or upset. The Dramatisation procedure consists first of description. The situation to be dramatised is described and the desired outcome made as clear as possible. Next, volunteers are sought for the parts or else individuals are selected for particular roles. Members should not however be forced to take part. The actors are then allowed a few minutes to discuss in general terms what they want to do. While this is happening they tell the others who constitute the audience, what to look for and ask them to withhold comments until the end. The action begins and once the important point has been made for discussion purposes, it is stopped. In the debriefing which follows, the focus is on the reasons why the action took the direction it did. Was the desired outcome achieved or about to be achieved? How did the behaviour of the actors influence the result? These points are then related to the job situation.

See also: Monodrama; Psychodrama; Role play; Dramatic skit; Surrogate client

SOCRATIC ENQUIRY

The Socratic method essentially involves the teacher eliciting correct answers from students by the sequencing of the questions he asks them. A modified form of Socratic Enquiry for use in the university classroom has been developed. The aim is to replace passive student behaviour, e.g. lecture attendance, with discussions for which the students have written the questions. Assigned reading is used and the characteristics of this determine the quality of the questions selected for classroom enquiry. These in turn directly influence the characteristics of the collective enquiry.

The focus of this method is on the asking of questions by students. What constitutes a good question? How can an existing question be improved? Questions are held to have certain characteristics: scepticism; philosophical understanding of the subject and concern for the nature of the subject as well as its informational base. Students design their own questions which are fed into the classroom sessions. Those which are not read or discussed in class may be introduced later by the lecturer as points of reference during the lectures. Lecture material can be focused around the questions. A class using this approach may be asked to submit a set of questions for the final exam. The best of these would be duplicated and distributed as study sheets and 25–50 per cent of the final exam might be comprised of student enquiry. At the beginning of the hour, the lecturer selects a few questions from those submitted by the students and he writes them on the board. He encourages the class to copy these questions for future reference and when they have finished he explains the reasons for his choice. He emphasises the merits of the questions chosen. These various activities provide stimulation for the class and subsequently the lecturer relies on the students to sustain the discussion because his behaviour is also modified in the process. He must conduct himself as unobtrusively as possible, except to clarify points in the discussion and to summarise different students' remarks.

The preparation of questions is an exercise in scholarly writing and a scholarly format is essential. Students must include pagination after questions where possible. 'Which page were you reading when the question appeared in your mind?' Inference, implication and colloquialism must be avoided. Questions on a single topic should be grouped together. The result of this is a limited amount of writing outside of the classroom on specific material and an assignment in which quality and quantity are directly related to thinking. The modified Socratic Enquiry method involves students more actively in the classroom, presupposes close reading of carefully chosen material, assumes that the learner and teacher are both there to learn, and considers that a dialogue is as effective as lectures and that students can learn from each other.

See also: Interrogation of experts; Questioning; Socratic questioning; Invitation to discover

SOCRATIC QUESTIONING

Socratic Questioning is a learning method which aims to check whether a student's knowledge is real. It involves the asking of questions and can be used with any subject matter. Different kinds of question can be asked and it is their purpose that matters. A Socratic teacher asks questions to test whether or not students really know what they think they know. The objective is to make students recognise their ignorance and stimulate their desire to learn. Socratic teaching begins after someone claims to know something. The first move in such teaching is always to ask someone to demonstrate the knowledge they claim to possess. Thus Socratic cross-examination differs from the usual sort of examination in which teachers test what students know. In a typical examination it does not matter whether or not a student has made a prior claim to know the material over which he is being tested. The examination is merely designed to test whether the student does know the material. In Socratic teaching, however, it is indispensible that the student claims to know the material before the examination begins.

The things which are tested in a Socratic examination include how much a person knows about a certain subject, and how much he knows about himself. Following a claim to know, the teacher tries to determine the accuracy of that claim, and whether it is true. If it is not then the student fails on two counts. He fails to know his subject matter and he fails to know himself. In terms of its effectiveness as a teaching strategy, Socratic teaching can in some cases change a student's attitudes towards learning. Some people become eager because they realise that they lack knowledge. But it depends on the students. Those who have a low opinion of themselves are unlikely to submit to public cross-examination. The same is true for those who do not care whether they answer the questions correctly or not. The method works best with strong, self-confident people who think they have the knowledge. Such people are often eager to be cross-examined. Moreover they have a strong sense of their own worth and do not feel downcast when their ignorance is revealed. If they cannot answer a question they will probably try to learn the answer because they do not like to think of themselves as ignorant.

See also: Questioning; Socratic enquiry; Invitation to discover; Interrogation of experts

STAFF MEETING ASSIGNMENT

Attendance at a staff or departmental meeting as an active participant can benefit many people especially if they are not expected to attend normally. The interplay between different individuals, conflicts of interests, subtleties, agreements and failure to reach agreement are all means of stimulating development. However, attendance at too many meetings deadens the energies of even the most ambitious. A variant of this developmental activity may involve an individual who has completed a project of some description, presenting his findings at a departmental meeting. This can then lead to a subsequent discussion of the report. It can be used to inject enthusiasm, especially into someone who might have become stale through overexposure to the same kind of work. Each subordinate either selects or is assigned a specific subject. This is normally, although not necessarily, related to his present departmental responsibility. He is then given a deadline to meet for presentation of findings at a departmental meeting. The method forces a person to reflect upon and classify his experience, to search for new information and to suggest viable improvements to present policies, methods or procedures. The fact that a presentation takes place before peers as well as superiors introduces a competetive element to which a moderate performer responds.

Bradford, L. P. (1976) *Making Meetings Work: A Guide for Leaders and Group Members*, Mansfield: University Associates of Europe

See also: Committee assignment; Development assignment; Proposal team assignment; Selection board assignment; Task force assignment

STEP-BY-STEP DISCUSSION

This involves teaching by a carefully prepared sequence of issues and questions to draw out the required information from students. The aim is to achieve knowledge of facts and understanding (especially logical argument or developmental sequence). The input may be a sheet of notes shared by the teacher and students or an audio or video tape. It has the possibility of embracing the function of the lecture and follow-up seminar in one class period. This method is of greatest value where a particular set of issues has to be covered. Each issue can be put on an overhead projector and assigned a pre-set discussion time.

See also: Case study method; Guided discussion; Step-by-step lecture

STEP-BY-STEP LECTURE

A Step-by-step Lecture is one organised around three to ten topics, each of which is talked about for a few minutes followed by discussion or another activity. It is used to impart information and develop problem solving skills. The student activity, frequent feedback, opportunities for rehearsal, the periodic relaxation from concentrated listening and the group discussion make it a useful method for classes of up to thirty. A variation of this method can be used when a course is built around problems projected onto a screen. Students attempt the questions and these are discussed with the lecturer before he proceeds to the next one. Questions are also supplied on a handout with space for students' notes so that a complete record of the course can be maintained.

McCarthy, W. H. (1970) 'Improving Large Audience Teaching: The Programmed Lecture' in *British Journal of Medical Education*, vol. 14, no. 1

See also: Step-by-step discussion; Lecture method; Buzz group

STRUCTURED SOCIAL SKILL SEMINAR

Developed by Lievegoed and colleagues at the Paedagogisk Institut in Holland, this form of seminar is a watered down form of T-group experience. Group members are equipped with a degree of organisation by first convening a planning session where the group without an outside observer agrees on a task they wish to tackle. An observer attends the working sessions, analyses and subsequently discusses with the group the interactions that he has seen emerging, and their development. In this approach, the learning process is conducted at a more explicit level, and in a form that more closely relates to the participants work situations. It helps them to integrate newly found insights with the technical and conceptual skills they already possess.

See also: Laboratory method; Micro-lab: Coverdale training; Action training; Process analysis

STRUCTURING SEMINARS

Developed by Wilson, this is a seminar design which is built around student readings. Its distinguishing feature is that a pattern system is used which enables students to participate in the structuring of the discussion. Various attempts have been made by teachers to improve different forms of structured group discussion with varying degrees of success. The presentation prepared by the single student on a set topic with a precise title is usually read too fast for others to learn from it and this means that other students do little reading. Giving all students some reading does provide a good resource base, but a lack of overlap of material can lead to a series of individual student-tutor interactions. A 'contract learning' approach based on the confrontation of issues of non-participation may be useful but still leaves the tutor as the only person with an overview on the whole subject.

The Structuring Seminar is based on an approach used originally to plan essay or exam answers. A pattern system is developed in which ideas radiate from a central issue. Links are drawn between related concepts and then the chunks of material can be identified and ordered. Applied in the seminar setting, at the end of a previous session, the tutor tells the students a little about the literature of the subject to be discussed next week. He gives pointers to the key names and about how sources are grouped into schools. There is no specific allocation of reading. At the start of the seminar in the following week, the tutor goes round the group and asks each student what he or she has read and what they thought about what they had read. Would they, for example, recommend it to other members of the group and if so with what provisos? If someone had not done some reading this would be accepted at first, but if this was continued the terms of the contract would be pointed out.

After an exchange of literature, a pattern is created. It may be written on an overhead projector or board by either the lecturer or a student. The topic for the session discussion is placed in the middle and the tutor asks the students what things need to be looked at today. Some ideas start to emerge. As suggestions flow, the tutor intervenes to ask if these constitute a separate item or if they are capable of being grouped alongside an existing idea already presented. The main headings are identified and subheadings placed under them. Links are also established between different points. As the suggestions slow up, students are asked to draw lines on the diagram enclosing the points that could be dealt with together. Often, other students suggest how this could be done. These 'chunks' are then placed in order ready for discussion. The entire procedure need take only between ten and fifteen minutes.

The advantages of this form of seminar organisation are that it produces participation; the students are involved in creating the structure of the discussion and thus their willingness to participate is increased. The pattern created can also act as a warming-up/ice-breaking process where ideas can be thrown in without searching questions following. Secondly, it sets a level. The student contributions to the planning give a guide to the appropriate level of the ensuing discussion. The headings also indicate where the tutor might offer explanation or check understanding. The approach offers cues. The fact that a student makes a suggestion at the start makes it easy for him to be brought in later or to make links between contributions. Because the agenda has been presented at the start, it is easier to plan the allocation of time during the session. A final advantage is that the session is given a structure which is clear to all students.

Wilson, A. (1980) 'Structuring Seminars: a technique to allow students to participate in the structuring of small group discussions' in *Studies in Higher Education*, vol. 5, no. 1, pp. 81–4

See also: Construct lesson plan; Learning through discussion; Seminar; Discussion guides; Data approach method; Guided group problem solving

STUDENT-PLANNED LEARNING
Student-planned Learning is one of several forms of independent study models in existence. The label has been used to refer specifically to the programmes of study designed by students themselves which lead to the award of a recognised diploma or degree qualification. Perhaps the best known programmes of this kind in the United Kingdom are those run by the School of Independent Study at the North East London Polythecnic (NELP) and at the University of Lancaster. Crudely defined, Student-planned Learning is a mixture of Contract Learning and the Project Method applied over a period of several years which leads to the award of a qualification. The NELP programme aims to develop general competence in the student, encourage in him the development of transferable skills and requires him to demonstrate his competence in both individual and collaborative situations. These objectives are achieved through individual study by students working on their

specialism, but also through group work which uses various project methods and skills workshops to develop their general competence in group situations.

There are several varieties of the approach. In one version the student plans his learning and the output of this is a form of learning contract which is called a 'learning statement'. This is a signed agreement between the student, the school and a specialised area. The statement is amplified by six appendices which are attached to it. The first three of these represent the student's formulation of the educational problem as it is perceived by him. The fourth and fifth represent the proposed detailed solution to the problem. The final one represents the basis on which the completion of the solution is to be tested. The student-designed programme is validated in three ways. The student's proposed personal and specialist tutors indicate the extent to which they feel able to support the learning statement. The school, through an internal validation board, endorses the tutors' views or not. Finally, a validating board external to the school considers it.

Cunningham, I. (1981) 'Self Managed Learning in Independent Study' in Boydell, T. and Pedler, M. *Management Self-Development: Concepts and Practices*, Aldershot: Gower

Stephenson, J. (1981) 'Student Planned Learning' in Boud, D. J. (ed.) *Developing Student Autonomy in Learning*, Kogan Page Ltd

Cornwall, M. (1981) 'Putting it into Practice: Promoting Independent Learning in a Traditional Institution' in Boud, D. J. (ed.), ibid

Sheldon, B. (1981) 'A Decade of Student Autonomy in a Design School' in Boud, D. J. (ed.), ibid

Percy, K. and Ramsden, P. (1980) *Independent Study: two examples from English Higher Education*, Guildford, Surrey: Society for Research into Higher Education

Stephenson, J. (1980) 'The Use of Statements in North East London Polytechnic' in Adams, E. and Burgess, T. (eds) *Outcomes of Education*, London: Macmillan

FitzHenry, M. (1979) 'My Experience of Dip.H.E' in *The NELP Experience of Independent Study*, North East London Polytechnic School for Independent Study

See also: Independent study; Course design as learning; Collaboratively designed courses; Learning community; Learning organisation; Project orientation

STUDY ASSIGNMENT

A Study Assignment is a form of in-company training in which the trainee is asked to study and subsequently write a report upon some specified company procedure or operation. He does this by using written material such as files and documentation and by observing the system or administrative procedure. In the process, the trainee may talk to the people who work in the areas being studied. He can study all facets of the subject and thereby is able to get an overall idea of how the system or procedure works. Depres (1980) has identified four key elements which are required for this form of development to be successful: a good question; the maximum use of documents and observation; an element of contrast and comparison, and finally, the writing of a report followed by a discussion. The purpose of a good question is to interest and thereby to motivate the trainee. It is intended to direct his attention and suggest ways in which he can tackle the task. Requiring the learner to compare and contrast different procedures or work practices can lead him beyond mere description into an evaluation of what he is studying. The emphasis on documentation and observation comes from the fact that this minimises the amount of time that other staff will be interrupted by the trainee's questions. Moreover, once the trainee has done the background work and does come to interview others, he is likely to be better prepared and more knowledgeable. The writing of the report clarifies thinking and provides a focus for the discussion of the assignment. It also introduces him to the writing and production of business reports. Additional skills may be developed if the trainee is asked to summarise his findings verbally. The discussion of the report gives an opportunity for the learner to have any doubtful points clarified and the Study Assignment can be placed in the context of the total operation of the company. In setting up such an assignment, the tutor must check that the learner is able to obtain the information required, and needs to clarify to himself the objectives of the assignment that he sets the trainee.

However, it is not just the newly recruited trainee who can benefit from a Study Assignment. Different levels of management can be given different types of questions to answer. The marketing manager may be asked to work alongside the production manager to suggest ways in which the product can be improved. When a Study Assignment approach is used as an in-company training method it is essential that all company staff understand the aims and implications of the approach, and that they are likely to be interviewed about their work. Departments must be prepared to accept the learner, be he a new recruit or experienced manager. They must also be prepared to have departmental files examined.

As a developmental tool, the Study Assignment has numerous advantages. It is practical since it is related directly to the working of the company and its content is designed to form part of the individual's job. Used in conjunction with a college course on management, it can help to balance out the abstractions and unreality of some management training which uses role plays and business games. The learning is individually geared and the initiative for making the assignment a success lies with the trainee. The production and presentation of a report helps him to develop both written and oral skills. Moreover, for the tutor it involves minimum use of his time while making the maximum effective use of the trainee's time.

Depres, D. (1980) 'A Study Assignment Approach to Training' in *Journal of European Industrial Training*, vol. 4, no. 3, pp. 14–16

Mumford, A. (1980) *Making Experience Pay*, London: McGraw Hill

BACIE Journal (1976), 'Study Assignments', vol. 30, no. 11, December, p. 203

See also: Development assignment; Research assignment; Consulting assignment; Research degree; Work sheet; Prompt list; Library assignment

STUDY SERVICE (Experiential Education, Service Learning)
Study Service was a word coined by Third World countries and disseminated by UNESCO. It refers to planned excursions by students into 'the bush' to contribute their specialisms to the country's development. This is therefore a form of experiential education for which academic credit may be granted. In Britain, Study Service has come to mean the doing of socially valuable work by students in secondary as well as higher and further education. This was normally done in their course projects and field attachments. In Britain, Voluntary Service Overseas (VSO) and the Peace Corps in the United States provided the organisation to send the nationals of one country to the aid of another.

While there is no absolute definition of Study Service, the term is used here to refer to projects and placements which, while they are educationally conceived for those participating, nevertheless provide service to the host region or country. The emphasis is on social, community and national development. In some ways, Study Service can be considered as an aspect of Cooperative Education. For the sake of clarity however, the latter label is reserved to designate student placements in business, commercial and professional organisations, most of which are companies. Both may use the same techniques such as

Internships. Examples of Study Service in Britain are numerous. Dental students have visited schools to teach children about dental care and secretarial students carried out research projects for a Social Services Department. In Salford, children in a secondary school have been involved in 'School Concern Project'. This was organised jointly by Community Service Volunteers, and Salford Council's Education and Social Services Departments. Pupils helped design aids for the physically disabled including an alarm clock for the deaf. Elsewhere in the world, Study Service operates as a block release or block despatch of students to the 'bush'. Here one can quote Ethiopia's 'University Year of Service' (conducted two-thirds of the way through the course); Iran's 'Army of Education' (an alternative to military service) and Nepal's 'National Development Service'. From the participants' viewpoint, Study Service provides a form of learning experience in which members contend with challenging real-world problems. In so doing they contribute to their own maturation and promote the service ethic. It involves students 'learning by doing', translating individual and institutional knowledge into a form useful for the community. It provides an opportunity to practise altruism based on the view that learning can be productive and contribute to the benefit of others.

Whitley, P. (1980) *Study Service in the United Kingdom*, report presented to the Department of Education and Science by the Community Service Volunteers, London: CSV

Dickson, A. (1973) 'Linking Study with Service' in *Journal of Educational Development International*

Dickson, A. (1980) *Study Service: Problems and Opportunities*, Paris: UNESCO

Dickson, A. (1979) 'Amelioration, Evasion and Concern' in *New Universities Quarterly*, Winter

Holman, R. (1971–72) 'Students and Community Activity' in *Universities Quarterly*, vol. 26, pp. 187–94

See also: Cooperative education; Internship; Teaching as learning

STUDY SKILLS TRAINING

In recent years there has been a growth in the forms of training which aim to help students develop their personal study skills and make them aware of the standards of work required of them on their diploma and degree courses. For many years books providing revision notes and information on 'how to pass exams' proliferated. While these continue to be published, the recent trend has been towards providing guidance to students on how to manage their own learning. A stimulus to this has been the growth of numbers of mature students, such as those studying for Open University degrees, who either have had no previous experience of self-disciplined study or whose experience was gained a long time ago. Study Skills Training therefore focuses on developing in the student the ability to organise and manage his way through a programme of study. Three broad models of Study Skills Training exist. There is the Resource Centre approach in which the individual works on his own with perhaps a tape slide programme and response sheet. This might be located in a room which contains books and learning packages on improving study methods. Another model utilises group discussion methods where the tutor takes groups of students through a series of structured exercises designed to help them organise their study time better, or to write better essays. Finally, there is the individualised approach where the student has an audio tape and a book, and learns about study skills at home. There is naturally a great deal of overlap between the three approaches.

Main, A. (1980) *Encouraging Effective Learning*, Edinburgh: Scottish Academic Press

Gibbs, G. (1981) *Teaching Students to Learn*, Milton Keynes: Open University Educational Enterprises Ltd

Gibbs, G. (1977) *Group Study Skills Learning*, Institute of Educational Technology, Milton Keynes: Open University Press

Elton, L. R. B., Hodgson, V. E. and O'Connell, S. (1980) 'Study Counselling in the University of Surrey' in Hills, P. (ed.) *Study Courses and Counselling*, Guildford, Surrey: Society for Research into Higher Education

Buzan, T. (1980) *Use Your Head*, BBC Publications

Preparing for Study, Milton Keynes: Open University Press, 1979

Gibbs, G. P., Morgan, A. and Taylor, E. (1980) *Understanding Why Students Don't Learn*, Study Methods Group Report No. 5, Milton Keynes: Institute of Educational Technology

See also: Confidence-building training

STUDYCADE

Participants sign up on a Studycade programme on some topic, for example, community development. They are given a reading list, then meet several times to discuss their reading and to identify questions for further study. They then travel in chartered buses to visit community development projects in the surrounding area. Finally, a series of discussions is held to consolidate their learning. The focus of the learning approach is the seeing, at first hand, of what it is that is being studied.

See also: Educational visit; Field trip; Outward bound training

SURROGATE CLIENT (Simulated Client, Programmed Client)

Originally developed in the area of medical teaching, the use of Surrogate Clients involves training people into patient roles so that they are able to exhibit certain behaviours. Sometimes the label Simulated Clients is used interchangeably with Surrogate. However, in medical teaching, Simulated Client has a separate and specialised meaning. It refers to the use of non-human, mechanical or electronic patient substitute systems. Thus a computer programme which simulated a patient's illness and gave the student information about the patient's status and options would be an example of a Simulated Client. To make the distinction, the term Surrogate is used here. Nevertheless, there remains an overlap between labels in use, as the definition below indicates.

Barrows has defined a Surrogate Patient as 'a person who has been trained to simulate a patient or any aspect of a patient's illness depending upon the educational need. A simulated patient can reproduce faithfully the psychological, emotional, historical and physical manifestations of a patient from observation, interview and examination'. The historical reasons for the development of this teaching method were twofold. First, there were insufficient patients coming with the diseases that could be shown to medical students for teaching purposes. Those who did come tended to have complex disorders and were seen by senior specialists. Second, it was felt that the affective/psychological problems in the doctor–patient interaction were not being dealt with adequately in the training. Students demonstrated an inability to obtain the relevant information about patients' histories in the time available; failed to elicit their real problems and did not pick up the verbal and non-verbal cues from the patient.

Surrogate Clients involve the use of actors who are briefed or 'programmed' with simple medical histories. They are the first real contacts that students have with a patient. The purpose of the training is not only medical, but also social. For example how to greet a patient, show concern for his problems, how to elicit spontaneous reporting by him of his state of health, and how to create quickly a climate of mutual trust. The emphasis is on the development of the social skills which help create an environment in which effective medical care can be provided. Surrogate patients are recruited from ordinary students, drama students and professional actors. While the last of these are expensive, they have been found to be good. They are able to 'turn on and off' the characters they play.

One of the most important aspects of the approach is that during an interview with a Surrogate Client, if the medical student is unhappy about the way it is going, he can call 'time out'. The action stops and both parties come out of their roles temporarily. During this break, the student may ask for feedback from the Client about his perceptions and feelings. The two discuss the impasse and the Client may help the student formulate a way out of his dilemma. The pair then get back into their roles and the interview continues. Following such role plays, there is a period of group discussion with feedback from the Surrogate Client, other students and the tutor. The purpose may be to make the students aware of the value of open-ended questions and to emphasise how they communicated through non-verbal cues. Students taught by this method felt they were better able to examine patients alone without supervision, and experienced less anxiety. It permitted the practice of patient examination techniques without tiring patients or aggravating their illness. It allowed repetitive examinations which gave each student experience of the same doctor–patient interactions and permitted the artificial termination of interviews so as to discuss matters at a time which would be educationally relevant to the student but therapeutically inappropriate to a real patient. It allowed some control of the variables in a patient examination situation and it provided a unique form of feedback to students from a hitherto ignored source.

Ostrow, D. N. (1980) 'Surrogate Patients in Medical Education' in *Programmed Learning and Educational Technology*, vol. 17, no. 2, pp. 82–9

Barrows, H. S. (1971) *Simulated Patients (Programmed Patients)* Springfield, Illinois: Charles C. Thomas

Barrows, H. S. and Abrahamson, S. (1964) 'Training of Simulated Patients' in *Journal of Medical Education*, vol. 39, pp. 802–7

See also: Simulation; Role playing; Role reversal; Sociodrama

SYMMETRICAL COMMUNICATION

Symmetrical Communication is a category of communication and interaction structuring. It is a structure of communication which allows all participants in a learning situation, teachers and students, to be partners in communication on equal terms despite their differences in status and knowledge. Cooperation and symmetrical communication are considered as a process of continuous effort. They are ideas to be strived for through course design, teaching/learning method selection and style of interaction. Thus the tutor would attempt to structure a given learning situation in such a way that both he and the students engage in a partnership of learning despite the institutional constraints and learners' expectations which would push him in the direction of expert-learner forms of interaction. This task is achieved by the application of a set of rules of communication. One of these is that the tutor refuses to present himself continuously as an expert, but takes instead the role of moderator or facilitator and acts as a catalyst. In interacting with students, the tutor would firstly aim to achieve a symmetry of communication before moving on to use the basis of that communication structure as the basis for further work. In the first stage, the tutor initiates interactions with students which are intended to prepare the partners involved for mutual understanding. He can do this in a number of ways. For example, by encouraging students who indicate their desire non-verbally to take part in the discussion. He might involve students by asking questions more frequently and maintaining longer silences after the questions have been asked, thereby giving a non-verbal cue which signals his desire for student participation. A second strategy used might stress the need of all the participants in the learning situation to understand each other's contributions to discussions before responding themselves. This is more than merely developing listening skills which, nevertheless, is important. It emphasises that in listening and seeking to understand another's contribution, one is valuing both the contribution and the person who makes it. The emphasis in this phase is on the encouragement of student contributions by a demonstration of their legitimacy. Two other forms of interaction are used in an effort to establish mutual understanding between learners and tutors. The latter seek to maintain fairness and tolerance by not letting a participant be offended or injured by unbalanced opinion. Finally, the tutor may take on temporarily the role of expert if specifically requested by the students.

Once a symmetrical structure of communication has been achieved, these overt strategies can be abandoned since the interaction will reflect the partnership in communication. Communication in the learning situation can become open and unreserved so that members feel able to share with others their thoughts and their feelings. Within such a climate, it is possible for negotiations to take place regarding the aims and strategies of learning. Described in this way, Symmetrical Communication can be considered as one of the first stages in the establishment of a Learning Community. However, its appliction goes beyond that particular approach. The notion cuts across the structures of academic hierarchy, and across the differences of status and knowledge attributed to the respective roles of students and teachers. Symmetrical Communication can be considered as a strategy which underlies the teaching and learning approaches such as Experience-based Learning, Project Orientation and Confluent Education. The theoretical background of this viewpoint is derived from American pragmatism including elements of symbolic interactionism. Charles Sanders Peirce's claim of a 'Community without definite limits, and capable of a definite increase of knowledge' was taken over by the German philosopher Karl-Otto Apel. Apel described an 'ideal' community as one being capable of defining its own rules of interaction and anticipating that there would be a consensus based on these rules. In a real community things are different. Human behaviour is shaped, according to this view, by the desire to reach this ideal community of man.

Werner, B. and Drexler, I. (1978/79) 'Structures of Communication and Interaction in Courses for Junior Staff Members of the Faculties of Engineering, TH Aachen' in *Bulletin of Educational Research*, nos. 16 and 17

Brandt, D. (1980) 'Notions and Strategies of Staff Development Programmes' in *Proceedings of the Sixth International Conference on Improving University Teaching*, University of Maryland, Lausanne, 9–12 July

See also: Learning community; Confluent education

SYMPOSIUM MEETING

A Symposium is a speech or lecture in which an audience listens to formal presentations given from a platform. A chairman usually opens the meeting with a few stage-setting remarks and then calls upon other platform members for each of their contributions. There may be two or more speakers each of whom is expected to deliver a formal or prepared talk on a subject. If the meeting closes after each has spoken, then a true Symposium will have been demonstrated. The objective of this form of event is to present many points of view on a particular subject and to help exploit all the possible aspects of a topic in the presence of an audience, thus broadening the flow of knowledge if each speaker is well prepared and keeps on the topic. Though each speaker's time is short, it is often possible to identify and explore problems quite thoroughly. Symposia are frequently more acceptable to an audience than speeches since they have many speakers thereby reducing boredom. The responsibility of the chairman is to introduce each speaker and ensure that each keeps within the time limit. There is no participation by the audience. Very large groups of up to 500 may attend. The ancient forms of Symposia were more participative. Up to twenty people met in someone's home to discuss informally a topic of mutual interest. Often it became a systematic study of a topic after the completion of a meal. Perhaps a managerial 'working breakfast or lunch' is the modern equivalent. It was also used by churches to gather people to discuss a topic. In the modern version, a group of much larger size meets to hear about a problem of common interest. Three to six members are assigned the task of developing short speeches which last a total of up to twenty minutes and are presented to the whole group. These are used to supply information to the audience. The Symposium is good for presenting an introduction to a group in an organised manner, for clarifying points and stimulating group thinking. The technique guards against the oversimplification of a topic and the shortness of the speeches forces the speakers to stay on their topic. However, the method may lack sufficient audience involvement, it is difficult to determine audience learning and if the speakers are uninteresting or incompetent, it can become boring.

See also: Colloquy meeting; Forum meeting; Brains trust; Panel discussion

SYNDICATE GROUP METHOD

The Syndicate Group Method refers to a form of learning where the class is divided into groups of about six members who work on the same or related problems with intermittent teacher contact and who write a joint report for the critical appraisal of the whole class. The approach involves a combination of lectures and group projects. Group projects are assigned to small groups of participants called Syndicates from subjects that follow from and are supported by lectures. Each Syndicate selects a chairman who conducts the discussions and leads his group in its work of preparing a report on an assigned task, topic or case study. A Secretary is also appointed who prepares the report. All syndicate members participate in the work and in the preparation of the report. Representatives are then nominated to make a presentation to the entire class. In the Henley model, the composition of the syndicates is changed from time to time to provide a stimulus and an opportunity to members to work with different people and to bring together or rotate those with specialist knowledge and/or experience. The term 'Syndicate' has in the past been loosely applied to any situation where a large class is broken up into small groups which go off to discuss some question(s) set by the tutor. Here, the term Syndicate Method is used to refer to an approach originally developed at the Administrative Staff College in Henley, England. In this purest form, a group of managers is given a subject brief or an agenda for discussion. One of the syndicate members is required to act as chairman. There is usually an oral and written report and the report of each group is discussed at a plenary session run by the tutor. The knowledge and experience of syndicate group members is supplemented by reading, films, and lectures given on the relevant subjects. The approach relies on the ability and willingness of people to learn from each other and appears to be most successful in the modification of attitudes.

As mentioned earlier, this original use has been adapted and, like the use of the term Case Study, rather generalised. Syndicate Discussion is the label now applied whenever groups of managers come together to discuss a question which is then followed by group reports and a plenary. This approach certainly promotes activity on the part of members, but this will not be shared equally since syndicate members do not contribute equally. The method helps people to disagree and learn by doing so. However, because of the generality of such discussions, ineffectiveness of most syndicate chairmen and low level involvement, the approach has been criticised and decribed as 'organising an exchange of ignorance'. If a series of syndicate groups are working simultaneously on a set of different problems, or even if they are working on different versions of the same problem, it is possible to vary the membership of the groups. Other meetings are held at which a member from one of the groups organises a relevant demonstration or presentation to which members of any syndicate group can come and participate in.

Evans, C. (1980) 'The Use of Student Led Groups or Syndicates in French Literature Classes' in *British Journal of Educational Technology*, vol. 11, no. 3, pp. 185–200

Collier, K. (1968–69) 'Syndicate Methods: Further Evidence and Comment' in *Universities Quarterly*, vol. 23, no. 4, pp. 431–6

Collier, K. G. (1965–66) 'An Experiment in University Teaching',

Universities Quarterly, vol. 20, no. 3, pp. 336–48

Lawrence, G. (1972) 'The Syndicate Method' in *Varieties of Group Discussion in University Teaching*, University of London Institute of Education

Bertcher, H. J. and Maple, F. F. (1977) *Creating Groups*, Sage Human Services Guide, London: Sage Publications Ltd

Adams, J. (1975) 'The Use of Syndicates in Management Training' in Taylor, B. and Lippitt, G. L. (eds) *Management Development and Training Handbook*, London: McGraw Hill

See also: Problem-centred group; Group discussion

SYNECTICS

Synectics is one of several available approaches to creativity training. It is however one of the oldest and best developed. It is based on a number of hypotheses. These are that creative efficiency in people can be markedly increased if they understand the psychological processes by which they operate; that in the creative process, the emotional component is more important than the intellectual, and the irrational more important than the rational view; and finally, that it is these emotional and irrational elements which can and must be understood in order to increase the probability of success in a problem-solving situation. It is believed that such releases of creativity can come by the use of certain structured problem-solving techniques which are introduced in special training programmes. The word 'synectics' comes from the Greek 'synektikos', meaning fit, to hold together, or the joining together of apparently irrelevant elements. It was developed by W. J. J. Gordon. It was George Prince who founded Synectics Inc. which made Gordon's theory into a practical technique. They used it to decribe a method of directing creative potential imagination towards solving technical and theoretical problems. Synectics is a problem-stating and problem-solving technique which is 'played' by a small closely-knit group trained for the purpose. A variety of techniques are used in Synectics training. Some change the climate of the work situation to release creative ability that is normally suppressed. The better climate also leads to improved communications, better teamwork, constructive resolution of conflict and higher morale. By working at the level of individual transactions, Synectics develops basic interpersonal skills and while it was originally developed to help improve creativity and problem-solving abilities, it has an application to every kind of situation which involves interaction between people.

A Synectics group consists of persons with a wide range of personalities, skills and interests since it is held that such heterogeneity of views can aid the search for new ideas. Within the group the techniques used force members to verbalise both thoughts and feelings. There are six steps in the Synectics approach to problem solving:

1 The problem as given is reviewed by members.
2 The problem is restated and reduced to essentials by members.
3 A connection is made by direct analogy between the key element in the problem and an object or organisation in a completely different field.
4 Following the direct analogy, a personal analogy is made. Having identified with the new analogous object or organism, members imagine how it might feel.
5 There is encouragement to analyse the perceptions and feelings in terms of intrinsic contradictions and to sum up the conflict in a two-word phrase.
6 Finally, there is a return to the problem as stated in the second step and the insights gained are used to obtain a new view of the problem.

Underlying the technique is the view that rational thinking tends to be judgemental, evaluative and tends to stay within known, safe areas where solutions are produced which 'make sense'. A Synectics approach aims to release the individual from the constraints of stereotypes and to widen the scope for solutions. The emotional, non-rational processes are emphasised, being seen as the source of new ideas and solutions. The tutor's role is to keep the group moving along through each of the steps outlined earlier and to encourage members' imaginative abilities and assist them to verbalise their thoughts and feelings about the problem.

Alexander, J. (1980) 'Synectics' in *Training*, vol. 6, no. 7, pp. 20–22

'Synectics' in *Industrial Training International*, August 1973, pp. 242–50

Gordon, W. J. J. (1970) *Synectics: The Development of Creative Capacity*, New York: Harper and Row

Prince, G. (1970) *The Practice of Synectics*, New York: Harper and Row

Alexander, J. (1979) 'Synectics, Problem-Solving and Interpersonal Skills' in *BACIE Journal*, vol. 33, no. 1, January

Rickards, T. and Freedman, B. (1979) 'A Reappraisal of Creativity Techniques' in *Journal of European Industrial Training*, vol. 3, no. 1

See also: Creativity training; Lateral thinking; Brainstorming

TALK

Abell has argued that lectures can fulfil a number of functions but that the transmission of information is not one of these. He argued that their most useful function was to inspire and stimulate listeners. Thus to distinguish 'non-information' lectures from the traditional type, the term Talk is used. Various types of 'Talks' were proposed by Abell. There is a 'come with me' Talk which is a narrative of enquiry in which the speaker describes the actual inquiry process which a group of researchers followed in making a discovery. Ideas for such lectures can be obtained from books on research projects, research papers or conversations with researchers who are asked to describe how they went about their studies, what clues they followed and how they felt. Watson's account of the discovery of the structure of DNA in *The Double Helix* would be a good example. In the 'glimpses of great men' Talk, a well known lecturer, manager, industrialist or researcher is invited to come and reminisce before a group of listeners. Video-tapes or films can be used if the persons themselves are not available. The 'flavour of the month' Talk is a case study or historical vignette about a company or industry which is intended to give an idea of how it is, or was, managed. In a 'dialogue, live interview or debate' Talk up to four people exchange views before a group, with or without its participation. Two lecturers may discuss a topic of interest, either semi-scripted or cold; for example, how new technology is introduced. The approach to the problem and the underlying thinking are more important than the particular information being conveyed. The 'paired antithetical' Talk is one in which two speakers with opposing viewpoints give separate lectures. These can be staged or real. The 'challenge' Talk can present evidence in support of a mistaken view, e.g. a lecturer delivers a talk proving that the earth is in fact flat. A variation of this is the 'ring' lecture in which a series of lecturers with differing viewpoints on the same topic take turns to present these. Each week a different lecturer makes his presentation. Not only challenging, the lecture may also bring new realism to old ideas by using theatrical techniques. The 'lecture-experiment' in which the speaker performs an experiment in front of an audience also has a long tradition. The 'analysis of news' Talk involves a major newspaper like *The Times*, *The Sunday Times* or *The Financial Times* being used as required reading and the lecturer probes and discusses the news. In a 'non-manager's look at management' Talk, a group of people from outside the world of management, e.g. ministers, musicians, artists, form a panel and discuss what's wrong with British management. Like a programmed text, a 'programmed lecture' is a Talk which is given in a programmed way. Such a method is useful if one has an auditorium equipped with direct student response capabilities (sometimes called a Feedback Classroom). The lecturer can ask for responses to questions, and these are punched in by listeners from their seats. These are tallied by a small computer and instant feedback is given to the tutor and students. A high percentage of incorrect answers means that the tutor will 'branch' in his lecture to cover in greater depth a point not fully understood by students.

At the margin of a Talk there is what Abell described as the 'concentrated visual experience'. This involves not merely illustrating one's Talk with slides but using slides or film to replace talk completely. These may be shown silently first and later with commentary. They can be followed by quizzes and repeated for immediate feedback. A colour slide might be shown and the students told: 'You have four minutes to describe what you see in this slide' or a series of slides are shown and the question asked: 'What is the most important thing in each of these slides?' or 'Interpret what you see in this slide'. These can be used for value clarification purposes by asking participants to make and defend choices. There need not be any correct answers, but the technique can produce a lot of interaction. A 'multisensory experience' or psychedelic lecture can be used to integrate perception, emotion and several kinds of subject matter. One can use slide projectors, bioscopes, polarising projectors, cassette recorders, cine projectors and multi-image systems to bombard participants with sensations.

Abell, D. (1970) 'On Lecturing Without Really Lecturing, Part 1' in *CUEBS News*, vol. 6, no. 3, February, Council on Undergraduate Education in the Biological Sciences, USA, pp. 7–10

Carl, J. and O'Brien, N. (1970) 'Classroom Debate' in *Journal of Geological Education*, vol. 18, p. 122

See also: Confluent education; Feedback classroom; Lecture method

TALKING WALL
A Talking Wall is a large group feedback device. It can be used at the end or in the middle of a course, seminar or conference to obtain participants' reactions to the proceedings. It is capable of being used with groups of

fifteen to sixty. The device is intended to be an enjoyable way of collecting participants' views and one which actively involves them both as initiators and respondents. The method also reflects members' rather than the organiser's perceptions of the important aspects of the event and can sample opinions on a wider range of topics than is usual at an end-of-event large group discussion. The approach involves the participants designing, answering and analysing a questionnaire. All participants are assembled in a large room and the procedure is explained to them. They each receive a handful of computer cards on the backs of which they write statements describing any significant features of the event they have been attending. One statement is written per card. For example, they may write 'Guest speaker rotten', 'Food excellent', 'Duplicating facilities crummy'. Usually, five or six cards are completed by each person. These are then attached to strips of sticky tape which hang on the wall from underneath a number of 'heading cards' which have been placed around the walls of the hall or room by the organiser. Before the activity begins, the organiser selects the six or so headings relevant to the event being evaluated, e.g. Facilities, Administration, Contributors. These are fixed to the wall with a strip of sticky tape (sticky side outwards) below. Participants walk around and stick their completed cards under the most appropriate heading so that they can be read by others. Once all members have placed their cards and read the others, the organiser invites participants to form roughly equal-size groups around each heading. The job of these small groups is to remove the cards, sort them and identify recurring themes. Five or six such themes might emerge and each one will be represented by a positive statement, e.g. 'Conference contributors were all of high quality'. All the statements are written on a single sheet of flip-chart paper leaving enough room on the righthand side for columns headed: strongly agree, agree, neutral, disagree, strongly disagree. The completed flip-chart questionnaire, based on individual cards, is then fixed to the wall. Each heading is now represented by such a sheet. The participants then go from chart to chart, read each of the statements on the chart, and indicate the degree of their agreement or disagreement by a tick or dot in the appropriate column. Once everybody has completed all the question-naires, the small groups for each heading reassemble briefly to total the responses, and then the entire membership meets in plenary. A representative from each group in turn reports a summary of results and a general discussion takes place.

See also: Fishbowl exercise; Process analysis; Instrumented feedback

TAPE/SLIDE PROGRAMME

Tape/Slide is the name given to an audiotape accompanied by a sequence of slides. In general, the audiotape contains, apart from the soundtrack, signals which make it possible for the slides to change automatically at prearranged points during the commentary. As well as being an ideal medium for student self instruction, Tape/Slide Programmes can be an effective lecture substitute for audiences of all sizes, and can be used in the teaching of skills as a viable supplement to, or substitute for, manuals. The material to be illustrated must be of the type that lends itself to visualisation, e.g. hazards to safety in factories. Tape/slide involves two channels of communication, visual and aural. Research shows that each has its own characteristics. If you overload both, or one at the expense of the other, then conflict will be created between channels and learning inhibited as a result. The visual will tend to dominate so the audio should be linked to it, but slavish descriptions of the visual with little other stimulation should be avoided. If possible each slide should make only one point, and the whole programme should not exceed twenty minutes.

Active involvement by the student in the learning process tends to increase response, either in oral or written form. Standard response sheets or accompanying booklets can also be provided. A major advantage of tape/slide is that the student can replay the material at will, as often as he needs to master it. The glamour of specially produced management training films and video has tended to put tape/slide into the shadow of late. Nevertheless, it does possess unique advantages over the other two methods, particularly in the areas of cost, simplicity of production and ease of updating. A number of companies produce tape/slide training packages on topics such as critical path analysis, decision making, report writing and industrial relations legislation.

Duncalf, D. (1978) *The Focal Guide to Tape Slide*, Focal Press

Towsend, I. (1976) 'Producing a Tape/Slide Package' in *Visual Education*, February, pp. 17–19; March, pp. 23–7; April, pp. 23–4

Hills, P. J. (1977) 'Tape/Slide Presentations and Teaching Packages for Library User Education', SCONUL, London

Jamieson, G. H. and Marchant, H. (1971) 'Learning by Tape/Slide; Linear Programme and Illustrated Booklet: A Comparative Study' in *Programmed Learning and Educational Technology*, vol. 8, pp. 245–50

See also: Programmed learning; Tape stop exercise; Audio-tutorial method; Autonomous learning group; Audio tape

TAPE STOP EXERCISE

Trainees sit around a tape recorder on which is played a conversation between two people, e.g. salesman and customer, appraiser and appraisee. From time to time the tape is stopped just as the key person is about to give a reply. The trainees' task is either to write down what they would say next if they were in that position, or to say out loud their response if the trainer points to them. A typical tape conversation might be as follows:

Union Rep:	My members are dissatisfied with the way in which Mr Smith has been treated.
Manager:	Mr Smith had been warned about his behaviour in the past.
Union Rep:	Past warnings don't give you the right to suspend him!
Manager:	?

The trainer stops the tape and points to one of the listeners who responds quickly and directly speaking the words the manager might use. The trainer may ask a number of participants to reply orally or in writing. He then has the choice of discussing responses or going on to find out what the manager actually says and evaluating the responses. Tape Stop exercises are easy to design and can be based upon the daily work activities of trainees.

See also: Interpersonal process recall; Trigger film

TAPE-ASSISTED LEARNING PROGRAMME

This involves groups of students being instructed by audiotapes. Such instructional programmes have been used in human relations training, e.g. to develop active listening, team development, problem solving and decision making skills. The key characteristic of this method is that it can be used by a group of students, working alone without the need for a tutor. During the session participants listen to the tape. This describes a structured activity for a group of nine to twelve people. The tape is stopped, and the activity carried out. The tape programme is designed to run up to a dozen sessions or more, and the same group may meet regularly for the entire set of sessions. A further sophistication is to add a tape/slide facility, and to link it to the feedback session on the performance of the structured activity. This makes it partially, a programmed learning situation.

Berzon, B. and Reisel, J., *Effective Interpersonal Relationships*, Mansfield: University Associates of Europe

Soloman, L. N. and Berzon, B., *Employee and Team Development*, Mansfield: University Associates of Europe

Tape Assisted Learning Programmes for Health Care Professionals, Mansfield: University Associates of Europe

See also: Audio tape; Audio tutorial method; Learning through discussion; Instrumented team learning; Media-activated learning group; Tape/slide programme; Tape stop exercise; Micro-lab

TASK FORCE ASSIGNMENT
Within a company, task force teams may be established to deal with particular topics or customers. Thus a major buyer may wish to computerise a large part of his manufacturing operation. A task force team from the computer company would be assembled to work on the customer's objective over a short period of time and the work may demand creative responses from members to the problems which arise. In this way, team members can gain an insight into topics such as problem solving and team work. A Task Force Assignment would involve the task force team in clarifying and agreeing on the objectives of the assignment, even where the overt objectives may have already been specified. The group may also need to agree on the process or learning objectives in addition to the content ones just mentioned.

See also: Development assignment; Committee assignment; Evaluation assignment; Proposal team assignment; Research assignment; Staff meeting assignment; Study assignment

TAVISTOCK CONFERENCE METHOD (Bion Group)
The Tavistock Working Conference is an educational event which has been run by the Tavistock Institute of Human Relations since 1957. These conferences have sometimes erroneously been considered as another type of T-group training. While a small group event is one of several aspects, the conference as a whole has an objective, theoretical base and methodology which is both separate and unique. Theoretically, it is grounded in the psychoanalytical work of Sigmund Freud and Melanie Klein. The working model owes much to Wilfred Bion's

therapeutic community approach to the treatment of psychological casualties during the Second World War. The emphasis throughout is at the group level (manifested in individual behaviour). The group is held to face always a choice between emotionality and work. It is this choice and how it is resolved in different contexts that forms the Tavistock Conference Method. The conference itself is designed to be a temporary educational institution in which group dynamics are examined. The focus is on the covert and overt processes which influence the way in which it behaves. The model emphasises and examines the concepts of role, task, authority, boundary and leadership within the context of a system. A Tavistock Conference consists of a series of different events (small group, institutional, large group, inter-group) in which about forty members participate.

Smith, P. B. (1980) *Group Processes and Personal Change*, London : Harper and Row

Rice, A. K. (1965) *Learning for Leadership*, London: Tavistock Publications

Trist, E. L. and Sofer, C. (1959) *Explorations in Group Relations*, Leicester University Press

Higgin, G. and Bridger, H. (1965) *The Psychodynamics of an Intergroup Experience*, London: Tavistock Institute of Human Relations, Pamphlet no. 10

Grinberg, L., Sor, D. and Tabak de Bianchedi, E. (1975) *Introduction to the Work of Bion*, Roland Harris Educational Trust, Strath Tay, Scotland: Clunie Press

Astrachan, B. M. and Flynn, H. R. (1976) 'The Intergroup Exercise' in Miller, E. J. (ed.) *Task and Organisation*, Chichester: John Wiley and Sons

Lawrence, W. G. (ed.) (1979) *Exploring Individual and Organizational Boundaries*, Chichester; John Wiley and Sons

Palmer, B. W. M. (1979) 'The Study of a Small Group in an Organizational Setting' in Babington-Smith, B. and Farrell, B. A. (eds) *Training in Small Groups*, Oxford: Pergamon Press

See also: Organisational laboratory; Power laboratory; Mini-society; Group dynamics laboratory; Human relations laboratory; Laboratory method; Personal development laboratory; Sensitivity (T-group) training; Team laboratory

TEACHING AS LEARNING (Cross-Age Tutoring, Inter-grade Tutoring, Peer Instruction, Youth Tutoring Youth, Each One Teach One)

The idea of students teaching other students goes back a long way in the history of education. While Peer Teaching is used to describe students teaching their colleagues and is described elsewhere, the label Teaching as Learning is reserved for a situation in which senior students teach younger ones. The approach is based on the theoretical proposition suggested by role theory that children learn more effectively from people nearer their own age than from teachers who are older and different in their general outlook and culture. Those doing the tutoring are likely to reinforce their own commitment to the material being taught and find their behaviour constrained by the role expectations of those whom they teach. Further, learning theory suggests that the young people will learn more effectively with the individual attention that tutoring can provide than with the normal high staff–pupil ratio.

An example of a study service scheme doing work of direct social value operates in the London Borough of Pimlico. Honours degree students in engineering from London University are required to do a project which involves a study of technical questions which are complicated by social, political or economic issues. Alternatively, they are required to study social problems to which engineers might contribute a remedy. As part of this project, twelve students visited a London comprehensive school for fifteen weeks during one academic year to help with the teaching of science. An evaluation of the tutoring provided constituted the subject of the group project. In this kind of method, various kinds of tutoring arrangements are possible. They range from in-class cooperation between pairs of pupils of approximately equal age (Peer Teaching), via cross-age, cross-class tutoring which involves regular meetings between older/abler pupils and younger/less able ones, to monitorial instruction in which older students move around the class assisting where necessary. The experiences and preferences of the London University students in the Pimlico experiment led them to a team-tutoring approach where teams of three to five undergraduates moved around the classroom as required, to help individuals or groups of pupils under the overall supervision and direction of the classroom teacher. The materials used by the students varied widely. Some were highly structured such as programmed texts, text books and worksheet-based approaches. The undergraduates worked with the pupils, discussing experiments with them, answering their questions, posing supplementary questions etc. To do this, the undergraduates were given a one-day training session using video, brainstorming problems and role playing. In terms of personal benefits, these students reported developing skills in the simple communication of scientific ideas and getting to know people from different social backgrounds. Secondary benefits included discovering how others perceived your subject and a feeling that one was doing something useful with what one had learned.

Goodlad, S., Abidi, A., Anslow, P. and Harris, J. (1979) 'The Pimlico Connection: Undergradutes As Tutors in Schools' in *Studies in Higher Education*, vol. 4, no. 2, pp. 191–201

Abidi, A. et al. (1976) *The Pimlico Connection*, Imperial College, London

Anslow, P. et al. (1977) *The Pimlico Connection: Phase 2*, , Department of Electrical Engineering, Imperial College, London

Goodlad, S., Atkins, J. and Harris, J. (1978) *Undergraduates as School Science Tutors: a report on a project in three inner London Comprehensive schools – including the 'Pimlico Connection', Phase 3*, Imperial College, London

Goodlad, S. (1979) *Learning by Teaching: An Introduction to Tutoring*, London: Community Service Volunteers

Klaus, D. J. (1973) *Students as Teaching Resources: a survey of teaching models using non-professionals*, Pittsburgh: American Institutes of Research

See also: Peer teaching; Cooperative learning; Study service; Project orientation; Internship; Field project/attachment

TEACHING OUTSIDE YOUR FIELD

This involves a lecturer in one subject, e.g. human behaviour, teaching in another, e.g. accounting. Within a single business school it may merely involve a subject change for the individual concerned. Over time it may develop a tendency for lecturers and their students to take a much broader point of view regarding management. Students benefit since they and the teacher are realistically 'learning partners' and can thereby mutually explore problems. The instructor may develop new approaches to the subject which can benefit students, since these teachers may have totally new ideas about proper organising principles, and may see new patterns and paradigms. It is further argued that new teachers are likely to choose texts that they found useful in course preparation whereas subject 'experts' are more concerned with completeness and organisation when selecting a text. Benefits are also held to accrue to the teaching staff who may become revitalised through the discovery of new material and in finding creative ways in which to teach it. The school or department may also benefit in that increased professional interaction across traditional departmental lines can stimulate new research questions and interdisciplinary interests. The general benefit is to the teacher who, in the role of the student, is more able to appreciate the learning problems of the subject material. However, the body of knowledge to be applied may be so unconnected to a lecturer's skills or interests that neither he nor the student benefit from this approach. In general therefore, such experiments might be limited to introductory courses in the different discipline fields.

Loper, M. and Armor, T. (1978) 'Teaching Outside Your Field' in *Management Education and Development*, vol. 9, no. 3, pp. 197–201

Hilgert, R. and Ling, C. (1974) 'Team Teaching a Course in Business and Society' in *Improving College and University Teaching*

Stoddart, J. (1975) 'Advance Needed in Business Education' in *Higher Education Review*, vol. 7, no. 3

See also: Team teaching

TEAM DEVELOPMENT (Team Training, Team Building)
Since individual managers spend much of their time working in groups, it is understandable that a great deal of energy and resources have been devoted in management development to the composition, development and functioning of teams. Particular forms of laboratory training are only one of several approaches used to improve team functioning. Team Development can be conducted in different ways. Structured interventions are frequently used to increase the effectiveness and thereby the performance of individual managers who work together on a daily basis. Frank and Margerison (1978) have explained that the team 'developed' may be the 'work family' (consisting of the manager and those who work immediately below him), a 'peer group' (managers at the same level of seniority heading different departments) or 'project teams' (groups brought together for a limited time or specific purpose).

Belbin, R. N. (1981) *Management Teams: Why They Succeed or Fail*, London: Heinemann

McLean, A. (1981) 'Organizational Development: A Case of the Emperor's New Clothes' in *Personnel Review*, vol. 10, no. 1, pp. 3–14

Woodcock, M. (1979) *Team Development Manual*, Aldershot: Gower

Stephens, C. and Young, D. (1976) 'Team Development' in *Journal of European Training*, vol. 5, no. 1, pp. 36–45

Honey, P. and Whiteley, P. (1976) 'So They Think They Want To Improve Their Teamwork?' in *Industrial and Commercial Training*, vol. 8, no. 12, pp. 473–7

Mangham, I. (1976) 'Team Development in Industry' in Cooper, C. L. (ed.) *Developing Social Skills in Managers: Advances in Group Training*, London: Macmillan

Industrial Training International, 1975, 'Developing More Effective Teams', Part 1 in vol. 10, no. 6; Part 2 in vol. 10, no. 7; Part 3 in vol. 10, no. 8; Part 4 in vol. 10, no. 9 and Part 5 in vol. 10, no. 10

Kilcourse, T. (1980) 'Team Building with Grids and Matrices' in *Training*, vol. 6, no. 3, pp. 4–9

Margerison, C. J. and Hunter, N. (eds) (1978) 'Group Training and Team Building' in *Management and Organizational Development Bibliography*, Section II, 2nd edition, Bradford: MCB Publications

Frank, E. and Margerison, C. (1978) 'Training Methods and Organizational Development' in *Journal of European Industrial Training*, vol. 2, no. 4, pp. 17–18

See also: Team laboratory; Coverdale training; Grid training; Tavistock conference method; Illuminative incident analysis

TEAM LABORATORY (Organisational Development Group)
Organisational teams often find it useful to use a laboratory in order to focus on the individual learning that appears in the context of working directly on real organisational problems. Laboratory learning can have a direct impact on the operations of the team involved. The subject matter for the team's discussions would be the real-life issues, problems and dilemmas that the team is experiencing. The learning inputs and

laboratory design would be aimed at helping the group to identify the issues more clearly as well as to generate solutions. The outcomes of such laboratories are twofold. One is the immediate advantage of sharpening the present operating procedures of the team. The second is the development of skills for dealing with such problems in the future.

Smith, P. B. (1980) *Group Processes and Personal Change*, London: Harper and Row

See also: Team development; Grid training; Illuminative incident analysis; Sensitivity (T-group) training; Laboratory method; Group dynamics laboratory; Human relations laboratory; Micro-lab; Mini-society; Organisational laboratory; Personal development laboratory; Power laboratory

TEAM TEACHING

Team Teaching is concerned with interdisciplinary, integrative presentations, e.g. lecture discussions, seminars, or case study sessions. It is a method of teaching by two or more tutors of different disciplines in combination. In order to work it appears that those involved must have a facility in their own discipline, be sympathetic to and have an understanding of one another and have a liking for this teaching method. Some of the difficulties that have been encountered in getting it started have included the choice of unsuitable material, over-preparation by teachers leading to synthetic changeover and the tutors always trying to be in agreement with one another. Surveys reveal that the method is time consuming in terms of material preparation, team member coordination and contact hour duplication. The need to clarify points of disagreement between tutors to the students may result in the learning going over students' heads. Problems also appeared to develop around the issues of status, conflict and interpersonal relationships among tutors. Team Teaching is an attempt to make management education less discipline-compartmentalised and, in various forms, is in widespread use in institutions concerned with management education. Potentially it offers students more depth of learning and the tutors can benefit from a wider understanding of management problems. When the team collaborates on a central lecture or discussion course, it may well be that each member may independently give seminars, or set and mark assignments. Lecturers may take seminars in a team teaching mode, but it may not be all the tutors. There is the possibility of various configurations of membership leading different types of learning experiences.

Pitfield, M. and Rees, F. M. (1972) 'Team Teaching – can it aid the integration of management education?' in *Management Education and Development*, vol. 3, no. 2, pp. 98–106

Howland, K., Hughes-D'Aeth, I. and Statler, J. (1974) 'Team Teaching in Business Studies', in *Technical Journal*, vol. 12, no. 9, Dec, pp. 14–15

Mansell, J. (1974) 'Team Teaching in Further Education', in *Educational Research*, vol. 17, 19–26

Shaplin, J. T. and Olds, H. F. (eds) (1975) *Team Teaching*, Harper and Row

Warwick, D. (1971) *Team Teaching*, University of London Press

See also: Teaching outside your field

TELEVISION PROGRAMME

Television Programmes regularly provide a source of material that can be used in management training and education. In general, the BBC offers more in this line than the independent stations, although an independent television station produced three programmes entitled 'Decision' which are regularly used by a number of business schools in the teaching of business policy. The BBC offers programmes in the areas of decision making, communication, small business management and industrial relations. The major difficulty with using transmitted broadcasts is that they rarely occur at a time suitable for teaching. For this reason they must be made available at some later date. The copyright rules on this are clear and should be studied to avoid copyright infringement. Open University programmes are also available on videotape which can be hired or bought. A number of other programmes regularly offer case studies or discussion material for management courses. In the past Panorama, The Money Programme, and The Risk Business have covered topics which would provide excellent teaching material. Some of these may be available for hire or purchase from BBC Enterprises.

Once a Television Programme has been obtained, there is then the problem of deciding what to do with it. Since programmes are usually self contained, the easiest approach is to show it in full and then discuss some of the issues raised. Where it lasts about 20–25 minutes this is possible. Longer programmes need to be broken up into smaller sections. Some documentaries on industrial issues can be divided up and 'what to do' and 'what are the issues' questions asked. Programmes may be difficult to use. Many of us watch television passively for relaxation and students may find it unexpectedly taxing to acquire the different frame of reference which may be needed to watch a Television Programme as a data source. Educational broadcasts demand an active response by the audience and are deliberately designed to be a resource for learning. Students may be expected to think, write or discuss. Difficulties may be experienced either because students cannot take the programme seriously (association with entertainment) or because its emotional impact is too great. Broadcasts proceed at a fixed pace which may be too fast or too slow for the individual learner.

It is possible to make one's own programmes using the video technology that is becoming cheaply available. Moreover, these can be made interactive. For example one can produce videos which are intended to be self-instructional. In these, short visual sequences are alternated with questions and activities. The activities may be mental, written or practical. It can provide useful training in observation and analysis as well as the type of stimulus contained in the Trigger Film.

Harris, D. (1975) 'Training Technology' in *Industrial Training International*, vol. 10, no. 2, pp. 49–51

Harris, N. D. C. and Austwick, K. (1973) 'TV or not TV?' in *Programmed Learning and Educational Technology*, vol. 10, no. 3, pp. 124–9

See also: Film; Trigger film; Audio tape

TEXT

Text is a term which has been used in a general way to refer to the use of written materials which the student studies as part of his learning task. The word usually refers to some pre-selected material which has either been chosen by the tutor or specifically prepared by him. Most distance learning programmes rely heavily on the use of specially prepared Texts. Texts may be accompanied by a supplementary visual programme, e.g. slides or film strip, or an audio programme, e.g. audio cassette. The key requirements for an instructional Text are, first, *interaction* in the form of self tests, activities and feedback. The isolated learner makes decisions and is not merely passive. Second, *carefully designed layout and format* and *objectives to clarify the task*. In terms of writing style it should include clear, interesting and unambiguous prose and finally it should *link to other work*.

Lewis, R. (1981) *How to Write Self Study Materials*, Guidelines No. 10, London: Council for Educational Technology

Rowntree, D. and Conners, B. (eds) (1979) *How to Develop Self-Instructional Material*, Milton Keynes: Open University Press

Hartley, J. and Burnhill, P. (1977) 'Understanding Instructional Text: Typography, Layout and Design' in Howe, M. J. A. (ed.) *Adult Learning: Psychological Research and Implications*, Chichester: John Wiley and Sons

Hartley, J. and Burnhill, P. (1977) 'Fifty Guidelines for Improving Instructional Text' in *Programmed Learning and Educational Technology*, vol. 14, no. 1, pp. 65–73

Fraser, L. T. and Schwartz, B. J. (1975) 'Effect of Question Production and Answering on Prose Recall' in *Journal of Educational Psychology*, vol. 67, no. 5, pp. 628–35

Rickards, J. P. (1976) 'Interaction of Position and Conceptual Level of Adjunct Questions in Immediate and Delayed Retention of Text' in *Journal of Educational Psychology*, vol. 68, no. 2, pp. 210–17

Hower, M. J. A. and Colley, L. (1976) 'The Influence of Questions Encountered Earlier on Learning from Prose' in *British Journal of Educational Psychology*, vol. 46, pp. 149–54

Rickards, J. P. and August, G. J. (1975) 'Generative Underlining Strategies in Prose Recall' in *Journal of Educational Psychology*, vol. 67, no. 6, pp. 860–5

See also: Handout; Guided study; Tutorial-tape-document learning package approach; Worksheet

THINK AND LISTEN SESSION
This is a group activity in which each person is given a set period of time in which to express himself on a given topic or anything else he would like to talk about. The grand rule is that other members do not interrupt, but give attention and support the person speaking.

Iles, C. D. (1981) 'Listening', in *Training*, vol. 7, no. 2, pp. 12–13

Stewart, A. and Stewart, V. (1976) *Tomorrow's Men Today*, London: Institute of Personnel Management, chapter 5

Jones, J. E. and Mohr, L. *The Jones-Mohr Listening Test*, Mansfield: University Associates of Europe Ltd

See also: Co-counselling; Group with ground rules; Buberian dialogue

3-D ORGANISATIONAL EFFECTIVENESS TRAINING

This management development approach is based upon the 3-D Theory of Managerial Effectiveness developed by W. J. Reddin. Its starting point is the research discovery that the task to be performed and the nature of the relationships between people constitute key elements in managerial style. A manager may be greatly or minimally task-oriented. Task orientation gives priority towards goal attainment. The stress is laid on planning, organising and controlling. Managers also have a degree of relationship orientation which gives priority to personal job relationships built on mutual trust. There is a respect for subordinates' ideas, suggestions and feelings. Managers emphasise one or other of these orientations. They can be greatly or minimally task- or relationships-oriented. Alternatively, both behaviours could be used together (labelled Integrating Style), Task Orientation can be used alone (labelled Dedicated Style) or each is used to a small degree (labelled Separated style). Research suggests that each style is more or less effective in different circumstances. None is more or less effective in itself. Thus each basic style has a less and more effective equivalent:

Basic Style	Less Effective Equivalent	More Effective Equivalent
Integrative	Compromiser	Executive
Dedicated	Autocrat	Benevolent Autocrat
Related	Missionary	Developer
Separated	Deserter	Bureaucrat

The eight management styles are not additional kinds of behaviour, but the names given to the four basic styles when used appropriately or inappropriately. 3D-Training involves teaching managers the theory and the way to read situations so as to be able to decide what kind of behaviour is required in a given situation in order for them to be effective. Managers are taught to increase their range of behaviour styles and their skill in changing situations.

Using this theory as a basis, Reddin has developed an intervention programme. This involves a group of managers discussing, in a structured way, their individual and team effectiveness criteria. The aim is to improve their methods of working together in a team. Reddin's programme has four stages. Managers are first taken away from their usual work colleagues and are assembled in an artificial group for a week (Managerial Effectiveness Seminar). Then an actual work team consisting of a boss plus subordinates discuss their roles and the way in which they operate together (Team Role Laboratory). A superior with a single subordinate then together consider effectiveness and objectives (Mangerial Objectives Conference). Finally, the programme concludes with the managing director and his executive directors coming together to discuss working relationships (Corporate Strategy Laboratory).

Reddin, W. J. (1971) *Managerial Effectiveness*, Maidenhead: McGraw-Hill

Reddin, W. J. (1966) 'The Tri-dimensional Grid', in *Canadian Personnel and Industrial Relations Journal*, January, pp. 13–20

See also: Action-Centred Leadership; Grid training; Interaction management

TRAINING TRANSFER TRAINING
Training Transfer Training refers either to a specific set of activities during a course or seminar, or to a separate seminar altogether. The primary aim of either of these activities is the application of previously acquired learning. In TTT sessions or seminars, participants are not provided with any new or additional knowledge or skills to do with a subject (e.g. using flow charts), but through a series of activities and exercises are helped to devise a strategy and practice the appropriate skills relevant to the application of their acquired subject knowledge in their work situation. Among the earliest developers of this approach was Miles (1959). In his book on group working he devoted a section to relating training to job experiences. He made a number of specific suggestions for activities which could assist trainees to apply their learning. These included theory of application sessions, situational diagnoses and planning, problem centred groups, intervisitation and many other techniques. Miles' ideas have been developed and elaborated

upon by Huczynski. He has suggested a five-stage transfer model which involved recall, selection, motivation, evaluation and practice. Through a series of structured activities, course participants are helped to reflect on their learning experiences so as to recall those most significant to them. From these they select several to work on for the purposes of transfer. Members identify motivational factors to spur them on to attempt a transfer of learning. The work environment is then evaluated as a source of support and the seminar concludes with participants practising their skills of influencing others to support their proposed changes.

Byham, W. C. and Robinson, J. (1977) 'Building Supervisory Confidence – A Key to Transfer of Training', in *Personnel Journal*, vol. 56, no. 5, pp. 248–250, 253

Miles, M. B. (1959) *Learning to Work in Groups: A Program Guide for Educational Leaders*, Bureau of Publications, Teachers College, Columbia University, New York

Huczynski, A. A. and Logan, D. W. (1980) 'Learning to Change: Organisational Change Through Training Transfer Workshops', in *Leadership and Organizational Development Journal*, vol. 1, no. 3, pp. 25–31

Huczynski, A. A. (1978) 'The Problems of Learning Transfer', in *Journal of European Industrial Training*, vol. 2, no. 1, pp. 26–29

Frank, E. and Margerison, C. (1978) 'Training Methods and Organisational Development', in *Journal of European Training/MCB Monographs*, vol. 2, no. 4, pp. 3–10

Leifer, M. S. and Newstrom, J. W. (1980) 'Solving the Transfer of Learning Problems', in *Training and Development Journal*, vol. 34, no. 8, pp. 42–46

See also: Post-course follow up; Application discussion group; Interaction management

TRANSACTIONAL ANALYSIS

Transactional Analysis (TA) was invented by Eric Berne. The central idea of TA is that people interact with each other on three levels which Berne called Parent, Child and Adult. The Child part of us manifests itself in behaviour that is acceptable and expected in young children (e.g.

desire for immediate gratification). Parent is that part of us which is entrenched with beliefs, attitudes, and values conferred on us by our own parents and accepted automatically. The Adult is the self-activating part of our personality, the mature part that considers each situation for itself and determines how to act appropriately.

Berne's PAC are behaviour patterns that can be consciously controlled and switched in and out of at will. We may demonstrate Adult-like behaviour at work, but Child-like behaviour at home. There is nothing wrong in slipping from one personality part to another. The problems develop when one person in a relationship is entrenched in a particular behaviour pattern. TA as a group therapy can help people recognise their own chronic behaviour patterns as well as those of other people. Once identified in this framework, such traits can be analysed and changed. TA has been widely applied in industry and personnel management.

Clements, R. (1980) *A Guide to Transactional Analysis: A Handbook for Managers and Trainers*, Insight Training Ltd.

Novey, T. (1979; *TA for Management*, Bradford: MCB Publications

Wellin, M. (1978) 'TA in the Workplace', in *Personnel Management*, vol. 10, no. 7, pp. 37–40

Berne, E. (1964) *Games People Play*, Grove Press Inc.; Harmondsworth: Penguin books (1968)

Harris, T. A. (1969) *I'm OK – You're OK*, New York: Harper & Row; Pan (1973)

Ryan, J. F. (1978) 'Transactional Analysis, The Aer Lingus Experience, in *BACIE Journal*, vol. 32, no. 9, October, pp. 158–61

Wright, D. (1978) 'Simplifying the Treatment of Transactional Analysis', in *Industrial and Commercial Training*, vol. 10, no. 6, pp. 238–44

Wright, D. and Whalley, P. (1978) 'Transactional Analysis', in *Industrial and Commercial Training*, vol. 10, no. 9, pp.371–7

Barker, D. (1978) 'What TA Can Do for You', in *Personnel Management*, vol. 10, no. 5, pp. 36–9

Barker, D. (1980) *TA and Training*, Aldershot: Gower

Kilcourse, T. (1978) 'TA Under Attack', in *Personnel Management*, vol. 10, no. 6, pp. 33–5 and 43

Kilcourse, T. (1977) 'Transactional Analysis: Some Concerns', in *Journal of European Industrial Training*, vol. 1, no. 2, pp. 1–5

Clary, T. C. (1980) 'Transactional Analysis', in *Training and Development Journal*, vol. 34, no. 6, pp. 48–54

Cox, M. and Cox, C. (1980) 'Ten Years of Transactional Analysis' in Beck, J. and Cox, C. (eds) *Advances in Management Education*, Chichester: John Wiley and Sons

See also: Interactive skills training

TRIGGER FILM

Trigger Films consist of short, high impact vignettes which aim to stimulate learning. They differ completely from the traditional management training films and should not be confused with them. These films are not a learning experience in their own right, but provide a means of initiating a subsequent activity. They are typically short (10-30 seconds), high impact vignettes designed to trigger an emotional response in the viewer. They are not primarily informative, discursive or instructional. Compared with most film material they appear incomplete and unresolved. They aim to place the person watching in the position of an active learner by presenting incidents which demand a response emotionally as well as intellectually. They try to encourage self reflection and personal engagement in the incident portrayed.

Boud, D. and Pearson, M. (1979) 'The Trigger film: A Stimulus for Affective Learning', in *Programmed Learning and Educational Technology*, vol. 16, no. 1, pp. 52–56

Fisch, A. L. (1972) 'The Trigger Film Techniques', in *Improving College and University Teaching*, vol. 20, no. 4

Powell, J. P. (1977) 'The Use of Trigger Films in Developing Teaching Skills' in Elton, L. and Simmonds, K. (eds) *Staff Development in Higher Education*, Guildford, Surrey: Society for Research into Higher Education

See also: Audio tape; Tape stop exercise; Video confrontation; Confluent education; Interpersonal process recall

TRUST EXERCISE

As the label suggests, Trust Exercises are an important sub-class of experiential exercises and can be closely associated with non-verbal approaches. The focus is on the feelings and attitudes of participants in relation to their trust of one another. Various structured activities are used to engender feelings relevant to the topic. Perhaps the best known of these are the 'Trust Fall' and the 'Trust Walk'. In the former, a group of students divides up into dyads. One stands with his back to the other and allows himself to fall. His partner than catches him. They exchange roles and, having completed the activity several times, share their feelings and experiences, first with each other and then with the other group members. In a Trust Walk, a blindfolded student is led around the building (or outside it) by his partner. Like non-verbal exercises in general, a Trust Exercise tends to produce strong emotions which can be the impetus for further learning.

See also: Experiential exercise; Non-verbal exercise; Tape stop exercise

TUTORIAL

In a Tutorial the instructor meets students individually or in small groups. The topics chosen for study are jointly agreed upon by the instructor and the students; the amount of lecturer guidance and lecturer–student interaction varies depending on the interests and needs of those involved. Students generally assume the primary responsibility for presenting and sharing ideas with the tutor, who then helps them sharpen their thinking. A written report or essay is frequently required to focus the preparation and subsequent subject discussion. The origin of the method is frequently attributed to William of Wykeham, Bishop of Winchester and founder of New College, Oxford. His method of providing for the teaching of the junior members by the senior members of his foundation gave rise to the tutorial system.

Tutorials are held to be one of the most valuable educational experiences. Whether they are one-to-one or small groups (e.g. 3–4), they offer students the maximum opportunity for individual attention and dialogue. Tutorials involve a number of activities. The Supervised Tutorial consists of a regular meeting of a teacher and a student during which the latter reads an essay he has written and defends it in argument. The strategy can provide an exceptionally able student with an excellent opportunity to deepen his understanding of a subject while advancing his mastery of the basic skills of scholarship. The approach depends heavily on a well-informed and sympathetic tutor and a student who has thoroughly prepared himself for the encounter. Group Tutorials arose from the need to make a more efficient use of staff time. Rarely are tutors sufficiently familiar with social psychology to exploit the full potentialities of the small group. During individual or group tutorials, different styles of teaching may be appropriate. Socratic methods appear appropriate when the student has all the information necessary to derive a correct solution to a problem, but needs to reorganise that information in order to reach the solution.

Didactic methods are effective when the learner lacks information in the subject matter to be acquired and has no foundation on which to build. Problem solving approaches are appropriate when student and teacher share common information and each has unique independent information. While learning activity may be highest in one-to-one tutorials, this high level of involvement may be inhibiting for some learners. Also the high demands made on student and tutor time, plus the need for the two to be broadly equated in terms of ability, have all meant that group tutorials are more generally favoured and employed in adult teaching. Students may need the support of a peer group to overcome inhibitions and express themselves in front of a figure of authority.

The variable contribution of different students may be a problem and some research suggests that most tutors monopolise discussion time, do not give students the opportunity to participate, turn the discussion into a lecture and generally forget that students are problem solvers and decision makers. The quality of group tutorials can be enhanced if: they are problem-centred rather than competitive; tutors act as mentors rather than judges; both students and tutor prepare beforehand; and the tutor has some knowledge of group processes. In these circumstances tutorials can achieve high order cognitive and affective objectives. Where students attend a series of supervised tutorials, these can be made more sophisticated. In the first of this series, the tutor and student negotiate an essay title from a field which the student has identified as being of interest to him and one that he wishes to explore further. In the second and third tutorials, the two examine together a proposed way in which the essay might be structured. They produce a structure plan for it. Finally, the student writes the essay and defends it in argument with the tutor.

Wood, A. E. (1979) 'Experiences With Small Group Tutorials', in *Studies in Higher Education*, vol. 4, no. 2, pp. 203–9

Bramley, W. (1977) *Personal Tutoring*, Guildford, Surrey: Society for Research into Higher Education

Ogborn, J. (ed.) (1977) *Small Group Teaching in Undergraduate Science*, London: Heinemann Educational Books

Axelroyd, J. (1948), 'The Technique of Group Discussion in the College Class', in *Journal of General Education*, vol. 26, pp. 200–207

McFarland, H. S. N. (1962) 'Education by Tutorial', in *Universities Review*, vol. 34, pp. 45–51

See also: One-to-one learning; Small group teaching; Tutorium; Questioning; Structuring seminars

TUTORIAL-TAPE-DOCUMENT LEARNING PACKAGE APPROACH

This is a scaled down version of a Keller Plan approach which is capable of being used by the individual lecturer. It was designed by November (1978) and is a learning system based on the use of tutorials, cassette tapes and printed materials. It consists of five components.

The audio cassettes contain information about what the student should do. They direct the student through the course. They can include a commentary on documents, anecdotes and other audio materials to stimulate the learners. The document file is an indexed collection of materials through which the student is guided. It can contain the aims of the course, diagrams, extracts from journals, cuttings from newspapers, photocopies of book pages and so on. Skeleton notes contain a minimum number of headings and include space for the student to take notes. At different points in the course, the audio tape directs students to complete an exercise which is then written up by them in their notes. Tutorials complete the package.

The class is divided into groups of about five who are seen weekly. In these meetings the tutor ensures that students are covering the ground and checks whether they are meeting the targets or encountering any problems.

The elements in the package are described to the students when they start the course. They are then divided into tutorial groups within which they share the tapes and document files. Everyone, however, receives his own copy of the skeleton notes. In this method the students have to manage their own learning. The pace of the course is governed by the distribution of the skeleton notes. The course content is divided into blocks and notes are issued at each tutorial. The tapes and documents contain more than one week's work. The materials are usually shared between three people and it is not necessary for the tutorial groups to correspond to these.

November, P. J. (1978) 'The Tape-Tutorial-Document Learning Package', in *Studies in Higher Education*, vol. 3, no. 1, pp. 91–95

See also: Circulated lecture notes; Handout; Personalised system of instruction; Guided study; Text

TUTORIUM (Seminar, Tutoring Group)

This label is used to distinguish a weekly one- or two-hour teaching seminar which is directed by a teaching assistant. Such an assistant is of a similar age and/or educational level to those being taught. Such seminars frequently supplement the large weekly lecture. Their purpose is to provide a link between the lectures (frequently given by professors) and the student body. They help to ensure that the material presented in the lectures is understood and permit students to ask questions, receive feedback and voice opinions. These objectives are similar to those sought in a traditional seminar or group tutorial which is led by a member of the academic staff and which seeks to involve the student actively.

There are several reasons for having a graduate student perform this task. One of these is the financial savings which accrue to the educational institution and another is the personal career development opportunities which the student tutor has. As far as the tutees are concerned, they are more likely to ask questions and admit to not having understood a point than perhaps they would be in the presence of a professor. Applications of this teaching method reveal an increase in the motivation and co-operation of students, a decrease in competitive behaviour and an increase in self-confidence and self-esteem for both students and tutors alike.

Since graduate students may be seen as just different authority figures, there has been experimentation with the use of final year undergraduate students. Results showed that staff and students rated undergraduate tutors as high as or higher than graduate teaching assistants.

Maas, J. B. and Pressler, V. M. (1973) 'When Students Become Teachers', in *Behavioural and Social Science Teacher*, vol. 1, no. 1, pp. 55–60

Gartner, A., Kohler, M. and Riessman, F. (1971) *Children Teach Children*, New York: Harper and Row

Wrigley, C. (1973) 'Undergraduate Students as Teachers: Apprenticeship in the University Classroom', *Teaching of Psychology Newsletter*, March, 5–7

Janssen, P. (1976) 'With a Little Help from their Friends', in *Change*, vol. 8, pp. 50–53

Lincoln, E. (1976) 'Everyman as Psychologist', in *Change*, vol. 8, pp. 54–57

Egerton, J. (1976) 'Teaching Learning While Learning to Teach', in *Change*, vol. 8, pp. 58–61

Vattano, F. J., Hockenberry, C., Grider, W., Jacobson, L. and Hamilton, S. (1972) 'Employing Undergraduate Students in the Teaching of Psychology', *Teaching of Psychology Newsletter*, March, pp. 9–12

See also: Tutorial; Peer teaching; Teaching as learning; Parrainage; Learning cell

UNIT BOX APPROACH
Developed by Batoff at the Jersey City State College, USA, the Unit Box involves each student assembling an inquiry-oriented, materials-centred, multi-media unit package built around a commercially available and tested unit of study. It was developed for use with schoolteachers but the idea can be applied to management training staff. The classroom tested units are modular in nature and are either teaching units, resource units or quasi-resource units. Students put together their Unit Boxes outside of the classroom time during a five- to six-week period prior to student teaching experience and use it when they begin their classroom teaching. Thus, the students are not required to write a unit, since their technical knowledge, skill level and the time available do not permit writing it, testing it, getting feedback and reviewing it. Instead they start with a good commercially available one and bring together all the hardware and supporting software necessary to make a good job of teaching it. The thrust of the UBA is implementation of tested and published materials. Participants therefore focus on the application rather than the production of materials. The emphasis is placed on the procurement, fabrication and improvisation of materials for the relevant

sized groups. The final output of a Unit box is a multi-media, multi-sensory, multi-level package of instructional materials. It is designed for in-depth use for a period of four to eight weeks. Each Box is custom made by the trainee teacher.

Batoff, M. E. (1974) 'The Unit Box Approach: a novel facet of elementary school science teacher preparation' in *British Journal of Educational Technology*, vol. 2, no. 5, pp. 88–95

Conkright, T. (1977) 'Guidelines for the Adaption of Course Materials' in *Journal of European Industrial Training*, vol. 1, no. 1, pp. 14–16

VALUES CLARIFICATION

The Values Clarification approach to teaching (VC) is not an attempt to teach 'right' or 'wrong' values but rather to help students to prize and act upon their freely chosen values. It is concerned with the process by which learners arrive at their values and not upon the content of their values. The decisions that a manager makes will always be partly based upon the values that he holds. Since they are part of the decision-making process, the educational experience should include making these explicit. It is argued that if students are to become motivated and receptive to learning, the educational process needs to be personalised with personal growth as well as intellectual development being given emphasis. To implement the VC approach, the teacher uses strategies which help students to choose their values freely, choose them from alternatives, choose them after weighing the consequences of each alternative, prize and cherish their values, share and publicly affirm their values, act upon their values and do so repeatedly and consistently. These steps are known as the valuing process of choosing, prizing and acting. In order to personalise education a number of approaches can be used. They include the personalisation of human relationships by developing a climate of trust, acceptance and open communication in the classroom; personalising goals by helping students to develop and clarify their values and goals; personalising the curriculum by making knowledge and cognitive skills serve student values, purposes and goals; finally, through personalising classroom organisation by using it to facilitate learning and personal growth.

Simon, S. B. (1974) *Meeting Yourself Halfway*, Illinois: Argus Communications

Koberg, G. and Bagnall, J. (1976) *Values Tech: a portable school for discovering and developing decision-making skills and self-enhancing potentials*, Los Altos, California: William Kaufmann Inc.

Raths, L., Harmin, M. and Simon, S. B. (1964) *Values and Teaching*, Columbus, Ohio: Merrill

Howe, L. W. and Howe, M. M. (1975) *Personalising Education: Values Clarification and Beyond*, Hart Publishing Company

Smith, M. (1977) *A Practical Guide to Value Clarification*, Mansfield: University Associates of Europe Ltd

Kirschenbaum, H. (1977) *Advanced Value Clarification*, Mansfield: University Associates of Europe Ltd

Bargo, M. (1980) *Choices and Decisions: A Guidebook for Constructing Values*, Mansfield: University Associates of Europe Ltd

Hunt, M. P. and Metcalf, L. E. (1968) *Teaching High School Social Studies*, New York: Harper and Row, chapter 6

See also: Confluent education; Jurisprudential model; Debate; Gestalt techniques

VESTIBULE TRAINING

The Vestibule Method of Training takes its name from the old vestibule school in industry which was a department in an industrial establishment where new employees were trained for the work which they would do in their regular jobs. The school was separate from the production facilities, its only function being to train employees in the performance of certain jobs before they were actually assigned to one of the regular production facilities or operating departments in the company. Vestibule Training closely approximates on-the-job training but it lacks the production requirements of the real situation. The instructor in Vestibule Training must be prepared to instruct. He prepares his trainees for instruction, presents the operation to the trainee, has each trainee perform part of the operation as taught and follows up on the training, making corrections and reinforcing the correct behaviours. The features which distinguish it from on-the-job training are that the trainer is a full-time instructor, rather than a supervisor or a full-time worker. The instructor teaches several persons at a time depending on the needs and sophistication of the skills taught. The training takes place away from the actual work area. Trainees learn the skills needed before they are assigned to production. Disadvantages include the added expense of professional instructors, devotion of space, materials and equipment strictly to training and the payment of wages for a period of time in which employees contribute nothing to the productive efforts of the company.

See also: Clarifying educational environment

VIDEO CONFRONTATION (Video Self-review)

Video recorders were undoubtedly the major educational innovation during the 1970s in the way that micro-computers and word processors are likely to be in the 80s. Recordings using video cameras have some significant advantages over 16 mm film. Pictures taken by video camera can be transmitted as they happen by cable or by wave transmission, to a large number of reception points. The replay of recorded pictures is immediate since there is no development in labs. They can be viewed in daylight while films are best shown in a darkened room. Unlike film, videotape is cheap and reusable. Electronic tricks, e.g. split screen, simple animation, reversed pictures, can be done immediately while film effects need to be done in the labs. The soundtrack of a television programme is recorded on the same piece of videotape as the pictures. Cinefilm and slides can be incorporated into a video programme. For all these reasons, video has been embraced by management teachers and trainees and it is now rare to find a business school or management training centre that does not possess its own video set-up. One of several important applications of this technology has been in the development of the technique of Video Self-confrontation. This is a term that is applied to the general process which allows the trainee to observe his or her own behaviour on a television screen, usually very shortly after it has been performed. The medium has been particularly useful in the training of managers in public speaking, group dynamics, interviewing and negotiating. Apart from this, video films are available in a convenient format. Those using the technique claim that just as people get a shock when they first hear their own voices on a tape recorder, so too when they first see themselves performing on television, they can be shattered by what they see. The confrontation needs to take place in a supportive atmosphere. It is essential for there to be assistance in interpreting and managing the seeing of oneself, and managing the affective dimension of the process.

Perlberg, A. (1975) 'When Professors Confront Themselves' in

Improving University Teaching International Conference Proceedings, Heidelberg, F. R. Germany

Finlayson, D. (1975) 'Self-Confrontation: A Broader Conceptual Base' in *British Journal of Teacher Education*, vol. 1, pp. 97–103

Fuller, F. F. and Manning, B. A. (1974) 'Self-Confrontation Reviewed: a conceptualisation for videoplayback in teacher education' in *Review of Educational Research*, vol. 43, no. 4, pp. 469–528

Nielson, G. (1964) *Studies in Self-Confrontation*, Cleveland, Ohio: Howard Allen Inc.

MacLeod, G. (1976) 'Self-Confrontation Revisited' in *British Journal of Teacher Education*, vol. 2, no. 3

Chipling, R. (1979) 'Are You Getting Value from your CCTV?' in *Journal of European Industrial Training*, vol. 3, no. 4, pp. 18–20

Perlberg, A. and O'Bryant, D. C. (1970) 'Videotaping and Micro-teaching Techniques to Improve Engineering Education' in *Journal of Engineering Education*, vol. 60, pp. 741–4

Smallwood, R. (1977) 'Using CCTV in Management Training' in *Journal of European Industrial Training*, Part 1 in vol. 1, no. 1, p. 6; Part 2 in vol. 1, no. 2, pp. 15–16 and Part 3 in vol. 1, no. 3, pp. 23–4

Biggs, S. (1980) 'The Me I See – Acting, Participating, Observing and Viewing and Their Implications for Videofeedback' in *Human Relations*, vol. 33, no. 8, pp. 575–88

See also: Interpersonal process recall; Trigger film; Micro-teaching;Self criticism

VISITING LECTURER
The emphasis here is on the manager either seeking, or taking the opportunity when it presents itself, to act as a visiting lecturer on either an in-company training course or on a course at the local college, polytechnic or university. The task of speaking in public, and the planning and preparation it involves, can develop the skills and knowledge of direct relevance to a manager's work. A role frequently allotted to a visitor by the course organiser is often that of expert. Where the training centre or college department lacks the necessary expertise, an outsider may be brought in on a one-off basis to make an input. For example, someone knowledgeable on company law or industrial relations legislation might be asked to contribute. Another role is that of

context-changer. Thus on an academic course in business studies, a practising manager may be invited to tell the students 'what it's really like'. Visiting Lecturer does imply that in general the manager will make a regular and continuous contribution to a course over a period of either a term or a year. While some managers may be naturally gifted speakers, others may require help and assistance from their company training department or from other managers in order to prepare themselves for this task.

See also: Interrogation of experts; Outside speaker; Short talks by students; Teaching as learning; Confidence-building training

WORK CARDS

If there are certain techniques and processes which all the students or trainees need to learn at some time, and these can be described easily in words and diagrams, and if each process is uncomplicated enough to go on one page, then it may be possible to use Work Cards for instructional purposes. Work Cards are sets of instructions mounted on to a stiff card, covered in plastic and proved by advance trials to be simple enough for the student to use on his own without needing the assistance of a tutor or trainer. A Work Card system can be designed to stimulate project and discovery work by posing questions or setting tasks as well as giving information. Work Cards can be used by students working either individually, in pairs or in small groups.

See also: Study assignment; Prompt list; Work-related exercise; Worksheet

WORK-RELATED EXERCISE

Work-Related Exercises are used to describe the types of activities that can be used with management students who are attending a diploma or degree course on a part-time basis. That is, the students continue their normal jobs while undergoing their studies. The method can however be used with full-time business management students in which case a 'work assignment' might be a more appropriate label. Essentially, WREs involve students searching out and obtaining from their home companies, information about some aspect of a course which is being studied. For example, a typical task might focus on labour turnover statistics when this topic is being discussed. In between the scheduled classes, students would be asked to find answers to the following questions. Who in your organisation is responsible for the collection of labour turnover figures? By what method is the data collected? On what basis is the figure for labour turnover calculated? What is considered the 'normal' turnover rate? What happens with the information once it is collected? Similar tasks can be assigned to students on subjects such as absenteeism, quality control data, sickness, industrial disputes, staff appraisal etc. The approach has several objectives. First, it aims to help to relate some concept, e.g. managerial control, to some well known organisational process (such as the appraisal system) or concrete organisational product, e.g. weekly production figures. Second, it helps students to get to know their organisations better and become aware of some of their unique features and the assumptions upon which company members behave. To achieve these aims it is necessary for course members to compare the information they have collected with each other. To ensure comparability of data, each student is issued with a common list of questions to be answered. This question list also provides the structure for the small group discussion.

Rendall, J. F. (1977) 'The Activity Record and Its Related Projects' in *Management Education and Development*, vol. 8, no. 2, pp. 69–78

See also: Prompt list; Work Cards; Worksheet

WORKSHEET
A Worksheet is a very simple and flexible method of structuring an active student learning programme within a variety of educational settings. Many museums now provide young visitors with a questionnaire and/or set of tasks which they can complete as they go around the exhibits. Within formal educational programmes, a Worksheet may not necessarily contain questions to be answered, but may give instructions about the nature, number and sequence of learning tasks that the student is required to engage in. This can involve the use of a range of different learning resources. The Worksheet is flexible, can individualise learning, uses simple technology and requires no investment in expensive equipment.

Ball, S. J. (1980) 'Mixed Ability Teaching: the worksheet method' in *British Journal of Educational Technology*, vol. 11, no. 1, pp. 36–48

See also: Prompt list; Work cards; Study assignment; Library assignment; Block method; Tutorial-tape-document learning package approach

WORKSHOP (Atelier)

A Workshop involves persons who are already experienced in a particular area coming together. They work on both concrete products as well as theoretical materials. Participants expect to learn primarily from one another, although most Workshops will contain an organiser who creates a working structure and some expert resource persons brought in specially for the event. A Workshop emphasises free discussion, exchange of ideas, demonstration of effort, practical implications of skills and principles mainly for adults who are already doing a job. The idea of learning from colleagues implies that participants are already competent in their particular role and are both capable and willing to switch from the role of learner to teacher and back again during the course of the event. There are several stages through which a Workshop runs. These refer to a Workshop in which only a general theme has been announced and where the arriving participants have not yet divided themselves into working groups. The first of these is the initiation phase. Ideally, participants should initiate the Workshop itself, although in practice it tends to be an institution which specifies the topic, selects participants, organises the details and designates the organisers. Once at the Workshop, participants are informed about their learning environment, meet each other and learn about each other's individual skills and interests. Members then seek to reach a consensus about which area of practice they desire to examine, and structure the content and organisation of the Workshop accordingly. Such an agenda can be achieved by the outlining and specification by the participants, organisers and experts of the general subject matter to be discussed. This is catalogued according to 'problem areas' and alternatives for solution. After a group discussion, topics of interest are selected for further work. The organiser may suggest that in addition to discussion, the Workshop group ought, by the end, to produce some concrete product, e.g. an action plan or a proposal.

Groups then form according to interests and expectations and proceed to work on certain problems, themes or to produce certain products. There is often a central information centre and experts are available to groups as required. They work on their task, and having completed it, evaluate the Workshop. A Workshop relies heavily for its success on the participants themselves. They play a crucial role to develop and structure it. Successful Workshops tend to contain members who are well informed, and motivated by their own learning, experienced in their field, and who are prepared to use their talents when working together with colleagues. The role of the organiser is to establish the working conditions to facilitate this process of mutual learning. He provides the necessary work materials, coordinates the technical procedures, selects the experts, offers help and information through personal consultation, papers and bibliographies, and other learning resources. In management education and development, the term Workshop has come to be more loosely applied and in some cases it is used synonymously with course. The reason may be to attract participants who do not mind 'sharing experiences' with colleagues, but who might feel offended at being 'taught'. Provided that all parties concerned are clear about expectations then there is no problem. The difficulty arises when members arrive at a Workshop expecting to exchange experiences and are then taught by a lecturer; or when the organiser prepares a structure to facilitate mutual learning and members arrive expecting to be taught by him.

Bates, W. T. G. and Farey, P. R. (1975) 'The Development of a Management Workshop' in *Journal of European Training*, vol. 4, no. 3, pp. 162–71

Chase, P. H. (1972) 'Creative Management Workshop' in *Personnel Journal*, vol. 51, April, pp. 264–9, 282

Mack, D. (1979) *The Workshop Way*, CCTUT Occasional Paper No. 1, Report of the Third National Working Conference, Co-ordinating Committee for the Training of University Teachers

See also: Learning community; Minicourse; Module; Residential

4
RESOURCES FOR TEACHING AND LEARNING

BOOKS

Berger, M. L. and Berger, P. J. (eds) (1972) *Group Training Techniques*, Aldershot: Gower
> A collection of articles by various authors describing the different uses of group approaches in the field of management education and training.

Boud, D. J. (ed.) (1981) *Developing Student Autonomy in Learning*, London: Kogan Page Ltd
> Each chapter is written by a different author and describes some of the ways in which they have attempted to increase students' autonomy in their learning. Includes descriptions of some approaches being increasingly used in management development such as Learning Contracts

Boydell, T. (1976) *Experiential Learning*, Manchester Monographs 5, University of Manchester, Department of Adult Education
> This short monograph considers what is meant by the term Experiential Learning. It also includes many useful references to sources of experiential learning materials.

Boydell, T. and Pedler, M. (eds) (1981) *Management Self-Development: Concepts and Practices*, Aldershot: Gower
> Another collection of chapters by different authors which describes the varying ways in which the concept of Self Development has been applied in management development programmes, degree courses, entrepreneurship training and other contexts.

Burgoyne, J. G. and Stuart, R. (1978) *Management Development: Context and Strategies*, Aldershot: Gower
> This is a collection of papers and journal articles written by members of Lancaster University's Centre for the Study of Management Learning. The papers contain descriptions of models, frameworks and research findings relevant to the design and conduct of management training and development programmes.

Drake, J., Margerison, C. and Hunter N. (1979) *Management and Organization Development Bibliography*, Bradford: MCB Publications, 3rd edition
> A detailed bibliography covering references to books and journal articles of relevance to everyone involved in both management development and organisational development.

Entwistle, N. (1981) *Styles of Learning and Teaching*, Chichester: John Wiley and Sons
> Essentially an educational psychology textbook, but one which is written in an attractive style. Introduces and illustrates the key concepts in undertanding how people learn.

Knowles, M. S. (1970) *The Modern Practice of Adult Education*, New York: Associated Press

Knowles, M. S. (1973) *The Adult Learner: A Neglected Species*, Houston, Texas: Gulf Publishing

Knowles, M. S. (1975) *Self-Directed Learning: A Guide for Learners and Teachers*, New York: Associated Press
> Some of the most comprehensive ideas on the subject of adult education have been written by Malcolm Knowles. Many of his ideas were ahead of their time and these books by him merit reading and re-reading.

Miles, M. B. (1959) *Learning to Work in Groups*, Bureau of Publications, Teachers College, Columbia University, New York
> Although written for schoolteachers, the book contains a great many ideas about the process of learning and also includes details of group activities and exercises.

Mumford, A. (1980) *Making Experience Pay*, London: McGraw-Hill
> Written by a company trainer, the emphasis is on the in-company and on-the-job techniques that can be used to help managers learn while they are fulfilling their organisational roles.

Rogers, C. R. (1969) *Freedom to Learn*, Columbus, Ohio: Charles E. Merrill Company
> One of the all-time educational 'classics' which emphasises student-centred learning. It should be read at least once by all educators and trainers, irrespective of whether they agree with Rogers' views.

Runkel, P., Harrison, R. and Runkel, M. (eds) (1969) *The Changing College Classroom*: San Francisco: Jossey Bass
> A provocative collection of contributions which emphasises new and innovative approaches. Although not dealing explicitly with management education and training, the contents do have an application.

Suessmuth, P. (1978) *Ideas for Training Managers and Supervisors*, Mansfield: University Associates of Europe Ltd
> A collection of useful, down-to-earth tips on how to organise and run a training session. It provides references to a wide range of resources and contains sections on setting up courses, class interaction, learner-centred teaching, evaluation, sample, lesson designs and audio visual aids.

Taylor, B. and Lippitt, G. L. (eds) (1975) *Management Development and Training Handbook*, London: McGraw-Hill
> Chapters contain descriptions of both training approaches, e.g. Action-centred Leadership and Grid Training, and general teaching and learning methods, e.g. Case Study and Syndicate Group Method.

Zoll, A. A. (1969) *Dynamic Management Education*, Reading, Mass.: Addison-Wesley

Zoll, A. A. (1974) *Explorations in Managing*, Reading, Mass.: Addison-Wesley
> These books are a valuable source of exercises and activities which can be used in management training. Zoll also suggests how one can design one's own case studies, action mazes and role plays.

ORGANISATIONS

Below are listed a number of organisations whose publications the writer has found useful in developing his skills and knowledge in the field of management education and training. This list does not in any way claim to be either comprehensive or exhaustive.

Australian Consortium on Experiential Education (ACEE),
PO Box 383
Leichhardt,
New South Wales 0240,
Australia

The ACEE is an Australian educational association which has an interest in the development and introduction of experiential learning approaches. Recently formed, it has published a number of papers on the subject of introducing experience-based learning approaches into the classroom.

British Association for Commercial and Industrial Education (BACIE),
16 Park Crescent,
Regents Park,
London W1N 4AP

BACIE provides a regular stream of information about training methods and designs through its monthly publication, *BACIE Journal*, and also through the books, booklets and monographs it publishes. It offers courses on training methods and runs an annual conference.

Centre for the Study of Management Learning (CSML),
Gillow House,
University of Lancaster,
Bailrigg,
Lancaster,
England

Conducts research into all topics related to management learning and has a wide-ranging list of publications on topics relevant to management trainers. In addition to providing short courses and workshops and a consultancy service, it also offers diploma and degree programmes.

Confluent Education Development and Research Centre (CEDARC),
3887 State Street,
Suite 13,
Santa Barbara,
California 93013,
USA

The purpose of this association is to disseminate the ideas and methods of Confluent Education through all levels of education. CEDARC publishes a regular newsletter containing information about confluent education techniques and lesson plans, as well as monographs and books on the subject.

Far West Laboratory For Educational Research and Development,
1855 Folsom Street,
San Francisco,
California 94104,
USA

The primary focus of the Far West Lab is on action research projects conducted in secondary schools. Its research papers however, are of interest beyond this specific education sector.

Society for Research into Higher Education,
University of Surrey,
Guidlford,
Surrey,
England

The Society produces a regular list of monographs on aspects of further and higher education in general, and on the use of teaching and learning methods in particular. It organises specialist topic interest groups and holds an annual conference.

Tavistock Institute of Human Relations,
Belsize Lane,
London NW3 5BA

This is a research and consulting organisation with an international reputation in the field of action research. It operates in a large number of fields including health organisations, education and management development. It publishes an annual report of its activities which includes a bibliography of recent publications.

University Associates of Europe Ltd,
Challenge House,
45–47 Victoria Street,
Mansfield
Notts NG18 5SU

UAE are perhaps best known for their series of the Pfeiffer and Jones Handbooks for Structured Experiences in Human Relations Training. In addition to producing a wide range of books, they also offer workshops, conferences and consultancy work in the field of human resource development, management development and organisational development.

JOURNALS

Below are listed a number of journals which regularly carry articles suggesting practical ideas on improving teaching and learning. Some of these publications are specific to management education and development while others are not.

BACIE Journal
British Journal of Educational Technology
Journal of European Industrial Training
Journal of Management Development
Leadership and Organizational Development
Management Education and Development
Personnel Review
Programmed Learning and Educational Technology
Studies in Higher Education
Teaching At A Distance
Training and Development Journal (USA)

5
ANALYTICAL FRAMEWORK FOR METHOD ASSESSMENT

The analytical framework is not a classification system, in that it does not present general category labels such as Interaction Rules or Learning Theories under which the entries in the book are grouped. Nor does the framework attempt to relate one method to another. What is presented can perhaps be described as a reflective tool which helps the tutor to think about the methods which he uses in his work. It does have the potential for relating the methods to each other through the agency of the reader himself. The framework presented here was developed by Main and Huczynski.

INTRODUCTION TO THE FRAMEWORK DIMENSIONS

The analytical framework is built around three dimensions of Content, Process and Setting. These are shown in Figure 5.1. To identify the primary content focus of a teaching or learning method used, one asks the question: 'What have I designed or adopted the method for?'. There are likely to be several answers to this question, but it is the most important of these which constitutes the primary focus. In column 1 of the framework, ten possible primary foci are suggested.

In a similar way, an indication of the primary process focus of one's method is obtained by asking the question: 'What does the method stress in its execution?'. Once again, eight possible process foci are suggested. The concern here is with how things are done. The third and final dimension is concerned with the ethos of the method of organisation. One's view or personal philosophy about how people learn and develop colours the setting in which the learning or teaching takes place. Seven potential setting foci are described to help the tutor reflect on his own ethos. The function of the framework is as a tool which can help the individual tutor or teacher reflect on the methods and approaches that he uses in his work and this personal reflection is structured around the foci of Content, Process and Setting. Whenever a tutor is asked to describe a learning situation which he designed, his description of it is likely to include a reference to the content of the method ('what he used it for') and to its process ('how things happened'). After further questioning, he is likely to reveal his philosophy of learning ('how he believes people learn'). It is therefore argued that a method-in-use, as opposed to some

abstract or 'ideal type' definition of it, can be described in terms of its
three primary foci (see Figure 5.2).

PRIMARY* CONTENT FOCUS	PRIMARY PROCESS FOCUS	PRIMARY SETTING FOCUS
Subject	Individual Learning	Teaching
Task	Self Learning	Learning
Learning	Group Learning	Counselling
Experience	Group Facilitation	Inspirational
Structures	Teacher/Trainer	Apprenticeship
	Community	Discipleship
Modelling	Resource Based	Revalatory
Mirroring	Feedback System	
Procedures		
Practices		
Principles		

*Also labelled 'Objectives' or 'Levels of Understanding'

Figure 5.1   Framework for analysing teaching and learning methods

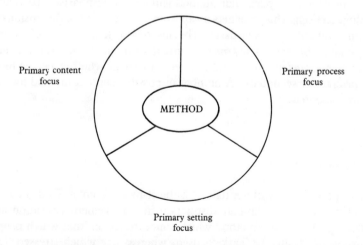

Figure 5.2   Teaching and learning methods defined by primary foci

PRIMARY CONTENT FOCUS

A teaching or learning method is not considered to be an abstract entity but is viewed as something that relates to actual *content*. Method can relate to content in at least two ways: first, in terms of subject content as for example in the study of finance, organisational behaviour, interviewing etc.; a second type of content is concerned with what you have designed or adopted the method for. This might be described as the content of the method. Looking at the Content column in Figure 5.1, a number of items in it would, in the eyes of many teachers, belong more properly in the Process list. In using the framework, the trainer can ask if his content objectives for a particular session are reflected in the process of the method, that is, in his involvement and that of his students. Modelling, for example, makes many assumptions about the appropriate types of activity and levels of involvement. In deciding on the primary content focus of a teaching or learning method, one needs to ask the question: 'What does the method stress in its concepts and activities?' It has to be answered with respect not only to concepts but also to activities. To omit activities would mean not accepting the assumption made here, that the very content of a method is bound up with its activities, i.e. those in which you are actually involved. Similarly, it is argued, one's learning objectives have always to be a part of what one is doing, rather than being perceived as being somehow 'out there'. The idea of a content focus is not intended to mean that content is separate from process or from setting; rather it is argued, that as one takes each dimension in turn, and considers it with respect to a method used, it is possible to identify the way in which the particular method will almost emphasise a particular thing. In doing this, one gets away from considering the dimensions as being mutually exclusive lists and begins to view them in terms of relative emphasis. Behind each *primary* content focus in the list there is also usually a *secondary* focus, and one needs to decide whether a given focus is primary or secondary. A number of possible content method foci are now presented.

Subject and Task

It is possible to differentiate a Subject-focus from a Task-focus in content. This is a familiar distinction in management education and training. A teaching method which concentrates on 'that which people have to do' would be Task-focused, whereas one which stressed 'that which people must understand or must assimilate into their knowledge structures' would be Subject-focused. When as a tutor one devises a learning activity, amongst the earliest decisions made is whether one will deal with people's behaviour or with helping them to learn knowledge or acquire understanding. There is no claim that these two foci are mutually exclusive, but in terms of primary focus such a distinction may be valid. Task is content in that if one uses a learning or teaching method in order to help people perform or do something, as opposed to know or accept something, then the primary content focus of the whole thing is the task which they are going to perform, even though they may not necessarily perform that task using the learning method. One has to examine and check that the process mirrors the content. For example, on training courses for new university staff, when a tutor lectures he is obviously using the teaching method of Lecture. When that lecture is about lecturing, then it is about task, i.e. the primary content focus of the lecture as a teaching method is the task of lecturing. The process itself is the task and the content is the task. They mirror each other and come together well. However, on the same course one may have a person lecturing about student learning. That is no longer Task-focused but becomes instead Subject-focused. The same would be true with counselling. When one lectures people about a university counselling system, then it becomes a Subject. If I lectured to you about counselling itself, the focus would remain Subject if you were not a counsellor, nor intended to be one, and your only interest in the topic was as a subject of study. However, if one learns about counselling and develops counselling skills through being counselled, then the focus becomes Task. Whenever a task is elevated into a 'bit of knowledge', one shifts from a Task-focus to a Subject-focus.

Experience and Learning

In considering Experience and Learning as content foci, one can see them as being one step removed from the previous two. Thus, Learning is one step away from Subject, while Experience is a step away from Task. Learning is to Subject what Experience is to Task. It is as if content had gone away from the specific subject matter towards a whole set of activities which surrounded the Subject. This would be the (personal) learning that people did of the subject. In the same way when they perform a Task they develop experience. Experience develops out of Task activity. Thus the primary content focus of a method may therefore be Experience rather than Task, or Learning rather than Subject.

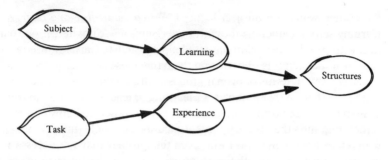

Figure 5.3 **Relationship of Subject, Learning, Task and Experience foci to Structures**

In a simulated group problem-solving Task such as the Lego-Man building exercise, the primary content focus for the observers is either on Learning or Experience depending on how the activity is designed by the tutor. In their role as observers, the teaching method as it applies to them is concentrating on Experience and Learning and not on Task or Subject. The primary content focus of most debriefing sessions will be Learning. An important point to mention is that in using a particular teaching method, one may have different phases in the use of that method in which the primary content focus changes. Thus in this list of proposed contents, the individual entries are not necessarily alternatives, but may be foci which flow into each other.

The relationship between Subject, Task, Learning and Experience has been described and one can see these four foci as constituting a single grouping which can be distinguished in qualitative terms from the next focus, Structures.

Structures

Structures refers to any kind of link, framework or logistical diagram the purpose of which is to help organise knowledge into some meaningful pattern for the learner. A Structures-focus in content may be concerned with the examination of the Structures that have evolved in the student's learning, or those links which may have evolved within a working group. It is possible to conceive of Subject moving out to Learning and then moving out still further to Structures. A similar progression may be observed with Task through Experience to Structures, as shown in Figure 5.3.

In a debriefing situation, one can concentrate the learner's mind on the structures of the learning that have been evolved. One can examine how knowledge has taken on a certain format in the learner's mind and question how relevant that is for a particular situation. Equally, the experiences that participants have derived from tasks can be examined in terms of their structures because one's experience relates to other people's, as in the case of a group or dyad. Equally the experiences of a person as a student, and that of another as a teacher in a teaching-learning situation can be structured, and to look at these structures may be important for further learning and development. In many experiential learning situations there are members who say that they enjoyed the activity, found the experience involving, learned a lot, but that their learning was very fragmented. In essence they are saying that they did not have a framework or structure within which to integrate their new knowledge. Without this, they are unable to relate it to anything else and are therefore unable to take it further. In such situations there would be a need for a debriefing session with the persons concerned, which could help them explore the possible links or logistics and provide them with an opportunity to both reflect on the learning and to integrate it. The participants who found a session enjoyable and useful but who felt unable to apply the learning may have 'blocked' on it; that is, they may have taken part in an exercise which was so far removed from their daily activities that they were unable to make the necessary jump in order to relate the two. They may need help to approximate to their work situation through finding metaphors and parallels in their own sphere of activity. Such activity concentrates almost entirely on the structures of knowledge and the structure of teaching as opposed to experience gained through doing a task or the learning which surrounds a particular subject.

Modelling and Mirroring

There is a second grouping of contents which is qualitatively different from the first which contained Subject, Task, Learning and Experience. In discussing Modelling and Mirroring, it is clear that one could easily be discussing a process and people usually use these terms in that way. For example, in Modelling one learns by copying someone else and in Mirroring one learns by observing oneself doing something and making an analysis of it. However, in the present list, Modelling and Mirroring are seen as content foci. This is because when a teacher devises a learning situation, he is frequently conscious of whether the whole thing is centred on an assumption about Modelling or Mirroring. For example, if one gives a lecture on the topic of lecturing, for most of the time one demonstrates the method, one also talks about the method and hopes that the demonstration of the method harmonises with what is being said about it. However, confusion can arise concerning the teacher's intentions. Does he want the audience to look at him and say, 'That's how I should lecture' or should they be thinking, 'Is the way he is lecturing the way I ought to be doing it'? In the first case the content is Modelling while in the second it is Mirroring. When the two elements are in harmony there is no problem. When however they become separated, as when the lecture runs over time, the overhead projector fails to work or when he cannot be heard at the back of the room, it is necessary to be clear about one's aims. Was the tutor wanting his listeners to model themselves on him, or did he want the listeners to take the ideas presented. The point here is that *it is not what the tutor does, but the content of what he does* which is the modelling situation. It is the content which focuses on the modelling. Moreover, it is not just the content of the tutor's lecture presentation which is being modelled, but also its structure, its ethos, its value structure and the preparation that went into it.

There are methods of teaching other than the lecture where the primary content focus is not Modelling but Mirroring. For example, the trainer may put individuals into a group and ask them to do certain things and take part in certain things. Here, he is not asking the participants to model, but rather to mirror by saying things and doing things to each other. The teacher creates a situation in which the primary content focus is the mirroring that the participants do for each other. One of several possible examples may be a group task which involves persons taking leadership roles. During the exercise, a member might reflect on whether the leadership behaviour being exhibited by another individual was the same as, or different from, his own. All of this is being achieved through the content of the method and not the process, because the facilitator has not explicitly stopped the activity to look at what has happened. It is content because, in constructing the situation, the tutor allowed the participants to concentrate on seeing themselves, observing themselves and judging themselves. A relevant question to ask here is whether the difference between Modelling and Mirroring in method content terms is dependent on the conscious design of the tutor or on what the learner chooses to take away from the activity. A response might be that what the learner takes away is more dependent on the process than on the actual content. Content can be viewed as the conscious design of the teacher. When he teaches a subject in a traditional way, such as how to use a pocket calculator, what the learner takes away from his interaction is the result of the process and not the content. The actual content is what the teacher puts in and in a sense is still there whether the student takes it away or not. Consider another example. In a method such as Guided Group Problem Solving, there exists the potential for mirroring rather than modelling. Most group situations, especially those in universities, tend to have modelling as the primary content focus. The group leader, usually a lecturer, wants people to behave according to his model of the 'good contributor'. In contrast, in the group problem-solving situation, there is the opportunity for participants to mirror their problem-solving skills.

Procedures, Practices and Principles

These three foci form the third grouping in the list of primary content foci. The distinction between procedures, practices and principles can be initially clarified with the use of an analogy. If one considers the *procedures* of the law, these have to do with the way in which the law is actually discharged. The focus is on how individuals are charged, how people are called to account, how they are dealt with in the courts etc. The *practices* of the law are one abstract step away from the procedures, but they are not yet the principles of the law. The practices have to do with the judgements that people make regarding the application of the principles. They are not, however, concerned with the 'hands on' aspects of the procedures. When one uses a particular teaching method, it is possible to concentrate a great deal on the procedures that people will have to go through, as opposed to emphasising the element of making judgements and seeing these judgements reach an action point. Equally, some teaching methods take principles as their primary content focus, and thereby move towards a Subject or Structures focus.

In any subject matter, be it chemistry, physiology or psychology, one can separate out procedures, practices and principles. Consider the operation of some problem-solving programmes which use a Problem-Solving Laboratory. The students who attend the programme will be exposed to a number of different primary content foci. Some of the teaching methods used, especially the more didactic ones which will precede some of the activity-oriented ones, will concentrate on the *principles* and theories of creative problem solving. They may stress the use of certain problem-solving strategies. Other approaches in the programme will use interactive methods when students examine problems together and observe each other's attempts to reach a solution. These would have practices as their primary content focus since they would be looking at how students have understood some of the principles and how they see them as relating to the particular subject matter or problem. In contrast, a third set of activities in the programme would involve the actual solution of problems and the testing of alternative solutions to problems. This would demonstrate a *procedures*-focus since what was being dealt with there would be the actual 'bits of equipment' that were not working, or with paper-and-pencil tests, circuit diagrams, chemical bonding or whatever the subject content was.

PRIMARY PROCESS FOCUS

The second column in the Figure 5.1 considers the Primary Process Focus of a teaching or learning method. The concern is with *how* things are done and the question is asked: 'What does the method stress in its execution?'. Process is concerned with 'doing'.

Individual Learning and Self Learning

In Individual Learning, the primary process focus is on the person *learning for himself*, but usually in a situation which has been structured by others. It is this emphasis on 'for himself' that distinguishes this process from other group learning situations where one may be learning *through* a group, *for* a group or even *with* a group. Individual Learning can be contrasted with Self Learning which is characterised by the student *learning by himself*. In Individual Learning the tutor may have devised some materials which the learner then uses to work on his own, whereas in Self Learning, the learner goes out and searches for the material himself. The material will not have been structured for him. The two foci may flow into each other. An example of Self Learning may be the manager who wishes to understand which type of leadership style he ought to use. He observes different managers working, notes their different styles and identifies their different interactional behaviours. Having done this, he may then indulge in Individual Learning in order to place his observation into some framework or perhaps in order to identify the different organisational contexts in which a particular leadership style might be most effective. To do this he may be supplied with notes, guided reading or a programmed text which he completes on his own.

Group Learning and Group Facilitation

Counselling skills may be acquired through Group Learning. For example, the manager may take part in different experiential activities where he finds out a great deal about himself through the group. Group Learning is distinguished from Group Facilitation by the fact that in the latter one becomes able to do certain things and acquires certain skills, not through taking part in experiential group activities, but by being part of a group which facilitates one's learning. For example, the membership of a certain work group may allow the manager to develop certain diagnostic skills rapidly. In Group Facilitation, the group concerned would not deliberately set out to teach its members specific skills or knowledge. The member would learn these informally through his group membership.

Teacher/Trainer

There is a well known process in which a teacher or a trainer is in command and it is he who directs and carries out a learning/teaching activity. Under this heading one would include not only didactic processes, ('get up and tell them'), but also those forms of group activity where the actual primary process is the trainer and not the group. In such circumstances, the trainer is not asking the group 'How is it?' but is saying, 'Do this, do that'. Examples of this primary process focus would include Micro-labs, Tutorials, and Seminars. In these cases, the Group Learning or Group Facilitation focus may be the secondary one.

Community

This label is intended to take in activites such as Teaching by Learning and Study Service where the focus is on the community-at-large. It may be in the form of students going out from the classroom situation to an activity which is outside of their learning. Community as a primary process focus is intended to be broadly defined. It takes in practical activities such as Placement, and some aspects of Sitting by Nellie as represented in the training of health visitors and district nurses. A community-focused process usually involves a larger group of people than merely the learners themselves. Moreover, it has to be a larger group to whom the learners relate in some structured way. All examples of Community-focused methods come from service occupations where the training demands a lot of feedback from those to whom the service is being provided. Doctors for example are community-trained, even though the community concerned may be the hospital.

Resource based

There are those methods where the primary process focus is on the resources and not on activities or experiences. Some rigid forms of Keller Plan teaching exemplify a situation where the resources take over completely and thereby de-emphasise the actual activities and interactions involved. Another example would be Programmed Learning which overlaps a little with what has been described as an Individual Learning focus.

Feedback system

Since Feedback Systems are involved to some degree in all the previous foci described, this has been left until last. There are some teaching and learning methods where the primary focus is on the feedback, and not on the group or the trainer or on the resources. For example, many forms of counselling training fall into this area, as does Interpersonal Process Recall, Video Confrontation, Micro-Teaching and Instrumented Laboratory.

PRIMARY SETTING FOCUS

The third dimension in the analytical framework concerns the *ethos* of the method of organisation and the orientation of its organisers and designers. It has to do with the way in which one puts things together and the philosophy and values which underlie that choice.

Teaching

The values inherent in the way in which you organise a teaching/learning situation can focus a great deal on Teaching. There is a whole educational philosophy which says 'I teach you something'.

Learning

On the other hand, there is another philosophy which says 'You learn and I will facilitate that learning'.

Counselling

Yet another philosophy says 'I listen and try to understand your learning needs and help you to identify not only those needs but also the resources which can help you fulfil those needs'.

Inspirational

Over and above the teaching ethos, it is possible to construct situations in which people really become motivated; not necessarily by the form of the teaching, although this is possible, but by the dynamics of the teaching. For example, there are some forms of confrontation and example building that can inspire people to learn. Equally there are forms of lecturing and problem-centred teaching which can be classed as inspirational.

Apprenticeship

The Apprenticeship model is also an ethos, since it is underpinned by a great many assumptions about how people learn and why they should learn in that way.

Discipleship

Discipleship is differentiated from Apprenticeship as an ethos because the latter tends to be more structured, more formal and usually has rules. Discipleship is a situation in which the learner attaches himself to a particular person, 'school of thought' or a group. There is the idea of 'following the leadership'. At one time medical education had a Discipleship ethos when each consultant had his own following. It was not Apprenticeship because the consultant did not deign to show his followers how to do things. They followed in his wake and tried to ape and imitate, but to also go beyond. Discipleship is an ethos which is usually characterised by an uncritical involvement of the learner.

Revelatory

A Revelatory ethos is common in many group learning situations such as counselling training or in group therapy. The ethos underlying this form of teaching is that there is no rigid pattern to people's learning, but there is an implicit belief that people will have insight. It goes back to the idea that a lot of learning comes from sudden flashes of inspiration and insight. This ethos can be seen in those modern learning methods which deal in experience and sharing and where people have revelations about what they ought to do next.

Depending on how one applied them in practice, the following methods might have the following 'profiles':

Method	Content Focus	Process Focus	Setting Focus
Study Skills Training	Learning	Individual Learning	Counselling
Sitting by Nellie	Experience	Feedback System	Apprenticeship
Trigger Film	Modelling	Group Facilitation	Revelatory
Role Playing	Experience	Group Learning	Revelatory

Because tutors are likely to use the same methods differently, the profile of their particular method-in-use is likely to differ. The purpose of the framework is not to group methods together, but to test the internal consistency of a method which one already uses. It might be used by the tutor in the following way. He thinks back over a recent learning method which he used and he asks himself the following questions:

Question	Primary Focus
What did the method put most stress on in its concepts and activities?	Content
What did it stress in its execution?	Process
What was the ethos of its organisation and the orientation of its user?	Setting

The answers to these questions can give a guide to the effectiveness or lack of effectiveness of a method. For example, the trainer may believe that he is being inspirational, but on analysis may discover that he is in fact being highly teaching-oriented, and that he places great emphasis on himself as the trainer and on structures. In such a situation it is possible to see why he was unable to motivate his students to either change or to innovate. The three columns suggest a complementarity. There are certain limited combinations of complementary Content, Process and Setting mixes. There are many other combinations which are incompatible. The triple column listing does not have the charcteristics of the well known 'Random Buzz Word Generator' where all mixes are possible. The reader is invited to consider which mixes are feasible. In the analytical framework described there may be other dimensions possible which have not been included. The framework is merely offered as a tool which the tutor and trainer can use to reflect on the teaching/learning methods that he uses in order to help his students to learn.

AFTERWORD

by John Morris
Professor of Management Development
Manchester Business School

If someone had asked you, before you had a chance to use this book, how many methods are currently being used in the field of management learning, what would your answer have been? If you had said 'Over 50', I raise my hat to you (or at least I would if I wore one). I would have thought about it for a while, wondered whether to question the question in the best academic tradition, and would finally have settled for a few dozen. How many dozen? Well, perhaps three or so. If I had been asked to draw up a list of those few dozen, I would have been even more embarrassed than I am now, as I contemplate the three hundred or more methods resourcefuly garnered and itemised by Andrzej Huczynski.

One fascinating thing about the methods is the splendid mix of labels used to describe them. There are some exotic foreign offerings. I particularly liked Parrainage and Tutorium, and the conferring of immortality on the innovators of particular approaches: Kepner and Tregoe, Phillips and Bion, Alexander and Socrates, Coverdale and Buber. In stark contrast to these warmly personal approaches, we have the technological thrust of Mathetics, Tape Stop Exercise, Micro-lab and Bio-energetics. The older reader might turn from these in some relief to the reassuringly firm ground of Lecture Method, Literature Search, Socratic Enquiry and Debate. Those who love a challenge, on the other hand, might alternate between the crisp technological labels and the apparent surrealism of the Talking Wall, the Action Maze (no, not Real Life, quite), Festival, Fishbowl, and Manager Shadowing. As an ageing academic in the field of management learning, I found it a useful precaution to look at Paid Educational Leave, Sick Leave and Holiday Replacement.

A useful aspect of the book is the inclusion of methods from related fields of work, such as medicine, biology, geology, and languages. It is good to see an already wide field being fruitfully extended in this way. The challenge that is faced in all these fields of professional learning is that of a discriminating set of fraternities, distinctly unwilling to become captive audiences for traditional methods of instruction drawn from compulsory education and training. These busy professionals seek help in developing their skills and their knowledge. Not least, they want to

337

foster their own ability to learn, with a minimum of expert control. Managers seem to have taken the lead, because their professional responsibilities require them to attempt to manage their fellow human beings, many of whom strongly object to being 'managed'.

Not surprisingly, managers have wanted to go well beyond the mastery of different fields of knowledge, into mastery of practice. They want to turn 'knowing about' something into 'knowing how' to get things done. And the most intractable area of 'know-how' is knowing how to understand, feel with, and work cooperatively with the people who surround us. The business manager has to add a further dimension of social understanding and skill, since he or she is often working competitively, with scarce resources, rather than cooperatively, in a supportive environment. Recent cutbacks in education and the social services have made this aspect of human affairs disturbingly relevant to the 'education manager' and the 'social services manager', if it were not already so.

The entries themselves are so intriguing that any reader could be forgiven for assuming that he has got hold of a dictionary of methods. But this book goes beyond the entries into listing resources for teaching and learning, and to providing a framework for assessing the methods. The list of resources is self explanatory, but I would like to comment briefly on the framework.

I agree whole-heartedly with the author's refusal to imprison these lively methods within a fixed classification. It is tempting for the tidy-minded to take a single dimension, such as 'learner-controlled ... teacher-controlled' and to place all available methods on it. Or, going a little further, to place two dimensions at right-angles to one another in a simple matrix and to place the methods into this slightly wider domain. In the framework we are offered here, there are three related ways of looking at a particular method, in relation to a chosen purpose. One can look at the *content* with which the method deals – that which hits the eye as 'input' or 'output' of materials. One can look at the *process* with which the method is concerned – the activities in which those engaged in learning take part. And one can look at the *value-context* within which the method is placed, and which gives it a particular meaning. I quarrel slightly with the author in calling this value-context a 'setting', since that word is often associated with space rather than values. But another word is hard to find.

These powerful concepts are handled very sensitively, and one sees clearly why it is impossible to pin down methods which change their form and content with each group of learners, with each 'learning consultant' and on each occasion that they are used.

The whole spirit of the book is liberating, and the notion of a liberating framework is difficult to comprehend. But as frameworks go, I found this one thought provoking. In particular, I like the notion that each aspect of a method can open up to wider considerations, until the method becomes part of the story of one's personal development. Perhaps the tables and diagrams that currently express the three dimensions of the framework could be seen as a cone-shaped spiral of personal and social development, moving from specific content-dominated modes of learning to deeply personal expressions of oneself in active engagement with the world.

For me, the test that such a book as this must pass is straightforward, but immensely difficult. Does it help the reader to understand better what he or she is doing, and to find ways of doing it better? From my experience, the book has passed this test triumphantly.

Making things for Children

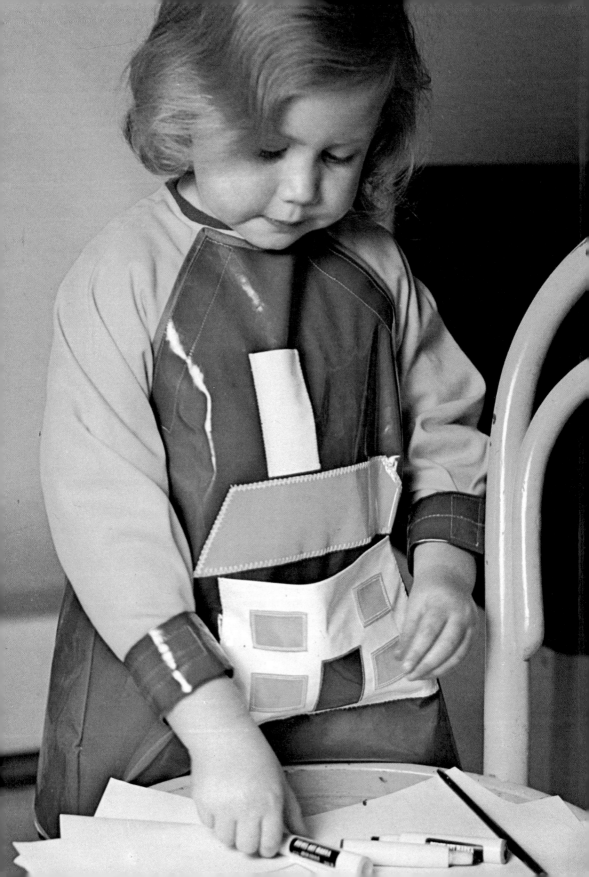

Making things for
Children

by Katie Dyson

Octopus Books

Acknowledgements

Katie Dyson and the publishers would
like to thank the following people for
their help in the preparation of this book:
Ethel Bowen
J & P Coats Ltd., machine and embroidery
threads
Joan O'Connor
Dylon, fabric and suede dyes
Jacqueline Dyson
Elna Sewing Machines Ltd., and
Hazel Chapman
Emu Wools Ltd., Emu yarns
French Wools Ltd., Pingouin yarns
Lucy Hedley
Patons & Baldwins, Patons yarns
Lister & Co., Listers Yarns
Robert Glew & Co., Robin yarns
Frances Rogers
Mary Stent
H. G. Twilley Ltd, Twilleys yarns
Childsplay, accessories.

First published 1974 by
Octopus Books Limited
59 Grosvenor Street, London W1

ISBN 0 7064 0347 9

Distributed in USA by
Galahad Books
a division of A & W Promotional Book Corp.
95 Madison Avenue, New York,
New York 10016

Produced by Mandarin Publishers Limited
14 Westlands Road, Quarry Bay, Hong Kong

Frontispiece: *Play apron (page 59)*

Printed in Hong Kong

Contents

Baby Things

Playtime and Partytime

Everyday Clothes

Nursery Accessories

Introduction

Half the fun of making children's clothes lies in adding an individual touch to an often simple pattern. This book is designed to be helpful in several ways. There are smocking, crochet, embroidery and other ideas to make basic patterns more exciting. There is also an invaluable range of money-savers in the form of colourful knitting, sewing and crochet patterns. These are practical things that are usually expensive to buy. There are cheerful play clothes, beautiful party things and an excellent everyday range, as well as a comprehensive selection of baby clothes and nursery accessories.

Use the book as an "ideas-bank". You will be able to come back to it again and again, making up the patterns in other sizes and different colours, or adapting the ideas to your own particular style.

The sewing machine is a willing ally. Make it work for you. Use it to its full potential to help speed up sewing work. This will give you more time to spend on the decorative touches; the knitting and crochet work.

The many patterns illustrate a wide cross-section of different methods and crafts used for making children's things. · As well as knitting, crochet, sewing and embroidery, there are instructions for patchwork, appliqué, collage, quilting, tie-dyeing and fabric painting. These are all original ideas, designed by a mother with young children for other mothers, grand-mothers and everyone who loves to make things at home.

Size note

Where more than one size is given follow 1st figures for 1st size and figures in brackets in order for other sizes. Where only one set of figures is given, read for all sizes.

Note

Where terms or materials may be different for overseas readers, an equivalent is given in parenthesis after the British term or material.

Knitting needle and crochet hook sizes

Equivalent American knitting needle sizes are given in brackets, throughout the knitting patterns, after the British sizes. Continental equivalents will be found in the chart below New International size crochet hooks are quoted in the crochet patterns, followed by the American equivalents in brackets. British sizes will be found in the chart below.

Crochet Hook Chart

Continental (New International Size)	American	British
2·50 mm	B/1	12
3·00 mm	D/3 or C/2	10/11
3·50 mm	E/4	9
4·00 mm	F/5	8
4·50 mm	G/6	7
5·00 mm	H/8	6
5·50 mm	H/8	5
6·00 mm	I/9	4

Knitting Needle Chart

British	American	Continental
3	10	$6\frac{1}{2}$ mm
5	8	$5\frac{1}{2}$ mm
7	6	$4\frac{1}{2}$ mm
8	5	4 mm
9	4	$3\frac{1}{2}$ mm
10	3	$3\frac{1}{4}$ mm
11	2	3 mm
12	1	$2\frac{1}{2}$ mm

Enlarging patterns

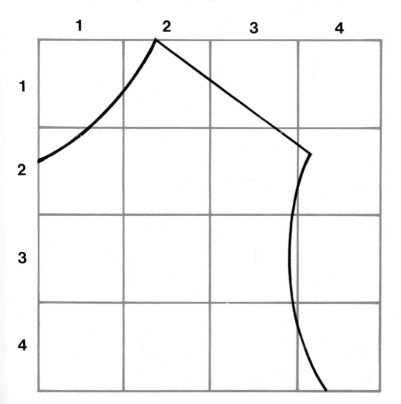

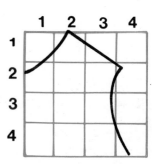

The important thing to remember when making your own patterns from the ones in this book is that 5 squares equal 4 inches (note pages 66, 89 and 98 differ). Seam allowances are included in the patterns. Before you start you will need:
dressmaker's squared paper, or large sheets of brown wrapping paper, with one inch squares drawn on (use a yardstick and set square to do this accurately).
ruler
sharp pencil
1. Number the squares along the top and side side of the pattern in the book. Mark corresponding numbers on the dressmaker's squared paper. Make sure there is sufficient

length and width of paper for each pattern. If not, tape pieces together.
2. Start from the top left corner and work downwards and across. Make an accurate full-size pattern by marking dots on the squared paper to correspond exactly with places where the pattern crosses the lines of the graph in the book.
3. Connect dots on the pattern to copy curves and use a ruler to draw in any straight lines.
4. Transfer any cutting instructions and details from the original graph and write what each piece of pattern is clearly—skirt, bodice front etc.
5. Now cut out the patterns you have drawn and they are ready for use.

Knitting and Crochet Abbreviations

Colours

M:	main shade mc: main colour
C:	contrast

Knitting

k:	knit
p:	purl
sts:	stitches
st st:	stocking stitch
g st:	garter stitch
alt:	alternate
foll:	following
inc:	increase
dec:	decrease
rep:	repeat
beg:	beginning
rem:	remain (ing)
ins:	inches
cont:	continue
tog:	together
SKPO:	slip 1, knit 1, pass slip stitch over
SK 2tog.PO:	slip one, K2 tog, pass slipped stitch over
m 1:	make 1
pw:	purlwise
K 21N:	K twice into stitch, i.e. first into front, then into back of stitch
patt:	pattern
tbl:	through back of loop
m st :	moss stitch
C 6f:	cable 6 front, i.e. slip next 3 sts on to cable needle and leave at front, k 3, then k sts from cable needle
C 6b:	as C 6f, but leave sts at back
sl:	slip
C 4b:	slip next 2 sts on to a cable needle and leave at back of work, k 2, then k 2 sts from cable needle
C 4f:	slip next 2 sts on to a cable needle and leave at front of work, k 2, then k 2 sts from cable needle
T2R:	k into front of second st on left hand needle, k first st slipping both sts off needle together
T2L:	k into back of second st on left hand needle, k first st slipping both sts off needle together
T2RP:	k into front of second st on left hand needle, p first st slipping both sts off needle together
T2LP:	p into back of second st on left hand needle, k first st, slipping both sts off needle together
C4BP:	slip next 2 sts on to a cable needle and leave at back of work, k 2, then p 2 sts from cable needle
C4FP:	slip next 2 sts on to a cable needle and leave at front of work, p 2, then k 2 sts from cable needle
y fwd:	yarn forward
yrn:	yarn round needle

Crochet

(American abbreviations in brackets)

ch:	chain
dc (sc):	double crochet (single crochet)
h tr (hdc):	half treble (half double crochet)
tr (dc):	treble (double crochet)
d tr (tr):	double treble (treble)
tr tr (d tr):	triple treble (double treble)
sl st:	slip stitch
yrh:	yarn round hook
sp:	space
gr:	group
dec:	decrease
inc:	increase
ML:	make a loop by inserting hook into next dc (sc), yarn over hook, and draw up a one inch loop on index finger of left hand, draw yarn through st, as in dc (sc), yarn over hook and draw through loops on hook
dec 1:	decrease 1 by inserting hook into next st, draw through a loop, insert hook into next st, draw through a loop, yarn over hook, draw through 3 loops on hook

Good stitches to know

A selection of stitches, some to make sewing work quicker, others to be used for decoration.

Three useful stitches for decoration

1. Chain Stitch

Stitches must be even. Make a stitch along the sewing line. Loop thread under needle point and pull needle through. Insert needle point next to exit of last stitch and bring needle out further along sewing line, looping thread under point. Use this stitch for decorative embroidery on clothes.

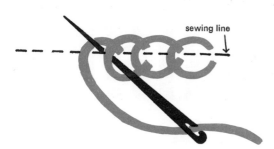

sewing line

2. Lazy-daisy Stitch

Once practised, this can be worked quickly freehand. Mark the daisy shape with tiny pencil points. Bring thread out at centre of daisy, stitch down into fabric from edge of "petal" and back up into centre on right side. Continue this way until daisy is completed. Use this stitch for all types of embroidery and especially for decorative embroidery on knitted baby clothes.

3. Knot a Fringe

Wind wool or thread on to card $\frac{1}{4}$ inch deeper than proposed length of fringe. Cut one edge. Fold one piece (two for thicker garment) of wool in half. Pull through garment hem with crochet hook (use needle threader if working on fine fabric). Pull ends of thread through loop until knot is firm. Use for making fringe on knitted or crochet things; on sewn play tunics, ponchos or capes.

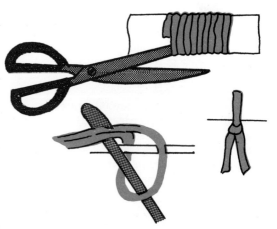

Short cuts with the sewing machine

1. Shirring Elastic

A gentle way of adding gathers to sleeve edges. Wind shirring elastic by hand on to bobbin, adjust upper tension and sew as for normal straight stitching. The shirring elastic will automatically gather the fabric.

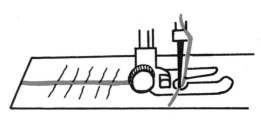

2. Speedy Gathers

A quick way of making neat gathers on skirts and particularly sleeve heads. Set the machine to a fairly wide zigzag. Cut two

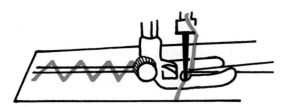

lengths pearl cord the same length as area to be gathered. Run cord under machine foot as you sew the zigzag stitch. The stitching will move along the cord so you can pull up fabric to required length.

3. Appliqué Work

Sew on appliqué with normal straight machine stitch. Trim edges neatly. Then sew all round edge with satin stitch. Use machine embroidery twist for smartest results. Put tracing or writing paper under fine fabrics while machining to give body to stitches and stop fabric from pulling.

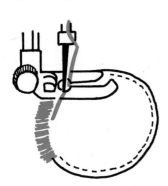

Six smocking stitches

Use these in any colour combination for effective patterning. For best effect, the stitches should not be sewn too deeply into the gathered pleats. Skim the tops of the gathers.

Note to left-handed people: Work all these stitches in reverse and study illustrations through mirror to get correct needle and thread positions. If instructions say "start at left", you should start at the right, and vice versa.

1. Single Cable

A good firm stitch for the top of a piece of smocking. Start from left. Bring thread out at left of pleat 1. Insert needle point on right-hand side of pleat 2. Stitch through back of pleat, bringing thread out parallel to first stitch and slightly above it on left of pleat 2. Make the next stitch downwards so thread comes out on a line with first stitch.

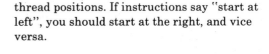

2. Trellis Stitch

Stitch this in the same way as single cable. Work along the pleats going 5 "steps" up and down to make a V pattern. The next row down and up turns this into a diamond shape. Thread should lie above needle when sewing downward steps and below needle when sewing upward ones.

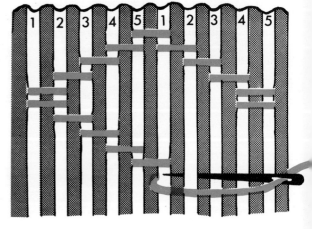

3. Vandyke Stitch

A good stitch for the base of a block of smocking. Work from right to left. Bring thread out on left of pleat 2. Stitch into right of pleat 1. Bring thread out on left of pleat 2, Take needle up and stitch into right of pleat 2 about ⅛th inch or slightly less above. Bring needle out horizontally on left of pleat 3. Take thread down and stitch into right of pleat 3. Bring needle out on left of pleat 4. Make the stitch more open at base of smocking by taking 2 or 3 steps up and 2 or 3 down at a time.

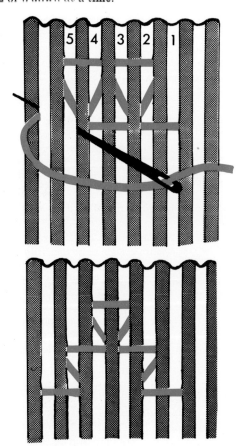

Open Vandyke.

4. Diamond Stitch

The first row makes the top of the diamond and the second completes it. Work from left to right. Bring thread out on left of pleat 1. Take thread across horizontally. Stitch through pleat 2 from right to left, bringing thread upwards, diagonally to right. Stitch from right to left of pleat 3. Take thread over

horizontally and stitch from right to left of pleat 4, bringing thread out below stitch. Sketch shows how to complete diamond shapes.

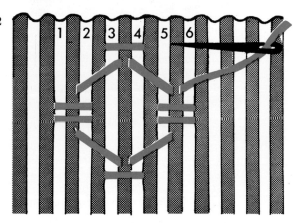

5. Outline Stitch

Begin with this stitch or use it before several rows of Vandyke stitch. Work from left to right. Bring thread out on left of pleat 1. Stitch diagonally downwards into right of pleat 2. Bring needle up and out on left of same pleat, in line with upper part of first stitch. Repeat the process, always taking thread diagonally down to right and pointing needle diagonally up to left.

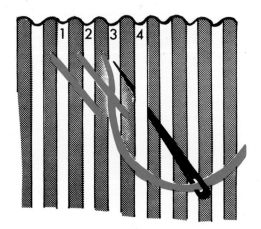

6. Feather Stitch

Work from right to left. Bring thread out on right front of pleat 1. Keep thread in front of needle. Take needle slightly down and stitch from right of pleat 1, through to left of pleat 2,

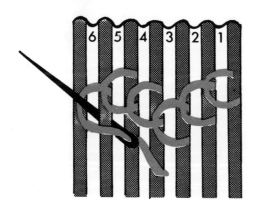

looping thread under needle. Hold thread down with left thumb so that it comes below thumb. Insert needle slightly below from right of pleat 2 to left of pleat 3. Loop thread under needle point. Continue working 3 stitches downwards and 3 upwards. When stitching a line of 3 upwards, hold thread down with left thumb so it comes above thumb while making the stitch. This stitch is particularly effective when a contrasting colour is worked just under the row.

Baby things

Knitted Matinee Set

This matinée set is ideal for a new baby girl. The dress has a decorative openwork stitch on the skirt and the coat, with an almost tweedy look, is a warm and practical idea. As an extra smart touch, the bonnet is decorated with a crochet flower motif. The set can be made up in a wide range of alternative colours, or the dress could be knitted in white and the coat and other accessories in navy blue and white or emerald green and white.

Materials

Lister Baby Bel 4-ply Courtelle or
Lee Target Lullaby 4-ply Courtelle,
(Fingering 3-ply)
25 gr balls:
Dress: 2 main colour, 2 contrast
Coat: 3 main colour, 2 contrast
Hat: 1 main colour, 1 small ball contrast
Bootees or mittens: 1 main colour
3 buttons for dress
4 buttons for coat
Ribbon for hat, mittens and bootees
Pairs of 10 (3) and 12 (1) knitting needles
No. 3·00 mm (D/3) crochet hook

Measurements To fit an 18 (20) inch chest.

Tension About 6 sts (1 complete patt) measures 1 inch.

Abbreviations, needle and size note
See pages 6 and 8.

Dress
Back

Using No. 10(3) needles and M, cast on 81(87) sts and work thus:

1st and 2nd rows K. Change to C.
3rd row K 1, sl 1 pw, * k 5, sl 1 pw. Rep from * to last st, k 1.
4th row P 1, sl 1 pw, * p 5, sl 1 pw. Rep from * to last st, p 1.
5th row K 1, sl 1 pw, * k 1, m 1, SK2tog.PO, m1, k 1, sl 1 pw. Rep from * to last st, k 1.
6th row As 4th row. Change to M.
7th and 8th rows K. Change to C.
9th row K 4, sl 1 pw, * k 5, sl 1 pw. Rep from * to last 4 sts, k 4.
10th row P 4, sl 1 pw, * p 5, sl 1 pw. Rep from * to last 4 sts, p 4.
11th row K 1, k 2 tog, m 1, sl 1 pw, * k 1, m 1, SK2tog.PO, m 1, k 1, sl 1 pw. Rep from * to last 4 sts, k 1, m 1, SKPO, k 1.
12th row As 10th row. Change to M.
These rows form patt. Cont straight in patt until work measures 7½(8) ins ending with a 2nd or 8th patt row. Break off C. Now use M. to complete the Back.
Next row (P 1, k 1) 1(4) times, (p 1, k 2 tog, p 1, k 1) 15(13) times, p 1, k 2 tog, p 1, (k 1, p 1) 0(5) times. 65(73) sts.
Next row * K 1, p 1. Rep from * to last st, k 1.
Cont in rib until work measures 8½(9) ins ending after a wrong side row.

Shape Armholes

Cast off 3(5) sts at beg of next 2 rows, then dec 1 st each end of every row until 49(53) sts rem. Cont in rib until work measures 10(11) ins ending after a wrong side row.

Divide for Back Opening

1st row (P 1, k 1) 13(14) times, p 1, leave rem 22(24) sts on a thread for other side. Work one row in rib.
Next row (buttonhole). Rib to last 3 sts, m 1, k 2 tog, p 1.

Cont in rib making a 2nd buttonhole 1¼ ins from base of first buttonhole and cont until work measures 12(13) ins ending at armhole edge.

Shape Shoulder

Cast off 6(7) sts at beg of next 2 armhole edge rows and leave rem 15 sts on a thread for neckband.

Return to other sts, rejoin yarn, cast on 5 sts for underflap and work to match other side, omitting buttonholes and reversing shoulder shaping.

Front

Work as for Back until armhole shapings are completed then cont in rib until work measures 11(12) ins ending after a wrong side row.

Shape Neck

1st row Rib 14(16) sts, k 2 tog, k 1, leave next 15 sts on spare needle for neckband and rem 17(19) sts on a st holder for other side.
2nd row P 2, rib to end.
3rd row Rib to last 3 sts, k 2 tog, k 1.
Rep 2nd and 3rd rows 3 times more, then 2nd row once more.

Shape Shoulder

Cast off 6(7) sts at beg of next row. Rib one row. Cast off rem sts.
Go back to other sts for other side.
1st row K 1, SKPO, rib to end.
2nd row Rib to last 2 sts, p 2.
Work to match other side, reversing shaping.

Sleeves

Using No. 12(1) needles cast on 49(55) sts, and work 6 rows in p 1, k 1 rib, thus beg and ending 1st row p 1, and 2nd row k 1.
Change to No. 10(3) needles and cont in rib until work measures 2 ins.

Shape Top

Cast off 3(5) sts at beg of next 2 rows, then dec 1 st at each end of next and every foll 4th row until 33 sts rem. Now dec 1 st each end of every row until 21 sts rem. Cast off 4 sts at beg of next 4 rows. Cast off rem sts.

Neckband

Join shoulders. Using No. 12(1) needles, rib across 15 sts of left side of Back, pick up and k 10 sts down left side of front, rib across 15 sts on spare needle, pick up and k 10 sts up right side of front, rib across 15 sts at right side of Back. (65 sts.) Work 5 rows in rib as set, working final buttonhole on 3rd row. Cast off in rib.

To make up

Press carefully, omitting ribbing. Join side and sleeve seams. Sew in sleeves. Sew underflap in position at lower edge. Sew on buttons. Press seams.

Coat
Back

Using No. 10(3) needles and M, cast on 63(69) sts and work in patt as for Back of Dress until work measures 8(8½) ins ending after a wrong side row.

Shape Armholes

Cast off 3 sts at beg of next 2 rows, then dec 1 st at each end of every row until 51(57) sts rem. Cont in patt until work measures 12(13) ins.

Shape Shoulders

Cast off 6(7) sts at beg of next 4 rows. Leave rem 27(29) sts on spare needle for neckband.

Left front

1st size only Using No. 10(3) needles and M, cast on 30 sts and k 2 rows. Change to C.
3rd row K 1, sl 1 pw, * k 5, sl 1 pw. Rep from * to last 4 sts, k 4.
4th row P 4, sl 1 pw, * p 5, sl 1 pw. Rep from * to last st, p 1.
Cont in patt keeping row ends correct until work measures same as Back to armhole shaping.
2nd size only Using No. 10(3) needles and M, cast on 33 sts and work in patt as given for Back of Dress until work measures same as Back to armhole shaping.

Knitted matinée set

Both Sizes. Shape Armhole

Cast off 3 sts at beg of next row, then work one row in patt. Now dec 1 st at armhole edge on every row until 24(27) sts rem. Cont in patt until work measures 10 rows less than Back to shoulder shaping, ending at armhole edge.

Shape Neck

1st row Patt to last 10(11) sts, k 2 tog, k 1, leave rem 7(8) sts on thread for neckband.
2nd row P 2, patt to end.
3rd row Patt to last 3 sts, k 2 tog, k 1.
Rep 2nd and 3rd rows 3 times more, then 2nd row once more.

Shape Shoulder

Cast off 6(7) sts at beg of next row. Patt one row. Cast off rem sts.

Right front

1st size only Using No. 10(3) needles and M, cast on 30 sts and k 2 rows. Change to C.
3rd row K 4, sl 1 pw, * k 5, sl 1 pw.
Rep from * to last st, k 1.
4th row P 1, sl 1 pw, * p 5, sl 1 pw.
Rep from * to last 4 sts, p 4.
Cont in patt as set and complete to match Left Front reversing all shapings and working SKPO in place of k 2 tog at neck edge.
2nd size only Work as Left Front, reversing all shapings and working SKPO in place of k 2 tog at neck edge.

Sleeves

Using No. 12(1) needles and M, cast on 35(39) sts and work in k 1, p 1 rib. Change to No. 10(3) needles.
1st row K 4(3), * K21N, k 2. Rep from * to last 4(3) sts, K 21N, k 3(2). 45(51) sts.
2nd row K.
Cont in patt as given for Back, beg with a 3rd row, until work measures 6(7) ins.

Shape Top

Cast off 3 sts at beg of next 2 rows, then dec 1 st at each end of next and every foll 4th row until 33 sts rem. Dec 1 st at each end

of every alt row until 21 sts rem. Cast off 4 sts at beg of next 4 rows. Cast off rem sts.

Left front band

Using No. 12(1) needles and M, cast on 7 sts and work in k 1, p 1 rib until band is long enough, slightly stretched, to reach neck shaping. Leave sts on holder for neckband. Sew band neatly in position.

Right front band

First place pins on Left Front Band for buttonholes, the first pin one inch below neck shaping, with 2 more pins 1¼ ins below each other. Work as Left Front Band ending on same row as rib on Left Front Band, working buttonholes when positions are reached thus:
Buttonhole row Rib 3, m 1, k 2 tog, rib 2.
Leave sts on holder for neckband. Sew band neatly in place.

Neckband

Sew up shoulder seams. Now using No. 12(1) needles and M, rib across 7 sts of Right Front Band, k across 7(8) sts on thread, pick up and k 10 sts up right front, k across 27(29) sts at back neck, pick up and k 10 sts down left front, then k across 7(8) sts on thread, and finally rib across 7 sts of Left Front Band. 75(79) sts.
Work 5 rows in rib, working final buttonhole on 3rd row.

To make up

Join side and sleeve seams. Set in sleeves. Sew on buttons. Press seams.

Bootees

Using No. 10(3) needles cast on 39 sts.
** **1st row** * P 1, k 1. Rep from * to last st, p 1.
2nd row * K 1, p 1. Rep from * to last st, k 1.
Rep 1st and 2nd rows until work measures 2 ins.
Next row P 1, * m 1, k 2 tog. Rep from * to end. Work 3 more rows in rib **.

Shape Instep
1st row K 25, turn.
2nd row K 11, turn.
Work 16 rows in g st on these 11 sts. Break off yarn. Rejoin yarn to lower edge of instep, pick up and k 14 sts up instep, k across 11 sts on needle, pick up and k 14 sts down other side of instep, and k rem 14 sts. 67 sts in all. K 5 rows across all sts.

Shape Foot
1st row K 2 tog, k 25, SK2tog.PO, k 7, SK2tog.PO, k 25, k 2 tog.
2nd and alt rows K.
3rd row K 2 tog, k 23, SK2tog.PO, k 5, SK2tog.PO, k 23, k 2 tog.
5th row K 2 tog, k 21, SK2tog.PO, k 3, SK2tog.PO, k 21, k 2 tog.
7th row K 2 tog, k 19 SK2tog.PO, k 1, SK2tog.PO, k 19, k 2 tog.
Cast off rem sts knitwise.

To make up

Sew up foot and back seam. Thread ribbon through holes in rib. Press carefully.

Mittens

Using No. 10(3) needles, cast on 31 sts and work as given for Bootees from ** to **. Work 24 rows in g st.

Shape Top
1st row (K 2 tog, k 4) 5 times, k 1.
2nd and alt row K.
3rd row (K 2 tog, k 3) 5 times, k 1.
5th row (K 2 tog, k 2) 5 times, k 1.
7th row (K 2 tog, k 1) 5 times, k 1.
Break yarn, thread through rem sts, draw up and fasten off.
Sew side seam. Thread ribbon through holes in rib.

Bonnet
Side pieces (Two required)

Using No. 10(3) needles cast on 45 sts and k 4 rows.
Continue thus:
1st row K 21, SK2tog.PO, k 21.
2nd and every alt row P.
3rd row K 20, SK2tog.PO, k 20.
Cont in st st dec 2 sts in centre of every alt row until 21 sts rem. Still dec in centre of row as before, dec 1 st at each end of every alt row until 5 sts rem. Cast off.

Centre piece

Using No. 10(3) needles, cast on 20 sts and cont in g st until work measures 5 ins. Dec 1 st at each end of next and every 4th row until 8 sts rem. K 3 rows. Cast off.

Motif

Using No. 3·00 (D/3) hook, make 4 ch, and join into a circle with a sl st.
1st round Work 10 dc (sc) into circle, join with a sl st.
2nd round 2 tr (dc) in each dc (sc) working into front loop of dc (sc) only, join with a sl st.
3rd round 3 d tr (tr) in each dc (sc) of 1st round, working into back loop only.
4th round * 1 dc (sc) in 1st d tr (tr) 5 tr (dc) in next d tr (tr). Rep from * all round. Fasten off.

To make up

Sew side pieces to centre piece. Sew motif in position. Sew ribbon at each side to tie. Press carefully.

Stripey Crawlers

This shows how you can turn a simple idea into something exciting. These crawlers are easy to make in stocking stitch. The bright colours make them fun for a baby to wear and the protective suede knee pads and soles will help the garment live longer. To simplify the pattern, make it up in just one gay colour.

Materials

Mademoiselle Pingouin (Fingering 3-ply) 50 gr balls: 1 ball each in colours A, B, C and D (blue, yellow, green and red)
Pairs of No. 10(3) and 12(1) knitting needles
Set of 4 No. 12(1) knitting needles, pointed at each end
4 buttons
Scraps of suede for kneepads and soles (optional)

Measurements To fit a 16(18:20) inch chest.

Tension 7 sts and 9 rows to 1 inch using No. 10(3) needles.

Abbreviations, needle and size note
See pages 6 and 8.

Stripe Sequence This is worked in st st of 2 rows B, 2 rows C and 2 rows D.

Right leg

** Using No. 12(1) needles and B, cast on 58(66:74) sts and work thus:
1st row In B, K 28(32:36) place a different coloured thread into next st as a marker, k to end.
Work straight in st st in stripe sequence until 10(12:16) rows from beg have been worked, then change to No. 10(3) needles and work for 8(10:12) more rows. Now inc 1 st at each end of next row and every 4th row until there are 84(90:96) sts. Work straight for 6(6:6) rows then dec 1 st at each end of

next row and every alt row until 66(72:78) sts rem, then every 4th row until 42(46:50) sts rem. Work straight until leg measures 15½(16¼:17) ins from beg, ending with a p row in D. Change to No. 12(1) needles and work 8 rows. Change back to No. 10(3) needles **.

Shape Foot
Next 2 rows K 36(39:42), turn, p 12(14:16). Work 22 more rows on these 12(14:16) sts. Break yarn. Rejoin C to inside of the 24(25:26) sts already knitted, pick up and k 14 sts along side edge of foot, k across 12(14:16) sts of foot, pick up and k 14 sts along other side edge of foot, k across rem 6(7:8) sts.
Next row P across all sts including 24(25:26) sts at other side of foot.
Work straight for 6(6:8) rows.
Next row K 4(5:6), k 2 tog tbl, k 2 tog, k 31(33:35), k 2 tog tbl, k 2 tog, k 27(28:29).
Next row P.
Rep these 2 rows 2(2:3) times more, but allowing for dec sts by placing the decreasings above the previous ones. Cast off rem sts.

Left leg

Work as for Right Leg from ** to **.

Shape Foot
Next 2 rows K 18(21:24) turn, p 12(14:16). Work 22 more rows on these 12(14:16) sts. Break yarn. Rejoin C to inside of 6(7:8) sts already knitted, then pick up and k 14 sts along side edge of foot, k across 12(14:16) sts of foot, pick up and k 14 sts along other side of foot, k across rem 24(25:26) sts.
Next row P across all sts including 6(7:8) sts at other side of foot.
Work straight for 6(6:8) more rows.
Next row K 27(28:29), k 2 tog tbl, k 2 tog, k 31(33:35) k 2 tog tbl, k 2 tog, k 4(5:6).
Next row P.
Rep these 2 rows 2(2:3) times more allowing for dec sts by placing decreasings above previous ones. Cast off rem sts. Sew together leg and foot seams, then sew together front and back seams.

Stripey crawlers

Back Bodice

Using No. 10(3) needles, A and with right side of work facing, pick up and k 57(65:73) sts across back, beg and ending with marker sts. Work in st st beg with a p row. Cast on 1 st at beg of first 2 rows, for side seams. Work straight for 17(17:21) more rows, thus ending with a p row. Break A. Change to the stripe sequence beg with B and work straight until 3 ins has been worked from picked up sts in A, ending after a p row **.

Shape Armholes

Next row Cast off 5 sts, work to last 5 sts, cast off 5. Break yarns.
Rejoin yarns and dec 1 st at each end of every row until 47(51:55) sts rem. Work straight until 4½(4½:4½) ins have been worked from picked up sts in A.

Shape Neck

Next row Work 16(17:17) sts, cast off next 15(17:21) sts for neck, work to end. Now finish each side separately, dec 1 st at neck edge on next 10 rows. Cont straight until armhole measures 3½(4:4½) ins from beg. Cast off.

Armhole and Neck Border

Using set of No. 12(1) needles, A, and with right side of work facing, pick up and k 38(40:42) sts round right armhole, 6(7:7) sts from shoulder, 67(73:81) sts round neck, 6(7:7) sts from shoulder and 38(40:42) sts round left armhole. Work in k 1, p 1 rib thus:
1st row Rib 38(40:42), inc 2 by working 3 times into next st, rib 4(5:5), inc 2 in next st, rib 67(73:81), inc 2 in next st, rib 4(5:5), inc 2 in next st, rib to end.
2nd and 3rd rows In rib.
4th row Rib 39(41:43), inc 2, rib 6(7:7) inc 2, rib 69(75:83), inc 2, rib 6 (7:7) inc 2, rib to end.
Cast off in rib.

Front Bodice

Work as for Back Bodice to **.

Shape Armholes and Neck

Next row Cast off 5, work 17(20:22) (including st on needle), cast off next 15(17:21) sts for neck, work to last 5 sts, cast off 5. Break yarns. Rejoin yarn and finish each side separately. Dec 1 st at neck edge on next 10 rows, *but at the same time*, dec 1 st at armhole edge on next 1(3:5) rows. Cont until armhole measures same as Back. Cast off.

Armhole and Neck Border

Using set of No. 12(1) needles, A and with right side of work facing, pick up and k 38 (40:42) sts round left armhole, 6(7:7) sts from shoulder, 83(89:97) sts round neck, 6(7:7) sts from shoulder, 38(40:42) sts round right armhole. Work in k 1, p 1 rib thus:
1st row Rib 38(40:42) inc. 2 as on Back, rib 4(5:5) inc 2, rib 83(89:97) inc 2, rib 4 (5:5) inc 2, rib to end.
2nd row Rib 38(40:42), cast off 2 for buttonhole, rib 6(7:7) cast off 2, rib 83(89:97) cast off 2, rib 6(7:7) cast off 2, rib to end.
3rd row In rib, casting on 2 sts over cast off sts of previous row.
4th row Rib 39(41:43), inc 2, rib 6(7:7) inc 2, rib 85(91:99) inc 2, rib 6(7:7) inc 2, rib to end.
Cast off in rib.

To make up

Do not press. Join side seams. Sew on buttons. Draw the outline of the baby's feet on scraps of suede to make soles for the crawlers. For knee pads cut 3½ in long oval shapes from the suede. Sew the soles and knee pads on with a quick overcast stitch.

Quick-knit Jumper

This pattern is an invaluable one to learn. It is knitted in one piece from sleeve to sleeve, instead of the usual method from waist to neck. The garter stitch pattern makes it speedy to knit and the decorative embroidery on the front adds a delicate note. With buttons all the way up the back, the jumper is particularly easy to put on a tiny new baby. An older baby will not be able to undo the jumper and there is also no danger of him being able to suck the buttons.

Materials

Pingouin Superbebe, (Fingering 3-ply) 50 gr balls: 1(2:2)
Pairs of No. 10(3) and 12(1) knitting needles
5 small buttons
¾ yd narrow ribbon
Embroidery wool (yarn)

Measurements To fit a 16(18:20) inch chest.

Tension 7 sts and 13 rows to 1 inch over No. 10(3) needles.

Abbreviations, needle and size note
See pages 6 and 8.

Begin at Centre Back
With No. 10(3) needles cast on 39(45:51) sts for Left Back and work in g st for 22 rows.
Next row (neck edge) K 7, k twice into next st, k to end.
Next row K.
Rep last 2 rows until there are 51(59:67) sts, ending at neck edge. K 12(16:20) rows straight for shoulder.
** Cast on 23(25:27) sts for sleeve, k these 23(25:27) sts, then k across 23(25:27) more sts, sl and leave last 28(34:40) sts on a spare needle.
Work on the 46(50:54) sleeve sts for 50(54:58) rows, k 2 tog at each end of last row. 44(48:52) sts on needle.
Change to No. 12(1) needles and work in K 2,

P 2 rib for 10 rows. Cast off in rib.
Return to shoulder edge of 23(25:27) cast on sleeve sts, and with right side facing, pick up and k these 23(25:27) sts, then k across 28(34:40) sts on spare needle.
Next row K to last st, pick up end st from first g st ridge on shoulder and k it tbl tog with last st on needle.
Next row K.
Rep last 2 rows (to form shoulder) until 7(9:11) sts have been picked up and worked tog with previous st, and ending at neck edge.
Next row K 7, k 2 tog, k to end.
Next row K.
Rep last 2 rows until 39(45:51) sts rem and ending at neck edge **.
Cont thus:
1st and alt rows K.
2nd row K 29(35:41), p 8, k 2.
4th row K 27(33:39), p 8, k 4.
6th row K 25(31:37), p 8, k 6.
8th row K 23(29:35), p 8, k 8.
10th row As 6th row.
12th row As 4th row.
14th row As 2nd row.
K 2 rows.
Next row K 7, k twice into next st, k to end.
Next row K.
Rep last 2 rows until there are 51(59:67) sts ending at neck edge.
K 14(18:22) rows straight, then rep from ** to **.
K 18 rows straight.
Next row K 6, * yrn, k 2 tog (for buttonhole) k 7 (9:11). Rep from * twice more, yrn, k 2 tog, k to end.
K 3 rows. Cast off.

Neckband
Using No. 10(3) needles and with right side of work facing, pick up and k 82(90:98) sts round neck.
Next row * P 2, k 2. Rep from * to last 2 sts, p 2.
Next row * K 2, yrn, p 2 tog. Rep from * to last 2 sts, k 2.
Work 3 more rows in rib. Cast off in rib.

Welt

Using No. 10(3) needles and with right side of work facing, pick up and k 118(134:150) sts round lower edge.

Next row * P 2, k 2. Rep from * to last 2 sts, p 2.

Next row * K 2, p 2. Rep from * to last 2 sts, k 2.

Rep these 2 rows twice more, then 1st row again.

Next row K 2, p 2 tog, yrn (for buttonhole) rib to end.

Work 3 more rows in rib then cast off in rib.

To make up

Do not press. Join sleeve seams. Sew on buttons. Using embroidery wool work small flower motifs in Lazy Daisy stitch with French knots for centres, on the stocking stitch part at front of neck. Thread ribbon through holes at neck, draw up to required size and tie in a bow.

Quick-knit jumper

Crochet Sleeping Bag

This is the sort of practical idea that is not always easy to buy. The sleeping bag is made in an airy cellular stitch, and in a cotton yarn which absorbs moisture, so that it will be cool in the summer and warm in the winter. The bag has a flap at the foot for easy nappy changing. When the baby is bigger, the flap can be removed and the garment used as a dressing gown. It is an ideal choice for a baby who throws off his bedclothes, as it will keep him warm at night.

Materials

Twilley's Aquarius: 6(7) 50 gr balls

No. 3·50 mm (E/4) crochet hook
16 in zip fastener
¾ yd Velcro or 6 strong press studs (snaps)

Measurements From birth to 1 yr (1 yr–18 months)
Length: 25(27) ins
Sleeve seam: 5½(6¾) ins

Tension 3 complete 'V's measure about 2 ins

Abbreviations, hook and size note
See pages 6 and 8.

Back

Using No. 3·50 mm (E/4) crochet hook work 83(91) ch.
1st row 1 dc (sc) into 3rd ch from hook, miss 3 ch, 1 tr (dc) into next ch, * miss 1 ch, 1 tr (dc) into next ch, miss 1 ch, then into next ch work 1 tr (dc), 3 ch, 1 dc (sc) into 3rd ch from hook to form picot, 1 tr (dc) (1 'V' formed.) Rep from * to end. 20(22) complete Vs.
2nd row 4 ch, * miss 1 V, then into next single tr (dc) work 1 V, 1 ch. Rep from * working 1 tr (dc) into top of last st.
3rd row 6 ch, 1 dc (sc) into 3rd ch from hook, 1 tr (dc) into first sp, * 1 ch, 1 V into ch sp. Rep from * to end.

4th row 4 ch, into next sp work 1 V, * 1 ch, 1 V into next sp. Rep from *, ending 1 ch, 1 tr (dc) into top of last st.
Rows 3 and 4 form patt. Rep them until back measures 21(22½) ins ending with a 2nd patt row (row 4).
Next row 5 ch, 1 sl st into top of picot, * 2 ch, 1 sl st into top of next picot. Rep from * ending 2 ch, 1 tr (dc) into end st. Fasten off.

Flap

With right side of lower edge of Back facing, rejoin yarn at base of 2nd V from right hand end.
Next row 6 ch, 1 dc (sc) into 3rd ch from hook, 1 tr (dc) into base of same V, * 1 tr (dc) into next tr (dc) (into next V work 1 V).
Rep from * until 2nd last V from main part has been reached, turn.
2nd row As 2nd row of Back.
Now work in patt rep 3rd and 4th rows 3 times.
Next row 4 ch, 1 sl st into top of picot, * 1 ch, 1 tr (dc), between Vs, 1 ch, 1 sl st into top of picot. Rep from * ending 1 ch, 1 tr (dc) in last st, turn.
Next row 1 ch, then work 1 dc (sc) into each ch sp, and 1 dc (sc) on each tr (dc) and each sl st, ending 1 dc (sc) on turning chain.
Work 3 rows of dc (sc), on dc (sc), but working into backs of loops and inc 1 st at each end of each row. Fasten off.

Side edging for flap
With right side of work facing, work 15 dc (sc) along one side of flap. Work 3 rows of dc (sc) into backs of loops inc 1 st on each row at lower end of flap to mitre corner. Work other side of flap in same way. Join shaped corners to top edge of flap.

Front

Using No. 3·50 mm (E/4) hook work 77(85) ch.
1st row 1 dc (sc) into 2nd ch from hook, * 1 dc (sc) into next ch. Rep from * to end, turn.

2nd row 1 ch, 1 dc (sc) into each dc (sc) working into back of loop only. Rep 2nd row twice more.

Next row 6 ch, 1 dc (sc) into 3 ch from hook, 1 tr (dc) in next dc (sc), then rep from * of 1st row of Back. 20(22) Vs.

Cont in patt from 2nd row as given for Back until work measures 3¾(5½) ins, ending with a 4th row.

Divide for Opening

1st row Work as for 3rd row working only 10(11) Vs including first V, turn.

Cont in patt on these sts only until front measures 18(19½) ins from lower edge ending with a 4th row.

Next row As given for last row of Back. With right side of work facing, rejoin yarn to sp on left of centre picot. Complete as for first side.

Sleeves and yoke

Beg at left cuff. Using No. 3·50 mm (E/4) hook work 7(8) ch.

1st row Into 2nd ch from hook 1 dc (sc) * 1 dc (sc) into next ch. Rep from * to end, turn.

2nd row 1 ch, into back loop only work 1 dc (sc) into each dc (sc) to end, turn.

Rep 2nd row 24(30) times more.

Next row Turn and work along one long side of ridged cuff, 1 ch, work 42(50) dc (sc) evenly along cuff. Cont thus:

1st row As given for 1st row of patt for front, turn. 11(13) Vs.

2nd row As given for 2nd row of Back.

Cont in patt until sleeve measures 6½(8) ins including cuff, ending with last patt row as given for flap before dc (sc) edging.

Work yoke

1st row 1 ch then working into back loop

only make 44(48) dc (sc) along row.

Work dc (sc) on dc (sc) for 12(14) rows.

Shape Back

1st row 1 ch, into back loop only work 20(22) dc (sc), turn and complete Left Back on these sts.

Cont working in ridged dc (sc), dec 1 st at neck edge on next 2 rows. Work 7(9) rows more. Fasten off.

Left Front Yoke

Miss 6 dc (sc) at neck edge and rejoin yarn to next dc (sc).

1st row 1 ch, working into back loop only work 17(19) dc (sc), turn. Cont in ridged dc (sc), dec 1 st at neck edge on next 4 rows. Work 3(5) rows more. Fasten off.

Work other sleeve in same way, reversing Front and Back yokes only

To make up

Join edges of Back yokes together. Join sleeve seams to within 1(1¼) ins of top edge of patterned section. Join back skirt to back yoke between sleeve seams. Join fronts to front yokes between sleeves. Seam sides of back and front skirts. Fold up flap to right side and stitch on wrong side at sides to within 1 in of top flap edge. Sew Velcro to right side of front lower edge and under side of flap top edge.

Neck Edge and Opening

Work 1 row dc (sc) around front opening.

Neck Edging

Work 1 row dc (sc) around neck.

2nd row * 3 ch, 1 dc (sc) into 3rd ch from hook, miss 1 dc (sc), 1 dc (sc) into each of next 3 dc (sc). Rep from * ending dc (sc) in last dc (sc). Fasten off. Sew zip into front opening.

Crochet Pram Cover

The crochet motifs on this bright pram cover have an unusual raised effect. This is an ideal pattern for a beginner as it is simple and quick to make. It will look smart on a pram or cot and could be backed with a light wool or Courtelle fabric for extra warmth.

Materials

Madame Pinguoin:
1 50 gr ball in orange (A), 2 in yellow (B), 2 in gold (C)

No. 3·50 mm (E/4) crochet hook

Measurements 25 ins by 15½ ins

Tension Each motif measures about 4 ins

Abbreviations and hook note See pages 6 and 8.

Using A make 6 ch and join into a ring with a sl st.
1st round 2 ch, 2 tr (dc) into ring, 1 ch, * 3 tr (dc) into ring, 1 ch. Rep from * 4 times more. Join with a sl st.
2nd round Turn work, (1 dc (sc) in 1 ch sp, 6 ch) 6 times, join with a sl st.
3rd round Do not turn. Join on C. [1 h tr (hdc), 2 tr (dc), 3 d tr (tr), 2 tr (dc), 1 h tr (hdc)] in each 6 ch loop, join with a sl st.
4th round Turn work. Join on B to 1st d tr (tr), * 3 h tr (hdc) on d trs (trs) 2 tr (dc) on 2 tr (dc), 2 d tr (tr) on last h tr (hdc) of group and 1st h tr (hdc) of next gr, 2 tr (dc) on 2 tr (dc). Rep from * all round, join with a sl st. Fasten off. One motif completed.

To make up

Do not press. Using B join motifs tog. alternating, 4 in one row, 3 in the next row, ending with 4 motifs in last row.

Edging

Working along a side long edge, join in B at a corner in the middle h tr (hdc) of motif. * Work 9 dc (sc) into next 9 sts, 2 ch, miss 2 sts, 1 tr (dc) in next tr (dc), 2 ch, miss 2 sts, 1 d tr (tr) in next tr (dc), 2 ch, miss 2 sts, 1 d tr (tr) in next h tr (hdc), 1 ch, 1 tr tr (d tr) on to join of 2 motifs, 1 ch, miss 2 sts, 1 d tr (tr) in next h tr (hdc), 2 ch, miss 2 sts, 1 d tr (tr) in next tr (dc), 2 ch, miss 2 sts, 1 d tr (tr) in next tr (dc), 2 ch, miss 2 sts, 1 d tr (tr) in next h tr (hdc), 1 ch, miss 2 sts, 1 tr tr (d tr) on to join, 1 ch, miss 2 sts, 1 d tr (tr) in next h tr (hdc), 2 ch, miss 2 sts, 1 d tr (tr) in next tr (dc), 2 ch, miss 2 sts, 1 tr (dc) in next tr (dc), 2 ch, miss 2 sts, 1 dc (sc). Rep from * twice more, work 25 dc (sc), [2 ch, miss 3 sts, 1 tr tr (d tr) onto join, 2 ch, miss 3 sts, 15 dc (sc)] three times, 1 dc (sc). Cont thus for other 2 sides of cover then join with a sl st.
Next round 1 dc (sc), * 4 ch, 1 dc (sc) in base of ch, miss 1 dc (sc), 3 dc (sc) in next 3 sts. Rep from * all round, join with a sl st. Fasten off. Press work very lightly.

Crochet Matinee Set

The loop stitch cape is simple to crochet and will keep a small baby warm on cold days. The smart jumper is long so will not come adrift at the waist. It also has an envelope neck that makes it simple to put on. Contrast colours and nautical motifs are the clever extras that make this little matinée set look so smart.

Materials

Robin Casino Crepe 4-ply (Nylon Sport Yarn), 25 gr balls:

Jumper: 4(5:6) balls white, 1 ball blue
Pants: 5(6:6) balls white, 1 ball blue
Mittens: 1 ball white

Robin Vogue Double Double:
(Knitted Worsted or Bulky) 50 gr balls:
Cape: 8(9) balls blue, 1 ball white
8 buttons for cape
Elastic for pants
Crochet hooks in sizes 2·50 mm (B/1),
3·00 mm (D/3), 5·00 mm (H/8) and 6·00 mm (I/9).

Measurements
Jumper To fit a 16(18:20) inch chest.

Pants Length at side, 18(19:20) ins.

Cape To fit birth–3 months (4–9 months).

Mittens Width across palm, 2 ins.

Tension About 13 dc (sc) to 2 ins using No. 3·00 mm (D/3) hook and 4 ply wool. 3 sts measure 1 inch, using No. 6·00 mm (I/9) hook and double double.

Abbreviations, hook and size note
See pages 6 and 8.
Extra abbreviation: W, white; B, blue.

Jumper

The Back and Front Alike
Using No. 3·00 mm (D/3) hook and B 4 ply make 54(58:62) ch.

Next row 1 dc (sc) in 2nd ch from hook, 1 dc (sc) into each ch to end, 1 ch turn. 53(57:61) dc (sc).
Work 3 more rows dc (sc) turning each row with 1 ch. Break B, join in W and work in patt thus:
Foundation row (right side), 3 ch, 1 tr (dc) in first dc (sc) * miss 1 dc (sc), 1 dc (sc) in next dc (sc), miss 1 dc (sc), [1 tr (dc) 2 ch 1 tr (dc)]—known as tr (dc) gr—in next dc (sc). Rep from * to last 4 dc (sc), miss 1 dc (sc), 1 dc (sc) in next dc (sc), miss 1 dc (sc), 1 tr (dc) in last dc (sc), turn. 12(13:14) tr (dc) grs.
1st patt row 1 ch, 1 dc (sc) in tr (dc) * 1 tr (dc) gr in dc (sc), 1 dc (sc) in 2 ch sp of previous row. Rep from * ending 1 tr (dc) gr in last dc (sc), 1 dc (sc) in tr (dc), turn.
2nd patt row 3 ch, 1 tr (dc) in dc (sc) * 1 dc (sc) in 2 ch sp, 1 tr (dc) gr in dc (sc). Rep from * ending with 1 dc (sc) in last 2 ch sp, 1 tr (dc) in last dc (sc), turn.
Rep 1st and 2nd rows until work measures 9½(10¾:12) ins from beg ending on a wrong side row.

Shape Armholes
Next row Sl st over 2 complete patts, patt to last 2 patts, turn.
Work 3 rows in patt, then work 1 row dc (sc), working 37(41:45) dc (sc) evenly across row. Break W. Join in B and work straight on these dc (sc) until armhole measures 2¼(2½:3) ins.
Work across 11(12:13) dc (sc), turn.
Work 2 rows.
Next row Sl st across 3 sts, work to end. Now dec 1 st at neck edge on every row until 2 sts rem. Fasten off. Miss centre 15(17:19) dc (sc), join yarn in next dc (sc) and work to match first side. Work 3 rows dc (sc) round each neck piece and along 2 dc (sc) at top. Fasten off.

Sleeves

Using No. 3·00 mm (D/3) hook and B, make 25(31:39) ch and work 4 rows dc (sc).

24(30:38) dc (sc). Break B, join in W and inc 1 st at each end of the next and every 4th row until there are 32(40:48) dc (sc). Work straight until sleeve measures 7(7½:8) ins. Fasten off.

To make up

Press work on wrong side with a warm iron over a damp cloth. Join side and sleeve seams leaving about 1 inch open at top of sleeve to set into armhole. Overlap shoulders as illustrated. Sew in sleeves, joining sleeve extension to sts left at armhole. Press.

Motif

(4 B and 1 W required for set)
Using No. 2·50 mm (B/1) hook make 6 ch and join into a ring, with a sl st.
1st round 6 ch, [1 tr (dc) 3 ch] in ring, 5 times, sl st into 3rd of 6 ch.
2nd round [1 dc (sc), 1 htr (hdc), 3 tr (dc), 1 htr (hdc), 1 dc (sc)] in each 3 ch sp all round, join with a sl st. Fasten off.
Sew W motif to front of jumper.

Mitts (both alike)

Using No. 3·00 mm (D/3) hook and W, make 15 ch. Work 1 dc (sc) into 2nd ch from hook, then 1 dc (sc) into each ch to end. Working into *back* of each loop and turning with 1 ch work 28 rows dc (sc). Fasten off. Join short ends together. Join yarn to edge, 2 ch, work 32 dc (sc), join with a sl st, 2 ch. Work 4 rounds in dc (sc).
Next round 2 ch, work across 12 dc (sc), miss 8 dc (sc) (for thumb) and work across 12 dc (sc), sl st to join. Work on these 24 dc (sc) for 7 more rounds.

Shape Top

Next round 2 ch, * dec 1, work across 8 dc (sc), dec 1. Rep from *, sl st to join.
Next round 2 ch, * dec 1, work across 6 dc (sc), dec 1. Rep from *, join with sl st.
Cont working 2 sts less between dec until there are 2 dc (sc) between each dec, break yarn, join ends together.

The Thumb

Join yarn and work 7 rounds dc (sc).

Break yarn and draw sts tog and fasten off. Press as jumper. Sew on B motifs as illustrated.

Pants

2 pieces alike as work is reversible.
Begin at top of one leg. Using No. 3·00 mm (D/3) hook and B, make 54(58:62) ch.
Next row 1 dc (sc) into 2nd ch. from hook, 1 dc (sc) into each ch to end. 53(57:61) dc (sc).
Work 3 rows in dc (sc), turning each row of dc (sc) with 1 ch. Change to W and work 3 rows dc (sc).
Next 2 rows Work across 40 dc (sc), turn, sl st into next dc (sc), work to end.
Next 2 rows Work across 32 dc (sc), turn, sl st into next dc (sc), work to end.
Next 2 rows Work across next 24 dc (sc) turn, sl st into next 1 dc (sc), work to end.
Next row Work in dc (sc) working 1 dc (sc) into each sl st. 53(57:61) dc (sc).
Work straight until short edge measures 2½(3:3½) ins. Now inc 1 st at each end of next and every 4th row until there are 61(65:69) sts, then inc 1 st at each end of the next 2(4:6) rows. 65(73:81) sts. Work 3(3:5) rows straight.

Shape Inside Leg

Dec 1 st at *beg* of every row until 40 (48:54) sts rem. Now dec 1 st at each end of every row until 30(38:46) st rem. Work straight for 4(4½:5) ins or as required. Change to No. 2·50 mm (B/1) hook and work 3 rows dc (sc). Change back to No. 3·00 mm (D/3) hook.

Shape Foot

Work across 20(26:31) dc (sc), turn.
Work across 10(14:16) dc (sc) for instep and work on these dc (sc) for 2(2:2½) ins. Now dec 1 st each end of next row. Fasten off. Rejoin at lower right side of instep, work 10(10:12) dc (sc) up side of instep, then work across the instep sts, then work 10(10:12) dc (sc) down the other side, dc (sc) to end.
Work 3(3:4) rows straight, then work another 3 rows but dec 1 st each end of work and 2 sts in centre of instep sts on every row. Fasten off.

To make up

Press as jumper. Join leg, crutch and foot seams. Press. Sew on motifs. Join elastic into ring and sew inside waist using a herring-bone casing stitch.

Cape

With No. 6·00 mm (I/9) hook and B work 73(79) ch.
Foundation row (right side) 1 dc (sc) into 2nd ch from hook, 1 dc (sc) into each ch to end, turn. 72(78) dc (sc). Continue thus:
1st row 2 ch (counts as 1st st), miss 1st dc (sc), ML (see abbreviations) in each dc (sc) to ch at end, 1 dc (sc) in ch, turn.
2nd row 2 ch, miss 1st dc (sc), 1 dc (sc) into each st to end, working last dc (sc) in ch at end, turn.
These two rows form the patt. Work 11 more rows thus, ending on a loop row.
Dec row 2 ch, miss first st, 1 dc (sc) into each of next 15(16) sts, (dec 1) twice (see abbreviations), 1 dc (sc) in each of next 32(36) sts, (dec 1) twice, 1 dc (sc) in each st to end, working last dc (sc) in ch at end, turn. 68(74) dc (sc). Work 7(9) rows straight.
Dec row 2 ch, miss first st, 1 dc (sc) into each of next 14(15) sts, (dec 1) twice, 1 dc in each of next 30(34) sts, (dec 1) twice, 1 dc (sc) in each st to end, working last dc (sc) in ch at end, turn. 64(70) dc (sc). Work 7(9) rows straight.
Dec row 2 ch, miss first st, 1 dc (sc) into each of next 13(14) sts, (dec 1) twice, 1 dc (sc) in each of next 28(32) sts, (dec 1) twice, 1 dc (sc) in each st to end, working last dc (sc) in ch at end, turn. 60(66) dc (sc). Work 7(9) rows straight.
Dec row 2 ch, miss first st, *2nd size only*, 1 dc (sc) in next st. *Both sizes* (Dec 1, 1 dc (sc) in each of next 2 sts) 3 times, (dec 1) twice, 1 dc (sc) into each of next 2 sts, (dec 1, 1 dc (sc) into each of next 2 sts) 6(7) times, (dec 1) twice, (1 dc (sc) into each of next 2 sts, dec 1) 3 times, *2nd size only*, 1 dc (sc) in next st. *Both sizes*, 1 dc (sc) in ch at end, turn. 44(49) dc (sc).
Work 1 row straight.

Dec row 2 ch, miss first st (dec 1, 1 dc (sc) in next st) 2(3) times, (dec 1) 3(2) times, 1 dc (sc) in each of next 2 sts, (dec 1, 1 dc (sc) in next st) 4(5) times, dec 1, 1 dc (sc) in each of next 2 sts, (dec 1) 3(2) times, (1 dc (sc) in next st, (dec 1) 2(3) times, (1 dc (sc) in chain at end, turn. 29(33) dc (sc).
Work 1 row straight. Break yarn and fasten off.

Hood

Using No. 6·00 mm (I/9) hook and B, make 43(49) ch and work foundation as given. 42(48) dc (sc). Cont in patt and work for about 4¾(5¾) ins from beg ending on a loop row. Break yarn and fasten off. Fold in half and join cast on ch edges together for back seam.

To make up

Press work lightly on wrong side using a warm iron over a damp cloth. Join short edges of hood to neck edge of cape, placing back seam of hood to centre back neck of cape and front edges of hood to centre front edges of cape. Press seam.

Edging

Using the 5·00 mm hook and W and with right side of work facing, begin at right lower edge and work 1 round dc (sc) around entire outer edge working 1 dc (sc) in each row and 1 dc (sc) to each st and 3 dc (sc) in each corner, join with a sl st. Place markers down right front for 8 buttonholes, 1 just below neck edge, 1 approx. 2½ (3½) ins from lower edge and the others spaced evenly between.
Next round (buttonhole round) 2 ch, dc (sc) to first marker, 2 ch, miss 1 dc (sc), * dc (sc) to next marker, 2 ch, miss 1 dc (sc). Rep from * 6 times more then cont. in dc (sc) working 3 dc (sc) in each corner dc (sc), join with sl st.
Work one more round in dc (sc) working 1 dc (sc) into each 2 ch sp and 3 dc (sc) in each corner dc (sc), join with a sl st.
Break yarn and fasten off. Press as before. Sew on buttons.

Dress and Pinafore

Baby dresses are fun to make, because they are so small and do not take long to sew. This one shows how decorative machine embroidery stitches can make a simple little pattern into something special. The set is made in a delicate lawn, the pale blue dress giving an attractive shadowed effect under the fresh white pinafore.

Materials

Dress 1½ yds fine cotton or lawn
Pinafore ¾ yd of same fabric in contrasting colour
¼ yd fine interfacing
Tracing paper
Bias binding
Thread and machine embroidery twist

Dress

1. After cutting out, overcast all seams, preferably using three-step zigzag on sewing machine. Gather along lines indicated on back and front of dress skirt.
2. Stitch centre back seam from dot to hem. Gather top of sleeve along lines indicated, using zigzag stitch over fine cord to give a controlled gather (see Good stitches to know, page 9).

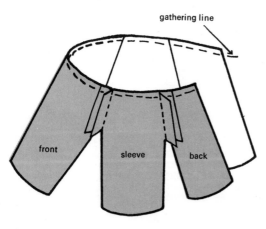

gathering line

front   sleeve   back

1

3. Stitch sleeves to front and back of dress, right sides together. Press seams towards bodice (diagram 1).
4. Baste or iron on fine interfacing to wrong side of yoke front and yoke backs. Stitch front yoke to back yokes at shoulder seams, then trim interfacing close to stitching. Pin yoke to dress, right sides together, adjusting gathers evenly along back, sleeve top and front (diagram 2). Insert zip in centre back seam. Press.

2

5. Stitch front lining to back lining at shoulder seams. Turn under small hem on back all round cut edges of lining. Then, placing right sides together, pin lining to neckline edge and stitch. Clip curve. Turn lining to inside and press. Slipstitch yoke lining into place, making sure it does not interfere with free running of zip.
6. Turn up hem as required. Baste tracing paper to underside of hem and use a machine embroidery stitch to decorate hem. The paper stops the fabric ruckling while it is being embroidered. Use a cam or disc for even stitches—shell stitch was used on the dress illustrated.
7. Stitch underarm seams of dress and sleeves. Turn narrow hem on bottom of sleeve, using either fine zigzag or overlock stitch on the

sewing machine. Stitch all round, cutting away surplus fabric afterwards. Run two rows of shirring elastic round cuff one inch from sleeve edge to form a shell (diagram 3).

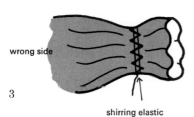

wrong side

3

shirring elastic

binding to form ties at either end. Join side seams. Stitch more bias binding down back edges and round hem.

8. Fold in lower edge of yoke lining and slipstitch neatly on inside. (diagram 4).

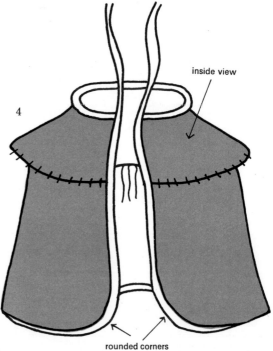

inside view

4

rounded corners

Pinafore

1. After cutting out, overcast all cut edges and continue as for step 1 of baby dress.
2. Attach interfacings as for yoke of dress. Stitch front yoke to back yoke at shoulder seams.
3. Neaten round armhole and along lower edge of yoke with bought bias binding.
4. Embroider decorative machine stitches to binding round edge of yoke, using the same stitch as on dress.
5. Pin skirt to yoke, adjusting gathers under binding evenly. Sink stitch gathers into place on line of join where binding meets yoke.
6. Join yoke linings at shoulder seams. Press and baste into position, wrong sides together.
7. Use the bias binding to attach yoke to yoke facing around neckline, leaving excess

9. Use the machine embroidery stitch to decorate binding at neck, back and hem. Work the decorative daisy motifs on yoke and hem with an automatic Elna machine daisy disc, which is quick to sew. The shapes are sewn on at random.

5 *squares represent 4 inches*

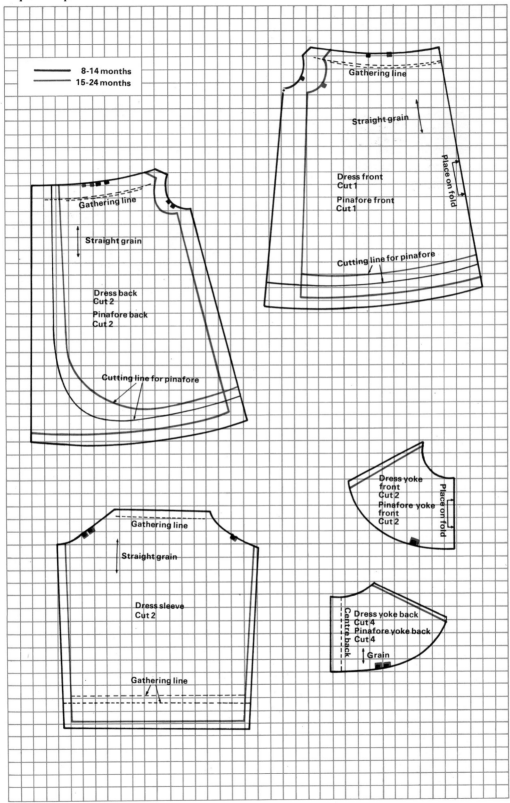

8-14 months
15-24 months

Gathering line

Straight grain

place on fold

Dress front
Cut 1

Pinafore front
Cut 1

Cutting line for pinafore

Gathering line

Straight grain

Dress back
Cut 2

Pinafore back
Cut 2

Cutting line for pinafore

Dress yoke front
Cut 2
Pinafore yoke front
Cut 2

Place on fold

Gathering line

Straight grain

Dress sleeve
Cut 2

Dress yoke back
Cut 4
Pinafore yoke back
Cut 4

Centre back

Grain

Gathering line

Dress and pinafore

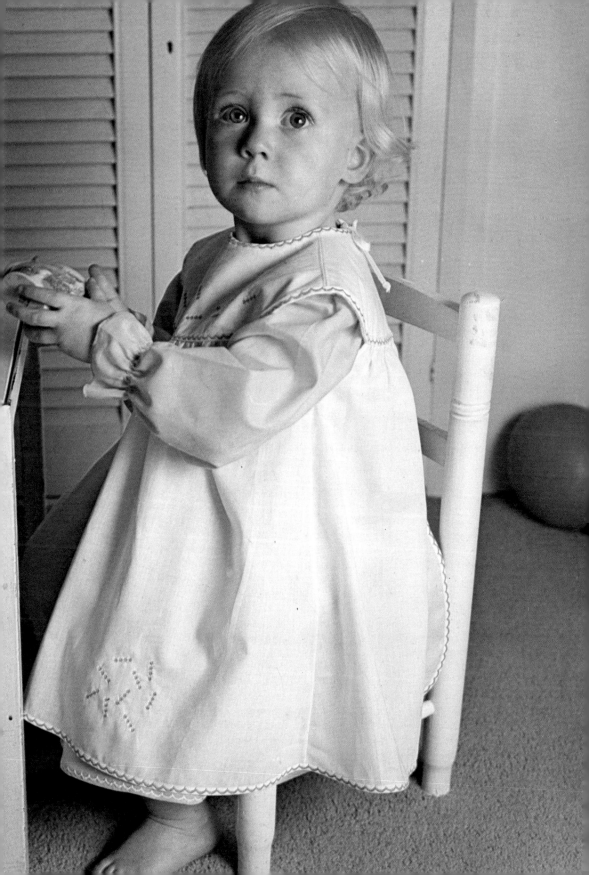

Lacy Wool Shawl

This beautiful shawl would make a perfect family heirloom. The centre pattern with its dainty flower motif is gossamer-fine, and the fringe helps to make it look graceful. Rather than use a pure wool yarn that may lose its freshness after frequent washing, the shawl has been made in a nylon yarn that is soft, yet wears well.

Materials

Patons Baby 2-ply, 100% Bri-Nylon (Fingering 3-ply) 20 gr balls: 13.
No. 2·50 mm (B/1) crochet hook.

Measurements Approx 36 ins by 36 ins square—excluding border and fringe.

Tension 4 patterns measure about 6½ ins.

Abbreviations and hook note See pages 6 and 8.

Using No. 2·50 mm (B/1) hook, make 288 ch loosely, turn.
Foundation row 1 dc (sc) in 2nd ch from hook, * 1 dc (sc) in next ch, 4 ch, miss 3 ch, 1 tr (dc) in each of next 4 ch, 4 ch, miss 3 ch, 1 dc (sc) in each of next 2 ch. Rep from * to end.
1st row 1 ch, 1 dc (sc) in 1st dc (sc), * 4 ch, 2 tr (dc) in next 4 ch sp, 1 tr (dc) in next tr (dc), 8 ch, miss 2 tr (dc), 1 tr (dc) in next tr (dc), 2 tr (dc) in next 4 ch sp, 4 ch, miss 1 dc (sc), 1 dc (sc) in next dc (sc). Rep from * to end.
2nd row 6 ch, * 2 tr (dc) in next 4 ch sp, 1 tr (dc) in next tr (dc), 4 ch, 1 dc (sc) in next 8 ch sp, 4 ch, miss 2 tr (dc), 1 tr (dc) in next tr (dc), 2 tr (dc) in next 4 ch sp, 2 ch. Rep from * ending last rep 2 tr (dc) in last 4 ch sp, 1 ch, 1 d tr (tr) in last dc (sc).
3rd row 3 ch, 1 tr (dc) in 1 ch sp, * 1 tr (dc) in next tr (dc), 4 ch, 1 dc (sc) in next 4 ch sp, 1 dc (sc) in next dc (sc), 1 dc (sc) in next 4 ch sp, 4 ch, miss 2 tr (dc), 1 tr (dc) in next tr (dc),

2 tr (dc) in next 2 ch sp. Rep from * ending last rep 1 tr (dc) in last tr (dc), 1 tr (dc) in last ch sp, 1 tr (dc) in 5th of 6 ch.
4th row 9 ch, miss next tr (dc), * 1 tr (dc) in next tr (dc), 2 tr (dc) in next 4 ch sp, 4 ch, miss 1 dc (sc), 1 dc (sc) in next dc (sc), 4 ch, 2 tr (dc) in next 4 ch sp, 1 tr (dc) in next tr (dc), 8 ch, miss 2 tr (dc). Rep from * but at end of last rep omit 8 ch and work 4 ch instead then miss 2 tr (dc), 1 d tr (tr) into top of 3 ch.
5th row 1 ch, 1 dc (sc) in first d tr (tr), * 4 ch, miss 2 tr (dc), 1 tr (dc) in next tr (dc), 2 tr (dc) in next 4 ch sp, 2 ch, 2 tr (dc) in next 4 ch sp, 1 tr (dc) in next tr (dc), 4 ch, 1 dc (sc) in next 8 ch sp. Rep from * ending last rep 1 dc (sc) in 4th of 9 ch instead of into 8 ch.
6th row 1 ch, 1 dc (sc) in 1st dc (sc), * 1 dc (sc) in next 4 ch sp, 4 ch, miss 2 tr (dc), 1 tr (dc) in next tr (dc), 2 tr (dc) in next 2 ch sp, 1 tr (dc) in next tr (dc), 4 ch, 1 dc (sc) in next 4 ch sp, 1 dc (sc) in next dc (sc). Rep from * to end.
The last 6 rows form patt. Cont straight until work measures about 36 ins ending after a 3rd patt row, turn. Now work in rounds thus:
Next round 1 ch, 2 dc (sc) in 1st tr (dc) [place a marker in first of these 2 dc (sc)] * 1 dc (sc) in each of next 2 tr (dc), 3 dc (sc) in next 4 ch sp, 1 dc (sc) in each of next 3 dc (sc), 3 dc (sc) in next 4 ch sp, 1 dc (sc) in each of next 2 tr (dc). Rep from * ending last rep 4 dc (sc) in 4 ch sp, instead of 3, then 1 dc (sc) in each of next 2 tr (dc), 3 dc (sc) in top of 3 ch [place a marker in 2nd of last 3 dc (sc)], now work in dc (sc) down 1st side edge making sure that the number of dc (sc) along this edge, including last marked st, is a multiple of 5, plus an extra 4 sts, now work 3 dc (sc) in first ch of original ch [place a marker in 2nd of last 3 dc (sc)], work 287 dc (sc) evenly along lower edge [thus working 1 dc (sc) into each ch of foundation], and working 3 dc (sc) in the last ch [place a marker in 2nd of last 3 dc (sc)], now work in dc (sc) up 2nd side edge to match corresponding edge, then work 1 dc (sc) in the first st worked into, sl st in first marked st [note that there should be a multiple of 5, plus

4 extra sts in between each set of marked sts].
Work border thus:

1st round 1 ch, [1 dc (sc), 7 ch, 1 dc (sc)] in
first marked dc (sc), [* 7 ch, miss 4 dc (sc),
1 dc (sc) in next dc (sc). Rep from * to next
corner, thus ending with 1 dc (sc) in next
marked dc (sc), 7 ch, 1 dc (sc) in same marked
dc (sc)] 3 times, ** 7 ch, miss 4 dc (sc), 1
dc (sc) in next dc (sc). Rep from ** ending
last rep, 3 ch, 1 d tr (tr) in first dc (sc).

2nd round 1 ch, 1 dc (sc) in top of d tr (tr),
* 7 ch, 1 dc (sc) in next 7 ch sp. Rep from
* ending last rep 3 ch, 1 d tr (tr) in first
dc (sc).

3rd round As 2nd round.

4th round As 2nd round, but working
[1 dc (sc), 7 ch, 1 dc (sc)] into each of the
4 corner 7 ch sp.

Rep last 3 rounds once more, then 2nd and
3rd rounds again.

Fasten off.

Block shawl out with pins and press lightly
using a *cool* iron and *dry* cloth. Cut remaining
yarn into 9 inch lengths and taking 5 strands
together each time, knot all round edge in
each 7 ch sp to form a fringe. Trim fringe.

Playtime and Partytime

Smocked Dresses

One of the most effective ways of decorating children's clothes is with colourful smocking. These dresses show two different and unusual ways of using it. The waist smocking goes all the way round and gives a flattering line to the garment. The elasticity of the smocking makes the dress extremely practical since the waistline will expand as the child grows. Add a generous hem and the dress can be used for a two- or even three-year period. The smaller dress shows how a block of smocking can be cut to shape over the shoulders, neck and round the armholes. It is worth trying this method, particularly on a small dress, as the smocking makes the dress fit so beautifully. Again the elasticity of the stitching means the dress can be worn over a longer growing period. Smocking is fairly slow, yet very simple to do. There are no short cuts for a perfect finish. It is an old craft but well worth learning. Page 10 shows how to sew a variety of smocking stitches used in the dresses illustrated.

Materials

Dress with smocked waist
Length of fabric for smocking should be three times the measurement of area to be smocked. For an 18 in waist, you need a 54 in length of fabric. The side measurement (for smocked waist and the skirt) should be from 2 ins above waist to 5 ins below knee, allowing generous hem for growth. Add on ½ yd for bodice and sleeves.

Lacy wool shawl

Broderie anglaise frill to line frill on sleeve and broderie anglaise edging for collar and sleeves.

Dress with smocked yoke
The same fabric requirements apply for smocked area. Measure chest front. Multiply by three and add on 3 ins at either side to work out the amount of fabric needed.
A 10 inch chest front needs a 30 inch wide block for smocking plus 3 ins at either side for underarm shaping and seams. For length, measure from top of shoulder to knee and add extra for hem and top turnings. Add on ½ yd for dress back, sleeves and lining. (The dress illustrated took 1½ yds fabric.)
Buttons for covering
Broderie Anglaise edging
For the Smocking (both dresses)
Smocking dot transfers
Coats embroidery thread
Fabric note: When selecting fabric similar to that illustrated, check that the lines of spots are straight on fabric before buying. The dots can then be gathered up without aid of transfers. Otherwise use the special transfers for all types of fabric. Buy yellow dots to show up on dark materials and blue ones to show up on pale colours.

The Smocking

The smocking is done before making the dress up. It is basically a way of decorating gathers. Cut out block of fabric for smocking (see under Materials needed for correct measurements). Iron smocking dots on to wrong side of fabric. Join up dots with rows of gathering stitches, to ensure even smocking. Warning: don't be tempted to try smocking "freehand" because fabric tends to gather unevenly. To join dots, use double thread, firmly knotted at one end (diagram 1).

and baste a line of double thread $\frac{1}{2}$ in inside cutting edge, ensuring the pattern runs straight. Make two rows of machine stitching just inside cutting edge of yoke sides and top (diagram 2) (the bottom edge should not be

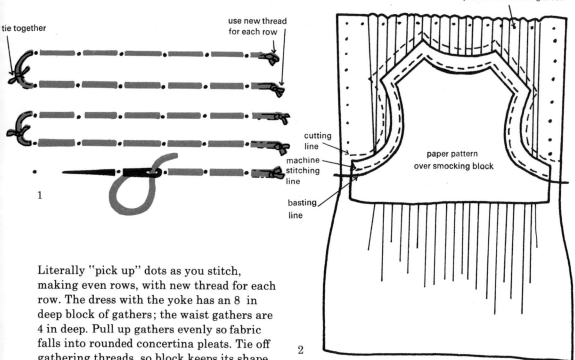

tie together

use new thread for each row

1

position of pins when basting pattern to smocking block

cutting line

machine stitching line

basting line

paper pattern over smocking block

2

Literally "pick up" dots as you stitch, making even rows, with new thread for each row. The dress with the yoke has an 8 in deep block of gathers; the waist gathers are 4 in deep. Pull up gathers evenly so fabric falls into rounded concertina pleats. Tie off gathering threads, so block keeps its shape. Now start the smocking. Page 10 shows a selection of different stitches. Use three strands of embroidery thread at a time (two for a finer fabric like organza and four for a heavier fabric like wool). Keep smocking stitches even, using the same tension all the way. Do not pull stitches up too tightly, otherwise dress will have no elasticity. When smocking is complete, remove original rows of gathers. Neaten off loose threads. The dresses can now be made up.

Dress with smocked yoke

1. Cut out front bodice facing, sleeves and back pieces.
2. Spread out block of smocking over blanket on bed. Stab pins through fabric into mattress to keep smocking stretched out evenly.
3. Place yoke paper pattern over smocking

cut because this incorporates the skirt). Cut away surplus material outside stitching and overstitch raw edges with zigzag or over-casting by hand. Remove paper pattern and basting.
4. Join front yoke facing to newly shaped smocking. Pin round side and top edges and machine.
5. Join bodice back and front, right sides together, at shoulders, plus back facings (diagram 3). Press shoulder seam open so back facing hides join.
6. Gather back skirt and join to back yoke.
7. Join side seams.
8. Gather fullness on sleeve tops. Sew sleeve seam and set in sleeves at armholes. Hem base of sleeves and sew broderie anglaise edging round wrists. Thread elastic through hem. Bind or overcast seam edges round armholes inside.

9. Stitch back yoke and facing, right sides together, down both sides of back opening. Turn and press.

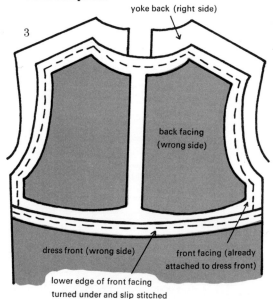

3

yoke back (right side)

back facing (wrong side)

dress front (wrong side)

front facing (already attached to dress front)

lower edge of front facing turned under and slip stitched

10. Cut a half inch wide bias strip, the same length as neck measurement plus one inch. Use this to neaten neckline, sewing it to right side first, then folding it over neck edge and slip stitching at inside.

11. Make buttonholes, cover buttons.

12. Cut 2 lengths 18 in by 3 in for sash. Fold in half lengthways and stitch (diagram 4). Turn right way out. Press flat. Neaten

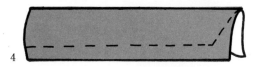

4

ends and stitch to dress over side seam just under arms.

13. Turn up hem and press.

Dress with smocked waistline

1. Cut out bodice, collar and sleeves.

2. Join bodice at shoulders and sides, with right sides facing.

3. Stretch out smocking and join skirt piece to bodice, right sides together, pinning, basting, then stitching. Make sure smocking is evenly distributed.

4. Join underarm sleeve seams. Cut out frills and broderie anglaise inner frills the same lengths. Join sides of frills and gather both together along upper edge. Attach to sleeve ends on wrong side, adjusting gathers to fit. Sew broderie anglaise edging to lower edge of outside frill.

5. Join collar pieces, right sides together. Stitch and turn right way out. Sew lower edge of collar to neckline, right sides facing. Turn in upper edge and sew it inside neckline.

6. Join bodice lining at shoulders (use silk or lightweight lawn for preference). Turn edge under and slipstitch into place inside bodice along neckline, round armholes, waist and back opening.

7. Make buttonholes. Cover buttons with matching fabric (optional) and sew to bodice opening.

8. Turn up hem. Press.

Note: When ironing smocking, press gently with a damp cloth under the iron.

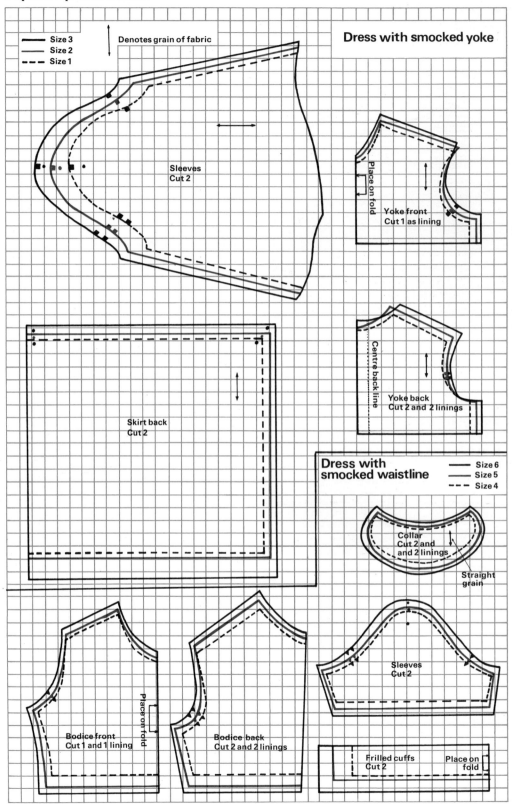

5 squares represent 4 inches

Dress with smocked yoke

Size 3
Size 2
Size 1

Denotes grain of fabric

Sleeves
Cut 2

Place on fold

Yoke front
Cut 1 as lining

Centre back line

Yoke back
Cut 2 and 2 linings

Skirt back
Cut 2

Dress with smocked waistline

Size 6
Size 5
Size 4

Collar
Cut 2 and
and 2 linings

Straight grain

Sleeves
Cut 2

Bodice front
Cut 1 and 1 lining

Place on fold

Bodice back
Cut 2 and 2 linings

Frilled cuffs
Cut 2

Place on fold

Smocked dresses.

Beach Clothes

These bright beach clothes in cotton are cool to wear and straightforward to crochet. The co-ordinated patterns make them ideal for a brother and sister. The neat little sun top is useful for boys or girls.

Materials

Twilley's Stalite (Coats and Clark Knit Cro-Sheen *or* Bali) in 50 gr balls:

Boy's trunks and top: 4 balls of hot orange (A) and 1 ball of almond green (B)
Girl's swimsuit: 2 of hot orange (A), 2 of fiesta pink (C), 1 of almond green (B)
Nos. 4·50 mm (G/6) and 4·00 mm (F/5) crochet hooks

Waist length of elastic for boy's trunks
One buckle for either model

Measurements To fit a 23(24:25) inch chest.

Tension 4 h tr (hdc) to 1 inch using No. 4·50 mm (G/6) hook.

Abbreviations, hook and size note
See pages 6 and 8.

Sun Top
Front

** Using No. 4·50 mm (G/6) hook and A, work 49(51:53) ch.
1st row Into 2nd ch from hook work 1 h tr (hdc), then 1 h tr (hdc) into each ch to end, turn. 48(50:52) h tr (hdc).
2nd row 2 ch, * 1 h tr (hdc) into next h tr (hdc). Rep from * to end working last h tr (hdc) into 2nd of 2 ch.
This last row forms patt. Rep until work measures 8½(9:10) ins from beg.

Shape Armholes
1st row Sl st over next 8(9:9) h tr (hdc),

2 ch, 1 h tr (hdc) into each of next 31(31:33) h tr (hdc), turn **.
Work 1 row on these centre sts.

Work Left Shoulder
1st row 2 ch, 1 h tr (hdc) into each of next 6(7:7) h tr (hdc), turn.
Complete left shoulder on these sts, and work straight until armhole measures 4(4½:4½) ins ending at armhole edge.

Shape Shoulder
1st row Sl st over next 3 h tr (hdc), 1 h tr (hdc) into each h tr (hdc) to end. Fasten off.
With right side of front facing, rejoin yarn to last 7(8:8) h tr (hdc) and work to correspond with other shoulder.

Back

Work as given for Front from ** to **. Work 7 more rows on these sts, then complete as for Front.

To make up

Join left shoulder seam. **Armhole Edging.** Using No. 4·00 mm (F/5) hook and B, work 1 row dc (sc) round armhole. Do not turn, but work 2nd row by working 1 row dc (sc) backwards along first row, omitting to work into corner sts of armholes. (This gives a firm edge.) Work neck edging in same way. Join right shoulder and work armhole to match first armhole. Join side seams.

Work Motifs
Apple Motif

Using No. 4·00 mm (F/5) hook and B, work 3 ch.
1st row 1 ch, then 2 dc (sc) into each of next 2 ch, turn. Working in dc (sc), inc 1 dc (sc) at each end of next 2 rows then on every alt row until there are 15 sts. Work

3 rows straight, then dec 1 st at each end of next 3 rows.

Next row 1 ch, 1 dc (sc) into next 2 dc (sc), sl st over 3 dc (sc) then 1 dc (sc) into each of last 3 dc (sc), turn.

Next row Sl st across all sts to last 2 dc (sc), 1 dc (sc) on each of last 2 dc (sc), turn.

Next row Sl st over 2 dc (sc), 1 ch, 1 dc (sc) into next st, turn.

Work 6 rows on 2 sts for stalk. Fasten off.

Leaf Motif

Using No. 4·00 mm (F/5) hook and B, make 8 ch.

1st row 1 ch, 1 dc (sc) into each of next 6 ch, 1 sl st into last ch, turn.

2nd row Sl st into next dc (sc), 1 dc (sc) into each dc (sc) to end, turn.

3rd row 1 ch, 1 dc (sc) into each of next 3 dc (sc), 1 sl st into next dc (sc), turn.

4th row As 2nd row. Fasten off.

Sew apple to front of top. Sew leaf to top of apple.

Press work lightly with a warm iron over a damp cloth.

Trunks
Right Leg

** Using No. 4·50 mm (G/6) hook and A work 59(61:63) ch.

1st row Into 2nd ch from hook, work 1 dc (sc), then 1 dc (sc) into each ch to end, turn. Turning each row with 1 ch, work 3 rows of dc (sc) on dc (sc) **.

Shape Body

1st row Sl st into 2nd dc (sc), 1 ch, 1 dc (sc) into each of next 53(55:57) dc (sc), turn.

*** Dec 1 st at each end of next row. Now dec 1 st at each end of next and every foll 8th row until 46(48:50) dc (sc) rem. Cont straight until work measures 6½(6¾:7) ins from beg of body shaping. Fasten off ***.

Left Leg

Work from ** to ** as given for Right Leg.

Shape Body

1st row Sl st into each of next 4 dc (sc),

1 ch, 1 dc (sc) into each of next 53(55:57) dc (sc), turn.

Complete as given for Right Leg from *** to ***.

Belt

Using No. 4·00 mm (F/5) hook and B, work 5 ch.

1st row Into 2nd ch from hook work 1 dc (sc) then 1 dc (sc) into rem ch, turn. Work in dc (sc) on dc (sc) until belt measures 26(27:28) ins, or required length. Fasten off.

Belt Tabs (4 required).

Using No. 4·00 mm (F/5) hook and B, work 8 ch.

1st row Into 2nd ch from hook work 1 dc (sc), 1 dc (sc) into each ch to end. Fasten off.

To make up

Join front and back seams. Work 2 rows dc (sc) round legs as given for Top armholes. Join leg seams. Sew 2 belt tabs to back and 2 to front. Sew buckle to belt end. Work a row of casing stitch around inside of waist edge and thread with elastic. Secure ends. Thread belt through tabs. Press very lightly.

Girl's one piece swimsuit
Right and Left Legs

Work as given for Boy's trunks.
Seam front and back seams together.

Top Front

Fold pants in half and mark sides (seams in centre).

Using No. 4·50 mm (G/6) hook and C, and with right side of pants front facing, join yarn to side.

1st row 2 ch, 1 h tr (hdc) in each dc (sc) across front to other side. 46(48:50) h tr (hdc) including first 2 ch, turn.

2nd row 2 ch. 1 h tr (hdc) into each h tr (hdc) to end. Cont in h tr (hdc) until top measures 6(6½:7) ins, inc 1 st at each end of 9th row.

Work as given for Boy's Top from armholes to completion.

Top Back

Using No. 4·50 mm (G/6) hook and C, and with right side of pants back facing, join yarn to side. Work as given for top front until 1 st has been inc at each end of 9th row. Work 1 row.

Divide for Back
1st row 2 ch, 1 h tr (hdc) into each of next 15(16:16) h tr (hdc), turn. Complete right back on these sts. Work until same length as front to armhole.

Shape armhole
1st row Sl st over next 8(9:9) h tr (hdc), 2 ch, 1 h tr (hdc) into each of next h tr (hdc) to end of row.
Cont on these sts, for Right Back until

armhole measures same length to shoulder as front, ending at armhole edge. Complete as for front shoulder. With right side of back facing, rejoin yarn to last 16(17:17) sts, and work left side to correspond with right side. Work Apple and leaf motifs, belt and tabs as given for Boy's Top and Trunks.

To make up

Work armhole and neck edgings in B as given for Boy's Top.

Leg Edgings
Work as for armholes only working dc (sc) into 2 out of every 3 sts along leg edge to draw leg opening in. Elastic may be threaded along this row if required. Seam legs. Sew on motifs and belt tabs. Sew buckle to belt and thread through tabs. Press lightly.

Beach clothes

Games Set

Something in the colours of a favourite team is sure to please almost any small boy. This is a good basic pattern for a V-necked sweater plus scarf and balaclava. A clever pocket adds interest to the sweater front, so children can keep their hands warm on cool days. The strips of cable stitching are a decorative and simple design note.

Materials

Robin Vogue Double Knitting:
(Knitting Worsted), 25 gr balls
Sweater: 8(9 10) balls of white
Balaclava: 3(3:4) balls of white
Scarf: 6 balls of white
The coloured borders: 1 ball each of gold and emerald
Pairs of No. 8(5), 10(3) and 11(2) knitting needles
No. 3·00 mm (C/2) crochet hook.
Cable needle

Measurements

Sweater: To fit a 22(24:26) inch chest.
Scarf: Length, 36 ins (excluding fringes).
It can, of course, be made longer.
Balaclava: To fit average size head for chest sizes.

Tension 6 sts to 1 inch using No. 8(5) needles.

Abbreviations, needle and size note

See pages 6 and 8.
Extra abbreviations, W—white; G—gold; E—emerald.

Sweater
Back

Using No. 10(3) needles and W, cast on 79(85:91) sts and work in k 1, p 1 rib for 16 rows. Change to No. 8(5) needles and beg patt.
1st row K.
2nd row P 12(15:18), k 2, p 6, k 2, p 35, k 2, p 6, k 2, p 12(15:18).

3rd row K 14(17:20), C 6f, k 39, C 6b, k to end.
4th row As 2nd row.
5th, 6th, 7th and 8th rows Rep 1st and 2nd rows twice.
These 8 rows form patt. Rep them until work measures 8(9:10) ins from beg ending on a wrong side row.

Shape Armholes

Keeping continuity of patt, cast off 6 sts at beg of next 2 rows *. Now dec 1 st at each end of every row until 55(61:67) sts rem, then work straight until armhole measures 4½(5:5½) ins ending after a wrong side row.

Shape Shoulders

Cast off 7(7:8) sts at beg of next 2 rows and 6(7:8) sts at beg of next 2 rows. Leave rem sts on spare needle.

Front

Work as for back welt, then break yarn.
Slip first and last 27(30:33) sts onto spare needles. Rejoin yarn to centre 25 sts and with No. 8(5) needles work 24 rows st st, ending after a p row.
Break yarn and leave sts on spare needle and fold back on welt. Rejoin yarn to beg of first set of sts on spare needle and with No. 8(5) needles, k across first set of sts, with same needle pick up and k 25 sts from the first row of pocket at back, k across sts on other spare needle. 79(85:91) sts.
Now beg with a 2nd patt row work 23 rows of patt as for Back ending on a wrong side row.
Next row K 27(30:33), now with pocket at front k tog 1 st from pocket and 1 st from main part, then k 27(30:33). Cont in patt across all sts and work as Back to *.

Divide for Neck

Next row K 2 tog, patt 28(31:34) k 2 tog, k 1, turn and leave rem sts on a holder.
Now dec 1 st at side edge on next 5 rows, *but at the same time* shape neck edge as set on every right side row. Keeping armhole

edge straight, shape neck as before until 13(14:16) sts rem. Cont straight until work measures same as back to shoulder ending at side edge.

Shape Shoulder
Next row Cast off 7(7:8) sts, work to end. Work 1 row and cast off.
Leaving centre st on safety pin, rejoin yarn to inner edge of rem sts, k 1, SKPO, patt to last 2 sts, k 2 tog.
Now work to match first side.

Pocket edges

Using No. 10(3) needles and W, rejoin yarn and pick up and k 25 sts evenly from side of pocket and work 2 rows in rib. Cast off in rib. Work other side in same way. Sew edges of rib into place.

Sleeves

Using No. 10(3) needles and W, cast on 32(34:36) sts, and work 2 ins in k 1, p 1 rib. Change to No. 8(5) needles and patt.
1st row K.
2nd row P 3(4:5), k 2 (p 6, k 2) 3 times, p 3(4:5).
3rd row K 5(6:7), C 6f, k 10, C 6b, k 5(6:7).
4th row As 2nd row.
5th, 6th, 7th and 8th rows Rep 1st and 2nd rows twice. These 8 rows form patt. Cont in patt inc 1 st at each end of next and every foll 6th row until there are 36(44:52) sts, working extra sts into st st, then every 4th row until there are 52(56:60) sts. Work straight until sleeve measures 9(10½:12) ins from beg ending on a wrong side row.

Shape Top
Cast off 6 sts at beg of next 2 rows, then dec 1 st at each end of next 4(6:6) rows. Now dec 1 st at each end of every right side row until 24(24:26) sts rem then 1 st each end of every row until 12(12:14) sts rem. Cast off.

Neckband

Join right shoulder. Using No. 10(3) needles and W, and right side facing, rejoin yarn and pick up and k 35(39:41) sts from side of

left neck, 1 st from safety pin (mark this st), 35(39:43) to shoulder seam, k across sts on spare needle, turn.
1st row With G, p to 2 sts before marker, p 2 tog tbl, p 1, p 2 tog, p to end.
2nd row Work in k 1, p 1 rib to 2 sts before marker, k 2 tog, k 1 SKPO, p 1, * k 1, p 1. Rep from * to end.
3rd row Rib to 2 sts before marker, p 2 tog tbl. p 1, p 2 tog, rib to end.
4th row With W, k to 2 sts before marker, k 2 tog, k 1, SKPO, k to end.
5th row As 3rd row.
6th row As 2nd row.
7th and 8th rows With E, rep 1st and 2nd rows. Cast off in rib dec as before.

To make up

Press work on wrong side using a warm iron over a damp cloth. Join left shoulder, neckband side and sleeve seams. Sew in sleeves. Press seams and edges.

Scarf

Using No. 8(5) needles and W, cast on 66 sts and work 16 rows in st st *. Change to G, and work 6 rows st st. Break G. Change to W and work 8 rows st st. Change to E and work 6 rows st st. Break E *. Change to W and work until scarf measures 10½ ins from beg ending after a p row. Rep. from * to * once more. Change to W and work until 23 ins are completed, ending after a p row. ** Change to E and work 6 rows st st. Break E. Change to W and work 8 rows st st. Change to G and work 6 rows st st. Break G. ** Change to W and work until scarf measures 31½ ins from beg, ending after a p row. Rep from ** to ** once more. Change to W and work 16 rows st st. Cast off. Press as sweater. Join side edges together with a flat seam. Turn scarf to right side and press with seam in centre. With W and No. 3·00 mm (C/2) hook work 1 row dc (sc) along edge working through both sets of sts, turn with 3 ch.
Next row * 1 dc (sc) in next dc (sc), 2 ch, miss 1 dc (sc). Rep from * to end, 1 dc (sc) in last dc (sc). Fasten off.
Work other edge in same way.
Cut yarn into 11 inch lengths in the 3 colours and knot through each chain sp alternating colours. Press and trim fringe.

Balaclava
Back

Using No. 10(3) needles and W, cast on
60(64:70) sts and k 4 rows.
Change to No. 8(5) needles. Work thus:
1st row K.
2nd row K 2, p to last 2 sts, k 2 *.
Rep these 2 rows until work measures
3(3:3½) ins from beg ending on a wrong side
row.

Shape shoulders
Cast off 7 sts at beg of next 2 rows and 6(7:8)
sts at beg of next 2 rows. Leave rem sts on
spare needle.

Left front

Using No. 10(3) needles and W, cast on
30(32:35) sts and work as Back to *. Rep the
last 2 rows 5(5:6) times more then the 1st
row again to end at neck edge.

Shape neck
Next row Cast off 7 sts, work to end.
Next row Work to last 2 sts, k 2 tog.
Next row Cast off 2 sts, work to end.
Dec 1 st at neck edge on every row until
13(14:15) sts rem. Work straight for a few
rows to same length as Back to shoulder
ending at side edge.

Shape Shoulder
Next row Cast off 7 sts, work to end.
Work 1 row. Cast off.

Right front

Work as Left Front but working 12 rows
before shaping neck.
Join shoulder seams.
With No. 10(3) needles and W and right side
facing, pick up and k 89(95:101) sts evenly
round neck edge.
Next row (wrong side) K 2, p 1, * k 1, p 1.
Rep from * to last 2 sts, k 2.
Next row K 3, p 1, * k 1, p 1. Rep from * to
last 3 sts, k 3.

Rep last 2 rows 3 times more, then first row
again.
Next row Rib 15 as before, and leave these
sts on safety pin. With No. 8(5) needles k to
last 15 sts, turn leaving 15 sts on safety pin.
Next row P, *but 1st and 3rd sizes only* inc 1
st at centre. *2nd size only* dec 1 st at centre.
60(64:72) sts.
Work in st st until 3¾(4¼:4¾) ins from top of
rib has been worked ending on a p row.

Shape Top
Next 2 rows K 44(47:53) k 2 tog, turn sl 1,
p to last 16(17:19) p 2 tog, turn.
Next 2 rows Sl 1, k to last 15(16:18), k 2
tog, turn sl 1, p to last 15(16:18), p 2 tog,
turn.
Cont dec in this way until all sts are on one
needle. Cast off.
Place marker in centre of cast off edge.
With right side facing, leaving first 5 sts on
safety pin, slip next 10 sts on to No. 10(3)
needles, join in G, work thus:
1st row K.
2nd row K 2, p 6, k 2.
3rd row K 2, C 6b, k 2.
4th row As 2nd row.
5th, 6th, 7th and 8th rows Rep 1st and 2nd
rows twice.
Rep these 8 rows until band fits to marker.
Leave sts on safety pin. Slip first 10 sts of
other side on to No. 10(3) needle leaving rem
5 sts on pin. Join in G and work to match
other side but working cable C 6f instead of
C 6b. Graft or cast off both sets of sts tog.
Sew cable band into place.
With No. 10(3) needles and E, k across 5 sts
on safety pin, then pick up and k 115(125:135)
sts evenly from edge of cable, k across 5 sts
on safety pin.
Next row K 2, p 1, * k 1, p 1. Rep from * to
last 2 sts, k 2.
Next row K 3, p 1, * k 1, p 1. Rep from *
to last 3 sts, k 3.
Rep last 2 rows once more. Cast off in rib.

To make up

Press as sweater. Join front edges together.

Tie & Dye Tunic

It is simple to use tie and dye work for making *individual fabric patterns. This craft is an economical way of utilizing odd scraps of plain fabric like old sheets. These can be made into clothes like our play tunic and cheered up with colourful tie and dye design. The pattern is made by folding and binding the fabric, then dipping it in dye, so the colour reaches some parts of the fabric and not others, giving a beautiful shaded effect. For a two, or three-colour pattern, parts of the folding are protected by strips of polythene. This prevents the dye from penetrating into the covered sections of fabric while it is dipped and re-dipped. Surplus dye is removed after each dip by washing and rinsing fabric, which then becomes completely colour fast. When making clothes, the dyeing is done after cutting out and before making up. Similar effects can be gained by dyeing ready-made white garments such as inexpensive tee shirts.*

Materials

Dylon Cold Dye: a tin each of Sahara Sun, Mandarin and Mexican Red
String, cord or tough elastic bands
Strips of polythene
1¼ yds white linen
5 in Velcro or 6 strong poppers (snaps)
Thread to match finished colour of dye

Measurements
Chest measurements 22, 23, 24 and 25 in.

1. Cut out fabric according to the pattern, preferably using pinking shears.
Alternatively finish off all raw edges with machine zigzag stitch before starting tie and dye work.
2. Mark centre of circle pattern on back, front and sleeves with a pin. Fold fabric back and furl it like an umbrella (diagram 1), then bind extra tightly in 3 places using rubber bands or string (diagram 2). Remove pins. Make the stripey pattern by folding

concertina pleats on the base of sleeves and hem on front and back pieces of tunic

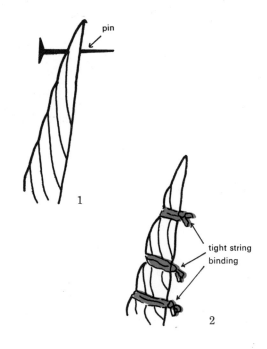

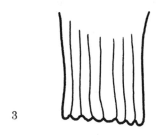

(diagram 3). Bind in 3 places and dye first in a pot of Sahara sun yellow. Wash and rinse the fabric pieces.

52

3. Cut one inch wide strips of polythene and bind these round each dyed portion of fabric, using string or elastic bands. Use two rows of polythene for each dyed portion and cover the "umbrella tips" with polythene too (diagram 4). Dye in a pot of Mandarin, then wash and rinse.

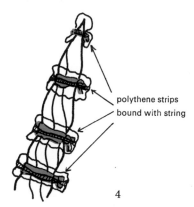

polythene strips bound with string

4

of sleeves. Attach sleeves to bodice. Neaten edge of sleeves. Turn up hem at the base of the tunic in the normal way or make a false hem.

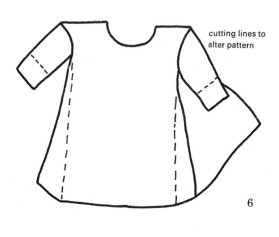

cutting lines to alter pattern

6

4. Leave the polythene in place. Tie new string loosely above each binding and remove original bindings where fabric is still white underneath. Dye in a pot of Mexican Red, then wash and rinse, before pressing thoroughly.

5. Make neck fastenings by folding under the shoulder tops on the back and front pattern pieces, making a $\frac{3}{4}$ in turning. Overlap the shoulder tops by 1 in and attach Velcro or poppers to fasten. Do up the Velcro or poppers and stitch along armhole for 3 ins on top of shoulders to attach front of tunic to back (diagram 5). Sew up sides and arms

7

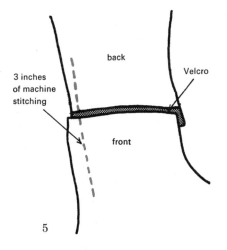

back

Velcro

3 inches of machine stitching

front

5

This pattern can be easily adapted for a boy by making the body less flared and the sleeves shorter (diagram 6), and by leaving a 4 in deep opening at the base of side seams for a casual look (diagram 7).

5 squares represent 4 inches

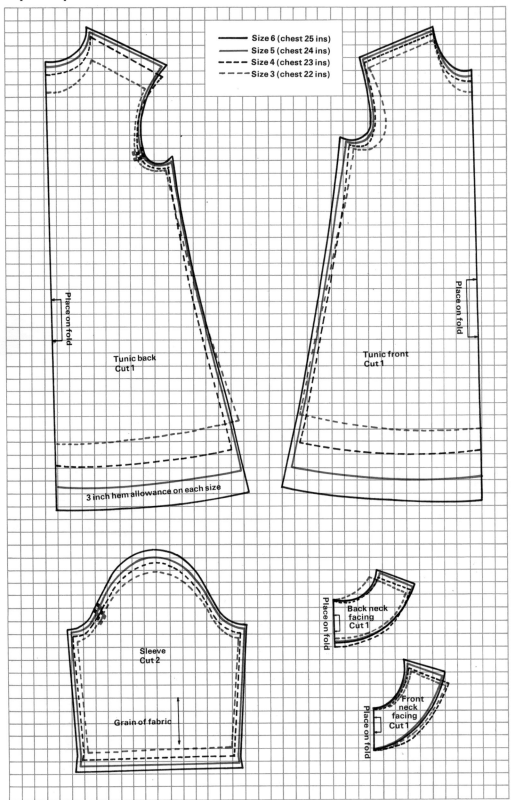

Size 6 (chest 25 ins)
Size 5 (chest 24 ins)
Size 4 (chest 23 ins)
Size 3 (chest 22 ins)

Place on fold

Tunic back
Cut 1

Place on fold

Tunic front
Cut 1

3 inch hem allowance on each size

Sleeve
Cut 2

Grain of fabric

Place on fold

Back neck
facing
Cut 1

Place on fold

Front
neck
facing
Cut 1

Tie and dye tunic

Party Cloak

This gorgeous party cloak is just what home sewing is all about. It should be almost impossible to buy a cloak like this ready-made, especially with the soft fluffy edging in crochet mohair. The cloak, with its matching lining, is easy to make and the crochet edging adds a smart touch of extravagance. Once you get into the swing of doing the looped crochet stitch, you will find it is the sort of straightforward work you can do while watching television or chatting in the evenings.

This pattern can be adapted for other uses in several ways. For instance, make a winter cloak from warm tweed and make the crochet edging in double knitting wool for a "fun fur" effect. The crochet edging pattern can also be used for adding a decorative touch to cuffs, collars and hems of dresses and coats.

Materials

Velvet and lining:
2½ yds of 36 in fabric
1¼ yds of 54 in fabric
Crochet edging:
5 balls of Emu Filigree

A No. 6·00 mm (I/9) crochet hook
Large covered hook and eye for fastening

Cloak

1. Cut out cloak, making sure pile of velvet faces up to neck of garment.
2. Stitch darts in back, press towards centre. Stitch side seams, notching over shoulders. Then, placing right sides together, stitch hood, notching curves. Fold along lines to make pleats.
3. Make hood lining in the same way and attach to hood right sides together. Stitch hood to neckline, right sides together.

Stitch back neck facing to front facing, right sides together. Stitch facings to neckline all round, right sides together. Grade turnings and turn to right side.
4. Make the cloak lining in the same way as step 2 and stitch into place just inside edge of facing.
5. Turn up hem, being careful not to mark velvet on right side. Slipstitch lining into place along hemline. Attach fastening to front edges of neckline, making an edge-to edge opening.
6. Slip-stitch crochet edging to cloak on right side using the same coloured sewing thread as the crochet and making sure the stitches do not go through the lining. Use a double thread and sew along centre of edging. It will be simple to remove, so garment and edging can be laundered separately.

Crochet Edging

Measurements 3½ yds long
Abbreviations see page 8
Work a chain 3½ yds long. If using a different yarn, the chain should be the same length as the required area to be edged. Instead of going all around the garment, it can be long enough to edge the hood alone, or to edge hood plus front.

1st row 1 dc (sc) in 2nd ch from hook, 1 dc (sc) in each ch to end, 1 ch, turn.

2nd row * Insert hook through next st, wind yarn twice round 2nd and 3rd fingers of left hand, clockwise. Now insert hook under top loops, yrh, pull through loops on fingers, yrh, draw through both loops on hook. Rep from * to end, 1 ch, turn.

3rd row 1 dc (sc) in each st of previous row, 1 ch turn.

4th row As 2nd row, but omitting 1 ch at end of row. Fasten off.

5 squares represent 4 inches

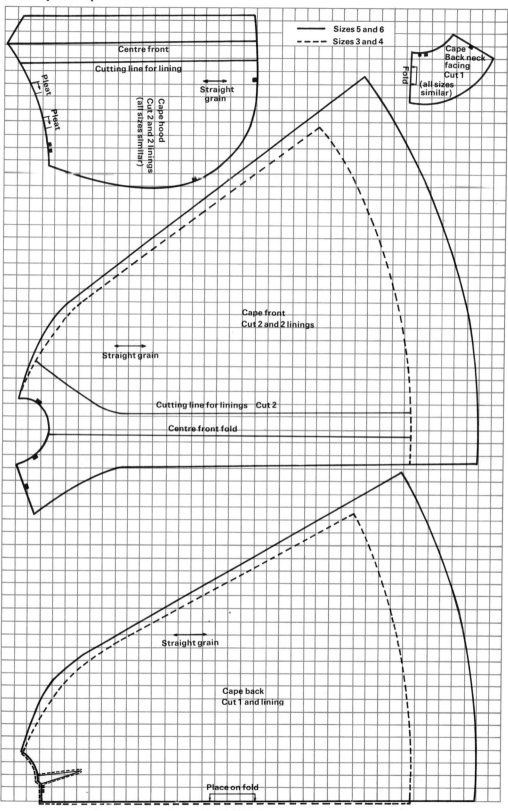

Sizes 5 and 6
Sizes 3 and 4

Centre front

Cutting line for lining

Straight grain

Pleat

Pleat

Cape hood
Cut 2 and 2 linings
(all sizes similar)

Cape
Back neck
facing
Cut 1
(all sizes
similar)

Fold

Cape front
Cut 2 and 2 linings

Straight grain

Cutting line for linings   Cut 2

Centre front fold

Straight grain

Cape back
Cut 1 and lining

Place on fold

Play Apron

This practical play apron is ideal for painting
or mealtimes and has a cunning hidden bonus.
The PVC overskirt and cuffs are attached
with Velcro, so can be removed in a trice if
paint or food has been spilt. It is a simple
matter then to wipe away the mark and the
whole garment will not need to be washed.
Underneath the PVC is a tough and protective
apron, made from sailcloth that is comfortable
to wear for play-school or when helping Mum
around the house. The velvet side of the Velcro
strip looks decorative stitched to the apron
front if the PVC overskirt is not in place,
and the appliqué on the apron is also a pocket.
This pattern is another good way of showing
how a simple garment can be turned into
something that is excitingly different as well
as being ultra-practical

Materials

Sailcloth or tough cotton:
1⅛ yds of 45 in fabric
PVC:
¾ yd of green for overskirt
¼ yd each of yellow and white for trims
6 yds of bias binding
Tracing paper and sticky tape for sewing PVC
1. Cut out sailcloth and overcast all seam
edges with three-step zigzag.
2. Stitch dart in head of sleeve and press.
Join sleeves to front and backs. Stitch sleeves
and side seams in one operation, right sides
together, clipping on curves.
3. Neaten all edges round neck, back opening
and hem by facing with bias binding. Leave
extra bias binding at back neck opening to
use as tie. Stop edges of tie fraying by
knotting.
4. Turn up ½ in hem on bottom of sleeves and
topstitch. Stitch Velcro on ends of sleeves so
that an inverted pleat will be formed when
closed. Also stitch a small oblong of Velcro
on back section of sleeve close to seam at
cuff edge (this is used to attach PVC cuff).
Attach Velcro to bodice front, close to
bodice/sleeve seam, also at centre back of
both pieces (diagrams 1 and 2).

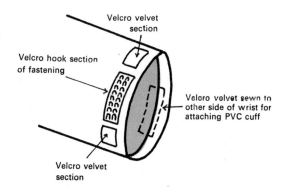

Velcro velvet
section

Velcro hook section
of fastening

Velcro velvet sewn to
other side of wrist for
attaching PVC cuff

Velcro velvet
section

1

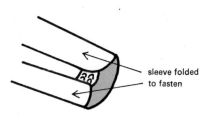

sleeve folded
to fasten

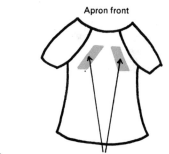

Apron front

2

sew Velcro velvet section here

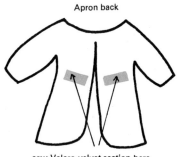

Apron back

sew Velcro velvet section here

5. Cut out PVC overskirt and join side seams.
6. Cut out the appliqué shapes and pieces of tracing paper the same size. The house is $7 \times 4\frac{1}{2}$ ins plus $\frac{1}{2}$in top turning. Door: $2 \times 1\frac{1}{2}$. Windows: $1 \times 1\frac{1}{2}$. Roof: 2 ins deep, 6 ins along top and 8 ins along bottom. Chimney: 3 ins $\times 1\frac{1}{2}$.
7. Use sticky tape instead of pins to hold PVC in place. Place the cut paper over appliqué sections to prevent PVC from sticking in sewing machine. A special roller foot for the sewing machine also helps. Tape door and windows in place over house and stitch round edges, over paper. Turn under top $\frac{1}{2}$in of white section and stitch. Attach this section, which will be a pocket for painting-things, to centre of apron front by stitching down sides and along bottom. Cut out roof and stitch to apron round all sides. Cut out white chimney, turning top under and stitching, before applying as a pocket for pencils. Trim back edges outside sewing lines and if required, overstitch with neat zigzag stitch, placing strips of tracing paper above sewing lines to facilitate sewing.

This appliqué method can be used for many different pocket ideas to decorate the apron front. The secret is to keep the shapes simple so the work does not become too fiddly.
8. Finish back edges and hem of overskirt with bias binding. Finish the top this way too, but leave enough bias at each end for ties. Apply the "hook" section of Velcro fastening inside top edge of overskirt. This will fasten up with the corresponding strip of Velcro on the yellow apron.

3

Removable PVC Cuff

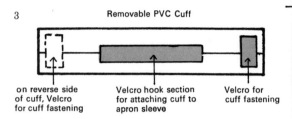

on reverse side of cuff, Velcro for cuff fastening

Velcro hook section for attaching cuff to apron sleeve

Velcro for cuff fastening

9. Fold cuffs, right sides together, and stitch, leaving opening on one side to turn. Turn and stitch along centre to secure. Apply Velcro as cuff fastenings and add another 2 in strip to the inside of each cuff. This will correspond with the strips already applied to apron sleeves (diagram 3).

5 squares represent 4 inches

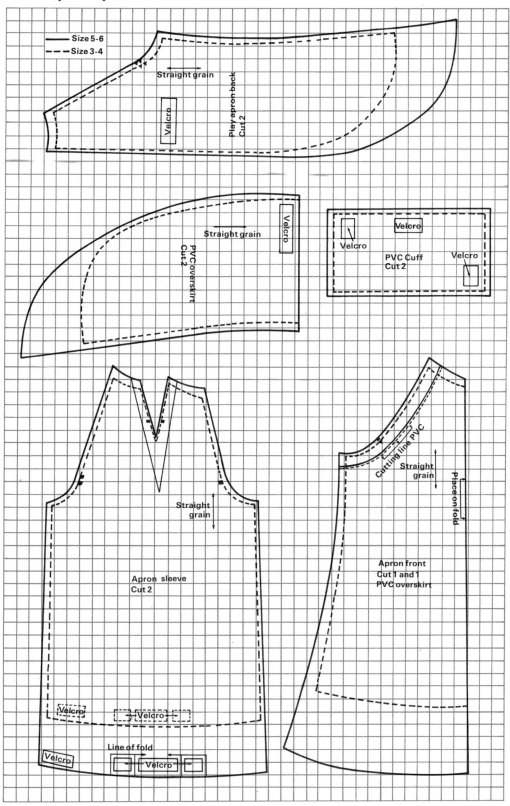

Hooded Play Jumper

Crochet borders, a gay fringe and smart cross stitch embroidery are the extra touches that make this warm play jumper unusual. The pattern is straightforward to knit in an extra thick yarn and an easy garter stitch. The cosy hood makes it an ideal garment for cool weather. It is loose fitting, allowing for plenty of movement and will be comfortable to wear over winter jumpers and trousers.

Materials

Robin Vogue Double Double
(Knitting Worsted *or* Bulky), 50 gr balls:
9(10:11) balls of red
1 ball each of blue and yellow
Pairs of No. 5(8) and 7(6) knitting needles
No. 4·50 mm (G/6) crochet hook
2 buttons

Measurements To fit a 22(24:26) inch chest.

Tension 4 sts to 1 inch over g st on No. 5(8) needles.

Abbreviations, needle and size note
See pages 6 and 8. Extra abbreviations:
R—Red; B—blue; Y—yellow.

Back

Using No. 5(8) needles and R, cast on 48(52:56) sts and work in g st until back measures 7(8½:9½) ins from beg.

Shape Armholes

Cast off 6(6:7) sts at beg of next 2 rows, 36(40:42) sts *. Cont straight until armhole measures 4½(5:5½) ins from beg.

Shape Shoulders

Cast off 5 sts at beg of next 2 rows and 4(5:5) sts on next 2 rows. Leave rem 18(20:22) sts on a holder.

Front

Work as Back to *, then work 2(4:4) rows straight.

Divide for Front Opening

Next row K 16(18:19), cast off 4, k to end. Work on last set of sts, ** work straight until armhole measures 3½(4:4½) ins ending at front edge.

Shape Neck

Cast off 3(4:4) sts at beg of next row and 3(3:4) sts on next alt row, then dec 1 st at same edge on next alt row 9(10:10) sts. Work straight until same length as back to beg of shoulder shaping ending at armhole edge.

Shape Shoulder

Cast off 5 sts at beg of next row, then work 1 row. Cast off rem sts.
Return to other sts, rejoin yarn at inner edge to rem sts and work to match first side working from ** to end.

Sleeves

Begin at shoulder.
Using No. 5(8) needles and B, cast on 36(40:44) sts and work in g st for 1¾(1¾:2) ins. Place marker at edge of last row. Work 4(6:8) rows more, then dec 1 st each end of next and every foll 8th row until 24(26:28) sts rem. Work straight until sleeve measures 7½(9:10½) ins from marker—or required length. Cast off.

Crochet Edgings

Join shoulder, side and sleeve seams. Using No. 4·50 mm (G/6) crochet hook, with wrong side facing and R, work thus round lower edges of back, front and sleeves.
1st round 1 dc (sc) into each st, join with a *sl st*.
2nd round In B as 1st round.
3rd round In Y as 1st round.
4th round As 2nd round.
5th round As 1st round. Fasten off.

Front Bands

Using No. 4·50 mm (G/6) crochet hook, R, and with wrong side facing, work 4 rows of

Hooded play jumper

dc (sc) turning each time with 1 ch—along right front edge. Fasten off.

Work left front to match but making 2 buttonholes in 2nd row by working 1 ch instead of a dc (sc), 3 sts in from each edge. In 3rd row work a dc (sc) into the *1 ch sp*. Stitch down side edge at base, left overlapping right.

Hood

Using No. 7(6) needles and R and with right side facing and omitting frontbands, pick up and k 12(13:13) sts from right front neck, k 18(20:22) sts from back neck and 12(12:13) sts from left front neck. 42(45:48) sts. Work 4 rows g st. Change to No. 5(8) needles.
Next row K 1, inc in next st, * k 2, inc. in next st. Rep from * to last st, k 1. 56(60:64) sts.
Work straight in g st until work measures 7(8:8½) ins or length required. Cast off. Fold cast off edge in half and join on wrong side.

Hood Edging
With right side facing, and R, work crochet edging as before but work in rows, cutting each colour at end of row and beg all rows at same edge. Work last row across each side edge for a neat finish.

To make up

Press lightly on wrong side using a warm iron over a damp cloth. Set in sleeves, sewing the part above marker to cast off armhole sts. Cut 5 inch lengths of each colour and, alternating colours, knot a fringe all round lower edge, along join of hood and down centre of back hood to neck. Turn back hood edging and tack down at each side of neck edge.

Cross stitch embroidery
Work over 1 st in width and 1 g st ridge in depth. Mark centre 2 sts between front band and first row of crochet edging in B. Work 4 crosses at centre, i.e. 2 rows of 2 in B, then using Y and leaving 2 g st ridges above and below and 2 sts at each side, work '1 box' of cross sts around centre and another 'box' in B at same intervals as before, as shown in photograph. Sew on buttons.

Peasant Dress

Bold embroidery makes this colourful peasant-style dress into something unusual. The dress is in fresh-looking and inexpensive calico, and the embroidery is worked with tapisserie wool. The secret of making effective use of embroidery on children's clothes is to keep it simple. The chain stitch is quick to sew, and the thread is colour fast and easily washable. There are many variations on this theme; use the flowers in a small cluster to decorate a collar on a plain dress or shirt; in a panel down the front of a shift dress or in a deep border round the hem of a party dress. Pastel-coloured flowers would look effective against plain fabric in a deep colour.

Materials

Calico—1¾ yds 36 in wide fabric
Coats Anchor Tapisserie Wool:
2 skeins green, 1 red, 1 blue, 1 yellow
½ yd muslin for lining bodice (optional)
4 buttons to cover

1. Cut out calico, overcast all cut edges and make up dress. Sew bodice darts first, then join bodice at shoulders.
2. Gather sleeves and sew to bodice. Stitch underarm seam of sleeves and bodice side in one.
3. Measure round neck and armhole. Cut half inch wide strips of calico in the same measurements, adding one inch to each for turnings. These must be cut on the *bias*.
4. Neaten neckline with the bias strips. Gather in fullness at sleeve edge and neaten with bias strip.

5. Join skirt, leaving a 4 in opening below waist at back. Gather skirt top, pin, baste and stitch to bodice, adjusting gathers evenly before stitching.
6. Turn up hem to individual size.
7. Sketch embroidery pattern on to dress with a pencil. Work embroidery in chain stitch (see page 9), using one strand of wool, following colours on our pattern or choosing your own.
8. With green, embroider chain stitch in a neat row round neckline and armholes, sewing along the binding. Embroider more green just above the hem as in photograph. At each side make small curves the same as those on the bodice centre waist.
9. To make bow, twist four 6 ft long strands of thread together evenly. Pin ends firmly to upholstered chair or tie them round a door handle while you twist the other ends round and round with one hand. When twists become tight, hold middle of skein with spare hand and let threads twist up on themselves so they become half their original length. Knot each end, untie threads outside knot to make a tassel. Clip away spare thread ends.
10. Cut out circles of calico to cover buttons. Embroider small daisy shapes with 3 petals in centre of each circle, using one strand of tapisserie wool and assorted colours. Use the circles to cover buttons so that embroidery lies in centre of button. Make the button-holes.
11. Cut bodice back and front shape from muslin and use this as lining to neaten inside bodice. Join lining at shoulders and slip stitch by hand to wrong side of bodice, turning raw edges under.

1 square represents 2 inches

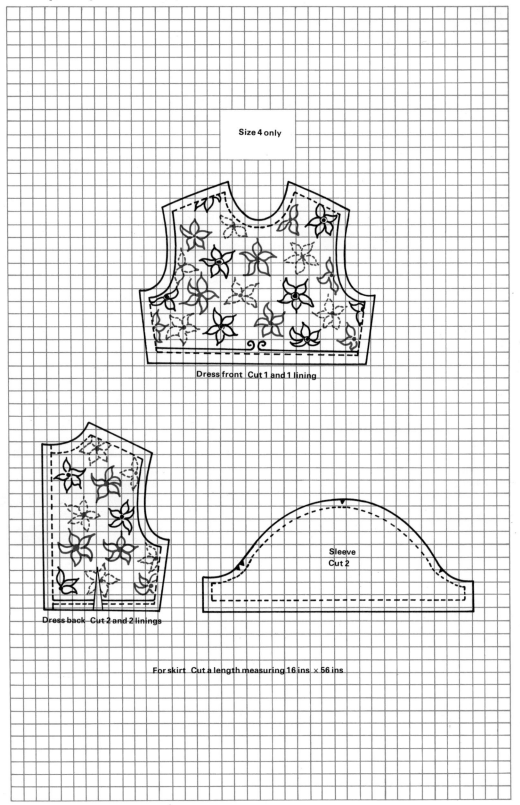

Size 4 only

Dress front Cut 1 and 1 lining

Dress back Cut 2 and 2 linings

Sleeve
Cut 2

For skirt Cut a length measuring 16 ins × 56 ins

Peasant dress

Quilted Waistcoat

The quilted velvet and shining metal buttons transform this straightforward pattern into party wear, fit for the best occasions. With the aid of a special foot on the sewing machine, quilting is quick to do at home, although it can also be done by hand. This is the sort of special garment that is always good to make because it becomes something that is quite individual.

Materials

Velvet, lining and Courtelle wadding:
1½ yds of 36 in wide fabric or
1⅛ yds of 45 in wide fabric
Matching thread
6 metal buttons
18 ins silk cord for button fastening

1. Cut out the pattern pieces in the three fabrics, allowing an extra inch all round pattern. Make sure pile of velvet is going up towards neck.
2. Place wadding under velvet and tack together. Using quilting foot and guide on the sewing machine, quilt velvet on the bias into inch squares, making sure that lines match up the front. If your machine has no quilting foot, rule the sewing lines with pencil and sew with an ordinary straight stitch.
3. Complete quilting, then re-cut front and back of waistcoat to the right size. Stitch front to back at side seams. Clip curves.
4. Stitch the side seams of the lining. Press under ⅝ in on shoulder edges. With right sides together, pin facing to vest, keeping raw edges even. Stitch all round except for shoulder edges and leave a 6 in. break in the stitching at the lower edge of back so the waistcoat can be turned the right way out. Trim all seams and corners. Clip curves. Turn and press. Either use a special velvet board, or lightly press using a Turkish towel as a base. Slipstitch back edge together along the 6 in break.
5. Sew shoulder seams of velvet with right

sides facing. Press seams open. Slipstitch shoulder edges of lining together.
6. Sew on buttons. Cut cord into 6 in lengths. Working one at a time, sew ends of

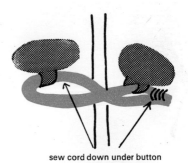

sew cord down under button
where it will not show

1

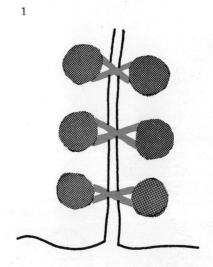

cord under buttons on right hand side, making three loops. These are then twisted once over the opening and looped round the left hand buttons for fastening (diagram 1).

5 squares represent 4 inches

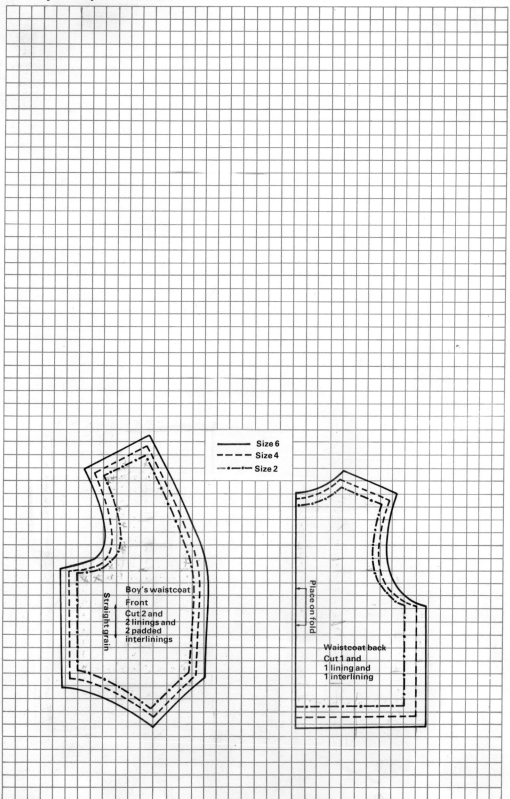

Size 6
Size 4
Size 2

Boy's waistcoat

Front
Cut 2 and
2 linings and
2 padded
interlinings

Straight grain

Place on fold

Waistcoat back
Cut 1 and
1 lining and
1 interlining

Simple Tabard

Beginners will find this crochet pattern an excellent one to try. It is quick, easy and practical. The tabard looks smart over play clothes, over matching tights and sweaters, or over long-sleeved blouses worn with trousers. There is a wide choice of alternative two-colour mixtures to think about, from scarlet with white to bright yellow with orange.

Materials

Pingouin Classique Crylor (Sport Yarn) 50 gr balls:

1(1:2:2) balls in dark shade (Dk), 1(1:1:1) balls in light shade (Lt)
No. 3·50 mm (E/4) crochet hook

Measurements To fit a 20(22:24:26) inch chest.
Length: about $11\frac{3}{4}(12\frac{3}{4}:15\frac{1}{2}:16\frac{1}{2})$ ins

Tension Motif measures $2\frac{3}{4}$ inches square
Note It is advisable to test tension before beginning garment and, if necessary, to change to a larger or smaller hook to obtain the correct tension.

Abbreviations, hook and size note
See pages 6 and 8.
Extra abbreviations, Dk—dark shade; Lt—light shade.

Motif

Using No. 3·50 mm (E/4) hook and Lt, make 6 ch and join into a ring with a sl st.
1st round Into ring work 2 ch [as 1st h tr (hdc)] 2 h tr (hdc), 3 ch, * 3 h tr (hdc), 3 ch. Rep from * twice, sl st to top of 2 ch.
2nd round Join on Dk, sl st to first sp, [2 ch, 2 h tr (hdc), 3 ch, 3 h tr (hdc)] into first 3 ch sp, * [1 ch, 3 h tr (hdc), 3 ch, 3 h tr (hdc)] into next 3 ch sp. Rep from * twice, 1 ch, join with a sl st.
3rd round In Lt, sl st to first sp, [2 ch,

2 h tr (hdc), 3 ch, 3 h tr (hdc)] into first 3 ch sp, * 1 ch, 3 h tr (hdc) into 1 ch sp, [1 ch, 3 h tr (hdc), 3 ch, 3 h tr (hdc)] into each corner sp. Rep from * ending 1 ch, 3 h tr (hdc) into 1 ch sp, 1 ch, sl st to join.
4th round In Dk, work 1 dc (sc) into each st all round, join with sl st and fasten off. This completes one motif. Work 24(24:40:40) motifs in all.

To make up

Do not press Form Back and Front of Tabard by joining 12(12:20:20) motifs tog for each side. Join 3(3:4:4) motifs in width and 4(4:5:5) motifs in length. With Dk, Work 2(4:3:5) rows in dc (sc) all round edges of Back and Front, working 1 extra dc (sc) in each corner on each row to keep work flat.
Work Shoulders (worked on one side of Tabard only)
1st and 2nd sizes only At one end of one side of Tabard, with Dk, work in dc (sc) to the centre of the first motif in row. Turn with 1 ch. Work 3(5) more rows in dc (sc) on this half motif, turning each row with 1 ch. Break yarn and fasten off. Rejoin yarn to centre of last motif in row and work in dc (sc) to end. Work to correspond with other shoulder.
3rd and 4th sizes only At one end of one side of Tabard, with Dk, work in dc (sc) across first motif in row. Turn with 1 ch. Work 7(9) more rows, turning each row with 1 ch. Break yarn and fasten off. Rejoin to beg of last motif in row and work in dc (sc) to end. Work to correspond with other shoulder. Join shoulders to other piece of Tabard.

Ties (4 required)

Using Dk, make a ch 12 ins in length and work 1 dc (sc) in each ch st. Break yarn and fasten off.
Now sew ties to sides of Tabard.

Everyday Clothes

Aran Sweater

This practical pattern, in the famous knitting style from the Aran islands, is useful to master. It can be used for both girls and boys. Especially warm and durable, it is a good money-saver when made at home as Aran-style clothes are expensive to buy.

Materials

Sweater 10(11:12:13) 25 gr balls of Lister Lavenda Double Knitting Wool (Knitting Worsted)

Pairs of No. 9(4) and No. 11(2) knitting needles

Measurements To fit a 24(26:28:30) in. chest

Tension 6 sts and 8 rows to 1 in using No. 9(4) needles

Abbreviations, needle and size note
See pages 6 and 8.

Back

Using No. 11(2) needles cast on 80(84:92:96) sts, and work 10 rows in k 1, p 1 rib. Change to No. 9(4) needles and work in pattern thus:
1st row (K 1, p 1) 2(3:5:6) times, T2R, p 2 (k 4, p 4) twice, k 4, p 2, T2R, p 3, k 1, T2R, p 4, T2L, k1, p 3, T2L, p 2, (k 4, p 4) twice, k 4, p 2, T2L, (k 1, p 1) 2(3:5:6) times
2nd row (P 1, k 1) 2(3:5:6) times, p 2, k 2, (p 4, k 4) twice, p 4, k 2, p 2, k 3, p 3, k 4, p 3, k 3, p 2, k 2, (p 4, k 4) twice, p 4, k 2, p 2, (p 1, k 1) 2(3:5:6) times
3rd row M st 4(6:10:12), T2R, p 2, (C4F, p 4) twice, C4F, p 2, T2R, p 2, T2RP, T2R, p 4, T2L, T2LP, p 2, T2L, p 2, (C4B, p 4) twice, C4B, p 2, T2L, m st 4(6:10:12).
4th row M st 4(6:10:12), p 2, k 2, (p 4, k 4) twice, p 4, k 2, p 2, k 2, p 1, k 1, p 2, k 4, p 2,

k 1, p 1, k 2, p 2, k 2, (p 4, k 4) twice, p 4, k 2, p 2, m st 4(6:10:12).
5th row M st 4(6:10:12), T2R, p 2, (k 4, p 4) twice, k 4, p 2, T2R, p 1, T2RP, p 1, T2R, p 4, T2L, p 1, T2LP, p 1, T2L, p 2, (k 4, p 4) twice, k 4, p 2, T2L, m st to end.
6th row M st 4(6:10:12), p 2, k 2, (p 4, k 4) twice, p 4, k 2, p 2, k 1, p 1, k 2, p 2, k 4, p 2, k 2, p 1, k 1, p 2, k 2, (p 4, k 4) twice, p 4, k 2, p 2, m st to end.
7th row M st 4(6:10:12), T2R, p 2, (C4F, p 4) twice, C4F, p 2, T2R, T2RP, p 2, T2R, p 4, T2L, p 2, T2LP, T2L, p 2, (C4B, p 4) twice, C4B, p 2, T2L, m st to end.
8th row M st 4(6:10:12), p 2, k 2, (p 4, k 4) twice, p 4, k 2, p 3, k 3, p 2, k 4, p 2, k 3, p 3, k 2, (p 4, k 4) twice, p 4, k 2, p 2, m st to end.
9th row As 1st row.
10th row As 2nd row.
11th row M st 4(6:10:12), T2R, p 2, k 2, (C4FP, C4BP) twice, k 2, p 2, T2R, p 2, T2RP, T2R, p 4, T2L, T2LP, p 2, T2L, p 2, k 2, (C4FP, C4BP) twice, k 2, p 2, T2L, m st to end.
12th row M st 4(6:10:12), (p 2, k 2) twice, p 4, k 4, p 4, (k 2, p 2) twice, k 2, p 1, k 1, p 2, k 4, p 2, k 1, p 1, k 2, (p 2, k 2) twice, p 4, k 4, p 4, (k 2, p 2) twice, m st to end
13th row M st 4(6:10:12), T2R, p 2, k 2, p 2, k 4, p 4, k 4, p 2, k 2, p 2, T2R, p 1, T2RP, p 1, T2R, p 4, T2L, p 1, T2LP, p 1, T2L, p 2, k 2, p 2, k 4, p 4, k 4, p 2, k 2, p 2, T2L, m st to end.
14th row M st 4(6:10:12), (p 2, k 2) twice, p 4, k 4, p 4, (k 2, p 2) twice, k 1, p 1, k 2, p 2, k 4, p 2, k 2, p 1, k 1, (p 2, k 2) twice, p 4, k 4, p 4, (k 2, p 2) twice, m st to end.
15th row M st 4(6:10:12), T2R, p 2, k 2, p 2, C4F, p 4, C4F, p 2, k 2, p 2, T2R, T2RP, p 2, T2R, p 4, T2L, p 2, T2LP, T2L, p 2, k 2, p 2, C4B, p 4, C4B, p 2, k 2, p 2, T2L, m st to end.
16th row M st 4(6:10:12), (p 2, k 2) twice, p 4, k 4, p 4, k 2, p 2, k 2, p 3, k 3, p 2, k 4, p 2, k 3, p 3, k 2, p 2, k 2, p 4, k 4, p 4, (k 2, p 2) twice, m st to end.

17th row M st 4(6:10:12), T2R, p 2, k 2, p 2, k 4, p 4, k 4, p 2, k 2, p 2, T2R, p 3, k 1, T2R, p 4, T2L, k 1, p 3, T2L, p 2, k 2, p 2, k 4, p 4, k 4, p 2, k 2, p 2, T2L, m st to end.

18th row M st 4(6:10:12), (p 2, k 2) twice, p 4, k 4, p 4, (k 2, p 2) twice, k 3, p 3, k 4, p 3, k 3, (p 2, k 2) twice, p 4, k 4, p 4, (k 2, p 2) twice, m st to end.

19th row M st 4(6:10:12), T2R, p 2, k 2, p 2, C4F, p 4, C4F, p 2, k 2, p 2, T2R, p 2, T2RP, T2R, p 4, T2L, T2LP, p 2, T2L, p 2, k 2, p 2, C4B, p 4, C4B, p 2, k 2, p 2, T2L, m st to end.

20th row As 12th row.

21st row As 13th row.

22nd row As 14th row.

23rd row M st 4(6:10:12) T2R, p 2, k 2, (C4BP, C4FP) twice, k 2, p 2, T2R, T2RP, p 2, T2R, p 4, T2L, p 2, T2LP, T2L, p 2, k 2 (C4BP, C4FP) twice, k 2, p 2, T2L, m st to end.

24th row As 8th row.

These 24 rows form patt. Cont in patt until work measures 9½(10:10½:11) ins ending after a wrong side row.

Shape Armholes

Keeping continuity of patt, cast off 5(4:5:4) sts at beg of next 2 rows.

3rd row K 2, SKPO, patt to last 4 sts, k 2 tog, k 2.

4th row K 1, p 2, patt to last 3 sts, p 2, k 1**.
Rep 3rd and 4th rows until 28(30:32:34) sts rem. Leave sts on spare needle for neckband.

Front

Work as for back to **, then rep 3rd and 4th rows until 42(46:50:54) sts rem.

Shape Neck

1st row (right side) K 2, SKPO, patt 10(12:14:16) sts, turn

2nd row P 2, patt to last 3 sts, p 2, k 1.

3rd row K 2, SKPO, patt to last 3 sts, k 2 tog, k 1.

4th row As 2nd row.

Rep last 2 rows until all sts worked off, working without edge sts as numbers decrease.

Return to other sts, sl next 14 sts on to a safety pin, rejoin yarn and patt to last 4 sts, k 2 tog, k 2

Next row K 1, p 2, patt to last 2 sts, p 2

Next row K 1, SKPO, patt to last 4 sts, k 2 tog, k 2.
Complete to match other side.

Sleeves

Using No. 11(2) needles, cast on 36(36:40:40) sts and work 14(14:18:18) rows in k 1, p 1, rib. Change to No. 9(4) needles.

1st row (K 1, p 1) 2(2:3:3) times, T2R, p 2, (k 4, p 4) twice, k 4, p 2, T2L, (k 1, p 1) 2(2:3:3) times.

2nd row (P 1, k 1) 2(2:3:3) times, p 2, k 2, (p 4, k 4) twice, p 4, k 2, p 2, (p 1, k 1) 2(2:3:3) times.

3rd row (K 1, p 1) 2(2:3:3) times, T2R, p 2, (C4F, p 4) twice, C4F, p 2, T2L, (k 1, p 1) 2(2:3:3) times.

4th row As 2nd row.

Cont in patt as now set, working cable patt as Back and inc 1 st each end of next and every foll 6th row working inc sts into m st, until there are 58(60:66:68) sts. Cont in patt until work measures 11(12:13:14) ins, or required length.

Shape Top

Work as Back armhole until 6 sts rem for each size. Leave sts on spare needle.

Neckband

Sew in sleeves, leaving Left Back armhole open. Now with right side of work facing and beg with left sleeve, rejoin yarn and using No. 11(2) needles, k across 6 sts at top of sleeve, pick up and k 14(16:18:20) sts down left front, k across 14 sts of front neck, pick up and k 14(16:18:20) sts up right front, k across 6 sts at top of sleeve and 28(30:32:34) sts at back neck. 82(88:94:100) sts.
Work 7 rows in k 1, p 1 rib. Cast off in rib.

To make up

Press work on wrong side with a warm iron over a damp cloth. Join left back armhole. Join side and sleeve seams. Press seams.

Fair Isle Pullover

Designs like this are always fashionable and always a pleasure to knit. A sleeveless pullover is excellent to make for either boys or girls.

Materials

Emu Machine Washable 4-ply wool:
(Fingering 3-ply):

Pullover: 2(3:3) balls of natural, 1 ball each of new white, Spanish gold and maize.
Pairs of No. 10(3) and 12(1) knitting needles

Measurements Measures 22(24:26) inches.
Length: 14(14½: 15) inches.

Tension 7 sts to 1 inch over stocking stitch.

Abbreviations, needle and size note
See pages 6 and 8.
Extra abbreviations, G—Spanish Gold;
W—White; M—Maize.

Back

** Using No. 12(1) needles and mc, cast on 77(85:93) sts and work thus:
1st row K 1, * p 1, k 1. Rep from * to end.
2nd row P 1, * k 1, p 1. Rep from * to end.
Rep last 2 rows 4 times more. Change to No. 10(3) needles and work in st st for 2 rows.
Beg patt.
1st row Using G, k.
2nd row P 1 M(3 G, 2 M : 2 M) * 5 G, 2 M.
Rep from * to last 6(3:0) sts, then 5 G, 1 M (3 G : 0).
3rd row K 2 M(2 G, 4 M : 3 M) * 3 G, 4 M.
Rep from * to last 5(2:6) sts, 3 G, 2 M (2 G : 3 G, 3 M).
4th row P 3 M(0 : 4 M) * 1 G, 6 M. Rep from * to last 4(1:5) sts, 1 G, 3 M (0 : 4 M).
5th row As 3rd row.
6th row As 2nd row.
7th row Using G, k.
8th row Using mc, p.
9th row K * 1 mc, 3 W. Rep from * to last st, 1 mc.

10th row P * 2 mc, 1 W, 1 mc. Rep from * to last st, 1 mc.
11th row K * 1 W, 1 mc. Rep from * to last st, 1 W.
12th row P * 1 W, 3 mc. Rep from * to last st, 1 W.
13th row K * 2 W, 1 mc, 1 W. Rep from * to last st, 1 W.
14th row Using mc, p.
15th row K 2 M (2 M, 1 mc, 3 M : 2 M) * 4 M, 1 mc, 3 M. Rep from * to last 3(7:3) sts, 3 M(4 M, 1 mc, 2 M : 3 M).
16th row P. 0 (1 M, 1 mc, 1 M, 1 mc : 0) * 5 M, 1 mc, 1 M, 1 mc. Rep from * to last 5(9:5) sts, 5 M, then for 2nd size only, 1 mc, 1 M, 1 mc, 1 M.
17th row K * 1 mc, 3 M. Rep from * to last st, 1 mc.
18th row For 1st and 3rd sizes only, 1 M, 1 mc, 1 M, 1 mc. All sizes * 5 M, 1 mc, 1 M, 1 mc. Rep from * to last 1(5:1) sts, 1(5:1) M.
19th row K 2(6:2) M, * 1 mc, 7 M. Rep from * to last 3(7:3) sts, 1 mc, 2(6:2) M.
20th row Using mc, p.
21st row K 5(1:5) mc, * 3 G, 5 mc. Rep from * to last 0(4:0) sts, k 3 G, 1 mc for 2nd size only.
22nd row P * 2 G, 1 mc, 1 G. Rep from * to last st, 1 G.
23rd row As 21st row.
24th row Using mc, p.
25th row K 5(3:1) W, * 1 mc, 5 W. Rep from * to last 0(4:2) sts, then for 2nd and 3rd sizes only, 1 mc, 3(1) W.
26th row P 1 mc (2 W, 3 mc : 3 mc) * 3 W, 3 mc. Rep from * to last 4(2:0) sts, then for 1st and 2nd sizes only 3 W 1 mc, 1st size and 2 W 2nd size.
27th row K 2 mc, 1 W (1 W : 4 mc, 1 W), * 5 mc, 1 W. Rep from * to last 2(0:4) sts, 2(0:4) mc.
28th row As 26th row.
29th row As 25th row.
30th row Using mc, p.
These 30 rows form patt and are rep throughout. Cont in patt until work measures 8½(9:9½) ins from beg ending with a p row **.

Shape Armholes

Keeping continuity of patt, cast off 4(6:8) sts at beg of next 2 rows, then dec 1 st at each end of next and foll 3 alt rows. 61(65:69) sts. Work straight until armhole measures 5½(5½:6) ins ending with a p row.

Shape Shoulders

Cast off 6 sts at beg of next 4 rows, then 5(6:7) sts at beg of next 2 rows. Leave rem 27(29:31) sts on a spare needle.

Front

Work as for Back from ** to **.

Shape Armhole and Neck

Next row Cast off 4(6:8) sts, patt 34(36:38) (including st already on right hand needle from casting off) turn, and leave rem sts on spare needle. Now dec 1 st at armhole edge at beg of foll 4 alt rows, *at the same time* dec 1 st at neck edge on next and every 3rd row. Keeping armhole edge straight, cont dec at neck edge as before until 17(18:19) sts rem. Work straight until front measures same as Back to shoulder, ending with a p row.

Shape Shoulder

Cast off 6 sts at beg of next and foll alt row. Work 1 row and cast off rem 5(6:7) sts. Sl centre st onto a safety pin, rejoin yarn to other sts on spare needle and patt to end. Work to match other side, reversing shaping.

Neckband

Join right shoulder. With right side of work facing, using mc and No. 12(1) needles, pick up and k 50(50:54) sts down left side of neck, k st from safety pin (mark this st with coloured thread) pick up and k 50(50:54) sts up right side of neck and k across 27(29:31) sts of back neck.

1st row Work in k 1, p 1 rib to within 2 sts of marked st, p 2 tog, p 1, p 2 tog tbl, rib to end.

2nd row Rib to within 2 sts of marked st, p 2 tog, k 1, p 2 tog, rib to end. Rep these 2 rows twice more. Cast off in rib, dec on this row as before.

Armbands

Join left shoulder. With right side of work facing, using mc and No. 12(1) needles, pick up and k 96(96:104) sts from armhole and work 6 rows in k 1, p 1 rib. Cast off in rib.

To make up

Press work on wrong side with a warm iron over a damp cloth. Join side and armband seams, matching patt. Press seams.

Knitted Dress

The decorative stitch on the full skirt makes this smart dress into something special. It is simple to knit and the close-fitting yoke and sleeves add a tailored touch. A simple variation on the style would be to make the yoke and sleeves in a contrasting colour to the skirt. The dress is made in a practical Tricel/nylon yarn that washes easily and holds its shape well.

Materials

Patons Kingfisher Tricel/Nylon 4-ply crepe

50 gr balls: 4(4:5)
Pairs of No. 11(2), 10(3) and 3(10) knitting needles
Cable needle
3 small buttons
3 press studs (snaps)

Measurements To fit a 22(24:26) inch chest. Length from top of shoulders, (approx) 17(19:21) ins. Sleeve seam, 8½(10:11½) ins, adjustable.

Tension 7 sts to 1 inch over st st using No. 10(3) needles.

Abbreviations, needle and size note
See pages 6 and 8.

Front

** Using No. 10(3) needles cast on 141(147:153) sts. Change to No. 11(2) needles and beg with a k row, work 4 rows st st. Change to No. 10(3) needles.
Next row (picot row) K 1, * y fwd, k 2 tog. Rep from * to end.
Beg with a p row, work 7 rows st st, dec 1 st in centre on last row. 140(146:152) sts.
Now work in patt thus:
Change to No. 3(10) needles.
1st row K.
2nd row P.

3rd row K 1, * C 6f. Rep from * to last st, k 1.
Change to No. 10(3) needles.
4th–10th rows Beg with a p row, work 7 rows st st.
These 10 rows form patt. Work 3(13:23) rows more in patt.

Shape thus:
Next row (P 14, p 2 tog) 3 times, p to last 48 sts, (p 2 tog, p 14) 3 times.
Work 29 rows straight in patt.
Rep last 30 rows once more, then 1st of these rows again. 122(128:134) sts. Cont straight in patt until Front measures 12½(14:15½) ins from picot row, ending after a wrong side row.

Shape armholes
Keeping continuity of patt, cast off 6 sts at beg of next 2 rows then dec 1 st at each end of next 3 rows, then on every alt row until 98(104:110) sts rem.
Cont straight until Front measures about 14½(16:17¾) ins from picot, ending with a 7th or 9th patt row. Cont in st st using No. 10(3) needles *only* for remainder of Front, working thus:
Next row P 10(11:12), (p 2 tog) 39(41:43) times, p 10(11:12). 59(63:67) sts **.
Beg with a k row, work 10(12:14) rows st st.

Shape Neck
Next row K 22(23:24) turn and leave rem sts on spare needle. Cont on rem sts for first half thus:
*** Dec 1 st at neck edge on every row until 17(18:19) sts rem. Work straight until Front measures 1½(1¾:1¾) ins from beg of neck shaping, ending at armhole edge.
Shape Shoulder
Cast off 6 sts at beg of next 2 armhole edge rows. Work 1 row straight then cast off rem 5(6:7) sts.
Return to other sts, sl centre 15(17:19) sts on a spare needle, rejoin yarn to rem sts and k to end.
Now work to match other half, working from *** to end.

Back

Work as Front from ** to **, then cont straight in st st until Back matches Front to shoulder edge, ending with a p row.

Shape Shoulders

Cast off 6 sts at beg of next 4 rows then 5(6:7) sts at beg of next 2 rows. Sl rem 25(27:29) sts on st holder.

Sleeves

Using No. 11(2) needles cast on 44(46:48) sts and work in k 1, p 1 rib for $1\frac{1}{2}$(2:2) ins. Change to No. 10(3) needles and cont in rib inc 1 st at each end of 1st and every foll 6th (6th:8th) row until there are 54 sts for each size, then each end of every 8th row until there are 60(64:68) sts, working inc sts into rib.
Cont straight until sleeve measures $8\frac{1}{2}$(10:$11\frac{1}{2}$) ins, or length required.

Shape Top

Cast off 6 sts at beg of next 2 rows, then dec 1 st each end of next and every alt row until 24(26:28) sts rem, then on every row until 18(20:22) sts rem. Cast off loosely in rib.

Neckband

First press yoke only on wrong side using a cool iron over a dry cloth. Join right shoulder. Using No. 11(2) needles and with right side facing pick up and k 16(17:19) sts along left front shoulder, 1 st from corner, 16(18:20) sts down left side of neck, k across centre front sts, dec 2 sts evenly across, pick up and k 16(18:20) sts up right side of neck, k across back sts, finally pick up and k 16(17:19) sts from left back shoulder. 103(113:125) sts.
Beg with a p row, work 3 rows st st, inc 1 st on every row at neck corner of left front shoulder. 106(116:128) sts.
Next row K 2, * y fwd, k 2 tog. Rep from * to end.
Beg with a p row, work 2 rows st st, dec 1 st in each row at neck corner. Cast off loosely.

To make up

Fold neck picot in half to wrong side and slip-stitch in position. Overlap front shoulder over back and tack together at armhole edge. Using a flat seam for ribbing and a fine back-stitch seam, join side and sleeve seams. Sew in sleeves. Fold picot at lower edge in half to wrong side and slip-stitch into position. Press picot borders and seams on wrong side. Sew press studs to shoulder picot, 1st to come $\frac{1}{2}$ inch from neck, remaining 2 spaced evenly. Sew buttons over press studs.

Everyday Dress

This handy little dress could not be easier to sew. It shows how to make exciting use of a bold fabric pattern. The fabric is also an ideal choice for a garment of this type as it is a tough and colourful furnishing cotton, which will wash and wear particularly well. A decorative pocket has been cleverly sewn to the dress front, so that it does not interfere with the pattern of the fabric. The zip is sewn on in a special way that is both decorative and quick to do.

Materials

Furnishing cotton: 1⅝ yds of 36 in fabric or 1⅜ yds of 45 in fabric
3 yds of bias binding
Thread and machine embroidery twist
8 in square scrap of iron-on Vilene

1. After cutting out, overcast all edges. Stitch back shoulder darts and press.
2. Place zip down centre front line on right side of fabric and sew round edge with decorative embroidery stitch or satin stitch, using the sewing machine for speed.
3. Iron Vilene on to wrong side of pocket. Overcast top edge and fold over a ½ in flap. Using straight machine stitch, sew round edge of pocket, following outline of fabric pattern. Cut raw edges back outside stitching line. Pin pocket in place over dress front so fabric matches pattern exactly. Oversew round edges in decorative stitch to match zip. The house roof above the pocket on the dress illustrated is also outlined with machine embroidery stitch to give a more finished effect to the dress.
4. Stitch shoulder and side seams.
5. Turn dress to wrong side and cut away excess fabric under zip so it can be opened and closed.
6. Gather sleeve head between dots, using a small zigzag stitch over cord to help make even gathers. Stitch sleeve seams and attach sleeves to dress in the normal way. Adjust sleeve length to individual fit. Make a small casing at wrists by turning up a ½ in hem, then insert elastic as required.
7. Overcast hem and stitch into place by hand or machine.
8. Neaten neckline with bias binding, folded over the neck edge and stitched. Leave enough binding on each side of neck opening to make a decorative tie. Small knots tied in ends of binding prevent fraying.

Cutting out note

Before cutting out, arrange pattern so the bold design is used to best advantage. The pocket is the same shape as the house on the

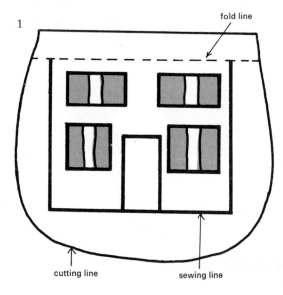

1

fold line

cutting line

sewing line

dress illustrated. To use this idea, which can be adapted for any bold fabric design, cut out a piece of fabric for the pocket which matches a section of the pattern on the dress front, allowing an extra ½ in on top and ¼ in round sides and bottom (diagram 1).

5 squares represent 4 inches

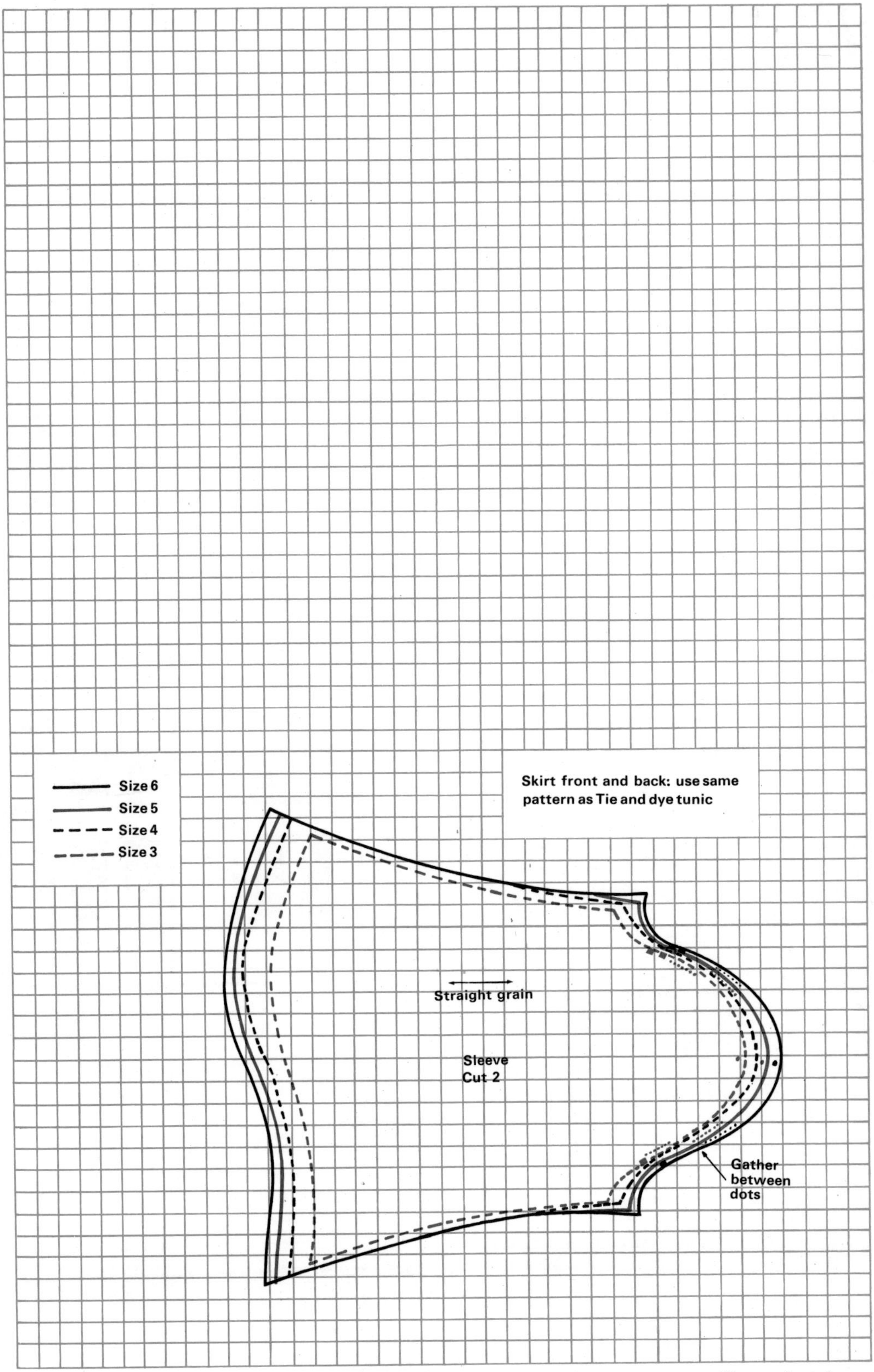

Size 6
Size 5
Size 4
Size 3

Skirt front and back: use same
pattern as Tie and dye tunic

Straight grain

Sleeve
Cut 2

Gather
between
dots

Everyday dress

Tucked Dress

This little dress shows how to make unusually effective use of check or striped fabrics. The decorative tucks on the bodice emphasize the colours and add a smart tailored look to a basically simple flared dress pattern. This idea can be used for all sorts of different fabrics, but is especially good for boldly striped cottons and colourful ginghams.

Materials

2 yds striped or check fabric
Thread to match
Zip fastener

1. Cut out a square of fabric for the dress front, 36 × 32 ins (size 6); 36 × 28 ins (size 4) or 36 × 22 ins (size 2).
Fold, pin, then baste tucks to make a dense block of colour in the centre of what will become the bodice front. The tucks should be folded so one of the fabric colours will be emphasized (diagram 1). The size of the tucks

fabric before tucking

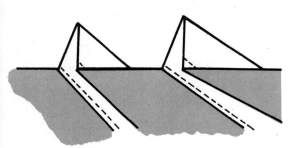

1   — — — — — sewing line

will depend on the fabric pattern you choose. When folded, the block of tucks should measure 11 ins wide (size 6); 9 ins wide (size 4) or 7 ins wide (size 2), not including the spare fabric on either side. Machine the tucks

down for 12 ins (size 6); 10 ins (size 4) or 8 ins (size 2). On the wrong side, iron the tucks with the folds pressed outwards. Mark the centre front line with basting. Pin the tucks down at what will be hem level, making

2

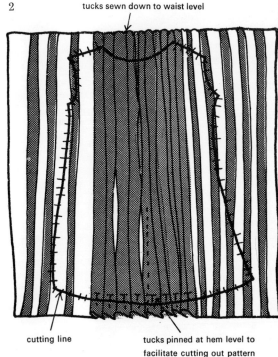

tucks sewn down to waist level

cutting line

tucks pinned at hem level to facilitate cutting out pattern

a square block of fabric that is now ready to be cut to shape (diagram 2).
(On the larger sizes if tucks are very deep ones using up most of the width of the fabric, it may be necessary to add 6 in panels on either side. This will make the material the right width for cutting out the dress front.)
Place the dress front pattern over the prepared piece of fabric, making sure the centre fronts coincide. Now cut out the dress front, stay stitching tucks on the shoulder and neckline.
2. Cut out back and sleeves and overcast all cut edges with zigzag stitching.

3. Join the two back pieces, right sides together. Make a seam from waist level and insert a zip fastener from the waist to the neck.

4. Make gathering stitches along upper edge of sleeves between notch marks. Pin sleeves to armholes, right sides together, adjusting gathers to fit and making sure notches match. The large notch in the centre top must match the shoulder seam.

5. Join the sides, right sides facing, making continuous seams from sleeves to hem.

6. Measure individual neck size and round top of arms. Cut strips of fabric the same length, adding on 2 ins for turnings. The strips must be cut on the bias and should be 1 in wide. Pin binding to neck edge, right sides together, baste and machine stitch. Trim edge. Fold binding over to inside. Turn in edge and oversew neatly. Add a hook and eye fastening at back of neck.

7. Join ends of sleeve binding to make a bracelet shape. Gather fullness at base of sleeve and pin it to binding, adjusting gathers evenly, right sides together. Machine the two together and finish off the inside as for neck binding.

8. Turn up hem to suit individual size.

5 squares represent 4 inches

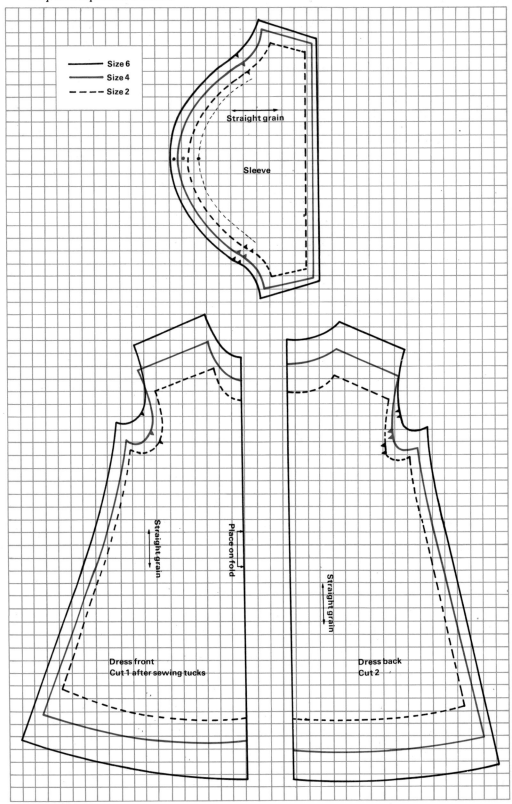

Size 6
Size 4
Size 2

Straight grain

Sleeve

Straight grain

Place on fold

Straight grain

Dress front
Cut 1 after sewing tucks

Dress back
Cut 2

Tucked dress

Dressing Gown

For something that is ultra quick to sew, try this practical pattern. With its warm towelling lining, the dressing gown is ideal for a child to wear after the bath or on the beach. The pattern is one large piece, with the addition of a collar and tab for front opening. With the minimum of seams, it is easy to make and illustrates how to make an original garment in a short time.

Materials

1¾ yds each of 36 in wide cotton and towelling
3 buttons

1. Cut out fabrics. Baste together, wrong sides facing and stitch round edge, following inner line drawn on pattern. Clip on curves.

Leave neck unsewn and use this opening to turn the fabric the right way out.
2. Baste round newly sewn edge to keep flat and machine stitch round edge again on the right side.
3. Cut out the two front tabs from cotton. Sew one edge of each tab, right sides facing to each side of the front opening. Fold tabs in half lengthways and turn raw edges under, slip-stitching into place inside the front opening. Overlap tabs at base of opening when stitching. On right side neaten lower and upper ends of tabs and oversew.
4. With right sides facing, sew along the upper edge and sides of collar. Turn collar right way out, baste and oversew with straight stitch round edge of join. Join collar to neck, using collar facing to neaten inside of neckline.
5. Join along underside of sleeves and sides of dressing gown by hand with oversewing.
6. Make buttonholes and attach buttons.

5 squares represent 6 inches

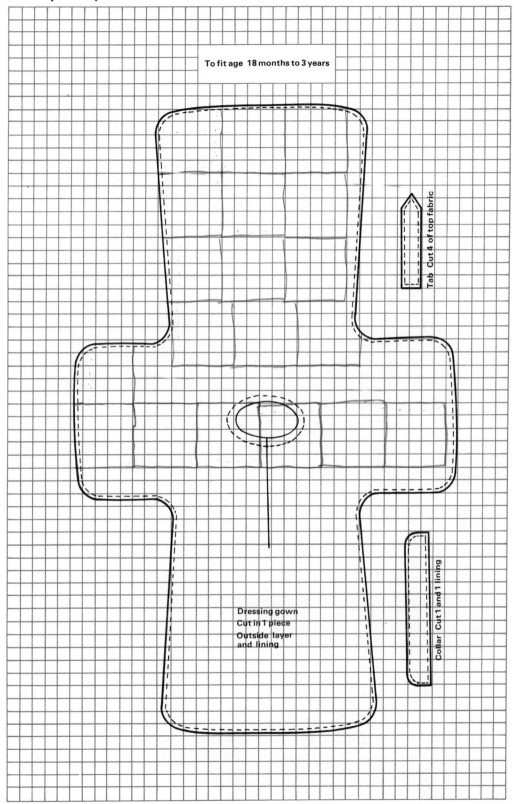

To fit age 18 months to 3 years

Tab Cut 4 of top fabric

Dressing gown
Cut in 1 piece
Outside layer
and lining

Collar Cut 1 and 1 lining

Dressing gown

Dungarees Sets

These patterns are excellent money-savers because they are so quick to make. The tough denim dungarees are ideal for active children at play. The toddler's pair has an easy fastening along the inner leg seams for quick nappy changing. The appliqué initials add an individual touch. The stretch towelling sweaters would be relatively expensive to buy ready-made, but are surprisingly simple to make at home.

Materials

Denim for dungarees:
Smaller sizes up to 3 years
1¼ yds of 36 in or 1 yd of 45 in fabric
Sizes 4 to 6 years
1⅜ yds of 36 in or 1⅛ yds of 45 in fabric
Buttons and suspenders for fastenings
Velcro or strip of poppers (snaps) for leg fastenings on toddler's sizes.
Two small strips of sweater fabric for cuffs on toddler's sizes
Scraps of towelling and iron-on Vilene for initials
Stretch towelling for sweaters:
1 yd of 36 in fabric

Dungarees

1. Cut out pattern and overcast all edges using three-step zigzag. Pin facing to front, right sides together. Stitch upper edges and armhole. Trim seams and corners where necessary. Clip curves. Press facing to inside of garment.
2. Stitch centre back seams, re-inforcing seam at crotch. Clip curves. With right sides together, pin facing to back. Stitch along upper edges and armhole. Trim seams, corners and clip curves. Press facing to inside.
3. Join side seams and stitch from edge of facing to underarm and down to ankle. Press facing to inside, baste and sew a neat row of machine stitching ¾ in from top edge of dungarees all the way round.

4. Using the green stretch towelling, apply motif to dungaree front. First iron on Vilene to wrong side of stretch towelling, then draw out initial on a piece of firm tracing paper. Pin fabric in position with paper under dungarees. Sew round outline of initial with small straight stitch. Cut away excess towelling round this stitching, leaving a clear outline. Sew satin stitch all round raw edges to prevent fraying. (For a good satin stitch, use machine embroidery thread, stitch width 3, length about ½).
5. Fold straps in half lengthwise, right sides facing. Make a ⅜ in seam, leaving opening halfway down, wide enough to turn fabric to right side. Turn straps and press, then slipstitch opening. Machine stitch straps to outside of trousers at back with a square of stitching. Attach suspenders to other end of straps and sew on buttons at front.
6. **On larger sizes,** stitch inside leg, and hem at ankle.
On toddler's sizes, turn in small hem on front and back of inside leg. Fold ankle cuff in half, right sides together, seam at either end, turn to right side and press. Stretch towelling whilst sewing and use a machine stretch stitch to attach cuff to trouser bottom. If the machine is non-automatic, attach cuffs by hand with back stitch. Stitch Velcro along entire front and back inside leg opening—from cuff to crotch to cuff, front and back.

Stretch Knit Sweaters

1. Cut out sweater, making sure width of fabric goes round body of garment and length of fabric goes up and down; otherwise garment will be unwearable. Maximum stretch must be on width of garment so it's easy to put on and will keep its shape properly.
2. Join sleeves to body of garment by placing wrong sides together then seaming and overcasting in one operation, using Elna superstretch stitch, disc no. 152, or a similar

special stretch stitch on an automatic sewing machine. With a non-automatic machine, seams must be joined by hand, using backstitch for elasticity. Then overcast cut edges by hand. Owners of automatic machines will score when they make this pattern, because it will take only about 15 mins to sew up the sweaters.

3. Seam from wrist to underarm and continue down side seam of sweater all in one operation.

4. Turn under $\frac{1}{2}$ in hem on bottom of sweater and on sleeves and again, (using superstretch stitch on machine, or overcasting, then backstitch for hand sewing), stitch turnings into place.

5. With *wrong* side of fabric facing, join neckband into a circle, again only leaving a narrow seam allowance. Fold band in half and with pins mark it into four equal sections. Mark neckline of sweater in the same way. Pin sweater and neckband together at quarter points. Then, using superstretch machine stitch or backstitch, seam sweater and neckband together, stretching neckband to fit garment as you sew.

5 squares represent 4 inches

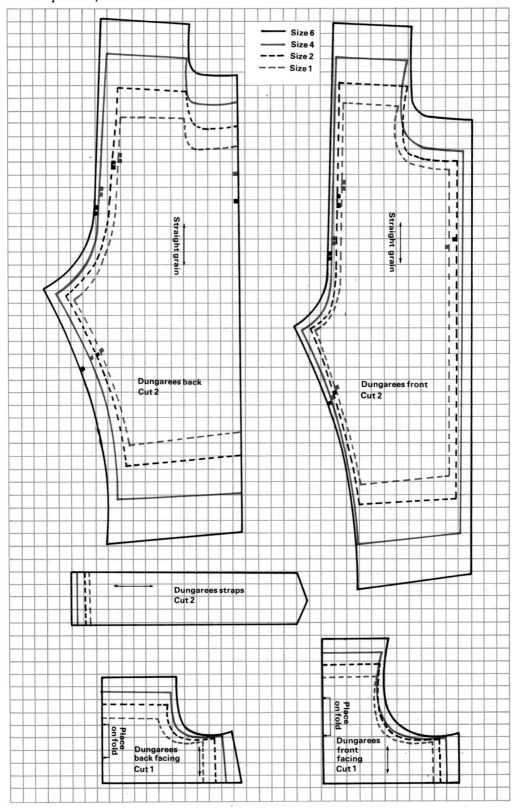

5 squares represent 4 inches

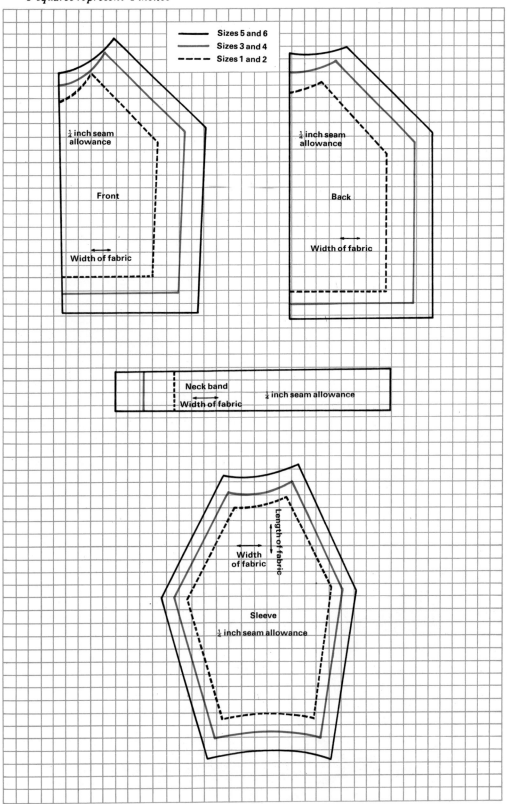

Sizes 5 and 6
Sizes 3 and 4
Sizes 1 and 2

$\frac{1}{4}$ inch seam allowance

Front

Width of fabric

$\frac{1}{4}$ inch seam allowance

Back

Width of fabric

Neck band

Width of fabric

$\frac{1}{4}$ inch seam allowance

Length of fabric

Width of fabric

Sleeve

$\frac{1}{4}$ inch seam allowance

Patchwork Robe

An ultra-feminine dressing gown is something most small girls long for. This one shows an unusual way of using patchwork and the finished result is something to treasure. Making a complete patchwork skirt for this dressing gown would take a long time, but using the hexagonal patchwork as flower shapes on the skirt takes much less time yet looks lovely. The skirt and bodice are lined with wadding for extra warmth. The dressing gown is made in practical cotton, with cotton patchwork and lining, and Terylene wadding so it will be easy to wash. This pattern could be adapted in several ways. Instead of the patchwork flowers, cut out animal shapes from cotton to appliqué round the skirt. If you want a quick "make", use warm ready-made quilting without the extra decorations.

Materials

Pink gingham: 1 yd 36 in or $\frac{5}{8}$ yd 45 in
Pink cotton: 2 yds 36 in or 45 in
Terylene or Courtelle wadding: 2 yds 36 in or 45 in
Scraps of cotton for patchwork
Thread
Buttons for binding

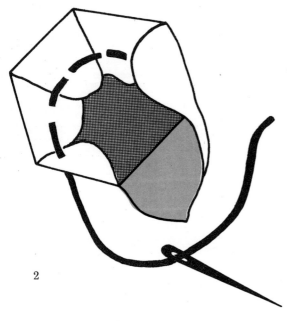

2

Patchwork

Use a one inch hexagonal template, or make your own from stiff card, using our pattern (diagram 1). Cut out a generous supply of

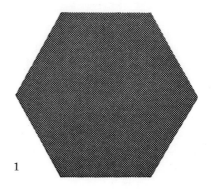

1

hexagonal patterns from old magazine paper. Now cut out a supply of cotton scraps, each one 1½ ins square. Place a paper pattern over a fabric square. Fold cotton over paper to make the hexagonal shape and baste securely (diagram 2). Assemble the patchwork flowers. Each flower is composed of one plain (for the centre) and six patterned patches. Join the patches along the folded edges, using neat overcasting stitch. When shapes are complete press firmly before removing basting and paper. Trim away any bulky excess material on underside. The flower shapes are now ready for stitching to the dressing gown.

Dressing Gown

1. Cut out the pattern pieces and overcast all cut edges, preferably using three-step zigzag on machine.
2. Join shoulder seams of yoke on both lining and garment.
3. Join side seams of both skirt and lining. Join side seams of wadding by butting edges and sewing with three-step zigzag so the join is flat. Sandwich wadding between skirt and

lining and press front edge of skirt inside along fold lines to form facing. Gather in fullness along skirt top between notches.

4. Pin skirt to yoke, drawing up gathers to fit. Stitch yoke to skirt.

5. Mark where flowers and stems will be sewn on dressing gown skirt, using a free-hand design. Make stems. Either appliqué them in the form of green cotton, or, as in the illustration, use a cording foot on the sewing machine and sew on close rows of green pearl cotton, using a three-step zigzag (diagram 3).

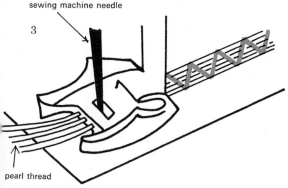

3

sewing machine needle

pearl thread

This is the quickest way with an automatic sewing machine. Sew leaves at random, following design, using tapered zigzag stitch. Cut out circular pieces of wadding a little smaller than the prepared patchwork flowers. Place wadding under flowers and baste to skirt. Sew round edge of flowers with straight stitch, and again round edge of hexagon in centre of each flower. Remove basting.

6. Gather head of sleeves between notches (see useful stitches, page 10). Stitch underarm seams of sleeves, clipping curves. Make narrow hems on bottom of sleeves and insert elastic to fit. With right sides together, pin sleeves into armholes, matching dots to shoulder seam on each side. Ease fullness and stitch along seam line. Press sleeve edge towards bodice.

7. Cut out a strip of gingham for frilled collar, measuring 36 × 3 ins. Fold the strip in half lengthwise. Stitch down each end of the folded strip, right sides together. Turn right way out and press firmly. Gather base of strip (diagram 4). Pull up gathers and pin collar to yoke neck, right sides facing, starting one inch from yoke front edge on each side and adjusting gathers to fit

(diagram 4a). Pin lining to yoke at neck, right sides facing, so frilled collar is sandwiched between the two. Then pin lining to yoke from neck edge to base of yoke on

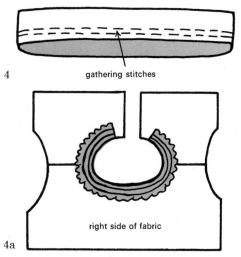

4

gathering stitches

4a

right side of fabric

both sides at front. Baste and stitch these layers together (diagram 5). Clip seams. Turn to right side, press. Turn under $\frac{5}{8}$ in seam allowance along both fronts, round armholes and along back of yoke lining and slip stitch into place.

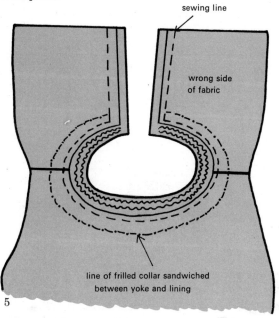

sewing line

wrong side of fabric

5

line of frilled collar sandwiched between yoke and lining

8. Turn up hem on lining and skirt and stitch into place.

9. Cover buttons in gingham. Stitch on to dressing gown. Make buttonholes.

5 squares represent 6 inches

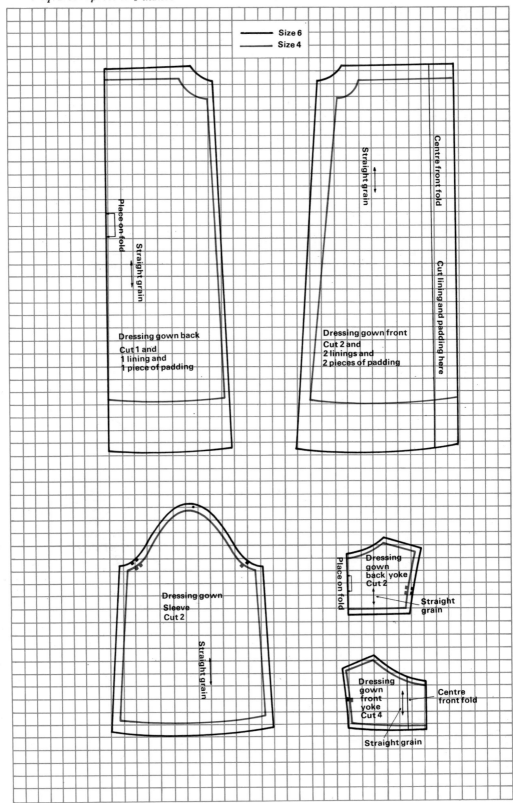

Size 6
Size 4

Straight grain

Centre front fold

Cut lining and padding here

Place on fold

Straight grain

Dressing gown back

Cut 1 and
1 lining and
1 piece of padding

Dressing gown front

Cut 2 and
2 linings and
2 pieces of padding

Dressing gown
Sleeve
Cut 2

Straight grain

Place on fold

Dressing
gown back yoke
Cut 2

Straight
grain

Dressing
gown
front
yoke
Cut 4

Centre
front fold

Straight grain

Patchwork robe

Nursery Accessories

Changing Mattress

Most mothers include one of these changing mattresses on their list of equipment for a new baby. It is easy to change a baby's nappies and to wash him when he is lying on a mattress like this one. The laminated surface makes it simple to wipe clean. The slightly raised sides will protect a young baby from draughts. However, an active baby may be able to roll off, so should not be left unattended if the mattress is on a table. The soft foam filling makes it comfortable for a baby to lie on. It is inexpensive and simple to make—the sort of job that can be done in an afternoon.

Materials

1¾ yds laminated fabric or PVC
Matching thread
1 in thick sheet of foam—15 by 24 in.
2 bags foam filling.
Sticky tape, and pattern or tissue paper
Size when completed—33 by 14 ins

1. Cut out the two pieces of fabric for the top and underside.
2. Place pieces of fabric together, right sides facing each other. Instead of pinning, bind together at intervals with strips of sticky tape. Machine round edge, leaving a ½ in seam allowance. Leave the base open and a 3 in gap for filling at the top end. Clip seam allowance on corners and turn mattress the right way out.
3. Place the foam sheet inside the mattress. With felt-tipped pen mark out the sewing line, ½ in from edge of foam. Pin carefully in three places along sewing line on each side. Remove foam.
4. Tape strips of paper over sewing line on both sides of mattress to prevent it from sticking when it is machined. Mark out the sewing line on the paper also and remove pins. Machine carefully, leaving base open. Remove paper and tape.
5. Slide foam sheet into place. Fill sides tightly with foam chips, using a rolling pin to help push filling into place. Fill top and neaten off seam with oversewing.

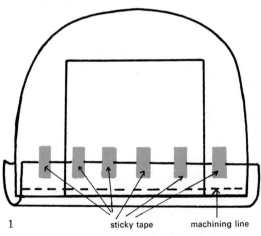

6. Secure the base with strips of sticky tape, so the top side is fixed to the underside. Place paper on both sides of mattress to cover sewing line. If necessary, mark sewing line with pen. Finish off base with row of zigzag stitch. Remove paper and sticky tape. Cut away remaining fabric below sewing line (diagram 1).

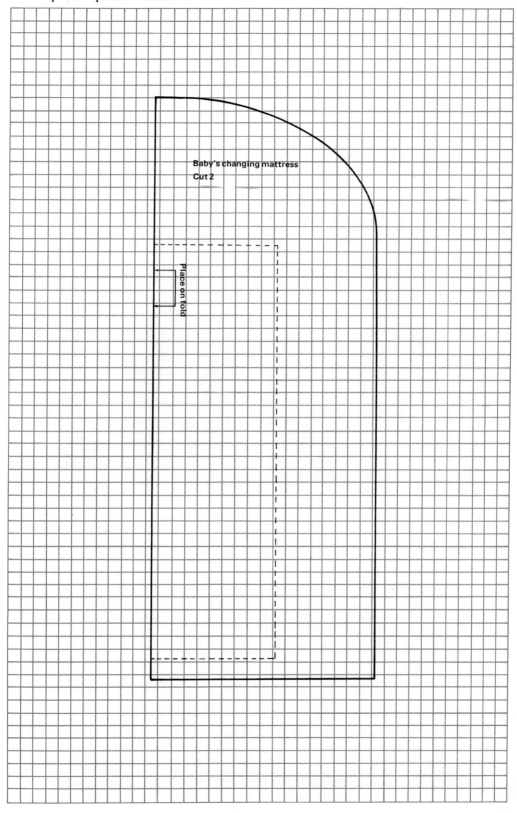

Baby's changing mattress
Cut 2

Place on fold

Wall Tidy

All the bits and pieces needed for changing
or bathing a baby can be stored in this
practical holdall. Use the big pocket for
cotton wool balls. Other pockets are specially
designed in an assortment of shapes to hold
everything from baby lotions to cotton wool
buds, nail scissors and medicaments. Later
on the holdall can be used as a desk tidy,
when it can be filled with homework equipment, like pencils and rulers. It is a good
space saver because it hangs so neatly on the
wall. This one is made in plastic-coated
fabric so that it can be wiped clean. However,
fabric of this type is quite awkward to sew
and the pattern could be used equally well
with a washable fabric like heavy canvas, or
gingham backed with Vilene. When using a
different fabric, sew pockets on with zigzag
stitch and attach the holdall to the frame back
with strips of strong poppers or Velcro so it
can be removed easily for washing.

Materials

Hardboard square 22 in by 28 in with $\frac{1}{2}$ in
battens pinned around edges to make a frame
(see diagram 2)
1$\frac{1}{4}$ yds PVC coated fabric or material of choice
Squared pattern paper or tracing paper
18 in length of tape
Scraps of fabric for appliqué (optional)
Reel of sticky tape (to be used on PVC fabric
instead of pins, which leave marks)

1. Cut out fabric for backing and pockets.
Fold raw edges of pocket tops under and
secure with short strip of sticky tape. The
shiny side of the PVC sticks to the machine
when it is being sewn, so fold strips of
pattern paper over the area to be sewn and
secure with strips of sticky tape. This helps
the fabric to run easily through the machine.
Machine pocket tops. Remove paper and tape.

Wall tidy and changing mattress

2. Cut pocket shapes neatly from the middle
of the backing pattern, then lay the backing
pattern over the material so the pocket
positions can be marked with faint pinpricks
or felt tipped pen (which wipes off).

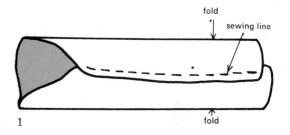

1

3. Make neat knife pleats on both sides of
each pocket. Secure pockets into position
with sticky tape. Tape the pocket outlines
(cut from the backing pattern) over each
pocket to make the PVC easy to sew. Machine

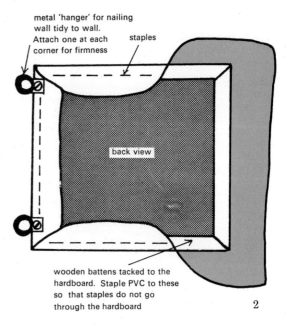

2

in place, using straight stitch. Remove paper and sticky tape. Complete one pocket before moving on to next. If the fabric shows signs of fraying, sew round edge of pockets with zigzag stitch.

4. Fold the paper roll holder in three, lengthways. Secure with tape and machine along centre to hold edges in place. Fold under the ends and machine. Machine one end on to backing fabric. Attach 9 in of the tape to the other end, and a further 9 in to the backing, so the holder can be undone easily when a new paper roll is needed (diagram 1).

5. Deal with safety-pin holder in the same way, machining it on to the backing at each end. Make slots to hold pins with short rows of stitching at half-inch intervals.

6. Tape appliqué into position (optional) under paper pattern, then sew—either with zigzag or straight stitch.

7. Pull holdall tightly over the hardboard square and staple tightly into position on the wood at the back (diagram 2).

▶

1 square represents 1 inch

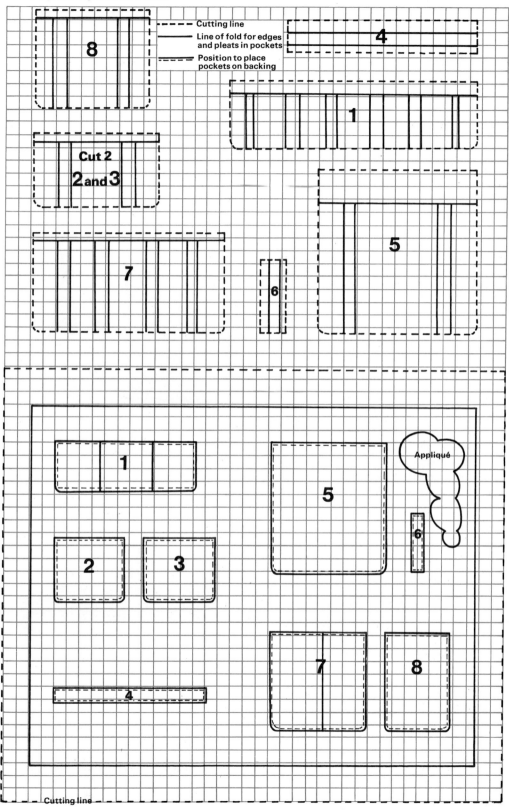

8

Cutting line
Line of fold for edges and pleats in pockets
Position to place pockets on backing

4

1

Cut 2
2 and 3

5

7

6

1

Appliqué

5

6

2

3

7

8

4

Baby's Cot

Covering the cot is one of the most pleasing preparations for a new baby. This pattern is simple to sew. The broderie anglaise frills and colourful ribbon bring a delicate finish. The skirts can be removed easily so the basket can be taken off its stand and used as a carry cot. All the coverings are simple to take off and wash. This method can be adapted for either round or square ended cots.

Materials

Cotton, Dacron or lawn for skirts (amount you buy depends on individual cot size and shape). For cot you need roughly 8 yds and for canopy another 3½ yds
Courtelle or Terylene wadding
Broderie anglaise frill trimming
Ribbon
Velcro
Brown paper

1. Use brown paper to make a pattern of the inside of the cot. A rounded cot needs two pieces to line sides and one for base. A square cot needs four pieces to line sides and one for base. When drawing up the pattern (use a felt tipped pen and trace shape of cot on to paper by feeling contours with pen through paper), add 4 ins along top edges so lining curves neatly over edge (diagram 1).
2. Cut out cot lining from covering fabric and wadding. The two layers should be the same. Pin, adjust fit, baste and stitch together with wadding beneath covering fabric.
3. Measure round outside top of cot, 2 in below edge. Cut a strip of fabric the same

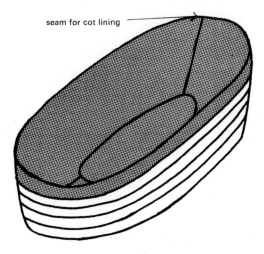

seam for cot lining

1

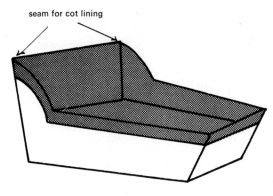

seam for cot lining

length plus 2 ins for turnings. The side measurement of this fabric should be 30 ins. This covers the cot outside. Gather trimming to go round top edge. This should be 1½ times or twice measurement round top edge of cot.

Baby's cot

Join it between cot lining and outside (diagram 2). Stitch these three layers together (diagram 3). Make a 1 in hem along bottom

half of the Velcro. Neaten sides of skirts and attach to cot under frill by pressing Velcro strips together.

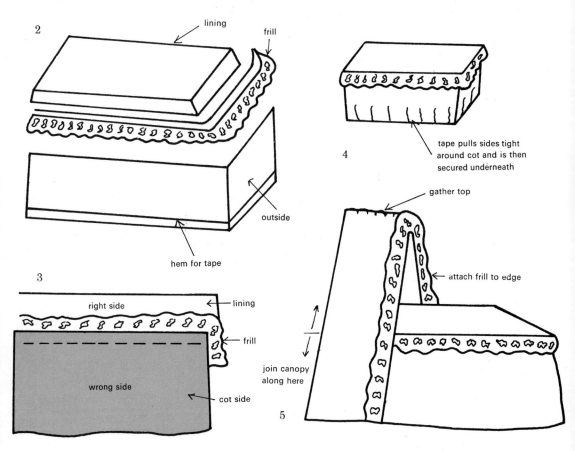

edge of cot side piece. Thread tape through this so sides can be pulled tight underneath (diagram 4).

4. Cut Velcro strip long enough to go round top of cot and sew velvet side of it under top frill.

5. Cut cot skirts—36 in wide and 1½ or 2 times length of Velcro strip. Hem one long edge and gather the other on to the other

6. Make canopy by cutting a straight length of fabric twice the height of canopy. Fold length of fabric in half. Join it up one side. Sew trimming and ribbon to unjoined edge. Gather fabric along fold so it fits over canopy top (diagram 5).

Sparkling Mobile

Babies love to lie in their cots and watch a nursery mobile like this one. The bright colours and the sequins catch the light and sparkle as the butterflies move. A gentle air current in the room is enough to make the mobile start twirling. This colourful idea is fun to make and much more simple than it looks.

Materials

½ yd organdie
Scraps of brightly coloured felt
Machine embroidery twist in shaded pink and green
Sequins in assorted shapes—12 large pink, 12 large green, a bag of small gold ones and a bag of sparkling flower shapes
Six sheets of writing paper
Fabric adhesive

Polythene covered garden wire:
1 piece 12 ins long
2 pieces 8 ins long

1. Cut out 12 organdie squares, measuring 6 ins by 6 ins.
2. Place 2 organdie squares together over a piece of paper the same size and baste round the edge, using a double thread. Repeat the process with the other sheets of paper. The paper gives more body to the embroidery and stops the light organdie from ruckling in the sewing machine.
3. Cut out a card butterfly shape from the pattern (diagram 1), and draw round the shape with pencil, transferring the design to each of the 6 prepared organdie squares.
4. Stitch round the butterflies' wings, one at a time, using a wide machine zigzag stitch

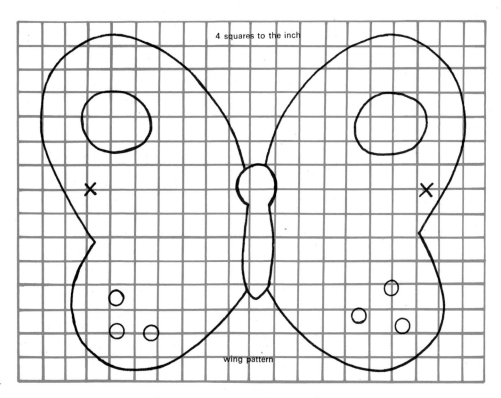

4 squares to the inch

wing pattern

1

with the stitches close together. If the butterflies are to be hand-made, use buttonhole stitch. Make 3 pink butterflies and 3 green.

5. Remove paper and basting. Trim away spare material outside sewing line.

6. Cut out the butterflies' bodies from the felt (diagram 2) to make six pairs.

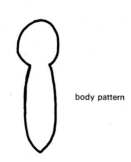

body pattern

2

diagram 1 for positioning. Use a pin point to apply adhesive.

9. Sew a 4 in long "handle" of cotton to each butterfly (diagram 3), to support the wings. Attach cotton to points marked X in sketch 1.

10. Twist a small circle in the centre of the

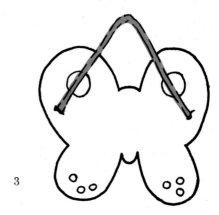

3

7. Sandwich each butterfly between two felt shapes. Baste in position and machine with a narrow zigzag stitch round the edge of the felt shapes. If hand sewing, use button-hole stitch for this.

8. Stitch the large circular sequins to the wings. Attach small ones with adhesive. See

longest piece of wire. Thread flower-shaped sequins at intervals on to long pieces of thread. Attach these to the "handles" and then to the wire (see picture). Wait until all butterflies are in place before tying off the cotton, so the lengths can be adjusted to get the correct balance.

Sparkling mobile

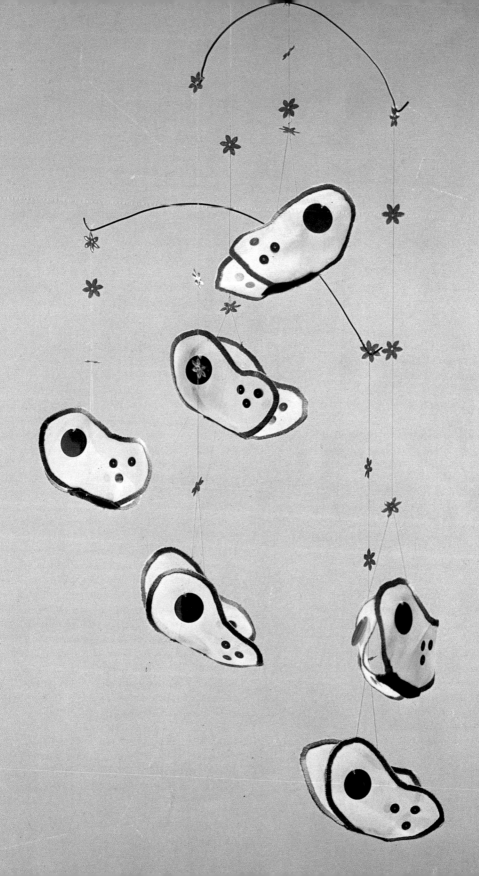

Collage

These are great fun to make and much loved by children. All you need are scraps of material and plenty of ideas. This collage is especially interesting because it incorporates several different crafts. The background is coloured with special dye paint, which is also used for the flowers and the pattern on Mrs. Bear's dress. The tree is effectively made from scraps of fabric that has been patterned with tie-and-dye work. Shoe dye is used to paint details on the suede bears and the tree trunks. The hessian house is appliquéd with embroidery thread to give the impression of bricks. Other details are made from scrap fabrics, glued into position. The shapes on the collage are purposely simple so they will be easy to copy.

Materials

¾ yd white cotton furnishing satin
4 sachets Dylon Paintex
4 sachets Dylon Cold Dye fix
Tins of Dylon Cold Dye in blue, green, navy, red and orange
1 bottle Miss Dylon (or other) suede dye in black smoke colour
Scraps of yellow velvet, hessian, felt, suede, rick-rack, lace
12 circular red buttons
1 square button or bead for door handle
Fabric adhesive
Piece of thick cardboard 26 in by 22 in

1. Sketch design on white fabric.
2. Make up blue and green Cold Dye with Paintex, following maker's instructions. Using an ordinary paint brush, paint in sky and grass, leaving white spaces for flowers, and window. Now make a darker green colour by mixing the made-up blue and green dye paint. Use this to paint in leaves for the flowers. Leave the fabric to dry, then wash and rinse to remove surplus paint. Press when dry.
3. Make two "tie-and-dye" trees from scraps of green fabric and brown suede. The dappled effect on the leaves is obtained by crumpling yellow velvet into a ball and then binding it tightly before dyeing it with the navy blue Cold Dye. Remove bindings. Crumple into a ball again and bind tightly. Dye a second time, using green Cold Dye. Untie bindings, dry velvet, then press lightly. Cut out 12 tree shapes (diagram 1). Cut out 2 tree trunks from scraps of brown suede and stick into position. Paint on the shadows with suede dye. Sew each of the red buttons on to a green velvet shape. Stick shapes in place so they overlap.
4. Cut out the three bears from scraps of brown suede. Stick them on to the collage. Paint in their faces, paws and toes with the suede dye.
5. Cut out Mr. Bear and Baby Bear's clothes from scraps of felt and stick on to collage.
6. Prepare the red and orange Cold Dye and mix with Paintex, following maker's instructions. Cut out Mrs. Bear's dress from yellow velvet. Paint on the pattern free hand, using the red and orange dyes. Use the red also for painting in flowers on the background fabric. Stick Mrs. Bear's dress in place.
7. Cut out the house from hessian, leaving a space for the door and window. Use orange felt for the roof and sun. Sew scraps of lace to background cloth where the window will go. Baste the house on top and stitch into place with blanket stitch to look like bricks. Sew long black threads across the window to to look like glazing bars. Cut out door from green felt. Sew on button for the handle. Stick door in place. Stick an orange felt roof, painting in tiles with suede dye. Add greenery by the door, made from scraps of tie-and-dye velvet.
8. Stick on sun rays, using scraps of yellow rick rack. Cut out a circular sun from orange felt and stick this in the centre of the rays.
9. Stretch the wall hanging over the cardboard base so that it looks smooth, then stick it firmly to the back of the cardboard.

1

4 squares to the inch

Collage

Rag Doll

This rag doll is made in a velvety towelling so she will be extra soft to hug. The little pinafore in calico is a good way of practising smocking. Her clothes are designed so she will be easy to dress and undress.

Materials

Doll
½ yd 36 in wide fabric, flesh coloured or white
Bag of foam chips or kapok type filling
2 buttons
Red and black stranded embroidery thread
¼ oz each of a dark and pale yellow knitting yarn or ½ oz of one colour

Her Clothes
½ yd 36 in wide fabric for dress and pants
¼ yd 36 in wide calico for pinafore and hat
Matching threads
3 buttons
1¾ yds cotton lace edging for dress and pants
1 yd broderie anglaise for hat edging
Shirring elastic for hat
Scrap of narrow elastic for pantaloons

Dimensions of Doll when finished
Overall length 23 ins. Waist 10 ins.

Doll

1. Cut out pattern pieces (p 120) ensuring there are 4 pieces each for legs and arms with two each reversed for left and right sides.
2. Seam head and body shapes together on wrong side, leaving seams open between dots for inserting arms and leaving under body open. Use small zigzag stitch for stretch fabric, or backstitch for non-stretch fabric. Turn right way out.
3. Stuff head and neck firmly.
4. Seam two arm pieces together on wrong side. Clip between fingers and thumb and trim seams. Turn to right side and stuff firmly. Make up second arm and legs in same way, using knitting needle to push stuffing in place.

5. Turn in seam allowance on open body seams and insert arms. Pin, baste and over-sew arms in place. Finish stuffing body.
6. Deal with legs similarly, making sure they are facing the right way with feet forwards.
7. Complete face by firmly sewing on two buttons for eyes. Ends of thread should be taken through to back of head and knotted for safety. Using stem stitch, sew mouth with 2 strands red embroidery thread and eyebrows with 2 strands of black.

Hair

Wind the two yarns together 50 times round a card 5 ins deep. Tie short length of yarn through the skein while it is on the card. Slip wool carefully off card and place it so upper fold of skein follows seam on top of doll's head. Stitch each loop down along this

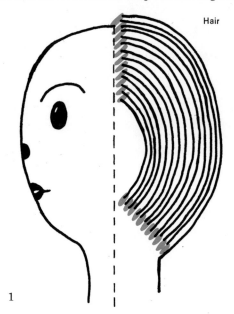

Hair

1

seam. Arrange wool to cover back of head and stitch each loop to neck (see diagram 1). Cut 8 pieces of wool, each 24 in long, using both colours for ringlets. Hold 4 ends in left hand and twist free ends until wool turns on itself and makes little ringlets. Hold both ends of twists in one hand and pull ringlets to even lengths. Repeat with the remaining 4 lengths. Stitch to doll's head on seam (see diagram 2).

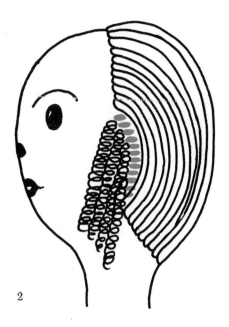

2

Wind the two yarns together 30 times round an 8 in deep card for side hair. Slip gently off card and tie round middle of skein which is then stitched in place to make a centre parting. Take loops round on both sides to cover tops of ringlets and stitch each loop in place under edge of back hair (see diagram 3).

3

Dress

Sew bodice back and front together on wrong sides, making a neat $\frac{1}{4}$ in hem down back opening. Cut a 26 in by 9 in strip of matching fabric for the skirt. Stitch lace to one long edge of this. Gather up top of skirt and join at back, leaving a 3 in deep neatened opening. Stitch skirt to bodice, with buttons and loops for back fastenings.

Sew lace to sleeves at wrist edge. Join under-arm sleeves and stitch to bodice from wrong side.

For neck frill, cut 1 strip of matching fabric 10 in by 1 in. Fold and press along the length. Neaten short ends and gather the two raw edges to fit bodice neck. Pin, baste and stitch in place.

Pinafore

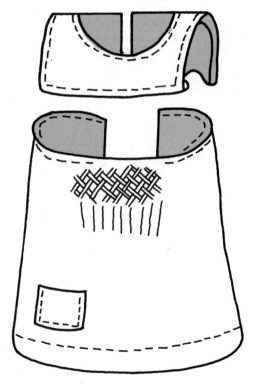

Pinafore

For the skirt, cut a strip of calico 9 in deep by 18 in wide. Gather up a $7\frac{1}{2}$ in long panel in the centre with 5 rows of stitching at $\frac{1}{2}$ in intervals. Pull threads up to make a $2\frac{1}{2}$ in

117

square block of gathering which can then be
smocked (optional). Page 10 gives smocking
stitch details.
Cut yoke patterns out from calico. Join at
shoulders and neaten neck and armhole
edges with machine or back stitching. Fold
and press a ¼ in turning on lower edge of
yoke. Pin over skirt, centring front over
smocked section. Top stitch this turning on
to skirt, starting at centre back.
Fold under and neaten back opening. Stitch
on button and loop, or tie fastenings.
Make a pocket from a 1½ in square of calico,
overstitched on to the skirt. Turn a 1 in hem
on skirt and overstitch to neaten. Add a 2 in
square handkerchief to pocket, made from
dress fabric.

Mob Cap

Cut an 8 in diameter circle of calico.
Gather up broderie Anglaise edging and pin
round calico. Attach with machine zigzag
stitch. One inch from edge of calico, sew two
rows of shirring elastic (see page 9 for
method). Finish the cap with a bow.

Hat   8 inch diameter circle

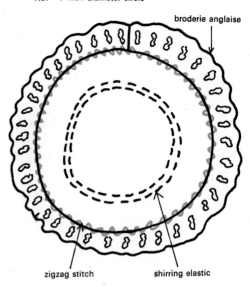

broderie anglaise

zigzag stitch   shirring elastic

Pantaloons

Cut out pattern in fabric to match dress.
Sew lace along leg ends. Stitch inside leg
and crutch seams. Make casing at waist and
insert elastic.

Rag doll

1 square represents 1 inch

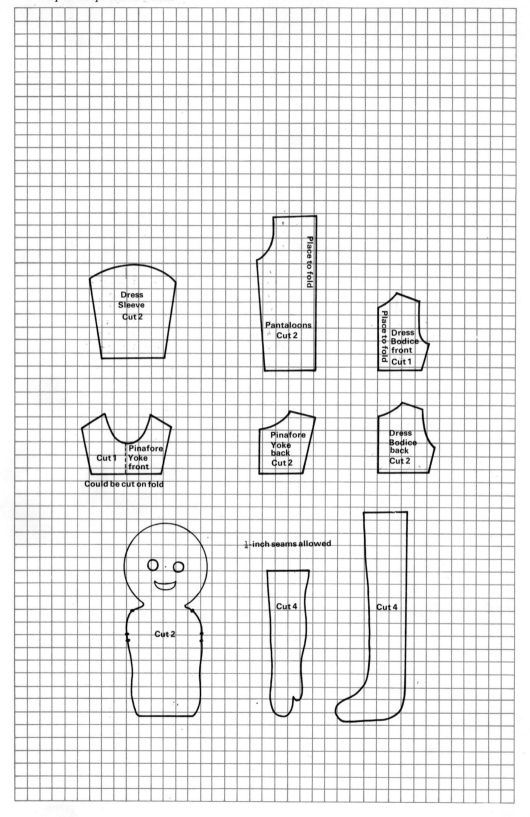

Dress
Sleeve
Cut 2

Place to fold

Pantaloons
Cut 2

Place to fold

Dress
Bodice
front
Cut 1

Cut 1 | Pinafore
Yoke
front

Could be cut on fold

Pinafore
Yoke
back
Cut 2

Dress
Bodice
back
Cut 2

¼-inch seams allowed

Cut 2

Cut 4

Cut 4

Pram Toy

Five colourful felt teddy bears are designed to be strung across a young baby's pram or cot. As he kicks, they spring around on elastic and the bells round their necks jingle. When the baby is about six months old, the bears can be taken off the elastic and hung on the nursery wall or kept with the soft toys.

Scraps of felt in bright colours
Kapok or Dacron wadding
2 ft round elastic
Thread to match felt colours
Strands of embroidery thread for faces
5 brass bells (small)
Bag of colourful macramé beads
Scraps of fabric for skirts
1 yd narrow ribbon

The bears are 4 ins high. Trace and cut out the required number of patterns from the felt scraps. Each of ours is in the dark and light shade of a different colour to give a kaleidoscope effect as the baby pushes the bears round and round on the elastic.
Sort the cut-out Teddies into pairs. Oversew each pair together firmly round the edge on the right side, stuffing each limb firmly as it is sewn. Leave an opening in the side to stuff the body and head. Use a pencil to help. Finish off side. Using pinking shears, cut scraps of fabric measuring 4 in by 1 in for the skirts. Gather these and sew up the openings on the wrong side. Stay stitch on to bears. Sew faces with 2 strands of embroidery thread on the needle, using French knots for eyes and stem stitch for noses and mouths. Cut 5 pieces of ribbon 7 in long. Thread a macramé bead and a bell on to each piece of ribbon. Tie ribbon round necks so each

bear has a bead at the back of his neck and a bell at the front, knotted into the bow. Stay stitch the bell, the bow and the ribbon knot firmly in place on to the bear so the baby will not be able to pull it off. Thread

4 squares to the inch

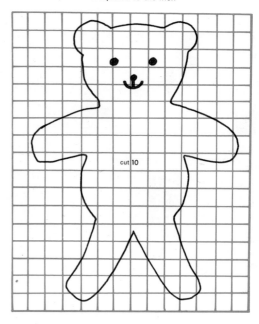

cut 10

elastic through beads at back of bears' necks, separating each bear with 20 beads. Sew loops at each end of the elastic and stay stitch beads at each end so they cannot be pulled off over the loops.

Pram toy

Crochet Rug

*The amusing tufted hedgehogs and dandelions
add an extra dimension to this little rug.
It shows how you can adapt crochet work for
furnishings. The pattern is especially simple
to follow and the rug is inexpensive to make
in a hard-wearing double knitting wool. For
added strength the rug can be backed with a
protective layer of felt.*

Materials

Monsieur Pingouin (Knitting Worsted), 50 gr
balls:

4 in orange, 2 in yellow and 1 each in rust
and green
A small amount of black double knitting wool
(knitting worsted) for the hedgehogs' face
and feet
A No. 5·50 mm (H/8) crochet hook
Strip of felt 18 in by 27 in for backing
(optional)

Measurements Approx 18 ins by 27 ins
(excluding fringe)

Tension 10 h tr (hdc) to 3 ins

Abbreviations and hook note See pages 6
and 8.

To make

Using orange make 81 ch.
Foundation row 1 h tr (hdc) into 3rd ch
from hook, 1 h tr (hdc) into each ch to end.
Next row 2 ch, 1 h tr (hdc) into each h tr
(hdc) to end.
Rep last row until work measures about
14½ ins. Fasten off.

Border

Turn and work in yellow. Join yellow into
last st worked, 2 ch for 1st h tr (hdc), 2 h tr
(hdc) into same st, work 1 h tr (hdc) into each
h tr (hdc) until 1 h tr (hdc) rems, 3 h tr (hdc)
into last st. Now work 52 h tr (hdc) down left
side of rug to foundation edge, work 3 h tr
(hdc) into 1st ch (at ch edge) then work
1 h tr (hdc) into each ch until 1 ch rems,
3 h tr (hdc) into last ch, work 52 h tr (hdc) up
right side of rug, sl st into 2nd ch.

2nd round Sl st into next h tr (hdc), 2 ch,
2 h tr (hdc) into same st, work 1 h tr (hdc)
into each h tr (hdc) and 3 h tr (hdc) into
centre of 3 h tr (hdc) at rem 3 corners, sl st
into 2nd ch.
Rep last round 3 times. Fasten off.

Now Work Tufted Hedgehogs
First wind rust wool over a piece of stiff
cardboard about 1½ ins wide, then cut at one
side, thus having strands of wool about 3 ins
long. Now work from left to right from chart.
Insert hook under a h tr (hdc)—working in
line now with this h tr (hdc) from left to right
and work a knotted loop by folding one
strand of wool in half over hook and draw
through a loop, pass the 2 ends through loop
and tighten knot. Follow chart using 1 strand
for hedgehogs, but use 2 strands together for
dandelions. Using green single, work stalks
and leaves in stem-stitch. Use the black wool
double, work nose, eyes and feet as shown in
photographs. Cut green yarn into 10 inch
lengths and knot 2 strands through every
alternate st along short edges. Trim fringe.
Cut felt back to size and sew in place with
overcasting stitch (optional).

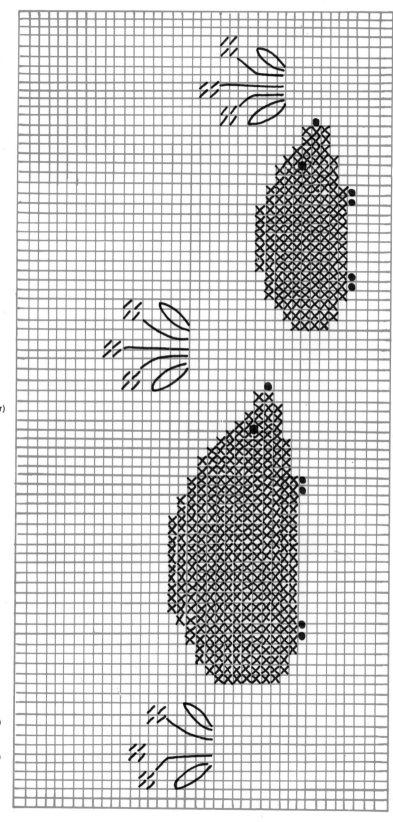

Centre of Rug (excluding Border)

X = rust
\ = yellow (use two strands)
• = black
◊| = stem stitch (embroidered)

Patchwork Bedspread

*This fresh-looking bedspread shows an
unusual and clever way of making patchwork,
using colourful cotton scraps. The circular
shapes are sewn in such a way that the
finished work has a nubbly three-dimensional
effect and does not need lining. The patchwork circles are joined to each other in four
places, instead of all the way round as in
traditional patchwork, which means it is
much quicker to sew. The method of joining
gives the bedspread a delicate cellular effect.
The nubbly side is the right side. The shapes
are easy to prepare at odd moments and the
patchwork can be used in several different
ways. Thin strips can be used as decorative
braid on curtains and long table cloths. The
patchwork would also make a colourful cot
or pram cover, or it could be used to cover a
drum-shaped lampshade, or even as a wall-
hanging.*

Materials

Plenty of cotton scraps
Thick piece of card for use as template
Thread

1. Make a template from thick card, the same
size as our pattern. Then cut out a good
supply of cotton circles (diagram 1).
2. Fold the cut edge of circle under and
gather fairly roughly, using double thread
with the ends knotted (diagram 2).

2

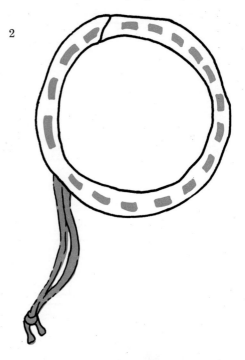

3. Pull up gathers tightly and tie off thread
neatly, passing it backwards and forwards
through neck of patch shape to make a firm
finish. This is important (diagram 3).

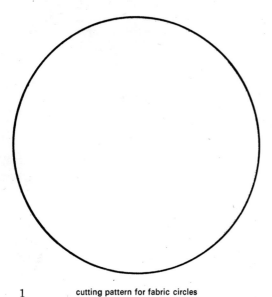

1   cutting pattern for fabric circles

3

Patchwork bedspread

4. Flatten the patchwork shape into a circle
(diagram 4).

4   profile of patchwork shape

top of patchwork shape

5. Join patches in groups of 9 or 16. Sew
patches together using overcasting stitches
with about $\frac{1}{4}$ inch of stitching in four places
round the now flattened circular shapes
(diagram 5).

6. Arrange the prepared blocks of patches so
colours mix well together. Carry on joining
up blocks until bedspread reaches required
size.

5